Pirkei Avot

Steinsaltz Center

KOREN

PIRKEI AVOT

WITH COMMENTARY BY
RABBI ADIN EVEN-ISRAEL

STEINSALTZ

The Steinsaltz Center
Koren Jerusalem

The Steinsaltz Mishna
Pirkei Avot
First edition, 2024

POB 8531, New Milford, CT 06776-8531, USA
& POB 4044, Jerusalem 91040, Israel
www.korenpub.com

Steinsaltz Center is the parent organization of institutions
established by Rabbi Adin Even-Israel Steinsaltz
POB 45187, Jerusalem 91450 ISRAEL
Telephone: +972 2 646 0900, Fax +972 2 624 9454
www.steinsaltz-center.org

Cover art: Eliyahu Misgav

www.steinsaltz-center.org

ISBN 978-965-7813-62-1, hardcover

Printed and bound in Turkey

TRACTATE AVOT

(*Ethics of Our Fathers*)

This book is tenderly dedicated to the
loving memory of my mother

Beverley Maron

whose teachings continue to light
my way through life's tapestry

To our cherished children,
Maya, Rachel, and Ari,
who embody the enduring wisdom
and loving-kindness she instilled in our hearts.

And to our brave soldiers,
whose valor is safeguarding our sacred legacy,
who will lead Am Yisrael to victory

Steinsaltz Center

Executive Director, Steinsaltz Center
Rabbi Meni Even-Israel

Editor-in-Chief
Rabbi Jason Rappoport

Translator
Rabbi Joshua Schreier

Editor
Rabbi Yaacov Francus

Copy-Editor
Ilana Sobel

Proofreader
Dvora Rhein

Hebrew Proofreader
Avichai Gamdani

Hebrew Edition Editors
Rabbi Yehonatan Eliav, *Senior Editor*
Rabbi Amechaye Even-Israel, *Managing Editor*

Technical Staff
Adena Frazer
Reut Hart
Shmuel Hart

KOREN

Design & Typesetting
Avishai Magence, *Editor-in-Chief*
Caryn Meltz, *Production Manager*
Rina Ben Gal, *typesetter*

Contents

INTRODUCTION TO *TRACTATE AVOT*

Tractate *Avot* is a compendium of sayings of wisdom and ethics stated by the "Fathers [*Avot*] of the World,"[1] the Torah Sages from the beginning of the Second Temple era through the period of the last Sages of the Mishna. As a book of ethics, the tractate serves as a guide, directing people in how they may reach human perfection in all areas of life, both in the private life of each and every person and in matters regarding society as a whole. Among the topics it addresses are the relationship between Torah and life and between study and action.

This tractate is substantively different from the rest of the tractates in the Mishna. All the others address matters of halakha, of fixed and defined laws delineating the standards that obligate every Jewish person: what he is commanded to do and what he is prohibited from doing, halakhot of marriage and acquisition, protocols of criminal and civil jurisprudence, the Temple service, and the halakhot of spiritual purity and impurity. By contrast, this tractate discusses general principles [*avot*] of conduct that, by their very nature, do not determine defined halakha. Rather, the tractate addresses approaches and attitudes, values, matters of wisdom, and arousal of the soul.

The tractate's content influences the manner in which it was edited. As opposed to other tractates, which cite tannaitic disputes and in which the details of the halakhot are organized according to defined topics and parameters, in tractate *Avot* there is no such order. This is due in part to the general nature of the directives therein, which include sayings of wisdom and ethics. It is also because each Sage who articulates his words of wisdom does not relate to the sayings of others, but rather, views matters from a completely novel perspective and formulates them in a unique manner, both in terms of content and in terms of form and expression.[2]

---

1. See Eduyyot 1:4.
2. At the same time, it is possible to very clearly discern the order and editorial policy of

"The Mishna of the Pious [*Ḥasidut*]"

A unique characteristic of tractate *Avot* is that it contains no defined laws or halakhic rulings. It does not address the basic halakhic obligations of each and every Jew, but rather the area characterized by the Sages as piety [*ḥasidut*], or what is beyond the letter of the law. This tractate does not say how one must fulfill the Torah laws in practice, but rather prescribes the direction and the effort required to transcend the obligatory to the realm of the appropriate, the desirable, and beyond. "The Mishna of the Pious," however we characterize it, is not a halakhic guide for every person, but it is primarily directed toward those who are capable of and seek to go beyond halakhic obligations to fulfill matters that are not typical of the standard person, but are on a more exalted level, *ḥasidut*, as it is stated in the Talmud, that "One who seeks to become pious ... should observe the matters of tractate *Avot*."[3]

Similarly, although from a different perspective, the Rambam explained the positioning of this tractate in the order of *Nezikin*, adjacent to tractate *Sanhedrin*. In his opinion, after tractate *Sanhedrin* teaches regarding the significance and the standing of the judges of Israel, tractate *Avot* constructs the appropriate ethical template and ways of conduct for those who issue rulings in Israel.

Tractate *Avot* and the Book of Proverbs

The Oral Torah in general and the Mishna in particular constitute a continuation of the Written Torah. Despite the differences in language, style, and other features, the continuity is implicit in the Oral Torah. Virtually every tractate in the Mishna contains a different formulation of one of the halakhot written in the Torah and greater detail about it.

Tractate *Avot*, too, is based on the Bible, and in certain respects is a continuation of it. But it continues not only the Torah itself;[4] it is to a large degree comparable to and a continuation of the book of Proverbs.[5]

---

the tractate. It consists of several parts, each with its own nature and structure regarding chronology, content, and form. In each of these parts, there is a discussion of a certain topic, such as wisdom, ethics, Torah, mitzvot, or etiquette, from different perspectives that complement one another. Together these parts constitute a single tractate.

3. Bava Kamma 30a.
4. It is especially conspicuous in the book of Deuteronomy, in which Moses, in his orations, serves as a teacher and guide, not only as a lawgiver and an arbiter of halakha and justice.
5. It is apparently no coincidence that just as the book of Proverbs consists primarily of a father's words of wisdom and ethics to his son, as in the verse: "Hear, my son, the admonition of your father" (Proverbs 1:8), so the Sages called this tractate "Avot," meaning fathers.

The primary conspicuous similarity is that just as the book of Proverbs contains guidance in instructive, pedagogical, and, to a large degree, even obligatory terms, even though this guidance is not formulated in legal terms, so too, the statements in tractate *Avot* are all sayings of counsel and guidance for ethical conduct and perfection of one's attributes.

The similarity between tractate *Avot* and the book of Proverbs is also manifest in the absence of one central topic. The book of Proverbs includes hundreds of statements of wisdom, ethics, and counsel in all areas, statements that in general act to form a specific character, although each verse in the book of Proverbs fundamentally constitutes a matter of wisdom in and of itself. Similarly, the *mishnayot* of tractate *Avot* are an unsystematic collection of counsel, guidance, and instruction in various areas that together create a template for the ideal character of man.

In addition, although the great majority of the book of Proverbs is ethical and practical guidance, it contains, primarily in its final chapters, matters that are not goal oriented but rather are matters of wisdom that expand horizons and provide knowledge of the world. Similarly, tractate *Avot* contains *mishnayot* and chapters that consist of matters of wisdom, summaries of matters that are found in the world, and explanations of how different matters in the world relate to one another. Interestingly, these portions of tractate *Avot*, too, are primarily located in the final chapter of the tractate.

Reciting Tractate *Avot*

There is an ancient custom among the Jewish people, dating back to the geonic period, to communally recite one chapter of tractate *Avot* on each of the *Shabbatot* between Passover and *Shavuot*, after the afternoon prayer, in honor of Moses, who died around that time. Likewise, it is said that reciting these chapters serves as preparation for the giving of the Torah on the festival of *Shavuot*.[6] In order to have it correspond to the number of the six *Shabbatot* between those holidays, the sixth chapter, "Acquisition of the Torah," was added. It is not strictly part of the Mishna, but is a *baraita* that contains a collection of statements in praise of the Torah and of those who engage in its study. Tractate *Avot*, thereby, entered into the prayer books throughout the Jewish Diaspora, and has been the object of many and varied commentaries.

---

6. The custom of Ashkenazic communities is to continue reciting the chapters of tractate Avot during the summer months until the Shabbat preceding Rosh HaShana.

Tractate *Avot* contains six chapters:

The first chapter, "Moses received," is primarily arranged chronologically, from the giving of the Torah until after the destruction of the Second Temple. The chapter begins with the chain of transmission of the Torah from Moses through the members of the Great Assembly at the beginning of the Second Temple era. From there, the chapter cites the statements of those who perpetuated the tradition: "pairs" of *tanna'im* from the Second Temple period; through those who filled the position of *Nasi*, from Beit Hillel through Rabban Shimon ben Gamliel, the father of Rabbi Yehuda HaNasi, redactor of the Mishna.

The second chapter, "Rabbi says," begins with the statements of Rabbi Yehuda HaNasi and his son, who were the last of the Beit Hillel dynasty during the period of the Mishna. Then the chapter returns to a discussion of Hillel and the chain of transmission of Hillel's students, i.e., Rabbi Yoḥanan ben Zakkai and his disciples.

The third chapter, "Akavya ben Mahalalel," is less defined in terms of chronology or content. It cites statements of the Sages who lived at the end of the Second Temple era and at the beginning of the functioning of Yavne as a center for Torah study. The three primary topics addressed in it are: engaging in Torah study both communally and individually, the relationship between wisdom on the one hand and action and fear of God on the other hand, and appropriate social ties.

The fourth chapter, "Ben Zoma," begins by citing statements of Sages who resided in Yavne but were not part of the court; the following generation, that of the students of Rabbi Akiva after the bar Kokheva revolt; and occasionally, later *tanna'im*. It concludes with words of reproach by Rabbi Elazar HaKappar, in the transitional generation between the *tanna'im* and the *amora'im*.

The fifth chapter, "With ten statements," is based primarily on unattributed statements and is constructed in descending numerical order beginning with ten. The chapter begins with matters of Creation and of providence over the Jewish people, and later places emphasis on the conduct of groups of people, both as individuals within the group, and as part of a large group. The chapter concludes by returning to the special matter of Torah study and cleaving to it.

The sixth chapter, "The Sages taught," is not from the Mishna per se, but is a *baraita*, apparently a very ancient one. The *baraita* is called "Acquisition of the Torah," referring to Torah study. The chapter, which contains statements that are somewhat more midrashic and detailed, addresses just the topic of the Torah – its virtue, its significance, and the methods to acquire it.

Chapter 1

Mishna 1

This mishna serves as an introduction to the entire tractate, and underscores the complex relationship between tradition and innovation. On the one hand, the entire Torah was transmitted through tradition, and on the other hand, sages in every generation discover and introduce matters of Torah in accordance with their own approach.

מֹשֶׁה קִבֵּל תּוֹרָה מִסִּינַי,

Moses our teacher **received** everything that can be categorized as **Torah**[N] **from** the mouth of God at **Sinai,**[N] when he was atop the mountain for forty days and forty nights (Exodus 24:18) and received the Torah in its entirety there (Deuteronomy 4:14).

NOTES

Moses received Torah – מֹשֶׁה קִבֵּל תּוֹרָה: The chain of tradition is cited specifically at the beginning of tractate *Avot* in order to teach that even though the statements in tractate *Avot* are usually cited without biblical support texts, they should not be underestimated, because their source is the tradition of the fathers [*avot*] (Meiri). Others say that the emphasis on these matters at the beginning of this tractate, whose primary focus is on the desired mode of conduct, comes to teach that Torah has no existence without proper conduct, and there is no proper conduct without Torah (*Tiferet Yisrael*, based on mishna 3:17; see *Melekhet Shlomo*). Some write that the point of the mishna is to emphasize that this tractate is unlike other books of wisdom and ethics, but addresses more exalted matters, which originated with the receiving of the Torah (Bartenura).

The line drawn between these two elements, the tradition from Sinai on the one hand and the personal statements of the Sages according to their topics and their time on the other hand, is the secret of the Torah in general. It has special significance specifically as an introduction to a tractate that discusses matters of ethics and perfection of the soul.

From Sinai – מִסִּינַי: The reference to Sinai is not to the place where Moses received the Torah, but to the One from whom he received it, i.e., the Holy One blessed be He, who revealed Himself at Sinai (Bartenura). This form of expression is a form of

וּמְסָרָהּ לִיהוֹשֻׁעַ,

And this Torah that Moses received, **he transmitted it to Joshua,** his primary disciple, who was chosen as his replacement and successor (see Numbers 27:18). Joshua was first to receive the Oral Torah in the chain of transmission.

וִיהוֹשֻׁעַ לִזְקֵנִים,

And Joshua transmitted the Torah that he received **to the Elders,** the leaders of Israel in his generation, who outlived him and continued his legacy (Joshua 24:1).

וּזְקֵנִים לִנְבִיאִים, וּנְבִיאִים מְסָרוּהָ לְאַנְשֵׁי כְנֶסֶת הַגְּדוֹלָה.

And the Elders transmitted it **to the prophets,**[N] who lived during the era of the Judges and thereafter, **and the** later **prophets transmitted it to the members of the Great Assembly,**[NB] who were their colleagues and disciples at the beginning of the Second Temple era.

NOTES

respect vis-à-vis the Holy One blessed be He, who is not mentioned by His name, but with an appellation, just as one says "the Omnipresent," or "Heaven," and the like (see *Midrash Shmuel*). Some write that this wording emphasizes that Moses received the Torah while he was on Mount Sinai, at a level that no person other than he was privileged to reach (Rabbi Moshe Alsheikh).

Jabel Musa, one possible location of Mount Sinai

And the Elders to the prophets – וּזְקֵנִים לִנְבִיאִים: The reference is to the Elders who stood at the head of the congregation "who continued living after Joshua" (Joshua 24:31). The commentaries disagree as to whether the reference is to the entire period of the Judges as well (Rashbatz, Meiri), or whether the Judges are not included among these Elders, but are included among the prophets (see *Maḥzor Vitri*, Vilna Gaon). Likewise, some hold that the period of the prophets begins in the days of Samuel the prophet, continues through the First Temple era, through Jeremiah and Ezekiel, who was exiled to Babylon, and concludes with the final prophets, who ascended in

The Ten Commandments as seen in a scroll from Qumran, first century BCE

הֵם אָמְרוּ שְׁלֹשָׁה דְבָרִים: הֱווּ מְתוּנִים בַּדִּין, וְהַעֲמִידוּ תַּלְמִידִים הַרְבֵּה, וַעֲשׂוּ סְיָג לַתּוֹרָה.

They, the members of the Great Assembly, **stated three matters:**[N] **Be deliberate in judgment,**[N] as the judges must precisely analyze every case that comes before them, even if it appears to them that the matter is clear and resolved. **And establish many stu-**

NOTES

the return to Zion: Haggai, Zechariah, and Malachi (see *Avot deRabbi Natan*, where the latter prophets are considered a group in and of themselves).

The prophets are mentioned here as part of the chain of transmission of the Torah. Although they hear the word of God, they are unable to innovate anything novel with respect to matters of Torah on the basis of their power of prophecy (Yaavetz).

And the prophets transmitted it to the members of the Great Assembly – וּנְבִיאִים מְסָרוּהָ לְאַנְשֵׁי כְנֶסֶת הַגְּדוֹלָה: Transmission appears explicitly twice in the mishna: "He transmitted it to Joshua…and the prophets transmitted it to the members of the Great Assembly." The first transmission marks the transition from the exalted status of Moses's prophecy at Sinai to the Sages of Israel with the giving of the Written Torah, and with it the tradition of the Oral Torah through the end of the First Temple era. The second explicit instance of transmission is at the beginning of the Second Temple era, from the prophets to the members of the Great Assembly, marking the transition from transmission of the Torah to the select leaders of the generation at the beginning of this period to the dissemination and teaching of the Torah to the multitudes by its end. Likewise, this marks the transition from the period during which the Torah was primarily Torah from Heaven, to a period where the Oral Torah was continually expanding and developing into a work crafted by the human intellect (*Beit Shaul*, Nathanson).

Three matters – שְׁלֹשָׁה דְבָרִים: The tally of "three matters" appears several times in the *mishnayot* of tractate *Avot* and in the words of the Sages in general. Three suggests completeness, like a triangle, which is the simplest shape that forms a structure. Scholars have written in this regard that in an abstract sense three reflects the dialectic of thesis, antithesis, and synthesis.

Be deliberate in judgment [*badin*] – הֱווּ מְתוּנִים בַּדִּין: Most commentaries explain that the reference is to issuing halakhic rulings, especially in monetary cases, which are typically referred to as *din* or *dinim*. Some explain that *din* in this context is a reference to an approach to study based on logic and reason through which one arrives at conclusions based on Torah verses, an approach that gradually developed during the Second Temple era. This approach is reflected in the talmudic phrases "from logical inference [*min hadin*]" and "could this not be derived through logical inference [*vehalo din hu*]." According to this, the mishna means that the members of the Great Assembly warned that although it is necessary and fitting to study and expand matters of Torah, one must do so very cautiously, as failure to exercise caution can lead to erroneous conclusions.

BACKGROUND

The Great Assembly – כְּנֶסֶת הַגְּדוֹלָה: The Great Assembly is the leadership group that functioned in Judah in the first part of the Second Temple era, from the days of Ezra the scribe at the time of the return to Zion, until the Greek conquest by Alexander the Great. Its character and identity are not perfectly clear, but it was apparently a council that convened from time to time and addressed matters on the communal and religious agenda. Since the names of the members of the Great Assembly were not preserved, some posited that the identities of the participants varied from session to session. Several ordinances are attributed to the Great Assembly, among them the institution of blessings, prayers, *kiddush*, and *havdala* (*Berakhot* 33a).

dents[N] in order to create a broad foundation of Torah study and Torah instruction. **And establish a fence [*seyag*] for the Torah**[N] These are ordinances and decrees enacted in order to distance individuals and society from transgressing mitzvot of the Torah.

Mishna 2

The Mishna continues recording the transmission of the Torah to a last member of the Great Assembly.

שִׁמְעוֹן הַצַּדִּיק הָיָה מִשְּׁיָרֵי כְּנֶסֶת הַגְּדוֹלָה.

Shimon HaTzaddik[P] **was among the remnants of the Great Assembly,**[N] one of the last of its Sages, and he continued the transmission of the Torah.

NOTES

And establish many students – וְהַעֲמִידוּ תַּלְמִידִים הַרְבֵּה: Some write that this matter, too, relates to the realm of teaching the Torah, as by means of increasing the number of students, the wisdom of the teachers is also increased and sharpened, as it is said: "From my students more than all of them" (*Maḥzor Vitri*, Meiri). Although this is true in every generation, it was especially so during the era of the members of the Great Assembly, whose primary role was establishing the stratum of Sages and their disciples.

Some note that in this regard, there is a moral determination regarding an issue that existed throughout the generations, especially between Beit Hillel and Beit Shammai, and was again manifest in the Yavne period (see *Berakhot* 28b): the question of how best to allocate teaching resources. Is it by forming an exclusive unit of extremely talented people or by teaching a large number of people with the understanding that greater quantity would produce greater quality (Rashbatz, Meiri, Rabbeinu Yona)?

And establish a fence for the Torah – וַעֲשׂוּ סְיָג לַתּוֹרָה: In addition to establishing ordered systems and instituting doctrines and principles for the Torah, the members of the Great Assembly also constructed a template of "fences for the Torah" (Meiri). In other words, they prohibited matters that were permitted per se, because of concern that people would err and violate Torah prohibitions due to habit or forgetfulness. This is because the difference between prohibited and permitted is sometimes very small. A large portion of the halakha that developed over the generations, especially during the Second Temple era, involves the creation of these fences. On the one hand, one is obligated to observe these fences, but on the other hand, one must remember that they are a rabbinic addition and not an intrinsic part of the mitzva.

Some explained that "and establish a fence for the Torah" is a continuation of "establish many students." Teaching the Oral Torah to many students itself preserved the Torah within certain frameworks and established a "fence" around it (*Notzer Ḥesed*).

הוּא הָיָה אוֹמֵר:

He would regularly say a fundamental principle that he would repeat:

עַל שְׁלֹשָׁה דְּבָרִים הָעוֹלָם עוֹמֵד, עַל הַתּוֹרָה, וְעַל הָעֲבוֹדָה, וְעַל גְּמִילוּת חֲסָדִים.

On the basis of three matters[N] **the world exists**; there are three foundational spiritual pillars upon which the world rests that enable it to exist: **on the basis of the**

NOTES

Among the remnants of the Great Assembly – מִשְּׁיָרֵי כְּנֶסֶת הַגְּדוֹלָה: This means that he was one of the last survivors, and in his days few of those Sages remained (*Maḥzor Vitri*, Meiri). In any case, the emphasis here is that he was considered one of the members of the Great Assembly. Through him, the live chain of tradition of the deliberations and activity of that institution continued (see Rashbatz).

On the basis of three matters – עַל שְׁלֹשָׁה דְּבָרִים: There are many explanations of the meaning and the identity of these pillars of the world, which are parallel to three "lines" of God's revelation, which are the mystical concepts of Kindness – acts of kindness; Might – Temple service; and Glory – Torah. This is an expression of the relationship between man and God. The Torah is the rational-intellectual component; the Temple service is the experiential-emotional component; and, in contrast to those two, which constitute a direct approach between man and God, performing acts of kindness is a manifestation of God's relationship with man, through one's relationship with other people.

Similarly, some explain that these three pillars correspond, respectively, to the power of study, faith, and virtues (Rambam). Others write that it corresponds to the three manners in which the soul expresses itself: speech, while engaging in Torah study; thought, in prayer service; and action, through acts of kindness (*Ḥesed LeAvraham*).

PERSONALITIES

Shimon HaTzaddik – שִׁמְעוֹן הַצַּדִּיק: Shimon HaTzaddik was one of the last survivors of the members of the Great Assembly. His place in the chain of tradition is significant, as he is the first of the Second Temple Sages whose name is known. Moreover, it is known that he was a High Priest, and as such he was also the most significant personage in the autonomous Jewish community in the Land of Israel at that time. He lived in the fourth century BCE and successfully oversaw a smooth transition between the period of Persian rule over the Land and the Greek conquest. It is related in the Talmud that for that purpose, he met with Alexander the Great, apparently during the latter's journey from the north toward Egypt (*Yoma* 69a).

Tradition holds that Shimon HaTzaddik served as High Priest for forty years. He was conspicuous in his extreme sanctity, which is also reflected in his title, "HaTzaddik," meaning, "the righteous." It is said that until the end of his life, protocols concerning sanctity and the Temple were conducted in the appropriate manner, and that after his death there was deterioration in these areas (*Yoma* 39a). A brief description of his character and his accomplishments is found in the Book of ben Sira, and ben Sira might have been his contemporary. The Book of ben Sira also includes words of personal praise of Shimon HaTzaddik, which were incorporated in lyrical form in the Yom Kippur prayers, in the liturgical poem: "How Splendid Was the Appearance of the High Priest." It is related that after his death, there was a crisis

Crypt of Shimon HaTzaddik in Jerusalem, with his statement in the mishna inscribed next to it

Torah,[N] i.e., studying it, knowing it, and engaging in it; **on the basis of** worship of God through **the** Temple **service;**[N] **and on the basis of acts of kindness,**[N] performing good deeds to benefit another person.

NOTES

concerning the succession to the High Priesthood (see *Menaḥot* 13:10 and 109b).

On the basis of the Torah – **עַל הַתּוֹרָה**: This is the first instance in the words of the Sages regarding the special place of Torah study as one of the pillars of the world. This mishna emphasizes Torah study as an independent value, in other words, not merely as a means to acquire knowledge of the mitzvot and their practical fulfillment, but a complete, absolute, and central world that exists in and of itself. This position of the Torah is one of the unique aspects of the Jewish world. The obligation to study Torah and the requirement to occupy oneself with it are an independent objective, a unique form of worship of God, and in its essence an act of ritual worship.

On the basis of the service [*haavoda*] – **וְעַל הָעֲבוֹדָה**: The plain understanding of the term *avoda* is Temple service, which is the unique aspect of worship of God emphasized in the Torah, the aspect of ritual worship and the connection and the drawing near of the person and the entire people to the Creator, and the entire world along with them. There is a reason that the prescribed offerings include all the strati of Creation: inanimate, vegetation, and living, which are all sacrificed and ascend heavenward. At the same time, prayer, which is characterized as "service of the heart [*avoda shebalev*]" serves, in certain respects, as a replacement for Temple service, because it is primarily a form of worship: direct worship of the Holy One blessed be He, which establishes the relationship between man and God (see Rabbeinu Yona and Rashbatz). Some write that service is a reference to fulfillment of all the practical mitzvot between man and God (*Tiferet Yisrael*, and so it is explained in Hasidic literature).

On the basis of acts of kindness – **וְעַל גְּמִילוּת חֲסָדִים**: In contrast to the mitzva of charity, "acts of kindness" include many matters that do not fall into defined halakhic categories (see *Pe'a* 1:1). It includes all aid extended to people, monetarily or physically, as the Sages said: Acts of kindness are greater than charity, as they can be fulfilled with all people, not just the poor, with both the living and the dead, and with both money and the body (see *Tosefta, Pe'a* 4:19). Included in "acts of kindness" are fostering peace between people, respecting others, organizing a wedding for a needy bride, accompanying the dead and arranging burial, consoling mourners, and more (Rashi).

Worshippers fill the Western Wall plaza, Yom Kippur eve, 2010

Sacrificing the daily offering

Mishna 3

Following Shimon HaTzaddik, who addressed matters upon which the world stands, his successor, Antigonus of Sokho, addresses the inner essence of each individual's worship of God.

אַנְטִיגְנוֹס אִישׁ סוֹכוֹ קִבֵּל מִשִּׁמְעוֹן הַצַּדִּיק.	**Antigonus** of the city of **Sokho**[P] in Judah **received** Torah **from Shimon HaTzaddik.**

PERSONALITIES

Antigonus of Sokho – אַנְטִיגְנוֹס אִישׁ סוֹכוֹ: Little is known about the life and personality of this Sage, who was a contemporary of the successors of Alexander the Great, in the first part of the third century BCE. It appears that he was a resident of the city of Sokho, in the lowlands of Judah (see Joshua 15:5). However, it is reasonable to posit that as a teacher of the multitudes and the head of the Sages, he also resided in Jerusalem.

The source of the name is the Greek Antigonus, a very common Greek name in those days, suggesting that Greek influence already existed at that time. It is possible that Antigonus was named after Antigonus I Monophthalmus, a prominent general of Alexander the Great and, for a certain period, his primary successor, much in the way that Jews called their sons Alexander in honor of that king.

In *Avot deRabbi Natan*, it is related that two of the disciples of Antigonus, Tzadok and Baitos, did not properly understand his statement as it was expressed in the mishna. They learned from it that a person does not receive reward for his good deeds at all. As a result, those disciples denied the existence of the World to Come, as well as denying the immortality of the soul and denying the Oral Torah in general. They established the sects of the Sadducees [*Tzedokim*] and the Boethusians [*Baitusim*], who strayed from the confines of tradition and for generations were enemies of the traditional Judaism of the Pharisees, the purveyors of the Oral Torah (see *Makkot* 1:6; *Menaḥot* 10:3; *Yadayim* 4:6–8, and elsewhere). According to what is related there, these sects' denial of the immortality of the soul caused them to live lives of luxury and hedonism. This divergence that resulted from the teacher's lack of clarity stands as the backdrop to several of the Sages' statements in this tractate that address the need to be cautious in choosing students and to convey material clearly.

The Ela Valley as seen from the top of Tel Sokho, commonly identified as Sokho

הוּא הָיָה אוֹמֵר: אַל תִּהְיוּ כַּעֲבָדִים הַמְשַׁמְּשִׁין אֶת הָרַב עַל מְנָת לְקַבֵּל פְּרָס, אֶלָּא הֱווּ כַּעֲבָדִים הַמְשַׁמְּשִׁין אֶת הָרַב שֶׁלֹּא עַל מְנָת לְקַבֵּל פְּרָס.

He would regularly **say: Do not be**, when fulfilling mitzvot and worshipping God, **like servants**[N] **who serve the master in order to receive a portion,**[N] in order to receive their portion of food, i.e., to receive reward for mitzvot, as that is not the ideal mode of service. **Rather, be like servants**[N] **who serve the master not in order to receive a portion.**[N]

וִיהִי מוֹרָא שָׁמַיִם עֲלֵיכֶם.

He added: Although you are not worshipping God in order to receive compensation, do not forget that you are servants of God, **and let the fear of Heaven be upon you.**[N]

NOTES

Do not be like servants – אַל תִּהְיוּ כַּעֲבָדִים: This statement provides guidance of great significance regarding the entire matter of observance of the mitzvot. In the Torah, the fact that there is reward for good deeds is mentioned many times; therefore, Antigonus saw the need to underscore that service of God should not be performed in order to receive that reward, but in order to perform the mitzvot for their own sake. Any intent to receive reward detracts from the virtue of the service, although it does not uproot it completely. That is, one should strive to arrive at a situation where his service will not be dependent upon receiving an external reward.

Portion [*peras*] – פְּרָס: Some explain that *peras* is a customary meal, a perpetual payment (Meiri and others). Others emphasize that it is a gift and is not characterized as the receiving of a payment (Rashi, Rambam, Bartenura). There are also those who explain it in homiletic fashion, as *peras* can mean "half," referring to thinking only of the reward in this world, which is half of what a person has (Rabbeinu Yosef Ḥayyim).

Rather, be like servants – אֶלָּא הֱווּ כַּעֲבָדִים: The reason Antigonus repeated his statement in two ways, one negative and one positive, was in order to emphasize that performing matters in the manner of "not in order to receive a portion" is not merely refraining from the negative, but it is a virtue in and of itself (Maharal of Prague). Moreover, there is another underlying emphasis. Although service of God that is not in order to receive a portion is primarily service motivated by love, nevertheless, "be like servants who serve the master." A person must consider himself like a servant, who does not work according to his own free will, but is subservient to his Master and worships Him with complete and fixed service.

Not in order to receive a portion – שֶׁלֹּא עַל מְנָת לְקַבֵּל פְּרָס: In ancient variant readings there is a more extreme formulation: "In order not to receive a portion." Some write that this version is referring to prominent people, while the version that appears in the mishna is directed to common people (*Notzer Ḥesed*). Conversely, it is referring to those of little faith, who, if they do not receive the portion, are likely to regret performance of mitzvot altogether (Rashbatz). In any case, this does not mean that there is no reward for mitzvot; rather, one must not perform them in order to be rewarded, but due to love (*Maḥzor Vitri*), and with complete identification with the purpose of the service (Yaavetz).

And let the fear of Heaven be upon you – וִיהִי מוֹרָא שָׁמַיִם עֲלֵיכֶם: This statement completes what was stated previously. A person who does not anticipate reward is ostensibly one who performs matters according to his will alone, from love. However, love alone is insufficient, as at times it waxes and at other times it wanes. This is why Antigonus adds that even if the most exalted action is one motivated by love, nevertheless, let the fear of Heaven be upon you (Rambam). Some write that the word Heaven in the expression "fear of Heaven upon you" comes to emphasize that the reference is not to fear of punishment, which is fundamentally parallel to receipt of reward, but to fear motivated by a sense of exaltedness (Yaavetz).

Mishna 4

Following Shimon HaTzaddik and Antigonus of Sokho, the mishna proceeds to the next stage of transmission of the Torah: five generations of "pairs."[B1]

יוֹסֵי בֶּן יוֹעֶזֶר אִישׁ צְרֵדָה וְיוֹסֵי בֶּן יוֹחָנָן אִישׁ יְרוּשָׁלַיִם קִבְּלוּ מֵהֶם.

Yosei ben Yo'ezer of Tzereida[P] and Yosei ben Yoḥanan of Jerusalem received from them.[N]

NOTES

Received from them – קִבְּלוּ מֵהֶם: The expression "from them" is difficult, as in the previous generation only the name of Antigonus of Sokho is mentioned. As a result, some explain that they received the oral tradition from Antigonus and the members of his court (Meiri, Rashbatz). Others explain that they received it from Shimon HaTzaddik and from Antigonus (Rabbeinu Yona, Rama). Rashbatz cites a variant reading, "received from him," which is the version in the Kaufman manuscript. He says that it is the simplest reading, but he was unable to determine whether it was the original version or a later emendation.

BACKGROUND

Pairs – זוגות: During the period from Yosei ben Yo'ezer and Yosei ben Yoḥanan until Hillel and Shammai, the Sages are cited in pairs. According to the Mishna (*Ḥagiga* 2:2), one of them was the *Nasi* of the Sanhedrin, while the other was deputy *Nasi*. Although undoubtedly there were other Sages in those generations, they are not mentioned in this list of the chain of tradition. According to the chronology, and inferring from mentions of some of these Sages, one can conclude that the period of the pairs continued from the days of Greek rule in the Land of Israel, through Hasmonean rule, and until the days of Herod. It is possible that the pairs were representative of two approaches, or two schools of thought regarding Torah study, each one sending its representative to the leadership of Israel, until, ultimately, many disputes developed between them, leading to a clear division into groups known as Beit Hillel and Beit Shammai (see *Tosefot Yom Tov*; *Ḥagiga* 2:2–3 and Jerusalem Talmud 2:2–3).

During the period of the "pairs," the Sages were not called by the honorific Rabban or Rabbi, but by their names alone. Due to the exalted status of those early Sages, they needed no honorific.

PERSONALITIES

Yosei ben Yo'ezer of Tzereida – יוֹסֵי בֶּן יוֹעֶזֶר אִישׁ צְרֵדָה: Yosei ben Yo'ezer was a priest, *Nasi* of the Sanhedrin, and of the first pair of Sages. He was a resident of Tzereida in western Samaria, adjacent to the site of the modern settlement of Peduel. Others identify Tzereida as the village of Surda in the region of Binyamin, west of Beit El. Due to his personal scrupulousness regarding the halakhot of ritual impurity, he was characterized as "the pious one of the priesthood" (*Ḥagiga* 2:7), and it is related that he, together with his colleague Yosei ben Yoḥanan,

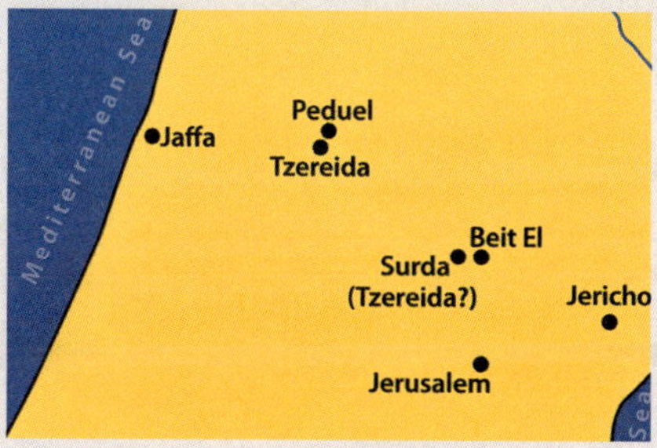

The village of Surda, possibly identified as the city of Tzereida

יוֹסֵי בֶן יוֹעֶזֶר אִישׁ צְרֵדָה אוֹמֵר: יְהִי בֵיתְךָ בֵּית וַעַד לַחֲכָמִים,

Yosei ben Yo'ezer says: Let your house be a meeting place[N] **for the Sages,** who will influence the atmosphere in your house;

וֶהֱוֵי מִתְאַבֵּק בַּעֲפַר רַגְלֵיהֶם,

and sit in the dust of their feet,[N] sit before them on the ground as students would sit before their teacher, and accept their authority;

PERSONALITIES

The curve of Wadi Shilo around the Balata ruins, possibly identified as Tzereida of the Second Temple era

instituted several ordinances regarding ritual purity. Nevertheless, because he attested that the ruling in several halakhot relating to ritual purity should be lenient, he was called "Yosei the lenient" (*Eduyyot* 8:4).

Yosei ben Yo'ezer was executed by the Greek authorities during the period of Antiochus's edicts, when his Hellenized nephew, Alkimos, served as High Priest under the auspices of the authorities and participated in the persecution and execution of many pious men (See *Bereshit Rabba* 65:22). In the Mishna (*Sota* 9:9) it is stated that Yosei ben Yo'ezer and Yosei ben Yoḥanan were the last of the *eshkolot*, people possessed of all positive attributes. Until the end of their lives, disputes did not endure in Israel, but were resolved according to the majority (*Sota* 47b).

NOTES

A meeting place [*beit vaad*] for the Sages – בֵּית וַעַד לַחֲכָמִים: Some explain it according to the standard meaning of *beit vaad*, a place where Sages sit and study (Rashi). Others explain it more broadly, that it is a place where the Sages assemble and engage in Torah or communal matters (Rambam, see Meiri). In essence, the statement means that it is not sufficient merely to hear the words of the Sages, but one must accord them great honor (Yaavetz) and be a virtuous person who performs good deeds so the Sages will agree to assemble in his home (Rashbatz). Moreover, if his house is a meeting place for Sages, inevitably he will absorb some of their Torah statements (Bartenura), as the atmosphere is affected by the guests who frequent his home and the discussions they conduct there. When Sages gather in his home, they influence the inhabitants and create an atmosphere of enlightenment in the house.

And sit [*mitabek*] in the dust of their feet – וֶהֱוֵי מִתְאַבֵּק בַּעֲפַר רַגְלֵיהֶם: In the days of the Mishna, the Sages would sit on a chair or a cushion while the students would sit on the ground at their feet. That is why the mishna specifies that although a person hosting the Sages in his home is the homeowner, he should not view himself as the Sages' equal, but should sit submissively on the floor before them and honor them (*Maḥzor Vitri*, Bartenura). In a broader sense, the statement means that he should accept their authority and learn from them. Rashi explains that the word *mitabek*, literally meaning to become dusty, serves to emphasize that one should serve the Sages even with menial tasks that are beneath him. By contrast, others write that *mitabek* is an expression referring to wrestling [*hitavkut*] and battle. Although in general a person should be submissive before his teacher, when it comes to matters of halakha, he

וֶהֱוֵי שׁוֹתֶה בְצָמָא אֶת דִּבְרֵיהֶם.

and thirstily imbibe[N] **their words,** listen to them attentively, with thirst and desire to hear what they have to say.

Mishna 5

Following the statement of Yosei ben Yo'ezer, who emphasizes opening one's house to Sages and thirsting after their words, Yosei ben Yoḥanan emphasizes the need to open one's house and one's heart to other people.

יוֹסֵי בֶן יוֹחָנָן אִישׁ יְרוּשָׁלַיִם אוֹמֵר:

Yosei ben Yoḥanan[P] **of Jerusalem says:**

יְהִי בֵיתְךָ פָּתוּחַ לִרְוָחָה,

Let your house be open wide[N] so that all the needy will be able to come to it.

NOTES

should express his opinion when he disagrees with them (*Ruaḥ Ḥayyim*).

Thirstily imbibe – שׁוֹתֶה בְצָמָא: This statement is a continuation of what was stated before. Since the mishna is referring to a person whose home is frequented by Sages, and he is constantly with them and learning from them, it is possible that he may become less sensitive to what they say, and he will no longer ascribe the appropriate significance to their words. That is why the mishna emphasizes that even though he is accustomed to hear the words of the Sages, he should conduct himself like one who thirsts and desires them (Rashi, Rabbeinu Yona, see Meiri).

Open wide – פָּתוּחַ לִרְוָחָה: Some explain this literally, to mean that the house should be open in all four directions, or, at least in the direction of the access road, as is related regarding Abraham and Job (*Avot deRabbi Natan*). Alternatively, one's house should be spacious and accessible, so the poor person will not think that the house is not roomy enough and be ashamed (*Maḥzor Vitri*). Some explain it as a figure of speech meaning that one should receive his visitors generously and warmly, as though he is capable of receiving an unlimited number of guests (Meiri, Yaavetz).

PERSONALITIES

Yosei ben Yoḥanan – יוֹסֵי בֶן יוֹחָנָן: Little information is known about him, other than that he was the deputy *Nasi* alongside the *Nasi* Yosei ben Yo'ezer, and what is stated regarding the two of them, both in terms of the ordinances that they instituted and in terms of their praise as well-rounded Torah personalities [*anshei eshkolot*] (see mishna 4).

His statement cited here may reflect the fact that he was a resident of Jerusalem, a large city. In a large city there are typically many guests and needy people, whereas this is less common in small, more remote villages.

Model of Jerusalem during the Second Temple period, Israel Museum

וְיִהְיוּ עֲנִיִּים בְּנֵי בֵיתְךָ,

And let the poor be members of your household;[N] receive them hospitably, so they feel like members of the household.

וְאַל תַּרְבֶּה שִׂיחָה עִם הָאִשָּׁה.

He qualifies the statement: Although your house and heart should be open to people, do not **speak excessively with a woman.**

בְּאִשְׁתּוֹ אָמְרוּ – קַל וָחֹמֶר בְּאֵשֶׁת חֲבֵרוֹ.

The mishna adds: **They said** this general prohibition **regarding one's wife,**[N] as excessive conversation between man and woman has the potential to lead to extreme frivolity and to sexual tension that is not beneficial in seeking to build a spiritual household. And **all the more so** must one **be careful** in this respect **regarding the wife of another,** as excessive conversation could lead to an inappropriate sense of intimacy and even deteriorate into forbidden actions.

NOTES

Let the poor be members of your household – וְיִהְיוּ עֲנִיִּים בְּנֵי בֵיתְךָ: Many explain based on what is stated in the Talmud, that instead of servants or slaves, it is preferable to have the poor in your house, to enable them to help a bit around the house during their stay (Rashi, Rambam, and others). Others explain that the poor should feel like members of the household, and not superfluous (Rabbeinu Yona). Or, that they will be able to enter without asking permission, due to a sense of intimacy (*Avot deRabbi Natan*), similar to the explanation in the commentary. Some explain otherwise, that one should not seek to avoid the poor, claiming insufficient resources. Instead, treat them as though they were members of your household, whose needs you always make certain to meet (*Ḥafetz Ḥayyim*).

They said regarding one's wife – בְּאִשְׁתּוֹ אָמְרוּ: Some write that this statement is a later addition by Rabbi Yehuda HaNasi, redactor of the mishna (Bartenura), and that is the explanation in the commentary. Some write that it is a continuation of the statement of Yosei ben Yoḥanan, who was relating to statements of the Sages who preceded him (*Tosefot Yom Tov*).

In explaining the crux of the matter, which is ostensibly difficult, as a man's wife is "your companion and the wife of your covenant" (Malachi 2:14), they explain that the emphasis is on specifically excessive speech, which is considered "idle speech" when there is no need for it (*Maḥzor Vitri*, Meiri). Alternatively, the mishna is referring to speech with an explicit or implied sexual overtone, especially when the wife is menstruating and excessive intimacy between spouses is problematic (see Rashi and Rabbeinu Yona).

מִכָּאן אָמְרוּ חֲכָמִים: כָּל זְמַן שֶׁאָדָם מַרְבֶּה שִׂיחָה עִם הָאִשָּׁה – גּוֹרֵם רָעָה לְעַצְמוֹ, וּבוֹטֵל מִדִּבְרֵי תוֹרָה, וְסוֹפוֹ יוֹרֵשׁ גֵּיהִנֹּם.

The mishna further adds: **Consequently, the Sages said: Any time one speaks excessively with a woman**, the longer the conversation lasts, the more **he causes himself harm,**[N] due to excessive intimacy that is liable to lead to sin or to lead to altercation or strife, **is idle from matters of Torah**, as this conversation usually comes at the expense of Torah study, **and ultimately inherits Gehenna**, as he caused harm to himself and was also idle from engaging in Torah study.

Mishna 6

Following the statements of the first pair, Yosei ben Yo'ezer and Yosei ben Yoḥanan, the mishna proceeds to the second pair in the transmission of the Torah from generation to generation.

יְהוֹשֻׁעַ בֶּן פְּרַחְיָה וְנִתַּאי הָאַרְבֵּלִי קִבְּלוּ מֵהֶם.

Yehoshua ben Peraḥya[P] **and Nitai HaArbeli received from them**, from Yosei ben Yo'ezer and Yosei ben Yoḥanan.

NOTES

He causes himself harm – גּוֹרֵם רָעָה לְעַצְמוֹ: This is because he thereby acquires the attribute of lust (Rambam). Rabbeinu Yona explains in a similar fashion, that the evil inclination overcomes him.

PERSONALITIES

Yehoshua ben Peraḥya – יְהוֹשֻׁעַ בֶּן פְּרַחְיָה: Yehoshua ben Peraḥya, who was apparently a priest, and perhaps the High Priest, was active during the reign of the Hasmonean kings, particularly in the time of John Hyrcanus (135–104 BCE) and King Alexander Yannai. The latter was in conflict with the Sages of Israel and tended to side with the Sadducees, arousing great resentment and various forms of revolt. Times were so tense that Yehoshua ben Peraḥya was ultimately forced to flee to Alexandria. Only sometime later did his disciple Shimon ben Shataḥ write to him that the situation was calmer and he could return to Jerusalem: "From Jerusalem the holy city to Alexandria of Egypt; my sister, my husband is found in your midst, and I am sitting desolate." According to the talmudic tradition, he had a disciple named Jesus. He ostracized him when he detected improper conduct in him (*Sota* 47a); that said, according to the chronology he was not the founder of Christianity.

Elsewhere an important statement is cited in the name of Yehoshua ben Peraḥya, although some attribute it to Yehuda ben Tabai, regarding the temptation associated with prominent status: Initially, anyone who would say: Ascend to the position of *Nasi*, I would bind him and place him before the lion. Now that I have become *Nasi*, anyone who tells me to descend from the position, I would cast a kettle of boiling water upon him (*Menaḥot* 109b).

יְהוֹשֻׁעַ בֶּן פְּרַחְיָה אוֹמֵר:

Yehoshua ben Perahya says matters relating to the type of relationships that one should forge with various other people.

עֲשֵׂה לְךָ רַב,

Establish for yourself a teacher,[N] even if is difficult for you to designate someone specific to be your teacher.

וּקְנֵה לְךָ חָבֵר,

Acquire for yourself, through effort and investment, **a friend**[N] with whom you can conduct close and reciprocal relations.

וֶהֱוֵי דָן אֶת כָּל הָאָדָם לְכַף זְכוּת.

And judge every person, in terms of his personality as a whole, **favorably**,[N] so that his shortcomings will not overshadow his positive characteristics.

NOTES

Establish for yourself a teacher – עֲשֵׂה לְךָ רַב: The plain understanding of this is that a person should acquire his Torah knowledge by learning it from another, as studying by oneself is not comparable to learning from another (Rashi, Rambam). *Avot deRabbi Natan* explains differently, that a person should acquire most of his Torah knowledge specifically from one teacher. In that way, the different areas of his study will be complete and orderly, "and the result is that this person will reside in his place and be filled with good and blessing."

The meaning of the command "establish for yourself" is that even if the teacher is himself unfit to be your teacher, you must study with him until he is fit to be your teacher (Rambam, Yaavetz), because it is dangerous for a person to be without a spiritual authority over him. Some explain that "establish for yourself" means that he should exert himself greatly to find a teacher who is suitable (Meiri).

Acquire [*ukne*] for yourself a friend – קְנֵה לְךָ חָבֵר: A relationship between friends is different from a relationship between teacher and student, or family relations. The way of acquiring such a relationship is complicated, as in order to find a true friend, one must find someone with whom there is a special intimacy. In that regard, Yehoshua ben Perahya advises not only to attempt to find a friend, but to acquire one – to invest a conscious and concerted effort to acquire him as a friend, and even to bear various costs to acquire a friend of that kind (Rashbatz). This friend should be a colleague in Torah, one who will spur you to do good and will offer you counsel (see Rambam). An additional, surprising explanation can be found in Rashi, who explains that the verb *ukne* is a reference to purchasing books for study. They are the "friend."

And judge every person [*kol haadam*] favorably – הֱוֵי דָן אֶת כָּל הָאָדָם לְכַף זְכוּת: In other words, whatever one hears about a person, he should say that the other's intent is for the best; and that is how one will be judged in Heaven (Rashi, based on *Avot deRabbi Natan*). The Sages derived this from the verse: "With righteousness you shall judge your counterpart" (Leviticus 19:15, see *Torat Kohanim* there). Some write that this is a continuation of the previous statement: If one judges another favorably, the friendship will be sustained (*Notzer Hesed*).

This statement is made regarding a person in general, of whom nothing is known about his actions and characteristics. However, if one knows that the other is righteous, he should make an even greater effort to find a favorable explanation. The opposite is true of a wicked person, who need not be judged favorably (Rambam, Meiri, Rabbeinu Yona).

In addition, as explained, the statement refers to

Mishna 7

Following Yehoshua ben Peraḥya's discussion of the preferred nature of ties with various people, his partner, Nitai HaArbeli, highlights the instances when it is appropriate to distance oneself from others.

נִתַּאי הָאַרְבֵּלִי אוֹמֵר: **Nitai HaArbeli**[P] says:

הַרְחֵק מִשָּׁכֵן רָע, **Distance** yourself **from an evil neighbor,**[N] refrain from residing near a wicked person, or minimize neighborly relations with a person of that kind, in order to avoid conflict with him or avoid his negative influence.

וְאַל תִּתְחַבֵּר לָרָשָׁע, Likewise, **do not associate with the wicked,**[N] even if he is successful and it appears

NOTES

the person in his entirety. Even though there are genuine flaws in that person, when one comes to assess him as a whole, one must view his positive aspects and judge him on their basis. Likewise, actions and characteristics can be interpreted positively or negatively. One must make an effort to interpret them for good and to search for the other's positive side.

Distance yourself from an evil neighbor – הַרְחֵק מִשָּׁכֵן רָע: The statement of Nitai HaArbeli regarding distancing oneself from evil completes the statement of Yehoshua ben Peraḥya, who spoke of drawing near to good (Rashbatz). An "evil neighbor" can be understood as one who treats people badly or who typically instigates quarrels and disputes; this is the reason it is recommended to keep one's distance from him. Alternatively, the reference is to a person who is a good neighbor but is a wicked man whose actions are evil; one must distance himself from him, so as not to learn from his evil behavior (Meiri, Yaavetz). *Avot deRabbi Natan* explains that "distance yourself from an evil neighbor" is stated not only regarding place of residence, but also regarding the owner of an adjacent field, or a colleague at work. They explained this on the basis of "woe unto the wicked, woe unto his neighbor," as when punishment befalls a wicked person, his neighbor is also harmed (see *Nega'im* 12:6).

Do not associate [*titḥaber*] with the wicked – וְאַל תִּתְחַבֵּר לָרָשָׁע: In other words, not only must one distance himself from being a neighbor to an evil neighbor, but one must refrain from any association with the wicked, as there are different types of interpersonal relationships, and one must distance himself from wickedness in all of them (Meiri). It is stated in *Avot deRabbi Natan* that this can be derived from the words of the prophet to Yehoshafat: "Because you allied yourself [*kehitḥaberkha*] with Aḥazyahu, the Lord has breached your works" (II Chronicles 20:37).

PERSONALITIES

Nitai HaArbeli – נִתַּאי הָאַרְבֵּלִי: Nitai HaArbeli is mentioned only here and in *Ḥagiga* 2:2. Nothing is known about him other than the fact that he was the deputy *Nasi* alongside Yehoshua ben Peraḥya. From the fact that he is from Arbel, it can be understood that during his lifetime there was already a populous Jewish settlement in the Lower Galilee, as well, and not only in and around Jerusalem.

that associating with him could bring one benefit and facilitate success.

וְאַל תִּתְיָאֵשׁ מִן הַפֻּרְעָנוּת.

And do not despair of divine punishment[N] of the wicked. Although it appears that the wicked one is successful in his wickedness, as though there is no justice and no Judge, know and believe that ultimately, the wicked will be punished.

NOTES

Do not despair of divine punishment [*puranut*] – אַל תִּתְיָאֵשׁ מִן הַפֻּרְעָנוּת: Despair means to give up on something, to think that it will never happen. The commentary is in accordance with the explanation of Rabbeinu Yona and others that a person who sees the wicked thrive must not despair due to the thought that there is no justice and no Judge in the world, and, as a result of that despair, to join forces with the wicked person; the reason is that ultimately punishment will be administered to him. Some explain that this statement is like what is stated in the previous mishna, "acquire for yourself a friend." Just as you must distance yourself from the wicked, so must you cleave to a good friend, because a calamitous [*puranut*] time is liable to eventuate in which you will need his help (Meiri). Others explain to the contrary: If calamity befalls you, do not despair, because salvation will soon come (Rashi).

Ruins of the ancient synagogue in the city of Arbel, second to fourth centuries CE

Mishna 8

This mishna continues on to the third "pair," whose statements are directed primarily toward judges sitting in judgment, although the moral lessons imparted are relevant to everyone, in his own place and context.

יְהוּדָה בֶּן טַבַּאי וְשִׁמְעוֹן בֶּן שָׁטָח קִבְּלוּ מֵהֶם.

Yehuda ben Tabai and Shimon ben Shataḥ received from them, from Yehoshua ben Peraḥya and Nitai HaArbeli.

יְהוּדָה בֶּן טַבַּאי אוֹמֵר:

Yehuda ben Tabai[P] **says** to judges:

אַל תַּעַשׂ עַצְמְךָ כְּעוֹרְכֵי הַדַּיָּנִין.

Do not render yourself, when you adjudicate between two parties, **like court advocates,**[N] who represent a particular party. Do not seek to represent and explain the positions of one of the parties, as in Jewish courts there are no advocates, just witnesses and judges.

NOTES

Like court advocates [*ke'orkhei hadayyanim*] – כְּעוֹרְכֵי הַדַּיָּנִין: Court advocates were part of the Greco-Roman judicial system, and the practice spread from there throughout the world. They functioned as lawyers do today, representing one of the parties and managing the course of the trial before the judge. Here, Yehuda ben Tabai cautions the judges to not be like the court advocates, who advocate on behalf of one of the parties, and, likewise, not to give legal counsel to one of the parties, who, as a result, is liable to deviate from the truth, e.g., by saying what the judge instructed him to say, in order to prevail in the trial. This was already stated in the Torah (Deuteronomy 1:17): "You shall not give preference in judgment" (see Rabbeinu Yona; *Ketubot* 52b).

Some cited a variant reading: "like arch-judges [*ke'arkhei hadayyanim*]," meaning like the most prominent judges. The mishna is addressing a student, cautioning him not to deliberate and speak before his teacher as though adjudicating the trial, or is cautioning a judge against coercing a litigant to be judged specifically before him (Bartenura). Some explain this as a directive to all people to avoid responding quickly when asked what is the ruling, as experts do (*Maḥzor Vitri*, based on *Avot deRabbi Natan*).

PERSONALITIES

Yehuda ben Tabai – יְהוּדָה בֶּן טַבַּאי: As with most of the Sages of the "pairs," very little is known about Yehuda ben Tabai. The *Tosefta* (*Sanhedrin* 6:6) relates an incident in which he erred regarding a halakhic matter and had a man unlawfully executed. After his colleague Shimon ben Shataḥ apprised him of the fact that he was mistaken, he accepted upon himself that he would not issue rulings without consulting Shimon ben Shataḥ. The version in the Talmud (*Ḥagiga* 16b) adds that from that time on, he would ascend each day to the grave of the person whom he sentenced to be executed, and weep there. Few other deeds are attributed to him; and in other places, those same actions are attributed to Yehoshua ben Peraḥya, so the attribution is uncertain.

וּכְשֶׁיִּהְיוּ בַּעֲלֵי דִינִין עוֹמְדִים לְפָנֶיךָ – יִהְיוּ בְעֵינֶיךָ כִּרְשָׁעִים.

When litigants stand before you, they should be wicked in your eyes. One should relate with suspicion to everything that they say and analyze it thoroughly.

וּכְשֶׁנִּפְטָרִים מִלְּפָנֶיךָ – יִהְיוּ בְעֵינֶיךָ כְּזַכָּאִין, כְּשֶׁקִּבְּלוּ עֲלֵיהֶם אֶת הַדִּין.

And when they depart from your presence after sentencing, transform your attitude toward both parties so **they would be innocent in your eyes**, and judge them favorably from **when they accepted the verdict upon themselves**[N] to rectify what needs to be rectified.

Mishna 9

Following the statement of Yehuda ben Tabai that cautions the judge about how to act and relate toward litigants, his partner, Shimon ben Shataḥ, addresses the conduct of the judge vis-à-vis the witnesses.

שִׁמְעוֹן בֶּן שָׁטָח אוֹמֵר:

Shimon ben Shataḥ[P] **says:**

הֱוֵי מַרְבֶּה לַחְקֹר אֶת הָעֵדִים,

You shall interrogate the witnesses extensively,[N] even beyond the basic questions, in order to precisely ascertain the matter and arrive at the true ruling.

NOTES

When they accepted the verdict upon themselves – כְּשֶׁקִּבְּלוּ עֲלֵיהֶם אֶת הַדִּין: It is the obligation of the judge to ensure that the trial will produce a just, practical decision in order to repair society, but he need not relate to the person standing before him as wicked or deceitful, other than for the purpose of his vigilance during the trial. Therefore, once the parties accepted the ruling and rectified what needed rectifying, through repayment of money, return of property, or payment of a fine, the judge may no longer judge the liable party unfavorably in the moral sense. He must again attribute to him the presumptive credibility and innocence that every person has (see Rashi, Rabbeinu Yona).

You shall interrogate the witnesses extensively – הֱוֵי מַרְבֶּה לַחְקֹר אֶת הָעֵדִים: In other words, one should not limit his questions to the fundamental information that must be included in the testimony, which the Sages characterize as interrogation [*ḥakirot*], but also regarding examinations [*bedikot*], in other words, minor, marginal questions. By increasing the number of questions, one is better able to ascertain the truth of the matter (Meiri, see *Sanhedrin* 5:1–2). Some write that the judge should ask many questions and ask them quickly and without interruption, so the witnesses will be unable to coordinate their testimony (*Midrash Shmuel*). These directives are especially significant in the Jewish judicial system in which there are no court advocates, as stated in the previous mishna, neither prosecutors nor defense attorneys, and the entire trial is conducted by the judges.

וֶהֱוֵי זָהִיר בִּדְבָרֶיךָ, שֶׁמָּא מִתּוֹכָם יִלְמְדוּ לְשַׁקֵּר.

And be careful with your statements when you interrogate the witnesses extensively, as that can also lead to problems; **lest from them**, from your words, **they learn to lie,** when they learn the judge's thought process and the potential conclusions that are likely to arise from their testimony.

Mishna 10

This mishna continues with the transmission of the Torah to the fourth generation of the "pairs."

שְׁמַעְיָה וְאַבְטַלְיוֹן קִבְּלוּ מֵהֶם.

Shemaya and Avtalyon[P] **received from them**, from Yehuda ben Tabai and Shimon ben Shataḥ.

PERSONALITIES

Shimon ben Shataḥ – שִׁמְעוֹן בֶּן שָׁטַח: Shimon ben Shataḥ was the brother of Salome Alexandra, wife of Alexander Yannai, who reigned 103–76 BCE, and there was a complex relationship between the Sage and his brother-in-law, the king. Shimon ben Shataḥ was active in many areas during his tenure: in the battle against the Sadducees, in improving the standards of testimony in court, in eradicating sorcery, in granting obligatory status to a woman's marriage contract, and more. After the king's death, Queen Salome assumed the throne, and Shimon ben Shataḥ was granted broad leadership authority. This period is etched in the memory of the Jewish people as one of the most idyllic periods in its history, as it was stable in terms of economics and security, and was accompanied by both spiritual and religious flourishing.

A relatively large number of stories are related about Shimon ben Shataḥ. Among others, it is related that due to exigent circumstances he resolutely utilized his great authority and sentenced to death a large number of women who engaged in witchcraft. Tradition holds that as a result, the relatives of these women caused his son to be falsely accused and executed (see Rashi on *Sanhedrin* 44b). It is possible that this event finds resonance in his statement regarding the importance of precision in interrogating witnesses.

Shemaya and Avtalyon – שְׁמַעְיָה וְאַבְטַלְיוֹן: According to the listed chronology of these generations, Shemaya and Avtalyon lived in the middle of the first century BCE, during the battle for power between the Hasmonean brothers Aristobolus and Hyrcanus, around the time of Herod's reign.

According to tradition, Shemaya and Avtalyon were proselytes or the children of proselytes (*Yoma* 71b). Some say that they did not pronounce the guttural letters properly, and some surmise that their country of origin was one where they did not speak a Semitic language (see *Eduyyot* 1:3 and Notes there). When they taught Torah in the study hall, they placed a guard at the door and demanded an entrance fee from those coming to study. Later, Hillel reprimanded the Benei Beteira, the most significant family of Sages at that time, saying that they did not sufficiently serve Shemaya and Avtalyon. The halakhic statements of this "pair" are not cited in the sources, and few testimonies and halakhot are cited by others in their name.

שְׁמַעְיָה אוֹמֵר:

Shemaya says matters relating to areas of life that a person should draw near to and those from which he should distance himself:

אֱהֹב אֶת הַמְּלָאכָה,

Love labor,[N] as it facilitates physical and mental health, and engaging in it helps settle the world.

וּשְׂנָא אֶת הָרַבָּנוּת,

Hate authority,[N] both communal and religious, as it involves the potential of evil and corruption.

וְאַל תִּתְוַדַּע לָרָשׁוּת.

And do not become intimate with gentile governmental **authorities,**[N] as their motives are different from yours, and your well-being is not their priority.

NOTES

Love labor – אֱהֹב אֶת הַמְּלָאכָה: This means that a person should not refuse to engage in labor because he considers himself important, and prefers to be supported by charity. Instead, he should engage in labor and thereby merit a long life (Rashi). Similarly, the Rambam writes that a person should be occupied by his labor, so he will have a way to earn his livelihood and will not come to engage in robbery or deceit. Moreover, when a person is idle from labor, it could lead to insanity and even to sin (see *Ketubot* 5:5 and below 2:2), as the only true rest is after exertion (Rabbeinu Yona).

Hate authority [*harabbanut*] – וּשְׂנָא אֶת הָרַבָּנוּת: *Harabbanut* refers to authority over the public and also to the attribute of arrogance and haughtiness. The reason that one should hate authority over the public is that it leads to envy and dispute, and it involves corruption of values and many tests of character (Rambam). Moreover, it ultimately causes the premature death of those who possess it (*Avot deRabbi Natan*). Some write that this directive is a continuation of what is stated above, "love labor." Even one who achieves prominence must love the labor aspect of his position and hate the authority and honor aspects that it entails (*Midrash Shmuel*).

Do not become intimate [*titvada*] with authorities [*larashut*] – וְאַל תִּתְוַדַּע לָרָשׁוּת: *Titvada* can be understood as indicating knowledge, that the government is aware of him. As a result, he becomes a target for unwanted attention, charges, and the like. But *titvada* can also be understood in the sense of intimacy. In the historical context of Shemaya's time and position, the authorities were certainly a foreign institution or at least alienated from the people as a whole. However, in any case, it is politics that shapes the character of the government, and there will always be an element of seeking personal gain and self-interest, as articulated below: "Be wary of the authorities, because they draw a person near only for their own purpose; they appear as friends when it benefits them, but they do not stand by a person in his hour of duress" (2:3). Therefore, one ought to keep as much distance from them as possible. Some write that one who begins to become intimate with the authorities will begin to be concerned exclusively with matters involving the authorities and become entangled with them (Rambam). Typically, associating with the government involves love of authority. Therefore, one must distance himself from both (see *Maḥzor Vitri*; Bartenura). Some explain *larashut* to mean a loan, perhaps because borrowing is associated with the poor [*rash*]; one should try to avoid taking loans in his business (*Tiferet Yisrael*).

Mishna 11

Following the statements of Shemaya, which consisted of guidance for everyone, the Mishna cites the statements of Avtalyon, which are directed to the Sages.

אַבְטַלְיוֹן אוֹמֵר:

Avtalyon[P] **says:**

חֲכָמִים, הִזָּהֲרוּ בְּדִבְרֵיכֶם!

Sages, who engage in issuing rulings to the public and to their students, **be careful with your statements,**[N] both in terms of their content and in terms of the form in which they are stated, especially regarding matters that can be misunderstood and lead to pitfalls.

שֶׁמָּא תָּחוּבוּ חוֹבַת גָּלוּת, וְתִגְלוּ לִמְקוֹם מַיִם הָרָעִים, וְיִשְׁתּוּ הַתַּלְמִידִים הַבָּאִים אַחֲרֵיכֶם וְיָמוּתוּ, וְנִמְצָא שֵׁם שָׁמַיִם מִתְחַלֵּל.

You must do so **lest you incur liability to be exiled,** both in the literal, physical sense and in the spiritual sense, **and you will be exiled to a place of bad water,** to a place or society in which influence of negative elements prevails. Even if you are not at all harmed, because you are wise and mature, there is a concern that your students will not be able to withstand that influence; **and**

NOTES

Sages, be careful with your statements – חֲכָמִים הִזָּהֲרוּ בְּדִבְרֵיכֶם: Although everyone must be careful with his statements, it is incumbent upon the Sages to be especially careful, because their statements enjoy greater circulation (*Midrash Shmuel*). This caution is vital, because on occasion a rabbi is tired or preoccupied and must be especially careful then to avoid error (*Notzer Ḥesed*).

This carefulness entails the Sage clearly articulating what he is saying, ensuring that there is nothing ambiguous in his words (Meiri). This is true not only in saying their own statements, but also in transmitting material that originated in previous generations (Rashi).

PERSONALITIES

Avtalyon – אַבְטַלְיוֹן: This name has no meaning in Hebrew. It sounds like a Greek name, although no parallel in the Greek language has been found for it. Some suggest that Josephus Flavius speaks of him in *Antiquities of the Jews*, and he is the one called *Patolyon* or *Poleyon* there.

the students who come after you[N] to those places **will drink** the "bad water," the foreign influences, **and die**, and will be totally corrupted, **and the name of Heaven will be desecrated,**[N] as those students continue to be associated, in their own eyes or in the eyes of their surroundings, with the teacher. Everyone will believe that it was due to his Torah that they ended up as they did.

Mishna 12

This mishna cites the statement of the fifth pair of leaders, the last of the "pairs."

הִלֵּל וְשַׁמַּאי קִבְּלוּ מֵהֶם.	**Hillel**[P] **and Shammai received from them,** from Shemaya and Avtalyon.
הִלֵּל אוֹמֵר:	**Hillel says:**
הֱוֵי מִתַּלְמִידָיו שֶׁל אַהֲרֹן,	**Be among the disciples of Aaron**[N] the priest, who was both a guide and teacher

NOTES

You will be exiled to a place of bad water...who come after you – וְתִגְלוּ לִמְקוֹם מַיִם הָרָעִים... הַבָּאִים אַחֲרֵיכֶם: Some explain simply that he will be exiled among the gentiles, or to a place of ignoramuses with wicked conduct. He will be isolated there, his students will be influenced by the actions and beliefs of their surroundings, and their actions will be corrupted (*Maḥzor Vitri*).

Some explain that the "place" is a place of heresy. A Sage must be careful not to say anything that can be interpreted as supporting heresy. If he errs in his statement, the resulting damage will remain even after his death, as his statements outlive him (Meiri). Moreover, when students who did not understand the matters properly rely on their understanding, they will elaborate on and develop the matters, and thereby exacerbate the initial damage (Rabbeinu Yona).

And die and the name of Heaven will be desecrated – וְיָמוּתוּ וְנִמְצָא שֵׁם שָׁמַיִם מִתְחַלֵּל: Here, too, this can be interpreted in two ways. Some explain that the students will die young due to their sin. People will say that the Torah that they studied failed to protect them, and will be unable to identify the true cause, that they themselves caused it with their actions (Rashi). Others explain that this is referring to spiritual death, as the name of Heaven will be desecrated by students attributing their misguided opinions to the teacher (*Pirkei Moshe*).

Among the disciples of Aaron – מִתַּלְמִידָיו שֶׁל אַהֲרֹן: This relates primarily to the instruction to act in accordance with Aaron's actions as they are articulated in the mishna, as it is written: "The Torah of truth was in his mouth, and injustice was not found on his lips;

of the multitudes, and a paradigm of a righteous person living in the midst of his people, as these were his qualities:

אוֹהֵב שָׁלוֹם, וְרוֹדֵף שָׁלוֹם,

He was one who **loves peace** and considers it a supremely important value, **and** also **pursues peace**[N] in a practical sense, as he makes efforts in order to increase its presence in the world.

NOTES

he walked with Me in peace and honesty, and he returned many from iniquity. For the lips of the priest will safeguard knowledge, and they will seek Torah from his mouth, as he is a messenger of the Lord of hosts" (Malachi 2:6–7). Some explain that he should be among the disciples of Aaron, who, despite being a prominent leader of his generation, nevertheless engaged in making peace between people (Yaavetz).

Loves peace and pursues peace – אוֹהֵב שָׁלוֹם וְרוֹדֵף שָׁלוֹם: "Loves peace" refers to his state of mind, and "pursues peace" means that he implements it in practice (Rabbeinu Yona). In any place that there is a quarrel of any kind, he makes the effort to reconcile the parties in any way that he can, whether through appeasement, an attempt at mediation, or an attempt to uproot the hatred embedded in their hearts. Similarly, it says in *Avot deRabbi Natan*: "And pursues peace" – even if you must pursue it from city to city, from metropolis to metropolis, from province to province – do not refrain from imposing peace."

PERSONALITIES

Hillel – הִלֵּל: Hillel, often referred to as Hillel the Elder, was a figure of great historical importance. Due to his great significance, much information about him was transmitted, including many incidents and facts.

According to the tradition, Hillel lived 120 years, from 113 BCE until 8 CE, and ascended from Babylon to the Land of Israel to study Torah. He was a scion of a prominent family, whose lineage traced back to King David. When he reached the Land of Israel, he lived in poverty as a wood chopper, and he set aside half of his meager wages in order to pay the entrance fee into the study hall. Hillel, thereby, became the model for the generations of a person who devotedly studies Torah in conditions of hardship and poverty (see *Yoma* 35b).

After the era of Shemaya and Avtalyon, there began a period of harsh persecution by Herod, who killed many of the Sages. At that time, members of the Babylonian family of Benei Beteira headed the Sanhedrin, apparently with Herod's backing. The members of this family were humble and decent. As a result, when a question of great public significance arose that they were unable to answer and for which Hillel alone was able to provide a solution, they resigned their positions and installed Hillel at the head of the Sanhedrin (*Tosefta*, *Pesaḥim* 4:14; *Pesaḥim* 66a).

As Hillel's personality incorporated love of people, humility, and great wisdom, he was widely admired. His descendants served in the position of *Nasi* for hundreds of years after him, and the halakha was established in accordance with the school of study that he established, Beit Hillel. Among his undertakings was defining the approaches to Torah study, the "Seven Principles of Hillel." Relatively many sayings are cited in Hillel's name in this tractate, and this is probably both because of his great prominence, and because he formulated many sayings as part of his common touch.

אוֹהֵב אֶת הַבְּרִיּוֹת, וּמְקָרְבָן לַתּוֹרָה.

This pursuit of peace is not undertaken in an isolated, arrogant manner, stemming merely from tolerance, but it grows out of the fact that he genuinely **loves people,**[N] because they are God's creations. Besides his love for them as they are, he takes action to elevate them to a higher level **and draws them near to the Torah.**[N]

Mishna 13

In this mishna, additional statements by Hillel the Elder are cited that address the appropriate way of life and the proper attitude toward Torah study, fulfillment of mitzvot, and performance of good deeds. These statements are in Aramaic, which was the spoken language at that time.

הוּא הָיָה אוֹמֵר: נְגַד שְׁמָא – אֲבַד שְׁמֵיהּ.

He, Hillel the Elder, **would say: One who glorifies his name, loses his name,**[N] because true glory stems from eternal, substantive matters, rather than from seeking instant publicity and glory, which do not endure over time.

NOTES

Loves people – אוֹהֵב אֶת הַבְּרִיּוֹת: In other words, his love for them is not due to their status or their actions, but because they are God's creations. He makes no distinction between great and inconsequential people or between the righteous and the wicked (*Tosefot Yom Tov*, *Tiferet Yisrael*). Some explain that it is a continuation of the previous matter, meaning that one who loves peace and pursues peace, loves people. When he rebukes them, he does so calmly and lovingly (Meiri).

And draws them near to the Torah – וּמְקָרְבָן לַתּוֹרָה: Some explain this as a continuation of the previous matter. Because he loves them he draws them near to the Torah. When he acts with fondness and intimacy toward a person who commits a transgression, that person experiences a sense of shame and repents (*Avot deRabbi Natan*; see Meiri). Some write that "loves people and draws them near to the Torah" are two separate matters, each one standing independently. He loves people as a mitzva in and of itself, even if he does not thereby change their ways. Besides that, he also "draws them near to Torah" (*Tanya*).

One who glorifies his name, loses his name – נְגַד שְׁמָא, אֲבַד שְׁמֵהּ: Most commentaries explain that the reference is to one who seeks to exalt his name, especially if he engages in Torah study to do so. Ultimately, he will lose his reputation (*Maḥzor Vitri*, Meiri, and others). The reason is that a good name, in any area of life, must have actual value and genuine actions behind it, and conversely, one who is engaged in efforts to exalt his name for public consumption concentrates on outward appearances and is not engaged in performing matters in the optimal, appropriate manner. Some explain that the reference is to one who uses the ineffable name

וּדְלָא מוֹסִיף – יָסֵיף.

One who does not increase, will lose,[N] as one who does not progress in his wisdom and in his character traits and behavior, but remains in the same place and in the same condition, will deteriorate and be lost.

וּדְלָא יָלֵיף – קְטָלָא חַיָּב.

One who does not study is liable to be put to death.[N] One who does not at all enter the gateways of Torah study, substantively undermines his very character as a Jew; his status is more severe than one who studied but discontinued his studies.

וְדִישְׁתַּמֵּשׁ בְּתָגָא – חֲלֵף.

One who exploits the crown[N] **will pass.**[N] One who exploits the crown of Torah for his own purposes to garner honor and wealth will pass from the world. This

NOTES

of God to perform supernatural actions (Rashi), as is described several times in rabbinic literature. As a result, this person will lose what little name he had.

One who does not increase, will lose [*yasif*] – **וּדְלָא מוֹסִיף, יָסֵיף**: This is one who does not seek to enhance his character or his Torah study (Maḥzor Vitri, Meiri), or who does not add at night to what he studied during the day (Rashi). *Yasif* means that since he stopped studying, he does not need life (Rabbeinu Yona). The version in *Avot deRabbi Natan* is "one who does not increase, loses [*pasid*]." It is the nature of the world that when a person does not continue to study the Torah that he learns, he slowly forgets it, until ultimately, he completely forgets it.

Some say that this saying is a continuation of "one who glorifies his name, loses his name"; if one who studies in order to exalt his name sees that he will not be able to exalt his name by means of the Torah, he will not continue to study. Then he would be lost and pass from the world (*Tosefot Yom Tov*).

One who does not study is liable to be put to death – **וּדְלָא יָלֵיף, קְטָלָא חַיָּב**: The commentary here is in accordance with most commentaries, that this is one who does not study Torah at all. That is why he incurs liability to be put to death. In Judaism, a person is required not merely to believe and act, but also to study. Failure to study is a substantive shortcoming in the character of the Jew. Such a person is not considered merely uneducated, but as one who has let go of a vital part of his soul and compromises his Judaism in general.

Some explain that the reference is to one who does not learn a lesson from the matters stated previously in the mishna; he incurs liability to be put to death (Rav Natan *Av HaYeshiva*). Some explain "does not study [*lo yalif*]" as a transitive verb, that he does not teach others (Rashi, *Tiferet Yisrael*).

One who exploits the crown [*tagga*] – **וְדִישְׁתַּמֵּשׁ בְּתָגָא**: The crown here is the crown of Torah, which is the only true crown (Rashi and others; see below 4:5). Some explain that the reference is to one who exploits a Torah scholar who is not his student. They said *tagga* is an acronym for the words, "student of another man" [*talmid gavra aḥerina*] (Rambam, Bartenura, see *Megilla* 28b). In *Avot deRabbi Natan* 12, it is explained that the reference is to one who invokes God's ineffable name, who has no share in the World to Come. This is derived from the case of Belshatzar, who used the Temple vessels and met his demise (see Daniel, chap. 5), and is all the more so true for one who exploits the special crown of the Holy One blessed be He.

Will pass [*ḥalef*] – **חֲלֵף**: This means that the person dies and passes from the world, as it is stated in *Avot deRabbi Natan* 12: "One who exploits the crown is lost and gone." Alternatively, the reward that he was

is because he is profaning the sacred and is exploiting a crown that is not his, but God's, for his own lowly, personal needs.

Mishna 14

This mishna continues citing statements of Hillel the Elder regarding a person's obligation to take responsibility for his actions and his future.

הוּא הָיָה אוֹמֵר:

He, Hillel the Elder, **would say:**

אִם אֵין אֲנִי לִי – מִי לִי.

If I am not for myself, who will be for me?[N] It is incumbent upon a person to take action and make an effort to ensure his success. If a person acquires a matter without investing effort or personal involvement, that acquisition is compromised.

וּכְשֶׁאֲנִי לְעַצְמִי – מָה אֲנִי.

And, on the other hand, **if I am only for myself, what am I?**[N] Alongside all his effort, the person must remember that he lacks the ability to act and succeed alone. He needs the support of his environment and the Holy One blessed be He.

NOTES

destined to receive in the World to Come has passed from him because he used it in this world (see Rashi). Some explain homiletically that *ḥalef* is an expression meaning exchange [*haḥlafa*], as one who does so exchanges the primary for the ancillary, the objective for the means (Yaavetz).

If I am not for myself, who will be for me – אִם אֵין אֲנִי לִי מִי לִי: Some explain that this means, "if I do not fulfill mitzvot, who will fulfill them on my behalf?" (Rashi, Yaavetz). Others explain it differently, as "if I do not spur myself to good, who will spur me?" (Rambam, Meiri). Ultimately, everything that a person can acquire, whether material or spiritual, is dependent upon the person himself. Items that a person acquires without effort are of no value, as long as he did not perform an action to secure them for himself. Just as a person cannot exist on the basis of what others consume, so a person cannot exist spiritually on the basis of others' studying or praying. If one remains on the margin and does not become involved, no one else can take his place.

And if I am only for myself, what am I – וּכְשֶׁאֲנִי לְעַצְמִי, מָה אֲנִי: There is nothing that comes exclusively from me; I need the help of Heaven. I, myself, cannot

וְאִם לֹא עַכְשָׁיו – אֵימָתַי? **And if not now, when?**[N] One must not wait with these matters and procrastinate until another time, as every other time will also be "now."

Mishna 15

Following the statements of Hillel the Elder, the Mishna cites the statements of his partner in the transmission of the Torah, Shammai.

שַׁמַּאי אוֹמֵר: **Shammai**[P] **says:**[N]

NOTES

achieve perfection (Rashi, Rambam, and others). This statement is the converse and completion of the opening statement; as important as it is for a person to perform and act himself, nevertheless, he must remember that he has no existence in isolation. His entire existence is dependent on others in a manner that ties him to all his surroundings, and on a more elevated plane, ties him to the Creator. Some explain that if I am "for myself," i.e., exclusively for my bodily needs, "what am I," meaning I am nothing more than an animal (Meiri).

And if not now, when – **וְאִם לֹא עַכְשָׁיו אֵימָתַי**: "Now," in this context, means the time in which I am alive, as in the World to Come one cannot perform good deeds (Rashi and others; see 4:17). Alternatively, if one postpones remedying matters to tomorrow, it is possible that this "tomorrow" will never arrive. Even if it does arrive, and he performs these actions the following day, he will not be able to compensate for the day of his life that he lost (Rabbeinu Yona; and see 2:4).

The Rambam explains that "now" in this context means when a person is young and he can refine his character relatively easily, as in his advanced years, it is very difficult to change and refine it (Rambam, Rashbatz).

Shammai says – **שַׁמַּאי אוֹמֵר**: These three sayings manifest a balance between, on the one hand, demanding of oneself constancy, precision, and commitment, a demand that requires moderation and restraint, and, on the other hand, internal kindheartedness that manifests through treating others well.

PERSONALITIES

Shammai – **שַׁמַּאי**: Little is known about the life of Shammai the Elder. He was apparently an architect, or a master builder, which is why he held a "builder's cubit" in his hand (*Shabbat* 31a). This may also have symbolic and emotional significance, as his approach was largely based on meticulous insistence on boundaries and measures. He was characterized by the Sages as "strict." However, that characterization is not a description of an angry personality, but rather, one of insistence on fixed, firm boundaries and definitions.

A school of study, ultimately called Beit Shammai, developed around Shammai. The common denominator of its members was meticulous insistence on tradition and adherence to a more stringent interpretation of halakha. Some also point to a commonality of zealous insistence on independence and on uniqueness and distinction from the surrounding nations and cultures (see *Shabbat* 1:4).

עֲשֵׂה תוֹרָתְךָ קֶבַע,

Make your Torah into a **fixed**[N] matter. Torah study shall be a foundation in your life more than any of your other pursuits.

אֱמֹר מְעַט וַעֲשֵׂה הַרְבֵּה,

Say little when you make a commitment to another, **and do much**[N] when you are carrying out that commitment.

וֶהֱוֵי מְקַבֵּל אֶת כָּל הָאָדָם בְּסֵבֶר פָּנִים יָפוֹת.

And receive every person, regardless of their actions or their status, **graciously,**[N] with a cheerful expression.

Mishna 16

From this point on, the Mishna presents the statements of later Sages, members of the dynasty of Hillel, who filled the role of *Nasi*.

רַבָּן גַּמְלִיאֵל הָיָה אוֹמֵר:

Rabban Gamliel[P] says[N] statements that provide clear and accurate guidance to a person regarding the manner in which to perform mitzvot.

NOTES

Make your Torah fixed – עֲשֵׂה תוֹרָתְךָ קֶבַע: The concept of "fixed" is explained in a variety of manners. Many explain that one must establish in his mind that Torah study is primary in his life, and that everything else will be done when he has the opportunity to do so (*Avot deRabbi Natan*). Some explain that one should set times for study each day in a fixed manner (Rashi and others). Others explain that this statement relates to issuing halakhic rulings, that one should do so with consistency and not rule leniently for himself and stringently for others (*Avot deRabbi Natan*, version B).

It is worth noting that in contrast to what is stated here regarding the Torah, which is limitless and must be accorded fixed status, it is stated in tractate *Berakhot* (4:4) that regarding prayer, for which the Sages established fixed times and a set structure, the opposite is true. One must take care that prayer does not become fixed, or routine. "One whose prayer is fixed, his prayer is not supplication" (*Berakhot* 4:4), and it loses its primary substance.

Say little and do much – אֱמֹר מְעַט וַעֲשֵׂה הַרְבֵּה: This means that if, for example, you say you will give charity, say little and give more than you promised, as that is the way of the righteous (*Avot deRabbi Natan*). The same is true regarding serving God. One must not verbally commit himself to do a great deal, but rather he should commit to a little, and if he is able, do much (*Tiferet Yisrael*).

Graciously [*besever panim yafot*] – בְּסֵבֶר פָּנִים יָפוֹת: *Sever panim yafot* is a joyous facial expression, which shows and expresses a good heart (*Maḥzor Vitri*). Some say that the mishna is emphasizing that even if one's heart is not joyful, he should show

עֲשֵׂה לְךָ רַב,

Establish for yourself a teacher,[N] whose halakhic decisions you can consistently follow.

וְהִסְתַּלֵּק מִן הַסָּפֵק, וְאַל תַּרְבֶּה לְעַשֵּׂר אוּמָדוֹת.

Avoid uncertainty;[N] perform matters in a way that is clear and certain. For example, **do not regularly tithe on the basis of**

NOTES

himself to be so (Meiri). It is stated in *Avot deRabbi Natan*: "If a person gave another all the great gifts in the world, and his face is downcast, the verse ascribes to him as though he gave him nothing. However, if one receives another graciously, even if he gave him nothing, the verse ascribes to him as though he gave him all the great gifts in the world."

Rabban Gamliel says – רַבָּן גַּמְלִיאֵל אוֹמֵר: Many explain, in the wake of the Talmud (*Shabbat* 15a), that this Rabban Gamliel is Rabban Gamliel the Elder, grandson of Hillel and son of Rabban Shimon ben Hillel. This deviation from the lineage sequence explains why the mishna does not say: "Rabban Gamliel received from…" Some said, to the contrary, that because he was Hillel's grandson it is obvious that he received the tradition from him, and there was no need to mention it (*Mirkevet HaMishne*).

Establish for yourself a teacher [*aseh lekha rav*] – עֲשֵׂה לְךָ רַב: This instruction was mentioned previously in the statement of Yehoshua ben Peraḥya (1:6). Commentaries explain that there the statement constituted a general instruction that a person should not study on his own, but from a teacher. By contrast, Rabban Gamliel's statement has a slightly different meaning: Make a clear decision as to whom you will consult and ask questions of as a mentor. In that way you will follow a defined path and a particular, consistent approach (Rambam, Meiri). The Sages state (*Tosefta*, *Eduyyot* 2:3) that a person must choose to follow either Beit Hillel or Beit Shammai, and then follow the path that he chose, for both leniency and stricture. Some interpret *rav* in the sense of "many," so that *aseh lekha rav* means that one should have others join him, so he does not sit in judgment alone (Bartenura).

Avoid uncertainty – וְהִסְתַּלֵּק מִן הַסָּפֵק: This instruction includes much more than the instruction "establish for yourself a teacher," as it means that one should not construct a world that is unclear and undefined and should not live in the reality of a world of that kind. Some explain that this is a continuation of the previous statement; after one establishes a mentor for himself, as a result he will avoid uncertainty (*Maḥzor Vitri*). Others explain that a person should have no uncertainty in his heart regarding the fundamental principles of faith and its foundations; rather, it should be certain in his eyes, obvious and established in his heart (Rashi).

PERSONALITIES

Rabban Gamliel – רַבָּן גַּמְלִיאֵל: Over the generations, there were several *tanna'im* with this name. It appears that the reference here is to Rabban Gamliel the Elder, who was Hillel's grandson and succeeded his father, Rabbi Shimon ben Hillel. Rabban Gamliel was *Nasi* during the first part of the first century BCE, and was the first *Nasi* with the honorific "Rabban." He was the spiritual leader of the Jewish people in the Land of Israel as well as in the Diaspora, to which he dispatched missives with instructions regarding intercalation of the calendar and other topics (*Sanhedrin* 11a). He instituted significant ordinances "for the betterment of the world," and in the matters of writs of divorce and *agunot*. It is said that when Rabban Gamliel died, honor of Torah ceased and purity and abstinence ceased. His son, Rabban Shimon ben Gamliel, served as *Nasi* while the Temple was still standing, and was apparently executed by the Romans. Some believe that the Rabban Gamliel mentioned here is Rabban Gamliel of Yavne, son of Rabban Shimon ben Gamliel and grandson of Rabban Gamliel the Elder.

estimates.[N] When tithing produce, do not tithe on the basis of an approximation, but on the basis of a precise measure or weight, as the Sages instituted to perform the tithe *ab initio*.

Mishna 17

Following the statement of Rabban Gamliel in the previous mishna, this mishna continues with the statement of his son and successor.

שִׁמְעוֹן בְּנוֹ אוֹמֵר:

Shimon, his, Rabban Gamliel's, **son,**[P] **says** matters that address the virtue of silence over speech in various respects:

כָּל יָמַי גָּדַלְתִּי בֵּין הַחֲכָמִים, וְלֹא מָצָאתִי לַגּוּף טוֹב אֶלָּא שְׁתִיקָה.

All my days I grew among the Sages,[N] who engage in matters of reason and wisdom, **and,** nevertheless, **I have found nothing for the body better than silence,**[N] as silence is preferable even to words of wisdom.

NOTES

Do not regularly tithe on the basis of estimates – וְאַל תַּרְבֶּה לְעַשֵּׂר אוּמָדוֹת: The tithe is a fixed portion separated from agricultural produce. First tithe would be separated for the Levites serving in the Temple, second tithe for consumption in Jerusalem, and the poor man's tithe as charity. Because the tithe is of fixed measure, its separation must be precise, and it should be separated based on number, measure, or weight (see *Terumot* 4:6). When a person does not have a measuring implement, he is allowed to separate tithes on the basis of an estimate. However, one should minimize estimates of that kind.

All my days I grew among the Sages – כָּל יָמַי גָּדַלְתִּי בֵּין הַחֲכָמִים: The meaning of this introduction is that, as a person who grew up among the Sages, Rabban Shimon could witness and discern the best character traits (Rabbeinu Yona). However, this statement also highlights that most of the activity of the Sages involves speech and is by means of speech. Some underscore a different aspect: One who grows among the Sages is privileged to hear many wise statements. Rabban Shimon comes to say that even regarding speech of that kind, he "found nothing for the body better than silence" (Yaavetz and others). In *Avot deRabbi Natan* it was added: "Silence is good for the wise, and all the more so for fools.

I have found nothing for the body better than silence – וְלֹא מָצָאתִי לַגּוּף טוֹב אֶלָּא שְׁתִיקָה: In other words, even in matters of Torah, it is preferable for one to be silent and learn from a Sage, who expounds and elaborates (*Maḥzor Vitri*). It is possible that the phrase "I have found nothing for the body" emphasizes that even when one discusses matters of Torah, which have value, one must pay attention to the body, to the person himself, to the meaning and the consequences of the words in the social, interpersonal context. Speech can cause great damage both to the one who speaks it and to the

וְלֹא הַמִּדְרָשׁ הוּא הָעִקָּר, אֶלָּא הַמַּעֲשֶׂה.

It is not study or rhetoric **that is principal,**[N] **but rather, action.**

וְכָל הַמַּרְבֶּה דְּבָרִים – מֵבִיא חֵטְא.

Anyone who speaks excessively engenders sin,[N] because the more one speaks, the more difficult it is to be cautious and precise regarding the content. One is consequently liable to gravitate in an undesirable direction, which will lead to sin and deception.

NOTES

one about whom it is spoken, and for a person who is demeaned, it is preferable for him to remain silent (Bartenura and others).

It is not study that is principal – וְלֹא הַמִּדְרָשׁ הוּא הָעִקָּר: This is another aspect of the virtue of silence. Even commendable speech is not an objective in and of itself, and it does not constitute a criterion for a person's worth. The test of a person and a society is in their actions, which are what determine the person or society's direction (see Bartenura). The commentaries note that this is the reason a person should not teach or expound unless he practices what he preaches. Similarly, some write that it is preferable to learn from a person's actions and not from his words (*Maḥzor Vitri*).

Anyone who speaks excessively engenders sin – וְכָל הַמַּרְבֶּה דְּבָרִים, מֵבִיא חֵטְא: This statement, too, teaches the virtue of silence. Not only is silence preferable and appropriate, but excessive speech engenders sin both in business and in interpersonal matters; as words gradually multiply, it is more difficult to maintain their truth and their effectiveness, and they are liable to lead to sin. Therefore, it is advisable to be brief even when speaking words of praise (*Maḥzor Vitri*) and even words of Torah (Rabbeinu Yona). A similar phenomenon took place during the sin of the Tree of Knowledge: They added to the original command, and this led them to sin (Bartenura; see *Sanhedrin* 29a).

PERSONALITIES

Shimon his son – שִׁמְעוֹן בְּנוֹ: The commentaries disagreed regarding the identity of the Sage in the mishna, as there were at least two significant Sages named Rabban Shimon ben Gamliel. This dispute is dependent upon the identity of Rabban Gamliel in the previous mishna. The straightforward understanding is that the previous mishna is referring to the first Rabban Shimon son of Rabban Gamliel, who headed the Sanhedrin when the Second Temple was destroyed. Among the actions and incidents attributed to him are the complex acts of juggling that he would perform during the Celebration of the Drawing of Water in the Temple (*Tosefta*, *Sukka* 4:4). A unique description of him from an external source was transmitted by Josephus Flavius, who was his contemporary. He relates that Rabban Shimon was "a wise and understanding man. In his wisdom, he knew how to smooth rough patches and to find a solution for even complicated matters" (*Life of Josephus*, chap. 38).

The first Rabban Shimon ben Gamliel died a tragic death. Although he was a member of the moderate leadership that sought to prevent the revolt against the Romans, he was executed after the conquest of Jerusalem, because in any event he was the official leader of the people. Therefore, in some places he is called "Rabban Shimon ben Gamliel the executed," and he is one of the first on the list of the "Ten Martyrs" (see *Avot deRabbi Natan* 38).

However, some hold that Rabban Shimon ben Gamliel in the mishna is the second Rabban Shimon ben Gamliel, who is mentioned in the following mishna as well.

Mishna 18

This mishna continues with the statements of the Sages from Beit Hillel, who filled the position of *Nasi*.

רַבָּן שִׁמְעוֹן בֶּן גַּמְלִיאֵל אוֹמֵר:

Rabban Shimon ben Gamliel[P] **says:**

עַל שְׁלֹשָׁה דְבָרִים הָעוֹלָם עוֹמֵד,

On the basis of three matters[N] **the world stands**; through them, the world, riven by dispute, continues to exist.

עַל הַדִּין וְעַל הָאֱמֶת וְעַל הַשָּׁלוֹם,

On justice, issuing rulings based on existing information; **on truth**, which is the guideline, which is not associated with one party or the other, and is complex to apply; **and on peace**,[N] which is the attempt to arrive at compromise, beyond the letter of the law.

NOTES

On the basis of three matters – עַל שְׁלֹשָׁה דְבָרִים: The Mishna states above (1:2), in the name of Shimon HaTzaddik, that there are three matters on whose basis the world exists: Torah, Temple service, and acts of kindness. These constitute the spiritual foundation of the world. Here, the reference is to matters that sustain and perpetuate the existence of the world and its proper social conduct (Bartenura, *Tiferet Yisrael*). According to some versions of the mishna, it reads, "the world exists." Some write that the primary difference between the statement of Shimon HaTzaddik and the statement of Rabban Shimon ben Gamliel is a function of the fact that Rabban Shimon ben Gamliel made his statement after the destruction of the Temple. He was saying that even though Temple service no longer existed, the world's existence was still due to the merit of these three matters (Yaavetz). The Rambam explains that these three matters refer to the appropriate conduct of a person and of the world: with action – justice; with the intellect – truth; and with character – peace.

On justice, on truth, and on peace – עַל הַדִּין, וְעַל הָאֱמֶת, וְעַל הַשָּׁלוֹם: These three constitute a dialectical triangle, with three different perspectives creating a stable structure that sustains the dispute-riven world. On one side is "justice," with connotations of stricture and a decisive determination of matters according to existing data, in order to arrive at a conclusion in a situation of dispute. By contrast, there is the path of "peace," a softer approach of creating harmony between contradictory elements, forging coexistence that includes them both. The third side is "truth," which is quite often much more complicated than judicial decision or compromise. Many times, the truth cannot be categorized to one side or the other, but rather is complex and not always possible to implement. In the Jerusalem Talmud (*Taanit* 4:2) it is stated that these three matters

שֶׁנֶּאֱמַר: "אֱמֶת וּמִשְׁפַּט שָׁלוֹם שִׁפְטוּ בְּשַׁעֲרֵיכֶם".

As it is stated: "Administer truth and justice, peace[N] in your gates" (Zechariah 8:16).

NOTES

describe a process that culminates with peace: "When justice is done, truth is done; when truth is done, peace is done."

Administer truth and justice, peace – אֱמֶת וּמִשְׁפַּט שָׁלוֹם: In contrast to the initial understanding, Rabban Shimon ben Gamliel expounds the words "justice, peace" as two disparate matters. Consequently, the three components, truth, justice, and peace, appear in the verse. In the *Tosefta* (*Sanhedrin* 1:3), Rabbi Yehoshua ben Korḥa teaches that "justice, peace" refers to justice that is accompanied by peace, i.e., compromise between litigants, because "in every place that there is true justice there is no peace, and in every place that there is peace, there is no true justice."

PERSONALITIES

Rabban Shimon ben Gamliel – רַבָּן שִׁמְעוֹן בֶּן גַּמְלִיאֵל: Rabban Shimon ben Gamliel in this mishna is apparently Rabban Shimon son of the second Rabban Gamliel, Rabban Gamliel of Yavne, and he was the father of Rabbi Yehuda HaNasi. He served during the most dire times for Israel, during the edicts of persecution issued by the Roman emperor against all the Jews after the failure of the bar Kokheva revolt during the fourth decade of the second century CE. In those circumstances, Rabban Shimon needed to restore the Jewish spiritual leadership and authority. His status was complicated, as among the Sages in his generation, the majority of whom were the remaining disciples of Rabbi Akiva, there were those who were greater that he was in Torah. Some even sought to oust him and install alternative leadership in his place.

Within that complicated framework that confronted him domestically and internationally, Rabban Shimon was able to establish a court that contained the disparate opinions of the Sages of that period, while integrating the qualities of leadership and humility. His leadership helped shape consensus halakhic opinions. Conceivably, this is one of the reasons for the opinion that, as a rule, the halakha is in accordance with the opinion of Rabban Shimon ben Gamliel when it is cited in the Mishna (*Ketubot* 77a, and elsewhere).

Chapter 2

This chapter continues to cover the dynasty of Sages from the house of Hillel the Elder who served as *Nasi*, until the end of the tannaitic era. The chapter then returns to sayings of the Sages tracing the transmission of the Torah from teacher to student. It enumerates the prominent Sages of that time, starting from Hillel the Elder until the disciples of his disciple Rabban Yoḥanan ben Zakkai, listing, among others, Rabbi Eliezer, Rabbi Yehoshua, and Rabbi Tarfon.

Mishna 1

The chapter begins with the statement of Rabbi Yehuda HaNasi, redactor of the Mishna. He was the son of the second Rabban Shimon ben Gamliel, whose statement was cited at the end of the previous chapter.

רַבִּי אוֹמֵר: אֵיזוֹהִי דֶּרֶךְ יְשָׁרָה שֶׁיָּבֹר לוֹ הָאָדָם? כֹּל שֶׁהִיא תִּפְאֶרֶת לְעוֹשֶׂיהָ, וְתִפְאֶרֶת לוֹ מִן הָאָדָם.

Rabbi[P] Yehuda HaNasi **says: Which is the upright path that a person should select for himself**[N] during his lifetime? It is **any-**

NOTES

Which is the upright path that a person should select for himself – אֵיזוֹהִי דֶּרֶךְ יְשָׁרָה שֶׁיָּבֹר לוֹ הָאָדָם: This instruction is not merely theoretical, but practical. It is the search for basic guidelines that can guide a person through the byways of his life. They encompass not only matters of Torah and mitzvot, or deciding between good and evil, but also determining the proper course of a person's life in general, and the criteria for making necessary decisions, e.g., choosing a profession and areas of interest, and more.

PERSONALITIES

Rabbi – רַבִּי: Rabbi is Rabbi Yehuda HaNasi, who was the *Nasi* of the Sanhedrin and the leader of Israel in his time. In contrast to the other Sages who served as *Nasi*, for whom the title Rabban was added to their

thing that strikes a balance between **glory for one who follows it,** meaning that he, himself, derives a sense of self-worth from his actions, **and glory for him** in the eyes **of man,**[N] as society approves of his actions and deems them significant.

וֶהֱוֵי זָהִיר בְּמִצְוָה קַלָּה כְּבַחֲמוּרָה, שֶׁאֵין אַתָּה יוֹדֵעַ מַתַּן שְׂכָרָן שֶׁל מִצְוֹת.

Be as meticulous with a mitzva that is considered **minor,** which does not entail great effort or does not appear significant, **as** you are **with** one that is considered **major,**[N] **as you do not know the reward given for mitzvot.**[N] It is an eternal matter, and we lack the criteria to assess it.

PERSONALITIES

name, he was called simply Rabbi, with no mention of his name, as his title was more elevated and reflected his role as the teacher of all Israel. During his lifetime, he was admired by everyone, and he was likened to Moses, as, like him, he was one in whom Torah and greatness were found in one place. His relations with the Roman authorities were very good, and there are many aggadic stories about the special relationship he enjoyed with the emperor.

Rabbi saw the combination of his personality and the time he lived in as fortuitous. He therefore undertook the great enterprise of redacting the Mishna, which, in many respects, is second in importance only to the Bible. He used the various anthologies of ancient *mishnayot* that the Sages wrote in the generations that preceded him, and he edited them, incorporating those disputes that he found relevant. Thus, Rabbi shaped the manner of Torah study in the generations that followed, and also edited one of the greatest and most important enterprises of the Hebrew language, in which he excelled. He, himself, is not mentioned frequently in the Mishna, specifically because he redacted and edited it.

As *Nasi* of Israel, Rabbi's household affairs were conducted lavishly and according to protocols of royalty; however, he personally lived a life of austerity and asceticism, due to which he was given the title of "Our Sacred Rabbi." His descendants continued serving as *Nasi* after him, for as long as that institution existed.

NOTES

Anything that is glory for one who follows it [*leoseha*] and glory for him in the eyes of man – **כֹּל שֶׁהִיא תִּפְאֶרֶת לְעוֹשֶׂיהָ וְתִפְאֶרֶת לוֹ מִן הָאָדָם**: "Glory for one who follows it" indicates a special matter that a person can take pride in accomplishing. There is a variant reading: "Glory for the One who made him [*leosehu*]," meaning that it is glorious in the eyes of the Holy One blessed be He (Rashbatz). In practice, it appears that the upright path is the golden mean that strikes a balance between a person's own feelings and beliefs regarding those matters he considers glorious and those matters that are significant and beneficial in the eyes of society (see Rambam).

With a mitzva that is considered minor as with one that is considered major – **בְּמִצְוָה קַלָּה כְּבַחֲמוּרָה**: People tend to sort mitzvot into categories of minor and major, on the basis of the degree of exertion or monetary expenditure they entail (see below), or their uniqueness (see Rambam), or other criteria tied to halakha and tradition or to social conventions.

As you do not know the reward given for mitzvot – **שֶׁאֵין אַתָּה יוֹדֵעַ מַתַּן שְׂכָרָן שֶׁל מִצְוֹת**: What we know or calculate according to our perspective does not necessarily reflect the true value of the mitzvot and their

וֶהֱוֵי מְחַשֵּׁב הֶפְסֵד מִצְוָה כְּנֶגֶד שְׂכָרָהּ, וּשְׂכַר עֲבֵרָה כְּנֶגֶד הֶפְסֵדָהּ.

Conversely, specifically because it is an eternal matter, **calculate the loss** entailed **in the** fulfillment of a mitzva, e.g., time or money, **against its reward,** which is incalculable, **and,** likewise, **the reward of a transgression,** like the pleasure involved in it, which is insignificant and limited, **against its loss,** which is also incalculable.

וְהִסְתַּכֵּל בִּשְׁלֹשָׁה דְבָרִים, וְאִי אַתָּה בָא לִידֵי עֲבֵירָה: דַּע מַה לְּמַעְלָה מִמְּךָ: עַיִן רוֹאָה וְאֹזֶן שׁוֹמַעַת, וְכָל מַעֲשֶׂיךָ בַּסֵּפֶר נִכְתָּבִין.

Look and constantly contemplate **three matters, and you will** thereby **not come to sin.** These matters are the details of a single principle: **Know what is above you,** as the Holy One blessed be He oversees all actions: **An eye** that **sees** all actions, **an ear** that **hears** all speech, **and all your actions are recorded in the ledger** and are never forgotten.

NOTES

actual reward. So said the Sages in the Jerusalem Talmud (*Pe'a* 1:1 and elsewhere): The Holy One blessed be He removed the [immediate] granting of reward from the performers of mitzvot, so they would perform them in good faith… the most minor of the minor mitzvot, this is the dispatch of the mother bird from the nest; and the most major of the major mitzvot, this is honoring one's father and mother. In both of them it is written, "and you will extend your days" (see *Ḥullin* 12:5), indicating that major and minor mitzvot are equally significant. The same is true of transgressions. While there is a hierarchical system of punishments for various transgressions, those relate to the considerations of the earthly court, not to their absolute value in the eyes of the Holy One blessed be He and the reward for refraining from these transgressions.

Burial cave of Rabbi Yehuda HaNasi, Beit She'arim

Mishna 2

Following the chapter's beginning, with the statement of Rabbi Yehuda HaNasi, the Mishna cites the statement of the next *Nasi*.

רַבָּן גַּמְלִיאֵל בְּנוֹ שֶׁל רַבִּי יְהוּדָה הַנָּשִׂיא אוֹמֵר:

Rabban Gamliel son of Rabbi Yehuda HaNasi[P] says:

יָפֶה תַּלְמוּד תּוֹרָה עִם דֶּרֶךְ אֶרֶץ, שֶׁיְּגִיעַת שְׁנֵיהֶם מְשַׁכַּחַת עָוֹן.

Engaging in **Torah study is best when combined with a** worldly **occupation, as endeavor,** exertion and toil **in both of them causes sin to be forgotten.**[N] It creates a healthy, balanced personality, and does not leave opportunity to engage in negative matters.

וְכָל תּוֹרָה שֶׁאֵין עִמָּהּ מְלָאכָה - סוֹפָהּ בְּטֵלָה וְגוֹרֶרֶת עָוֹן.

Any Torah that does not have labor with it, that one engaging in it has no worthy occupation for earning a livelihood, **is ultimately null and void** due to the constraints of subsisting, **and** this even **leads to sin.** When a person is in a state of economic duress and is idle from Torah study, he is drawn to matters that border on sin, whether in the financial arena or in other areas.

NOTES

Torah study is best...with a worldly occupation...causes sin to be forgotten – יָפֶה תַּלְמוּד תּוֹרָה עִם דֶּרֶךְ אֶרֶץ...מְשַׁכַּחַת עָוֹן: This is similar to the statement of Rabbi Yehuda HaNasi in the previous mishna, that the path that a person selects for himself should synthesize matters that have intrinsic value, on the one hand, and significance in the eyes of society, on the other.

Some explain that when a person engages in the mitzvot of the Torah and also does not need money because of his labor, he does not covet the money of others and is not tempted to rob them (Rashi). Others write that exerting oneself in both Torah and labor exhausts the body, so it will not be able to overcome his self-discipline and incite him to transgression (Rashbatz). There are also those who note that although the wording of the mishna might lead to the conclusion that Torah is ancillary to a worldly occupation, that is not the meaning of the mishna. Torah must certainly be primary.

Here Rabban Gamliel begins to discuss those who engage in tending to communal needs. He speaks from experience, due to his role as a leader and *Nasi*.

וְכָל הָעֲמֵלִים עִם הַצִּבּוּר – יִהְיוּ עֲמֵלִים עִמָּהֶם לְשֵׁם שָׁמַיִם, שֶׁזְּכוּת אֲבוֹתָם מְסַיַּעְתָּן, וְצִדְקָתָם עוֹמֶדֶת לָעַד.

All who toil on behalf of the community,[N] communal leaders, **should toil on their behalf for the sake of Heaven.** They should not view their labor as a source of livelihood or social standing. **As,** when they engage in communal matters for the sake of Heaven, **the merit of their ancestors,**[N] the ancestors of the community, **assists them** in their sacred work, even if their abilities do not seem up to par for engaging in politics and communal needs. **Moreover, their righteousness endures forever,** because they engage in the work for the sake of Heaven. Although their actions appear to be merely for temporal needs, they have eternal value.

NOTES

All who toil on behalf of the community – וְכָל הָעֲמֵלִים עִם הַצִּבּוּר: Some explain that this is stated as a continuation of the initial statement in the mishna. Although those who engage in the needs of the community are not free to engage in Torah and mitzvot to the proper degree; nevertheless, if they engage in tending to community needs for the sake of Heaven, they will be greatly rewarded for their actions, and they too will be spared from sin (*Tiferet Yisrael*).

Should toil on their behalf for the sake of Heaven, as the merit of their ancestors – יִהְיוּ עֲמֵלִים עִמָּהֶם לְשֵׁם שָׁמַיִם שֶׁזְּכוּת אֲבוֹתָם: Some explain that the merit of the ancestors is a rationale of sorts for toiling on behalf of the community for the sake of Heaven, as their successes result not due to their merit, but due to the merit of the ancestors of the community (Rashi, Bartenura, and others). According to another interpretation, it is due to the merit of the ancestors of those engaged in tending to the needs of the community (*Mirkevet HaMishne*). The commentary here is in accordance with the many commentaries that write that this provides encouragement for those who engage in the needs of the community, assuring them that they will succeed in their endeavor with the help of the ancestors' merit, which forever stands with the community. This is especially true of the three patriarchs, Abraham, Isaac, and Jacob, to whom it was promised that the nation will exist forever (see Maharal of Prague).

PERSONALITIES

Rabban Gamliel son of Rabbi Yehuda HaNasi – רַבָּן גַּמְלִיאֵל בְּנוֹ שֶׁל רַבִּי יְהוּדָה הַנָּשִׂיא אוֹמֵר: This Rabban Gamliel was the eldest son of Rabbi Yehuda HaNasi and his successor. The Sages said: Although he was not his equal in wisdom, and although his younger brother Shimon was greater than he was in Torah, he was his father's successor in terms of fear of sin (*Ketubot* 103b). Little is known about the events of the life of this Rabban Gamliel, but from his wise statements it is clear that his primary vocation was public leadership, which included work within the Jewish community as well as contact with the government. This mishna, which cites the statements of Rabban Gamliel, is unusual and anomalous, because the Mishna was redacted and concluded by Rabbi Yehuda HaNasi, and later Sages are typically not cited in it.

The son and successor of Rabban Gamliel was also a renowned Sage in his generation. He was the second Rabbi Yehuda HaNasi, who is generally called Rabbi Yehuda Nesia.

Now Rabban Gamliel addresses himself directly to those who engage in tending to communal needs, speaking, as it were, in the name of the Holy One blessed be He.

וְאַתֶּם, מַעֲלֶה אֲנִי עֲלֵיכֶם שָׂכָר הַרְבֵּה כְּאִלּוּ עֲשִׂיתֶם.

And you, do not regret the fact that you are not as free to engage in Torah and mitzvot as you would have wished, as **I ascribe to you great reward, as though you had done so.**[N] Through your efforts you enable these matters to be realized in the world, and it is as though you performed them yourself.

Mishna 3

This mishna continues citing words of wisdom of Rabban Gamliel son of Rabbi Yehuda HaNasi to those engaging in communal needs. He speaks from his experience of contact with the Roman empire in his time, but his words are relevant for every person in every circumstance.

הֱוּוּ זְהִירִין בָּרָשׁוּת, שֶׁאֵין מְקָרְבִין לוֹ לָאָדָם אֶלָּא לְצֹרֶךְ עַצְמָן; נִרְאִין כְּאוֹהֲבִין בִּשְׁעַת הֲנָאָתָן, וְאֵין עוֹמְדִין לוֹ לָאָדָם בִּשְׁעַת דָּחְקוֹ.

Be wary of the governmental **authorities,**[N] even if they relate to you amicably. Do not delude yourselves that you have genuine, strong friendship with them, and rely upon it. This is **because they draw a person near**

NOTES

And you, I ascribe to you great reward as though you had done so – וְאַתֶּם, מַעֲלֶה אֲנִי עֲלֵיכֶם שָׂכָר הַרְבֵּה כְּאִלּוּ עֲשִׂיתֶם: For example, those appointed to be in charge of charity must not think that they themselves accomplish nothing and that the reward goes exclusively to those who gave the charity. Rather, the charity is ascribed to them as though they gave it from their own money (Rashbatz). Likewise, if, as a result of their work on behalf of the community, they were remiss in performing some mitzvot, God ascribes to them reward as though they did what needed to be done (Rambam and others). Some explain this in the context of "the merit of their ancestors assists them"; although their success was due to the merit of the ancestors, it is considered for the communal leaders as though it were accomplished due to their own efforts, because their intent was for the sake of Heaven.

Be wary of the authorities [*barashut*] – הֱווּ זְהִירִין בָּרָשׁוּת: This statement may be seen as a continuation of the earlier statement by Shemaya, who said:

only[N] **for their own purpose,** due to concern for the interests of their rule. Although **they appear as** though they are **friends,**[N] that is only **when it benefits them** and they derive benefit from the person who approaches them. **But** when that person is no longer of use to them, and he needs their help, **they do not stand by a person** to help him **in his hour of duress.**

NOTES

"Do not become intimate with authorities." Some explain that there, Shemaya addresses people who do not need to interact with the authorities, cautioning them not to become known to the authorities. By contrast, here Rabban Gamliel ben Rabbi Yehuda HaNasi addresses communal leaders, who, due to their positions, must have ties with the authorities, and he offers guidance on how they should conduct themselves with them (Rashbatz, Bartenura).

Some explain homiletically that one must be vigilant regarding matters that are optional [*reshut*], even though they are not a mitzva (*Notzer Ḥesed*, *Midrash Shmuel*), or that the mishna is referring to the enticement of the evil inclination, which appears as though it is an independent entity [*rashut*] and not subjugated to the truth and the Holy One blessed be He (citing Maharit).

Because they draw a person near only – שֶׁאֵין מְקָרְבִין לוֹ לָאָדָם אֶלָּא: The plain understanding of the statement appears to be defamation of the monarchy. However, some comment that this can be expounded as praise of the monarchy as well, as a king does not need to fear or flatter individuals and thus is free to administer the law honestly based on the needs of the people. In any case, one must understand that this is the way of the world, and act accordingly (Rabbeinu Yona).

They appear as friends – נִרְאִין כְּאוֹהֲבִין: Some infer from the language of the mishna that even when friendship benefits the authorities, they are not actual friends, but they only make themselves seem like friends, and they do not love others even when those others can benefit them. Moreover, even their pretense does not look like actual friendship, but they only "appear as though they are friends," with limited resemblance to true friendship (*Pirkei Moshe*, and see Rashbatz).

Coin minted on the occasion of Hadrian's arrival in Judea in the second century CE. On the coin there is a Latin inscription: "In honor of the emperor's arrival in Judea."

Mishna 4

This mishna begins with additional statements of Rabban Gamliel son of Rabbi Yehuda HaNasi.

הוּא הָיָה אוֹמֵר: עֲשֵׂה רְצוֹנוֹ כִּרְצוֹנְךָ, כְּדֵי שֶׁיַּעֲשֶׂה רְצוֹנְךָ כִּרְצוֹנוֹ.

He, Rabban Gamliel son of Rabbi Yehuda HaNasi, **would say: Render His will,** the will of God, **your will,**[N] **so that He will render your will His will.** A person's complete identification with the will of the Holy One blessed be He leads to the Holy One blessed be He assisting him in realizing his wishes, especially since his life and his desires are already in accordance with the will of God.

בַּטֵּל רְצוֹנְךָ מִפְּנֵי רְצוֹנוֹ, כְּדֵי שֶׁיְּבַטֵּל רְצוֹן אֲחֵרִים מִפְּנֵי רְצוֹנְךָ.

Similarly, **void your will before His will,** even if at that moment it is not convenient for you, **so that** in reward **He will void the will of others**[N] **before your will.** Even if you are unable to completely identify with the will of the Holy One blessed be He, but fulfill it only as one accepting a burden, you will be rewarded by the Holy One blessed be He voiding the will of others before your will.

NOTES

Render His will your will – עֲשֵׂה רְצוֹנוֹ כִּרְצוֹנְךָ: In other words, when you perform His will, act as though you are engaged in matters that are for your own purposes, with desire and effort (Rabbeinu Yona and more). Some explain that even when you perform actions "according to your will," for your own needs, do them for the sake of "His will" (Rashi). Others read this as a continuation of the admonition for communal leaders to engage in their matters for the sake of Heaven, indicating that their will in performing their leadership actions should be like the will of the Holy One blessed be He, i.e., for the benefit of all Israel (Maharal).

Still others suggest a completely different explanation, that this is a continuation of the guidance regarding the prudent attitude toward the authorities. Although everything they do is for their own benefit, if one serves them with alacrity and loyalty, they will help him and will render his will to be their will in certain respects (*Mirkevet HaMishne*).

Void your will…so that He will void the will of others – בַּטֵּל רְצוֹנְךָ...כְּדֵי שֶׁיְּבַטֵּל רְצוֹן אֲחֵרִים: Some explain that this expression also applies regarding the Holy One blessed be He, meaning that He will void His will, like evil edicts that He decreed, due

To this point, the Mishna presented the statements of the dynasty of Sages who served as *Nasi*, the descendants of Hillel the Elder until the conclusion of the redaction of the Mishna. Here, the Mishna returns to the tradition of transmission from teacher to student during the period of the Sages of the Mishna. In doing so, it once again begins with the statement of Hillel.

הִלֵּל אוֹמֵר: אַל תִּפְרֹשׁ מִן הַצִּבּוּר,

Hillel says: Do not diverge from the community.[N] Instead, participate with them in their joy and in their pain, and do not conduct yourself in a different or divergent manner.

וְאַל תַּאֲמִין בְּעַצְמְךָ עַד יוֹם מוֹתְךָ,

Do not have confidence in yourself[N] that you will not fall into sin, **until the day of your death,** even if you have followed the straight and narrow path over the course of many years. Until a person's death, he has the potential to change for better or for worse.

NOTES

to your will; however, it is not respectful vis-à-vis Heaven to write that explicitly. Therefore, the mishna expressed this idea with the expression, "the will of others" (Rashbatz and others).

Hillel says: Do not diverge from the community – הִלֵּל אוֹמֵר אַל תִּפְרֹשׁ מִן הַצִּבּוּר: In other words, it is worthy for a person to include himself in the troubles of the community, and in that way, he will also share in their joy (Rashi; see *Taanit* 11a). This is of great importance, to the point that the Sages considered one who diverges from the community as the wicked who are sentenced to an eternity in Gehenna (*Rosh HaShana* 17a). The commentaries note that the mishna is not referring to a corrupt community, as a person has no recourse other than to diverge from them (see Rambam, *Hilkhot Deot* 6:1). Rather, the reference is to a standard community; even if it is not perfect, a person must not diverge from it, because the merit of the community is greater than that of an individual (see Rashbatz and *Midrash Shmuel*).

Do not have confidence in yourself – וְאַל תַּאֲמִין בְּעַצְמְךָ: In Berakhot 29a it is written: "As Yoḥanan the High Priest served in the High Priesthood for eighty years and ultimately became a Sadducee." Moreover, a person should not think that he knows the rationale for the mitzvot and does not need the "fence" that the Torah circumscribed around them to ensure that they would not be violated, as King Solomon stumbled because he was overly reliant on himself (Rashbatz, *Tiferet Yisrael*). Some write that this statement is juxtaposed to the previous statement, to mean that one should not diverge from the community because he believes in himself and thinks that he does not need the merit of the community as protection, or its support in his time of trouble.

וְאַל תָּדִין אֶת חֲבֵרְךָ עַד שֶׁתַּגִּיעַ לִמְקוֹמוֹ,

Do not judge your counterpart until you reach his position,[N] until you reach a situation of understanding of and identification with the entirety of the circumstances in which he is found. This refers to the place and the society in which he lives, as well as to the entirety of the situations and inner experiences that he has undergone.

וְאַל תֹּאמַר דָּבָר שֶׁאִי אֶפְשָׁר לִשְׁמֹעַ, שֶׁסּוֹפוֹ לְהִשָּׁמַע.

Do not say privately **something that cannot be heard,** that you do not want other to hear, **as ultimately**[N] **it will be heard** and revealed.

וְאַל תֹּאמַר: "לִכְשֶׁאֶפָּנֶה אֶשְׁנֶה", שֶׁמָּא לֹא תִפָּנֶה.

Do not say: When I will be unoccupied with my present affairs or troubles, **I will study** Torah, **lest you not be unoccupied** and you will be unable to accomplish that. Instead, do what needs to be done now, when it is certainly possible to do it.

NOTES

Until you reach his position – עַד שֶׁתַּגִּיעַ לִמְקוֹמוֹ: The simple explanation is that one should not judge another for his evil deeds without knowledge of his situation and standing; one does not know whether he himself would have been more successful in withstanding the test, because, as stated before, a person should not have confidence in himself until the day of his death. One should think how he would judge himself were he to stumble in that situation. Some write that the matters are stated in the other direction as well. One must not rush to judgment regarding a stranger who conducts himself with greatness and prominence, as though that is what he is, until you reach his place and see that he is not a pretender (Meiri).

Do not say something that cannot be heard [*lishmo'a*], as ultimately – וְאַל תֹּאמַר דָּבָר שֶׁאִי אֶפְשָׁר לִשְׁמֹעַ שֶׁסּוֹפוֹ: Some explain that one should not reveal a secret, thinking that it will not be heard and be revealed to others (Rashi, Rabbeinu Yona). Others explain that one should not say things in a manner that is difficult to understand and will be understood only later (Rambam). One should speak to people according to their present ability to absorb the content. Besides the fact that this is true in and of itself, matters might be misunderstood and cause error or mishap. Some explain that this counsel is addressed not to the one teaching but to the one being taught. He should not say that he is unable to understand [*lishmo'a*], because ultimately, if he sets his mind to it, he will be able to understand (Abravanel, *Pirkei Moshe*, and others). Some suggest that it is like the statement that follows, "Do not say: When I will be unoccupied, I will study"; as when you have the opportunity to learn something, do not postpone it with the thought that "it cannot be heard" at this point and "ultimately it will be heard" in the future. Instead, learn it now (Meiri).

Mishna 5

This mishna continues citing the statements of Hillel the Elder.

הוּא הָיָה אוֹמֵר:

He, Hillel the Elder, **would** typically **say** regarding the behaviors and character traits that form the basis of refraining from sin and of study, wisdom, and performance of good deeds:

אֵין בּוּר יְרֵא חֵטְא, וְלֹא עַם הָאָרֶץ חָסִיד,

An ignoramus, a person lacking education and knowledge of Torah, **cannot be one who fears sin,**[N] who takes precautions not to sin, as he does not know which sins he must refrain from. **An am *haaretz,*** an unrefined person with a basic education, one who is not meticulous in his actions and does not seek to expand his knowledge, **cannot be a *ḥasid,***[N] a person who goes beyond the standard obligations vis-à-vis God and man. Performing the actions of a *ḥasid* does not fit his general conduct.

NOTES

An ignoramus [*bur*] cannot be one who fears sin – אֵין בּוּר יְרֵא חֵטְא: Generally, a *bur* is a person who is lacking education, especially Torah education, and who has not mastered even a specific occupation. He is like a fallow [*bur*] field, in which nothing grows (see Rashi and Rambam here and 5:6). A person like that cannot be one who fears sin, because his lack of knowledge prevents him from discerning what is a sin and what is not a sin. Therefore, even when he attempts to the best of his ability to avoid sins, a substantive obstacle prevents him from doing so (Rashi, Rashbatz).

An *am haaretz* cannot be a *ḥasid* – וְלֹא עַם הָאָרֶץ חָסִיד: The meaning of the term *am haaretz* is a person who is not very educated, even though he has certain positive character traits (Rambam). This is a person who is occupied by matters of the world and labor. It is conceivable that this person will fear sin, as he is likely to have knowledge of many and various matters. However, he cannot be a *ḥasid*, who not only fulfills all the standard demands and obligations, but also performs matters that go beyond his obligations. Since an *am haaretz*, however he is defined, has a substantive shortcoming, then even when he seeks to become a *ḥasid* in a particular area, he appears to lack credibility and may even seem ridiculous, because of the dissonance with his general ways.

וְלֹא הַבַּיְשָׁן לָמֵד, וְלֹא הַקַּפְּדָן מְלַמֵּד,

Similarly, regarding the study of Torah and wisdom, **the shy cannot learn,** as his shyness leads him to refrain from questioning what he does not understand. Therefore, he cannot progress in his studies. **And** on the other hand, **the strict,** one who is impatient and angry, **cannot teach**[N] properly, because his students will fear asking him questions and seeking clarification. That will lead to deficits and gaps in their studies that they will be unable to overcome.

וְלֹא כָּל הַמַּרְבֶּה בִסְחוֹרָה מַחְכִּים.

Not everyone who engages in commerce extensively becomes wise,[N] even though he thereby becomes familiar with many people, different situations, and a variety of cultures. This is because wisdom is not acquired solely through exposure to matters, but only when the person has the ability to understand, absorb, and utilize the matters that he encounters.

NOTES

And the strict cannot teach – וְלֹא הַקַּפְּדָן מְלַמֵּד: The commentary follows the simple explanation, that it is a reference to one who becomes angry with his students when they ask many questions (Rashi, Rambam, and others). However, it can be understood otherwise, that the reference is to a person who is fastidious regarding the order of matters and that they be stated precisely. He cannot teach others, as their knowledge, character, and level of education differ from one another. The result is that the character and the conduct of the strict one, who insists on his orderly principles of teaching and is inflexible in their regard, lead to his not adapting to his students, and they will remain with deficiencies and gaps that will prevent them from learning.

Not everyone who engages in commerce extensively becomes wise – וְלֹא כָּל הַמַּרְבֶּה בִסְחוֹרָה מַחְכִּים: Some explain this as relating to Torah study, as one who engages in commerce extensively spends considerable time preoccupied with it, creating difficulty in studying his Torah regularly (Rashbatz, Meiri). The Sages say on the verse: "And it is not across the sea" (Deuteronomy 30:13), that the Torah cannot be found among merchants, shippers, and those who engage in commerce generally (*Kalla Rabbati* 5:5). Some broaden the interpretation to include wisdom and education in general. Although the merchant must know and understand his occupation, he does not gain wisdom, because his heart is not free to engage in matters of wisdom (*Tiferet Yisrael*). In order to acquire wisdom, one must engage in all matters of world affairs, including additional disciplines beyond commerce (Rashi), and especially gain knowledge in areas that are not merely commercial and financial.

Others see this as a continuation of the previous statement about the strict person; while, unlike the strict person, one who engages in commerce theoretically could teach, he cannot actually make his students smarter, as in order to do so he must be a wise man who diligently studied and analyzed (*Pirkei Moshe*, *Tosefot Yom Tov*).

וּבְמָקוֹם שֶׁאֵין אֲנָשִׁים – הִשְׁתַּדֵּל לִהְיוֹת אִישׁ.

In a place where there are no people,[N] leaders, **seek to be** such **a person,** even if you do not consider yourself worthy of it.

Mishna 6

This mishna continues to cite the statements of Hillel the Elder, and describes an incident in which his statement, regarding an evildoer and his punishment, was made in Aramaic, the language spoken at that time.

אַף הוּא רָאָה גֻּלְגֹּלֶת אַחַת שֶׁצָּפָה עַל פְּנֵי הַמַּיִם,

He, Hillel the Elder, **too, saw**[N] **one skull** of a person **that was floating on the water surface.**

אָמַר לָהּ: "עַל דַּאֲטֵפְתְּ – אַטְפוּךְ, וְסוֹף מְטִיפַיִךְ – יְטוּפוּן".

He said to it:[N] **Because you drowned others they drowned you,**[N] **and ultimately,**

NOTES

In a place where there are no people – וּבְמָקוֹם שֶׁאֵין אֲנָשִׁים: The commentary follows the straightforward interpretation, that the mishna is referring to leadership, to attending to the needs of the public and instructing the masses (see Numbers 13:3 and Rashi there); if there is no one to engage in these activities, you should engage in them. Some explain in a slightly different direction, that in a place where there are no worthy people, one should make the effort to become a person of standing and value, a person who is complete in his actions (*Midrash Shmuel*), and not allow himself to be trampled by lesser people (Meiri; see Yaavetz and *Tiferet Yisrael*).

This statement can also be understood in the converse manner. In a place where there are people, do not engage in public affairs, but study Torah (Rashi and others). The Rambam writes that this statement refers to Torah study, which was referred to previously. When there is no one to teach you, make certain to teach yourself.

He too saw – אַף הוּא רָאָה: Some explain that Hillel knew the person whose skull was floating, and knew that he was a murderer. But it can be explained that he did not know that person, but it was evident that he was a person who was killed in a violent incident.

He said to it – אָמַר לָהּ: Hillel did not merely think these words, but said them out loud so that the people with him would learn a moral lesson. He spoke in Aramaic because it was his mother tongue, just as he said his sayings cited earlier (1:13; Yaavetz). Some say that he actually addressed the skull, as for a certain period after death, the soul hears what is being said to it. He spoke in Aramaic, because it was the language understood by the simple people and the murder victim was one of them (*Hon Ashir*).

Because you drowned others, they drowned you – עַל דַּאֲטֵפְתְּ אַטְפוּךְ: This means that with the measure that a person measures, he is measured, and he receives a punishment commensurate to the crime (Rashi; see *Sota* 1:9). Moreover, it serves to teach that although he incurred liability to be put to

those who drowned you[N] **will be drowned.** In other words, the cycle of violence ultimately returns and harms those who hurt others. But it does not stop there, as when he receives his punishment, the cycle of violence is continued.

Mishna 7

This mishna cites a series of brief sayings of Hillel that relate to the consequences of performing actions beyond the standard measure, for good or for bad. At times this can lead to a result that is dissonant and even contrary to the desired objective.

הוּא הָיָה אוֹמֵר:

He, Hillel the Elder, **would say:**

מַרְבֶּה בָשָׂר – מַרְבֶּה רִמָּה.

One who increases flesh,[N] who eats much during his lifetime and becomes fat, gains no advantage from that. But the certain consequence is that upon his death this **increases maggots**[N] in his grave, and they are the ones who gain from this.

NOTES

death, his killers will also be punished, as they did not do so with the mandate of the court (Rashbatz). The Rambam writes that this statement serves to teach the converse as well. One who generates good for another will ultimately benefit from the results of that good.

Ultimately those who drowned you – וְסוֹף מְטִיפַיִךְ: Some say that the word "ultimately" comes to underscore that although, at times, murderers are not killed and they die in peace, ultimately the punishment will reach the evildoer, whether in this incarnation or in another incarnation. Furthermore, the plural indicates that if there were many participants in the act, each will be punished for his part (*Midrash Shmuel*).

One who increases flesh – מַרְבֶּה בָשָׂר: Some note that the matters in this mishna are listed chronologically. Initially, it considers the person himself, then it mentions his assets. When he has assets, he wants wives; the wives need maidservants; and managing the household requires slaves (Rashbatz, Bartenura).

One who increases flesh increases maggots – מַרְבֶּה בָשָׂר מַרְבֶּה רִמָּה: The Tiferet Yisrael explains that this is a form of deterrence, as even after a person's death, his soul senses the decomposition of the body and suffers from it. This is based on the verse: "But his flesh on him is painful, and his soul mourns over him" (Job 14:22; *Berakhot* 18b). Some explain that a person suffers during his lifetime when he thinks of what will befall him after his death (*Tosefot Yom Tov*). Others add that excessive flesh causes illness during one's lifetime and shortens his life (*Mirkevet HaMishne* and others).

מַרְבֶּה נְכָסִים – מַרְבֶּה דְאָגָה.

One who increases possessions because he is covetous or seeks a sense of security and tranquility is not happy as a result. He primarily **increases worry**[N] about how to maintain and cultivate his belongings.

מַרְבֶּה נָשִׁים – מַרְבֶּה כְשָׁפִים.

One who increases women, who takes many wives in the belief that he will thereby attain happiness or increase the variety in his life, **increases sorcery**[NB] and intrigue, as his wives will utilize these techniques in order to compete for his heart.

מַרְבֶּה שְׁפָחוֹת – מַרְבֶּה זִמָּה.

One who increases maidservants, who are predominantly young, unmarried women of low standing and lacking in self-esteem, **increases lewdness**[N] that is engaged in with them, whether with their master or with other people.

NOTES

One who increases possessions increases worry – מַרְבֶּה נְכָסִים מַרְבֶּה דְאָגָה: So it is written in the verse: "Sweet is the sleep of the worker, whether he eats little or much, but the satiation of the wealthy does not allow him to sleep" (Ecclesiastes 5:11).

One who increases women increases sorcery – מַרְבֶּה נָשִׁים מַרְבֶּה כְשָׁפִים: At that time it was accepted for a man to marry multiple wives. Inevitably these women would compete with one another for his attention and love, using any means at their disposal. One of these means, throughout the generations, was the use of sorcery, whether to cause the husband to love this wife, or to cause harm to another.

One who increases maidservants increases lewdness – מַרְבֶּה שְׁפָחוֹת מַרְבֶּה זִמָּה: In the past, it was common for families of means to have a maidservant, who would perform some or all of the household tasks (see *Ketubot* 5:5). An especially wealthy household might employ more maidservants than they actually needed. The presence of several young, lower-class, idle, unmarried women constituted a great sexual stumbling block for their master and for others, who could easily take advantage of these low-status women.

BACKGROUND

Sorcery – כְשָׁפִים: Over the generations, acts of sorcery and magic were common in Jewish society, as in the surrounding nations, and amulets and incantations were accepted as a means of coping with various illnesses and problems. The Sages believed in the curative powers of magic, but were concerned about its pagan influence. The determination that "most sorcery is in women" (*Mekhilta* of Rabbi Shimon bar Yoḥai on Exodus 22:17) and that "the most upright of women is a sorceress" (*Soferim* 15:7), alluded to in this mishna, is repeated elsewhere in the sources as well. That said, from many testimonies scattered throughout rabbinic literature, it is clear that men engaged in sorcery no less than did women.

מַרְבֶּה עֲבָדִים – מַרְבֶּה גָזֵל.

One who increases slaves[B] **increases robbery,**[N] as the slaves, without status and human dignity, lack restraint and illegally take money, whether from the master's property or from the property of others.

After citing the negative aspects that stem from an increase in material acquisitions, the mishna proceeds to cite a corresponding list of spiritual acquisitions and activities. Increasing them adds goodness and blessing.

מַרְבֶּה תוֹרָה – מַרְבֶּה חַיִּים.

One who increases his study of **Torah** and his engagement in it **increases life.**[N] Although it appears as though it takes up a person's time and places restrictions on his life, Torah elevates life. In contrast to material acquisitions, for which increase presents problems, the Torah brings life to the world.

מַרְבֶּה יְשִׁיבָה – מַרְבֶּה חָכְמָה.

One who increases sitting[B] in study and analysis, especially with others, **increases wisdom,**[N] for himself and for the world.

NOTES

One who increases slaves increases robbery – מַרְבֶּה עֲבָדִים מַרְבֶּה גָזֵל: The presence of multiple slaves, too, beyond the number needed by the household, creates a stratum of people with a mentality of idleness, and lacking in means and basic dignity. This stems from the fact that typically, they have no private property, and are also not responsible for their fate the way that a free person is. Therefore, at times, they steal items from the house in which they work, and sometimes they steal from others. The result is that owning multiple slaves brings with it an increase in robbery and theft instead of an increase in labor.

One who increases Torah increases life – מַרְבֶּה תוֹרָה מַרְבֶּה חַיִּים: Although, ostensibly, it appears that Torah diminishes one's life force, as it is stated: "Torah saps a person's strength" (*Kalla Rabbati* 5:2; see mishna 2), ultimately it adds life, as the verse states: "To love the Lord your God, to hearken to His voice…for He is your life and the length of your days, so that you may live in the Land" (Deuteronomy 30:20), and in many additional verses (Bartenura and others).

One who increases sitting increases wisdom – מַרְבֶּה יְשִׁיבָה מַרְבֶּה חָכְמָה: Some explain that this is stated regarding the teacher. By increasing the number of students who sit and study with him, he increases his own wisdom, as his students make him sharper, and he also increases wisdom in the world, as he makes his students wiser (Rashbatz, Bartenura).

מַרְבֶּה עֵצָה – מַרְבֶּה תְּבוּנָה.

One who increases counsel, seeking advice from others and hearing different opinions, **increases understanding.** As a result of the multiplicity of opinions and advice, he has a better understanding of reality and the ability to resolve unfamiliar problems.

מַרְבֶּה צְדָקָה – מַרְבֶּה שָׁלוֹם.

One who increases charity and acts of kindness to others, with his possessions or with his person, **increases peace,**[N] as he thereby prevents distress, and distress is liable to engender quarrels.

NOTES

Others maintain that this is stated regarding the one studying, as studying with Sages promotes acquisition of wisdom (Maharal of Prague and others). Rabbeinu Yona has a reversed reading: "One who increases wisdom increases sitting," meaning that if one becomes wise, many people come to learn from him.

Some comment that this saying is parallel to what is stated in mishna 5, that "not everyone who engages in commerce extensively becomes wise" despite traveling extensively, as "one who increases sitting increases wisdom" (*Avodat Yisrael*).

One who increases charity increases peace – מַרְבֶּה צְדָקָה מַרְבֶּה שָׁלוֹם: The verse states in this regard: "The act of charity will be peace and the effect of charity will be quiet and security forever" (Isaiah 32:17). Want and famine cause strife; therefore, one who increases charity, even from compulsion, causes peace in the world (Rashbatz). Some explain that giving charity demonstrates the giver's attributes of agreeableness and generosity. These are the opposite of insistence on strict implementation of the law, which stands at the foundation of dispute and quarrel (Maharal of Prague).

BACKGROUND

Slaves and maidservants – עֲבָדִים וּשְׁפָחוֹת: The Sages' assumption of questionable moral standing of slaves and maidservants stemmed from the lowly social background that led them to be sold into slavery or to be born to a slave. In terms of their personal status, slaves were considered property, like animals, and it was accepted that the norms, mitzvot, and values that characterize the society of free people did not apply to them. That is why it is possible to find in rabbinic literature general statements about slave society, e.g., "a slave, licentiousness is preferable for him" (*Gittin* 13a; see *Tosefta*, *Horayot* 2:10). It is also stated that "there is no trust in slaves." At the same time, rabbinic literature also testifies to the existence of slaves who were considered trustworthy, and were punctilious in fulfillment of mitzvot that they were not obligated to fulfill, like the slaves of the house of the *Nasi* (see *Berakhot* 2:7, *Sukka* 2:1; Jerusalem Talmud, *Nidda* 2:1, and elsewhere).

One who increases sitting [*yeshiva*] – מַרְבֶּה יְשִׁיבָה: A yeshiva, an institution in which Torah is studied, derives its name from the fact that students sit together there and jointly engage in Torah study. The source of this concept is apparently in the Babylonian institution of the *metivta*, from the Aramaic root meaning sit, in which many students studied and in which there was an authoritative, elected head. By contrast, study groups and study halls are mentioned in the Jerusalem Talmud, but not a yeshiva. As a result, in many manuscripts this passage does not appear, as well as additional passages from this mishna.

קָנָה שֵׁם טוֹב – קָנָה לְעַצְמוֹ.

One who acquires a good name through his good deeds, his wisdom, or his eminent personality, **acquires it for himself.**[N] This is the asset that belongs to a person completely in this world. By contrast, other people sometimes benefit more from one's material assets than the person himself does.

קָנָה לוֹ דִּבְרֵי תוֹרָה – קָנָה לוֹ חַיֵּי הָעוֹלָם הַבָּא.

Furthermore, **one who acquires matters of Torah for himself** did not make an acquisition that is limited to this world, but **he has acquired life in the World to Come for himself,** as the matters of Torah touch upon the eternal.

Mishna 8

Following the previous mishnayot, which cited the statements of Hillel the Elder, this mishna continues tracing the chain of transmission of the Torah.

רַבָּן יוֹחָנָן בֶּן זַכַּאי קִבֵּל מֵהִלֵּל וּמִשַּׁמַּאי.

Rabban Yoḥanan ben Zakkai[P] received from Hillel and Shammai.

NOTES

One who acquires a good name acquires it for himself – קָנָה שֵׁם טוֹב קָנָה לְעַצְמוֹ: Most acquisitions are not permanent, and often one discovers that, in fact, others enjoy his acquisitions more than he does, whether they are family members, heirs, or strangers. But a good reputation is a personal acquisition that remains in one's possession and belongs to him alone, as it is written: "A name is preferable to great wealth, and good grace to silver and gold" (Proverbs 22:1; Rashbatz).

Some note that one aspect of the phrase "acquires it for himself" is that it is a personal acquisition and not a general or eternal one. By contrast, one who acquires Torah acquires matters that transcend this world, with its priorities and pleasures. He acquires a stake in eternity (*Tosefot Yom Tov*).

Slave's collar, Roman Empire

הוּא הָיָה אוֹמֵר: אִם לָמַדְתָּ תּוֹרָה הַרְבֵּה – אַל תַּחֲזִיק טוֹבָה לְעַצְמְךָ, כִּי לְכָךְ נוֹצָרְתָּ.

He would regularly **say: If you studied much Torah**[N] **do not give yourself credit**[N] and consider it a matter worthy of special recognition, **as it is for this that you were**

NOTES

If you studied much Torah – אִם לָמַדְתָּ תּוֹרָה הַרְבֵּה: Some note that Rabban Yoḥanan is the one who emphasized this matter because he studied much Torah, as it is stated in *Avot deRabbi Natan* 14; see *Sukka* 28a): "He did not neglect Bible, Mishna, Gemara, halakhot and *aggadot*, *Tosefta*, inferences of the Torah and inferences of the scribes, and all the hermeneutical principles of the Sages, and each and every Torah matter; there was nothing that he left unstudied" (Rashi and others). Others cite a variant reading: "If you performed much Torah," as it appears in *Avot deRabbi Natan* and ancient manuscripts. Rabban Yoḥanan thereby incorporated the statements of his two teachers, Hillel and Shammai, who spoke against exploitation of the honor of Torah (see, e.g., 1:13) and in praise of action (*Mirkevet HaMishne*).

Do not give [*taḥazik*] yourself credit [*tova*] – אַל תַּחֲזִיק טוֹבָה לְעַצְמְךָ: Some noted that Rabban Yoḥanan fulfilled this saying himself, conducting himself with great humility, as related in the Talmud: "No one ever preceded him in issuing a greeting, not even a gentile in the marketplace" (*Berakhot* 17a). Some write that *tova* in this context is Torah, which is the quintessential good [*tova*]. One who studied much Torah should not keep it [*taḥazik*] to himself but should teach it to others (*Lev Avot*).

PERSONALITIES

Rabban Yoḥanan ben Zakkai – רַבָּן יוֹחָנָן בֶּן זַכַּאי: Rabban Yoḥanan ben Zakkai was a prominent personage from the tannaitic period, with historic significance. He was the only Sage accorded the title "Rabban" who was not a descendant of Hillel. Apparently, Rabban Yoḥanan ben Zakkai was a priest, and lived most of his life in Jerusalem, although he was not born there. While this mishna lists him as a disciple of Hillel and Shammai, he was the primary disciple of Hillel and was his successor. It is stated that he lived a long life, 120 years according to tradition, and in the course of his life he engaged in commerce, studied Torah, and taught the masses (*Rosh HaShana* 31b).

Rabban Yoḥanan saw himself as carrying the responsibility for preserving the character of the Jewish nation in his generation and in the future. Before the destruction of the Temple, he acted forcefully to have the Pharisee tradition be the prevalent one, and he battled the Sadducees. When he foresaw the impending destruction, he began developing the Torah center in Yavne. During the Great Revolt, he opposed the steps of the Zealots, and was smuggled out of the besieged city with the help of his disciples Rabbi Eliezer and Rabbi Yehoshua. Rabban Yoḥanan encountered Vespasian and requested that he not harm the Torah center in Yavne and the dynasty of Rabban Gamliel in the institution of the *Nasi* (*Gittin* 56a–b). After the destruction, Rabban Yoḥanan instituted many ordinances designed to establish an alternative means of enabling religious life even without the Temple, while preserving its memory (see *Rosh HaShana* 4:1–4), and for all intents and purposes, he was among the great designers of Judaism after the destruction. It is related that before his passing, his students addressed him with the honorifics: "Lamp of Israel, right pillar, mighty hammer" (*Berakhot* 28b). It is also stated that after he died, "the glory of wisdom ceased" (*Sota* 9:15).

Monument at the crypt of Rabban Yoḥanan ben Zakkai, Tiberias

created.[N] This is the purpose of a person of Israel. You have merely fulfilled the obligation incumbent upon you.

The mishna continues tracing the chain of transmission of the Torah, to Rabban Yoḥanan's disciples, each with his own unique characteristic.

חֲמִשָּׁה תַלְמִידִים הָיוּ לוֹ לְרַבָּן יוֹחָנָן בֶּן זַכַּאי, וְאֵלּוּ הֵן: רַבִּי אֱלִיעֶזֶר בֶּן הוֹרְקְנוֹס, וְרַבִּי יְהוֹשֻׁעַ בֶּן חֲנַנְיָה, וְרַבִּי יוֹסֵי הַכֹּהֵן, וְרַבִּי שִׁמְעוֹן בֶּן נְתַנְאֵל, וְרַבִּי אֶלְעָזָר בֶּן עֲרָךְ.

Rabban Yoḥanan ben Zakkai had five outstanding **disciples** who were especially close to him and were considered his successors, **and these are they: Rabbi Eliezer ben Hyrcanus, Rabbi Yehoshua ben Ḥananya, Rabbi Yosei HaKohen, Rabbi Shimon ben Netanel, and Rabbi Elazar ben Arakh.**

הוּא הָיָה מוֹנֶה שִׁבְחָן:

He would recount their praise and characterize the special virtue of each of his disciples:

רַבִּי אֱלִיעֶזֶר בֶּן הוֹרְקְנוֹס – בּוֹר סוּד שֶׁאֵינוֹ מְאַבֵּד טִפָּה.

Rabbi Eliezer ben Hyrcanus he characterized as **a plastered cistern**[NB] **that never loses a drop,** due to his phenomenal memory. Due to his memory, he became a receptacle for the entire Torah of Israel.

NOTES

For this that you were created – לְכָךְ נוֹצַרְתָּ: In other words, you were born into the world for this purpose, and a great obligation is incumbent upon you. This is not a matter for which a person can take credit (Rashi, Rabbeinu Yona). Some explain that if a person succeeded in garnering much Torah, this was because he was created from the outset with the requisite abilities and skills (*Midrash Shmuel*).

A plastered cistern – בּוֹר סוּד: This means that his memory was so great that it was like a cistern coated with plaster, from which no water can seep (Rashi). In the version cited in *Avot deRabbi Natan* 14, they add his praise: "A tarred jug that preserves its wine." Some write that he possessed this virtue because he loved matters of Torah so much that he never forgot them (*Tiferet Yisrael*). Moreover, beyond the fact that he never lost any of his Torah knowledge, he was careful not to innovate anything on his own. It is related in his regard (*Tosefta, Yevamot* 3:1) that he would not say anything that he did not hear from his teachers (Rabbi Matitya HaYitzhari).

רַבִּי יְהוֹשֻׁעַ בֶּן חֲנַנְיָה – אַשְׁרֵי יוֹלַדְתּוֹ.

Rabbi Yehoshua ben Ḥananya – happy is the one who bore him.[N] This description, which the book of Proverbs applies to the wise son, who is the pride of his parents, depicts Rabbi Yehoshua's wisdom, cleverness, and character traits.

NOTES

Happy is the one who bore him – אַשְׁרֵי יוֹלַדְתּוֹ: Rabbi Yehoshua ben Ḥananya was a prominent Sage, and was expert in everything, both Torah and worldly matters. He was known as the greatest of the Sages in the eyes of the emperor. That is why this praise was expounded in his regard, based on the verse: "The father of the righteous will revel with happiness, and the begetter of the wise will rejoice in him. Your father and your mother will rejoice, and she who bore you will be happy" (Proverbs 23:24–25). Some say, based on the words of the Jerusalem Talmud (*Yevamot* 1:6), that his mother would bring him to the study hall when he was a small child (see Rashi). The Rambam says that the special virtue attributed to Rabbi Yehoshua was the perfection of his character traits, and some add that this is the reason the praise is directed to his parents (*Mirkevet HaMishne*).

Crypt of Rabbi Yehoshua ben Ḥananya

BACKGROUND

A plastered cistern – בּוֹר סוּד: In order to prevent seepage of water from cisterns, they would coat the walls of the cistern with plaster, a sealing agent made of burnt limestone.

Cistern whitewashed with plaster, Masada

רַבִּי יוֹסֵי הַכֹּהֵן – חָסִיד.

Rabbi Yosei HaKohen was a **ḥasid,** a person who performs actions that are beyond the standard obligations vis-à-vis other people or God.

רַבִּי שִׁמְעוֹן בֶּן נְתַנְאֵל – יְרֵא חֵטְא.

Rabbi Shimon ben Netanel was **one who fears sin;**[N] he conducted himself with extreme caution, to avoid sin.

וְרַבִּי אֶלְעָזָר בֶּן עֲרָךְ – מַעְיָן הַמִּתְגַּבֵּר.

Rabbi Elazar ben Arakh was **an ever-flowing spring,**[N] a description pointing to his originality and creativity.

הוּא הָיָה אוֹמֵר: אִם יִהְיוּ כָּל חַכְמֵי יִשְׂרָאֵל בְּכַף מֹאזְנַיִם, וֶאֱלִיעֶזֶר בֶּן הוֹרְקְנוֹס בְּכַף שְׁנִיָּה – מַכְרִיעַ אֶת כֻּלָּם.

Despite his praise for all five disciples, **he,** Rabban Yoḥanan ben Zakkai, **would say: If all the Sages of Israel would be on** one **pan of a scale and Eliezer ben Hyrcanus on the second pan,** Rabbi Eliezer would outweigh them **and overcome them all,** as he is greater in his Torah and his sanctity than all the rest of the Sages of his generation.

NOTES

Ḥasid…one who fears sin – חָסִיד...יְרֵא חֵטְא: Regarding the praise of Rabbi Yosei HaKohen, the version in *Avot deRabbi Natan* 14 states that he was the "*ḥasid* of the generation" and would keep extreme distance from sin (see Rashbatz). Rabbi Shimon ben Netanel is praised for establishing many fences around permitted matters (Rashbatz). He feared sin itself, out of a desire not to violate the commands of the Holy One blessed be He, rather than due to the reward or punishment that sin entails (*Tiferet Yisrael* and others). In *Avot deRabbi Natan* he is described as "a furrow in the wilderness that holds its water."

Rabbi Elazar ben Arakh was an ever-flowing spring – רַבִּי אֶלְעָזָר בֶּן עֲרָךְ מַעְיָן הַמִּתְגַּבֵּר: In Avot deRabbi Natan 14, a variant reading states about him: "A continuous river and an ever-flowing spring, whose waters intensify and are dispersed abroad, to fulfill what is stated: 'May your springs be dispersed abroad, and streams of water in the streets' (Proverbs 5:16)." It is related there that when Rabban Yoḥanan's son passed away, his five disciples entered to comfort him. The only one of them who was able to say words of consolation that comforted him was Rabbi Elazar ben Arakh.

The Ḥermon (Banyas) River, an ever-flowing river

אַבָּא שָׁאוּל אוֹמֵר מִשְּׁמוֹ: אִם יִהְיוּ כָּל חַכְמֵי יִשְׂרָאֵל בְּכַף מֹאזְנַיִם, וְרַבִּי אֱלִיעֶזֶר בֶּן הוֹרְקְנוֹס אַף עִמָּהֶם, וְרַבִּי אֶלְעָזָר בֶּן עֲרָךְ בְּכַף שְׁנִיָּה – מַכְרִיעַ אֶת כֻּלָּם.

The Mishna comments that **Abba Shaul,**[P] one of the Sages, **said in his,** Rabban Yoḥanan ben Zakkai's, **name**[N] a different version: **If all the Sages of Israel would be on the pan of a scale and even were Eliezer ben Hyrcanus with them, and Elazar ben Arakh on the second pan, he,** Elazar ben Arakh, would outweigh them **and overcome them all,** as his great innovative ability exceeds the greatness of Rabbi Eliezer.

NOTES

Abba Shaul said in his name – אַבָּא שָׁאוּל אוֹמֵר מִשְּׁמוֹ: Some comment that the difference between the traditions surrounds the question of the relative value of innovation versus outstanding memory (Rashbatz). This is similar to the talmudic discussion over what is preferable – "Sinai," who is expert in all the Torah, or "one who uproots mountains," who is extremely sharp and analytical (*Tiferet Yisrael*; see *Berakhot* 64a). Others say that there is no dispute between the traditions; regarding breadth of knowledge Rabbi Eliezer prevails, and regarding in-depth study Rabbi Elazar prevails (Bartenura). Alternatively, when speaking to the masses, Rabban Yoḥanan highlighted the virtue of Rabbi Eliezer, who excelled in his knowledge, but he mentioned privately to his disciple Abba Shaul that the sharpness and creativity of Rabbi Elazar was even greater in his eyes than the ability of Rabbi Eliezer (*Lev Avot*).

PERSONALITIES

Abba Shaul – אַבָּא שָׁאוּל: The name "Abba" was an honorific given to early Sages, especially to those known for their piety. Abba Shaul was a *tanna*, and many of his halakhot and his aggadic statements are embedded in the Mishna, the Babylonian Talmud, and the Jerusalem Talmud. Nevertheless, so little is known about his life that there is a dispute regarding the generation in which he lived. Some date him as early as the end of the Second Temple era, because it is related that he was older than Rabbi Tarfon (*Bemidbar Rabba* 9:24), but according to others, he was younger than Rabbi Akiva and cited halakhot in his name (*Tosefta, Sanhedrin* 12:10). In certain places it is related that Abba Shaul's occupation was gravedigging. In other sources he transmits halakhot relating to the Temple and its service, including the tradition regarding the daily schedule in the Temple that was integrated into the passage of the sacrifices, recited before prayer (see *Yoma* 33a). In several places the Mishna cites a variant reading of Abba Shaul in addition to the primary version. This fact suggests that Rabbi Yehuda HaNasi had "the Mishna of Abba Shaul," an earlier compilation of tannaitic material, before him when he redacted the Mishna.

Mishna 9

This mishna continues to discuss Rabban Yoḥanan ben Zakkai and his disciples, focusing on the manner in which he developed them and directed them to search for truth and a worthy life. In doing so, the mishna reveals each one's unique opinions and character traits.

אָמַר לָהֶם: צְאוּ וּרְאוּ, אֵיזוֹהִי דֶּרֶךְ יְשָׁרָה שֶׁיִּדְבַּק בָּהּ הָאָדָם.

He, Rabban Yoḥanan ben Zakkai, **said to them,** his five disciples: **Go out and see,**[N] search and consider, **which is the upright path, to which a person shall adhere?**[N] What is the fundamental point through which and by means of which a person can unlock his good character traits and his conduct in general?

רַבִּי אֱלִיעֶזֶר אוֹמֵר: עַיִן טוֹבָה.

Rabbi Eliezer says: A generous eye,[N] a positive perspective regarding other people and matters in general.

NOTES

Go out and see – צְאוּ וּרְאוּ: This formulation is meant to urge students to abandon other topics and engage in a specific problem. This is probably because to do so, one must leave the study hall and look at people in order to ascertain the upright path to follow (see Maharal of Prague), or go out to observe matters that are relevant to all people and not only to Sages (*Midrash Shmuel* and others). Some explain to the contrary, that one should leave matters relating to the body and instead clarify this matter through intellectual analysis (*Mirkevet HaMishne*).

The upright path to which a person shall adhere – דֶּרֶךְ יְשָׁרָה שֶׁיִּדְבַּק בָּהּ הָאָדָם: In mishna 1, it was taught in the name of Rabbi, who lived a generation later: "Which is the upright path that a person should select for himself?" Some explain that Rabbi's use of the word "select" refers to choosing one path and forsaking any other, while here the mishna refers to the path to which he should especially adhere, even though the other paths may also be good (Rashbatz). Alternatively, Rabbi directed that in every path that a person follows, he should conduct himself in a way that renders it a glorious path, whereas here the mishna is referring to a specific path to which a person shall adhere (*Tosefot Yom Tov*).

A generous eye – עַיִן טוֹבָה: The essence of a generous eye is that a person is satisfied with what he has and does not envy another's success (Bartenura and others). By contrast, a miser, in whose regard it is stated: "A miserly man rushes after wealth" (Proverbs 28:22), is not happy with his lot and is upset at other people's success. Others explain that one with a generous eye is openhanded and gives of his own to others, as it is stated: "A generous eye will be blessed, for he gives of his bread to the impoverished" (Proverbs 22:9; Rashbatz). Some explain that one with a generous eye sees only the good in others (Maharal of Prague).

רַבִּי יְהוֹשֻׁעַ אוֹמֵר: חָבֵר טוֹב.	**Rabbi Yehoshua says:** A person must begin with finding **a good,** personal **friend,**[N] who will help him follow the right path.
רַבִּי יוֹסֵי אוֹמֵר: שָׁכֵן טוֹב.	**Rabbi Yosei** HaKohen **says: A good neighbor,**[N] as the social influence of a neighbor is especially significant.
רַבִּי שִׁמְעוֹן אוֹמֵר: הָרוֹאֶה אֶת הַנּוֹלָד.	**Rabbi Shimon** ben Netanel **says: One who foresees consequences.**[N] This is the ability to assess long-term consequences of one's actions, which enables him to overcome temptation and avoid reacting immediately; rather, he chooses his path advisedly.
רַבִּי אֶלְעָזָר אוֹמֵר: לֵב טוֹב.	**Rabbi Elazar** ben Arakh **says: A good heart.** In other words, nothing external is likely to resolve problems sufficiently. One must generate change within himself and identify with good.
אָמַר לָהֶם: רוֹאֶה אֲנִי אֶת דִּבְרֵי אֶלְעָזָר בֶּן עֲרָךְ מִדִּבְרֵיכֶם, שֶׁבִּכְלַל דְּבָרָיו דִּבְרֵיכֶם.	**He,** Rabban Yoḥanan, **said to them,** to his disciples: **I prefer the statement of Elazar ben Arakh over your statements, because your statements are included in his statement.** One who achieves a good heart and internal perfection will have a generous eye; he will certainly choose for himself a good friend and a good neighbor; and he will also be able to assess the long-term consequences of his actions.

NOTES

A good friend – חָבֵר טוֹב: A friend's counsel will help save one from errors of judgment caused by one's personal involvement in a matter (Rashbatz). Alternatively, a person should make himself a good friend to all people (*Leḥem Yehuda*), or befriend the Sages so that he will adhere to them (*Midrash Shmuel*). Some say that this alludes to finding a good wife (*Notzer Ḥesed*).

A good neighbor – שָׁכֵן טוֹב: One's neighbor influences him more than a friend does, as he sees him and can affect him at all times, day or night (Rashi and others); therefore, both parties can help one another (Rabbeinu Yona). Choosing a neighbor is a more significant choice than choosing a friend, as one is choosing the society in which one establishes his life (see 1:7). The variant reading in *Avot deRabbi Natan* 14 is, "a good neighbor, a good inclination, a good wife."

One who foresees consequences – הָרוֹאֶה אֶת הַנּוֹלָד: This is not referring to some extraordinary mental ability, but to a way of life of paying attention to the consequences of one's actions (Rambam), as

אָמַר לָהֶם: צְאוּ וּרְאוּ, אֵיזוֹהִי דֶּרֶךְ רָעָה שֶׁיִּתְרַחֵק מִמֶּנָּה הָאָדָם.

Moreover, **he,** Rabban Yoḥanan, **said to them: Go out and see, which is the evil path,**[N] **from which a person shall distance himself?** This is the primary point that is likely to cause deterioration in all areas.

רַבִּי אֱלִיעֶזֶר אוֹמֵר: עַיִן רָעָה.

Rabbi Eliezer says: An evil eye, the quality of looking at other people or things in order to find their flaws.

רַבִּי יְהוֹשֻׁעַ אוֹמֵר: חָבֵר רָע.

Rabbi Yehoshua says: An evil friend.

רַבִּי יוֹסֵי אוֹמֵר: שָׁכֵן רָע.

Rabbi Yosei HaKohen **says: An evil neighbor.**

רַבִּי שִׁמְעוֹן אוֹמֵר: הַלֹּוֶה וְאֵינוֹ מְשַׁלֵּם. אֶחָד הַלֹּוֶה מִן הָאָדָם, כְּלֹוֶה מִן הַמָּקוֹם בָּרוּךְ הוּא, שֶׁנֶּאֱמַר: "לֹוֶה רָשָׁע וְלֹא יְשַׁלֵּם, וְצַדִּיק חוֹנֵן וְנוֹתֵן".

Rabbi Shimon ben Netanel **says: One who borrows but does not repay,**[N] who makes commitments but does not honor them. This indicates a lack of foresight in addition to ingratitude toward one who performed an act of kindness for him. He elaborates: **One who borrows from a person is like one who borrows from the Omnipresent, blessed be He.** Receiving gifts from the Holy One

NOTES

according to Rabbi Shimon ben Netanel, the obstacles that a person encounters on his spiritual path are due to his preferring immediate stimuli and enticements, which do not take the future into account. When he pays attention to their consequences, he will choose the good path.

Which is the evil path – אֵיזוֹהִי דֶּרֶךְ רָעָה: Some good paths are not obligatory, but rather go beyond the letter of the law. Similarly, there could be a middling path between a generous eye and an evil eye. Therefore, Rabban Yoḥanan also asked his disciples the opposite question: What is the evil path from which every person must distance himself (Rabbeinu Yona and others).

One who borrows but does not repay – הַלֹּוֶה וְאֵינוֹ מְשַׁלֵּם: This is an example of one who does not "foresee consequences," as if he does not pay his debt, others will not lend to him again (Rambam), nor will they help him in other ways (Rabbi Matitya HaYitzhari). Some explain that he does not pay because he did not foresee consequences when he took the loan, as he did not think ahead about how he would be able to repay it (*Midrash Shmuel*). Even if others agree to lend to him on another occasion; nevertheless, he is wicked, as he did not pay his debt (Rashbatz). Moreover, beyond the fact that he did not foresee the consequences, he harms and treats badly one who did him a favor (Maharal of Prague). Rabbi Shimon ben Netanel mentioned this specific behavior, and did not merely say in general that one who does not foresee consequences is on an evil path, because it is conceivable that a person will not foresee consequences but will nevertheless manage his life without harming others (Bartenura).

blessed be He can also be viewed as taking a loan, which carries an obligation to repay it, in other words, to utilize it for good and for the sake of Heaven. From where is it derived that "one who borrows but does not repay" characterizes the evil path from which a person must distance himself? It is **as it is stated:**[N] **"The wicked one borrows and does not repay; the righteous one is gracious and gives"** (Psalms 37:21); this verse defines the point that distinguishes between the righteous and the wicked.

רַבִּי אֶלְעָזָר אוֹמֵר: לֵב רָע.

Rabbi Elazar ben Arakh **says:** The evil path from which one must distance himself is **an evil heart.**

אָמַר לָהֶם: רוֹאֶה אֲנִי אֶת דִּבְרֵי אֶלְעָזָר בֶּן עֲרָךְ מִדִּבְרֵיכֶם, שֶׁבִּכְלַל דְּבָרָיו דִּבְרֵיכֶם.

Here, too, **he,** Rabban Yoḥanan, **said to them,** to his disciples: **I prefer the statement of Elazar ben Arakh**[N] **over your statements** for the same reason as before: It is **because your statements are included in his statement.** The deficiency in one's heart manifests later in various forms: ingratitude, shortsightedness, an evil eye, choosing inappropriate friends and neighbors, and lack of commitment.

NOTES

One who borrows from a person is like one who borrows from the Omnipresent, as it is stated – **אֶחָד הַלֹּוֶה מִן הָאָדָם כְּלֹוֶה מִן הַמָּקוֹם... שֶׁנֶּאֱמַר**: Some explain that if one borrows from another and does not repay him, it is as though he borrowed from the Holy One blessed be He, as the Holy One blessed be He, who is righteous, is gracious and repays the lender what the borrower did not return. Therefore, the borrower's debt is to God (Rashi). Although, on occasion, the court absolves the poor man from the obligation to repay his loan to his creditor, because they see that he has nothing with which to repay, nevertheless, he is obligated by the laws of Heaven; he is called wicked, and retribution will be exacted from him for borrowing and failing to repay (Rashbatz; see *Mirkevet HaMishne*). Others explain that this is said regarding all of a person's actions, because "the earth is the Lord's, and all that it holds" (Psalms 24:1). Everything from which one benefits in this world is a loan of sorts from the Holy One blessed be He, given to be used appropriately. The wicked do not repay this "loan," while the righteous add to it beyond what they were asked (*Avodat Yisrael*, *Tiferet Yisrael*: see 3:16).

I prefer the statement of Elazar ben Arakh – **רוֹאֶה אֲנִי אֶת דִּבְרֵי אֶלְעָזָר בֶּן עֲרָךְ**: This statement of Rabban Yoḥanan ben Zakkai lends support to the statement of Abba Shaul in the previous mishna that Rabban Yoḥanan considered Rabbi Elazar to be the greatest of his disciples and the equivalent of all the rest of them together.

Mishna 10

After discussing the character traits and the way of life of the disciples of Rabbi Yoḥanan ben Zakkai, the Mishna cites statements of each of them.

הֵם אָמְרוּ שְׁלֹשָׁה שְׁלֹשָׁה דְבָרִים.	**They,** the five disciples of Rabban Yoḥanan ben Zakkai, **each made three** notable **statements** regarding matters of ethics.
רַבִּי אֱלִיעֶזֶר אוֹמֵר:	**Rabbi Eliezer**[P] **says:**[N]
יְהִי כְבוֹד חֲבֵרְךָ חָבִיב עָלֶיךָ כְּשֶׁלְּךָ,	**Let the honor of another be** at least **as dear to you as your own**[N] honor.
וְאַל תְּהִי נוֹחַ לִכְעֹס.	**Do not be easily** and quickly **angered.**[N]
וְשׁוּב יוֹם אֶחָד לִפְנֵי מִיתָתְךָ.	**Repent one day before your death,**[N] as after death it is no longer possible.

NOTES

Rabbi Eliezer says – רַבִּי אֱלִיעֶזֶר אוֹמֵר: Ostensibly, Rabbi Eliezer's statement contains more than three matters. The commentaries explained this matter in several ways. The Rambam writes that Rabbi Eliezer said the first three matters on his own, and that what he said thereafter, from "Warm yourself," are matters that he heard from others. Rabbeinu Yona explains that Rabbi Eliezer would commonly state the first three matters, but that the others he said only occasionally. Rashi contends that "let the honor of another" and "do not be easily angered" are actually one matter, and the third matter is: "Warm yourself opposite the fire" (see Meiri).

Let the honor of another be as dear to you as your own – יְהִי כְבוֹד חֲבֵרְךָ חָבִיב עָלֶיךָ כְּשֶׁלְּךָ: Some explain that when another is accorded honor, you should consider it as though the Holy One blessed be He is honoring you as well (*Notzer Ḥesed*). Or, if a person dishonored another, defend him as you would act with regard to your own honor (*Midrash Shmuel*). Some cite a variant reading of the mishna: "The honor of your student" (Meiri; see *Tosefot Yom Tov*).

Do not be easily angered – וְאַל תְּהִי נוֹחַ לִכְעֹס: Even a person who has a bad temper by nature should distance himself from anger, or, at least, he should try not to be easily angered. Alternatively, although at times a person has a reason to get angry, he should try not to be easily angered, as it is written in the verse: "Do not precipitate your spirit to become angry" (Ecclesiastes 7:9); only a special circumstance should justify anger (Rabbeinu Yona). Some write that this admonition is stated as a continuation of "let the honor of another [*ḥaverekha*] be as dear…," because a person gets angry specifically at those closest to him, i.e., his friend [*ḥaver*] (Yaavetz).

Repent one day before your death – וְשׁוּב יוֹם אֶחָד לִפְנֵי מִיתָתְךָ: There are two aspects to this. First, one must think each day that the day of his death is approaching, so he must do what needs to be done in preparation, as in the dialogue related in *Avot deRabbi Natan* 15: "His students asked Rabbi Eliezer: Does a person know what day he will die, so he can repent? He said to them: All the more so! Let him repent today lest he die tomorrow. Let him repent

In addition, Rabbi Eliezer said additional matters regarding how one should relate to Sages.

וֶהֱוֵי מִתְחַמֵּם כְּנֶגֶד אוּרָן שֶׁל חֲכָמִים. וֶהֱוֵי זָהִיר בְּגַחַלְתָּן שֶׁלֹּא תִכָּוֶה, שֶׁנְּשִׁיכָתָן נְשִׁיכַת שׁוּעָל, וַעֲקִיצָתָן עֲקִיצַת עַקְרָב, וּלְחִישָׁתָן לְחִישַׁת שָׂרָף, וְכָל דִּבְרֵיהֶם כְּגַחֲלֵי אֵשׁ.

Warm yourself opposite the fire of the Sages. Draw near to them and receive Torah from them, just as a person draws near to fire for warmth. **However, be careful of their coals,** be careful not to get too close to them, **so you will not be burned** by treating them with disrespect; **as their bite,** the bite of the Sages, **is the bite of a fox,** as even though it is not terribly painful at the outset, it intensifies with the passage of time, **and their sting is the sting of a scorpion, and their hiss,** when they speak in anger or impatience, **is the hiss of a** venomous **serpent.**[NB] **And,** in general,

NOTES

tomorrow, lest he die the following day. The result is that he spends all his days in repentance." Tractate *Shabbat* (153a) added to this, quoting a verse: "At all times, let your garments be white, and may the oil on your head not be lacking" (Ecclesiastes 9:8), indicating that he should always repent his sins. The second aspect is that repentance, even one day before death, is effective (*Yaavetz*).

The hiss of a serpent – לְחִישַׁת שָׂרָף: Some write that what is notable about this serpent is that it cannot be placated, as it is stated: "Like the venom of a serpent, like a deaf cobra blocking its ear, which does not hear the voice of charmers, skillful casters of spells" (Psalms 58:5–6), and so too a Torah scholar who gets angry, it is impossible to placate him (Rambam and others). Moreover, his bite kills immediately (*Tiferet Yisrael*). Some write that the serpent is capable of killing one who is distant from him, and the Sages have a similar ability (*Mirkevet HaMishne* and others).

PERSONALITIES

Rabbi Eliezer – רַבִּי אֱלִיעֶזֶר: Rabbi Eliezer ben Hyrcanus was called Rabbi Eliezer the Great even during his lifetime. From a wealthy family, he was twenty years old when he left home to study Torah with Rabban Yoḥanan ben Zakkai in conditions of poverty and hardship. With his persistence and diligence, combined with his special talent for comprehension and memory, he was acknowledged as one of the great leaders of Israel. He married Imma Shalom, sister of Rabban Gamliel of Yavne. Alongside his tremendous memory, Rabbi Eliezer was characterized by his extraordinary insistence not to say anything that he did not hear from his teachers. Besides his great prominence in Torah, he was also considered a holy man. He also engaged in Torah mysticism, and the aggadic midrash *Pirkei deRabbi Eliezer* is attributed to him.

Despite his close relationship with Rabban Yoḥanan and the house of the *Nasi*, who descended from Beit Hillel, he himself tended toward the approach of Beit Shammai. That is why he is sometimes called "Shamuti," in other words, "one who tends toward the opinion of Beit Shammai." It was also one of the reasons that he found himself in dispute with many of his contemporary Sages. When he did not agree to accept the majority opinion, the Sages had to ostracize him. His most outstanding student was Rabbi Akiva.

BACKGROUND

The bite of a fox, the sting of a scorpion, the hiss of a serpent – נְשִׁיכַת שׁוּעָל, עֲקִיצַת עַקְרָב, לְחִישַׁת שָׂרָף: The commentaries explain that a fox bite was notable due to a fox's crooked teeth; in order to treat wounds

all their words are like fiery coals,[N] which illuminate and warm; however, one must treat them with great caution.

BACKGROUND

from its bite, it is necessary to make an incision over a wide area. Alternatively, its teeth are far from one another, necessitating separate treatment of each puncture that it causes. In the common fox today, there is no significant difference in the structure of its mouth from that of a dog.

The common fox, *Canis aureus*, is considered in many cultures, since ancient times, as a symbol of cleverness and slyness. This is due, in part, to its cleverness in escaping hunters and its ability to play dead in order to attack prey. There is great variety in its habitats and the types of food included in its diet. Its reputation for cleverness may be the reason it was chosen to symbolize the damage caused by the Sages. It appears that the mishna warns of the punishment exacted by the Sages due to the difficulty in avoiding it.

Why is the bite of a fox described as being so damaging? It does not have the teeth of a lion or a leopard, nor jaws with the crushing power of a hyena's. However, since the mishna mentions the bite of a fox in the same context as the sting of a scorpion and the hiss of a serpent, which is the sound made by a serpent when it delivers its venom, it is apparently referring not to physical damage but to chemical or viral harm, i.e., the scourge of rabies. Foxes are among the main disseminators of rabies in Israel (R. Natan Slifkin).

The sting of a scorpion can be explained similarly, as it is enumerated among the three matters that affect a person when he is distracted (*Sanhedrin* 97a). The serpent also symbolizes slyness, as it is stated: "The serpent was more cunning than any beast of the field that the Lord God had made" (Genesis 3:1). It is able to overcome obstacles in its path and to bite suddenly, without warning.

Fox

Nebo *hierichonticus* scorpion, Jericho

Cerastes cerastes, a venomous serpent that lives in Israel, among other places

NOTES

And all their words are like fiery coals – וְכָל דִּבְרֵיהֶם כְּגַחֲלֵי אֵשׁ: Rashi writes that Rabbi Eliezer is underscoring that all the Sages' words, even those that appear to be inconsequential, are like fiery coals, and one must be very careful in their regard. On that subject, some write that being burned by coals is worse than being burned by the flame itself (Rashbatz). Others explain that just as a coal can cause a burn even when there is no flame, and even if the coal is buried in the dirt, so one must be careful with the words of the Sages, even after their death (*Mirkevet HaMishne*; see Maharal of Prague).

Fiery coals

Mishna 11

This mishna continues citing statements of the disciples of Rabban Yoḥanan ben Zakkai, each of whom made three statements.

רַבִּי יְהוֹשֻׁעַ אוֹמֵר:

Rabbi Yehoshua[P] **says** three matters that a person must be careful to avoid. Each of them is a topic in and of itself:

עַיִן הָרָע, וְיֵצֶר הָרָע, וְשִׂנְאַת הַבְּרִיּוֹת, מוֹצִיאִין אֶת הָאָדָם מִן הָעוֹלָם.

The evil eye,[N] looking upon people or things with the intent of finding fault with them; **the evil inclination,**[N] all the various inclinations that tempt a person to perform all sorts of transgressions; **and hatred of people**[N] that

NOTES

The evil eye – עַיִן הָרָע: This is desire and the coveting of money, including miserliness. Alternatively, it is one who hates his friend or his enemy, and seeks to find flaws in everything (see mishna 9). Conduct of this sort is damaging to oneself and one's surroundings, and shortens one's life. Some write that the mishna is referring to an evil eye of the mind, when a person is agnostic and denies the fundamentals of faith (*Tiferet Yisrael*).

The evil inclination – וְיֵצֶר הָרָע: The Rambam writes tersely that the evil inclination constitutes increased desire. The Rashbatz expanded on the matter, and said that realizing the lust for food, drink, and sexual relations causes a person to die soon.

Hatred of people – וְשִׂנְאַת הַבְּרִיּוֹת: Rashi writes that this is baseless hatred. Some write that the mishna is referring to one who acts in a way that causes people to hate him (Bartenura), or one who refrains from performing acts of kindness for people (*Tiferet Yisrael*). The Rambam writes that the reference is to the personality trait of melancholy, which causes one to shy away from people and live a life of isolation, which is perilous for him.

PERSONALITIES

Rabbi Yehoshua ben Ḥananya – רַבִּי יְהוֹשֻׁעַ בֶּן חֲנַנְיָה: Rabbi Yehoshua ben Ḥananya was a Levite, and in his youth served in the Temple as a singer. In a sense, Rabbi Yehoshua is the preeminent disciple of Rabban Yoḥanan ben Zakkai. He is the person who preserved the approach of Beit Hillel in the most complete fashion, and he apparently stood at the head of the group that led the academy in Yavne to adopt the opinion of Beit Hillel as the halakha. As a result, the halakha was adopted in accordance with his opinion in most of his disputes with his colleague, Rabbi Eliezer.

Rabbi Yehoshua was renowned for his great wisdom, not only among the Jewish people, but also in the emperor's palace, where he was considered the wisest person they ever encountered. It is related that no person ever bested him in a debate (*Eiruvin* 53b). Rabbi Yehoshua continued Rabban Yoḥanan's political philosophy and leaned toward avoiding confrontation with the government in Rome (see *Bereshit Rabba* 64:10). Indeed, the great battle against the Romans, the bar Kokheva revolt, took place after his death.

Little is known about the events of his private life, other than the fact that he worked with coal or was a blacksmith. It is stated that when he died, "counsel and thought ceased from the world" (*Sota* 9:15).

is not for any particular reason but due to a general sense of enmity and alienation. These three **drive a person from the world,** both this world and the World to Come. This is because his life is full of enmity and evil, and after his death, he is destined to be punished for the resulting sins.

Mishna 12

This mishna continues citing three statements from each of the five disciples of Rabban Yoḥanan ben Zakkai.

רַבִּי יוֹסֵי אוֹמֵר: יְהִי מָמוֹן חֲבֵרְךָ חָבִיב עָלֶיךָ כְּשֶׁלְּךָ.

Rabbi Yosei[P] HaKohen **says three** statements: **The property of another should be as dear to you as your own.**[N] Protect it, and when you are dealing with it, do not cause it to be wasted or squandered.

וְהַתְקֵן עַצְמְךָ לִלְמֹד תּוֹרָה, שֶׁאֵינָהּ יְרֻשָּׁה לָךְ.

Prepare yourself to study Torah; you must exert yourself to that end, **as it is not your inheritance.**[N] Every person must toil to acquire it for himself, even if he grew up in a family of those who study Torah.

NOTES

The property of another should be as dear to you as your own – יְהִי מָמוֹן חֲבֵרְךָ חָבִיב עָלֶיךָ כְּשֶׁלְּךָ: He should care for the other's possessions, return his lost items, and make certain to prevent any potential financial harm from affecting him (Rashbatz, *Avot deRabbi Natan*). He must also not denigrate another's belongings, to distance potential buyers from them (Meiri).

Prepare yourself to study Torah, as it is not your inheritance – וְהַתְקֵן עַצְמְךָ לִלְמֹד תּוֹרָה שֶׁאֵינָהּ יְרֻשָּׁה לָךְ: Some emphasized that "prepare yourself" refers not only to studying, but also to preparing one's soul, to reach the level of *ḥasidut* (Rabbeinu Yona). The simple understanding of the phrase "as it is not your inheritance" is that Torah knowledge is not like an inheritance that comes to a person without effort, but rather, one acquires it through exertion. Others explain that this statement is made specifically vis-à-vis those who grew up in families of Sages with distinguished lineage (Rashi and others). Although a verse says that the Torah is an inheritance, as it is stated: "Torah, Moses commanded us, a heritage of the assembly of Jacob" (Deuteronomy 33:4), it is not an inheritance for a specific person or a specific family, but for the entire Jewish people (*Tiferet Yisrael*).

וְכָל מַעֲשֶׂיךָ יִהְיוּ לְשֵׁם שָׁמַיִם.

All your actions, regarding both sacred and non-sacred matters, **should be for the sake of Heaven,**[N] in the name of God and in His honor.

Mishna 13

This mishna continues citing three statements from each of the five disciples of Rabban Yoḥanan ben Zakkai.

רַבִּי שִׁמְעוֹן אוֹמֵר:

Rabbi Shimon[P] ben Netanel **says** three matters:

הֱוֵי זָהִיר בִּקְרִיאַת שְׁמַע וּבִתְפִלָּה.

Be vigilant in reciting Shema and the *Amida* **prayer,** to make certain to perform them at their proper time and not to skip them.

NOTES

All your actions should be for the sake of Heaven – וְכָל מַעֲשֶׂיךָ יִהְיוּ לְשֵׁם שָׁמַיִם: For every mitzva that one performs, he should intend it to be for the sake of Heaven, and not for the sake of profit or some ancillary benefit. In his other actions, too, all non-sacred matters and optional acts should be for the sake of Heaven (Bartenura and others). In *Avot deRabbi Natan* this was derived from a verse: "In all your ways be cognizant of Him, and He will smooth your paths" (Proverbs 3:6). It is stated in *Berakhot* 63a that this verse is "a brief passage upon which all fundamental principles of Torah are dependent."

PERSONALITIES

Rabbi Yosei HaKohen – רַבִּי יוֹסֵי הַכֹּהֵן: Rabbi Yosei HaKohen was one of the five great disciples of Rabban Yoḥanan ben Zakkai, who said in his regard that he was a "*ḥasid* of the generation." This is not the same Rabbi Yosei who is typically cited in the Mishna without a patronym. That *tanna* is Rabbi Yosei ben Ḥalafta, one of the disciples of Rabbi Akiva, who lived two generations later. He is mentioned in few places, and in the Mishna is mentioned only one other time, in tractate *Eduyyot* (8:2). Virtually nothing is known about his actions and his Torah legacy.

Rabbi Shimon – רַבִּי שִׁמְעוֹן: Very little is known about Rabbi Shimon ben Netanel, who was primarily a private person and not a teacher of the multitudes. Like his teacher and his colleagues, he also engaged in Torah mysticism. From another source, it emerges that he was a priest and was very exacting regarding the laws of the priesthood. In addition, he was the son-in-law of Rabban Gamliel the Elder (*Tosefta, Avoda Zara* 3:10).

וּכְשֶׁאַתָּה מִתְפַּלֵּל – אַל תַּעַשׂ תְּפִלָּתְךָ קֶבַע, אֶלָּא רַחֲמִים וְתַחֲנוּנִים לִפְנֵי הַמָּקוֹם בָּרוּךְ הוּא, שֶׁנֶּאֱמַר: "כִּי חַנּוּן וְרַחוּם הוּא אֶרֶךְ אַפַּיִם וְרַב חֶסֶד וְנִחָם עַל הָרָעָה".

When you pray, although prayer is incumbent upon you as a permanent obligation with defined halakhot, **do not render your prayer fixed,**[N] like a rote requirement, **but** recite it with intent and from the depth of the heart as **a plea for mercy and supplication before the Omnipresent, blessed be He.** In that way He will accept it, because He is merciful and responds to supplication, **as it is stated: "As He is gracious and merciful, slow to anger, abounding in kindness, and reconsiders harm"** (Joel 2:13).

וְאַל תְּהִי רָשָׁע בִּפְנֵי עַצְמְךָ.

Do not be wicked in your own eyes,[N] because a person who characterizes himself as wicked descends into sadness and despair, which prevent him from doing what he is obligated to do. Moreover, because he feels that he is wicked, he sees no reason to engage in mitzvot.

NOTES

When you pray do not render your prayer fixed – וּכְשֶׁאַתָּה מִתְפַּלֵּל אַל תַּעַשׂ תְּפִלָּתְךָ קֶבַע: This completes Rabbi Shimon ben Netanel's first statement. Even when you are punctilious with regard to the halakhot and the times for reciting *Shema* and the *Amida* prayer, do not relate to the prayer as a burden and as fulfillment of a mere technical obligation (see *Berakhot* 4:4). This is derived from the verse cited in this mishna, which indicates that the essence of prayer is not in its external manifestations, but in the inspiration of the heart and words of supplication (see *Taanit* 2:1). This latter statement is stated regarding prayer, not regarding the recitation of *Shema*, as reciting *Shema* is primarily a mitzva of rote and recital, and not service of the heart. Some explain that one must not place the main emphasis on prayer, because the main focus must be on the Torah. He should pray appropriately, entreating for mercy and with supplication, but his main emphasis must be on matters of Torah (*Midrash Shmuel*. See also statement of Shammai, 1:15: "Make your Torah permanent."

Do not be wicked in your own eyes [*bifnei atzmekha*] – וְאַל תְּהִי רָשָׁע בִּפְנֵי עַצְמְךָ: A person should not think of himself as wicked, because if he does he will be lax in observing the Torah and mitzvot and he will not refrain from performing all sorts of lowly actions (Rambam, Rabbeinu Yona, and others). Some write that this warning is a continuation of the previous statement, about prayer. Do not think that because you sinned, you are wicked, and there is no value to your prayer (*Mirkevet HaMishne*).

Another interpretation is, do not perform an action that over time will cause you to consider yourself wicked (Rashi). Others understand this to mean that one should not seclude himself and live alone [*bifnei atzmekha*], and be wicked in that regard (Rashbatz, Bartenura). There are also those who explain that you should not think that your sins are your personal concern, because every person is part of the collective, and the wickedness of one condemns the collective (*Midrash Shmuel*).

Mishna 14

This mishna continues citing three statements from each of the five disciples of Rabban Yoḥanan ben Zakkai.

רַבִּי אֶלְעָזָר אוֹמֵר: **Rabbi Elazar**[P] ben Arakh **says** three matters:

הֱוֵי שָׁקוּד לִלְמֹד תּוֹרָה. **Be diligent in studying Torah.** Never stop studying, with toil and diligence, even if it is not for a specific purpose of knowledge or skill, as the study itself constitutes service of God.

וְדַע מַה שֶּׁתָּשִׁיב לְאֶפִּיקוֹרוֹס. But on the other hand, **know what to respond to a heretic** [***epikoros***]. [NB] It is not sufficient to

NOTES

Know what to respond to a heretic – וְדַע מַה שֶּׁתָּשִׁיב לְאֶפִּיקוֹרוֹס: The heretic is one who repudiates faith, although he often has Torah knowledge. In order to respond to him appropriately, one must be well versed both in Torah and in outside philosophies (Rambam, Meiri). Some infer from this mishna that one should not initiate a debate with a heretic; rather, one should know what to respond to him if he approaches you (Yaavetz). Others cite a variant reading in which this is a continuation of the first matter: "Be diligent in studying Torah so you will be able to respond to a heretic" (Ramban on Leviticus 3:9). In an ancient version of the Mishna (Kaufman manuscript), the reading is: "Be diligent in studying what to respond to a heretic."

PERSONALITIES

Rabbi Elazar – רַבִּי אֶלְעָזָר: As explained in this chapter, this is Rabbi Elazar ben Arakh, the most brilliant and creative of the disciples of Rabban Yoḥanan ben Zakkai. Despite his special standing among his colleagues, both in halakha and in Torah mysticism (see *Tosefta*, *Ḥagiga* 2:1), virtually no statements attributed to him remain.

An explanation for this can be found in an incident that is related about him. After the passing of Rabban Yoḥanan ben Zakkai, Rabbi Elazar ben Arakh separated from his colleagues, who were concentrated in Yavne, and went, apparently following his wife, to a place of therapeutic springs and pleasure, where there were no Torah scholars. This choice caused him to remain alone, without students following him, and ultimately for him to forget his learning. The incident served for generations as an object lesson, that a Sage must be in constant conversation with his colleagues, which includes reciting and reviewing statements of the Sages. Without them, not only will he not continue to develop greatness, but his prominence will decline.

BACKGROUND

Epikoros – אֶפִּיקוֹרוֹס: The term *epikoros* comes from the name of the Greek philosopher, Epicurus (341–270 BCE). His philosophy was considered to be contrary to the Greek religion, and aroused the wrath of the masses. At the center of his approach was happiness and avoiding suffering as the primary objective of human life. Epicurus denied the existence of the Creator, of Divine Providence, and of life after death. Due to the fact that his philosophy ran counter to the principles of religious faith, the name *epikoros* became a

Bust of the Greek philosopher Epicurus; Roman restoration, third century BCE

confine your Torah study to the defined circle of the principles of thought and methods of study of the study hall. Rather, you must also be capable of addressing problems and questions that originate from the outside, from another kind of world, considering both worlds simultaneously.

וְדַע לִפְנֵי מִי אַתָּה עָמֵל, וְנֶאֱמָן הוּא בַּעַל מְלַאכְתְּךָ שֶׁיְּשַׁלֶּם לְךָ שְׂכַר פְּעֻלָּתֶךָ.

He adds: Although the results of diligence and toil in Torah are not recognized according to the criteria of this world, **know before whom you are toiling,**[N] the Holy One blessed be He Himself, **and that He is your employer who will pay the reward** that you deserve **for your actions,**[N] and even more.

Mishna 15

After the mishna concludes citing the sayings of Rabbi Yoḥanan's five disciples, it cites the statements of Rabbi Tarfon, who was their contemporary.

רַבִּי טַרְפוֹן אוֹמֵר:

Rabbi Tarfon[P] would **say**[N] a saying in the form of a parable, which comes to rouse a person to consider his existence in this world:

BACKGROUND

derogatory epithet for the heretics among the Greeks. With the influence of the Aramaic term for anarchy [*afkiruta*], the term permeated Hebrew and Jewish sources with a similar meaning.

NOTES

Know before whom you are toiling – וְדַע לִפְנֵי מִי אַתָּה עָמֵל: Some explain that this is a continuation of: "Know what to respond to a heretic." Although you study outside areas of philosophy to know what to respond to a heretic, do not be drawn in by their statements. Instead, "know before whom you are toiling," the One who examines your inner thoughts and feelings (Rambam, Bartenura, and others). In some variant readings, and in *Avot deRabbi Natan*, the version is: "Know who is your ally."

Who will pay the reward for your actions – שֶׁיְּשַׁלֶּם לְךָ שְׂכַר פְּעֻלָּתֶךָ: Although it is best to serve God "not… in order to receive a portion" (1:3), a person should keep in mind that the Holy One blessed be He will pay a reward. This will help him appreciate the importance of serving God and be strengthened in that service.

Rabbi Tarfon says – רַבִּי טַרְפוֹן אוֹמֵר: Here Rabbi Tarfon concisely formulates the great facets of life.

הַיּוֹם קָצָר, וְהַמְּלָאכָה מְרֻבָּה, וְהַפּוֹעֲלִים עֲצֵלִים, וְהַשָּׂכָר הַרְבֵּה, וּבַעַל הַבַּיִת דּוֹחֵק.

The day is short,[N] referring to this world, and the lives of people in it are brief. **The task** that is incumbent upon them in Torah study and reforming the world **is substantial. The laborers,** people, **are lazy, the reward** for this labor **is great,**[N] **and the employer,** the Holy One blessed be He, **is insistent,**[N] and is motivating people to perform their labor and their roles.

NOTES

On the one hand, people experience obligation, necessity, and reward, but on the other hand, they are subject to the human weaknesses of lack of time and a natural tendency toward laziness.

The day is short – הַיּוֹם קָצָר: The commentary follows the straightforward explanation, that Rabbi Tarfon is referring to life in this world (Rashi). Some write that it comes to underscore that the day is actually short, like the short winter days, while the task is substantial, so that even on a long summer day there is not enough time to perform the task (Rashbatz). Others write that the mishna used this language in order to spur people to consider that a person might not have much more time, and that this might be his final day, similar to what Rabbi Eliezer said (mishna 10): "Repent one day before your death" (*Midrash Shmuel*).

The reward is great – וְהַשָּׂכָר הַרְבֵּה: On the simplest level, the labor of the Torah and mitzvot is labor that, in and of itself, has great reward. However, some write that the mishna is saying that because the day is short, the task is substantial; laborers are lazy; and there is a special, great reward for those who expend effort in performing that task (*Avodat Yisrael*). Others write that the mishna means that even the most industrious are called lazy, relative to the immensity of the reward (*Midrash Shmuel*).

The employer is insistent – וּבַעַל הַבַּיִת דּוֹחֵק: Rashi cites proof from the verse: "This book of the Torah shall not depart from your mouth, and you shall ponder it day and night" (Joshua 1:8), whereas Rashbatz mentions the verse: "You shall observe the commandment, and the statutes, and the ordinances that I command you today, to perform them" (Deuteronomy 7:11) as support. The crux of the matter is that you should not say: I may be losing reward, but the employer Himself is not so insistent about this matter; rather, He wants it to be done and so is insistent that the labor be done quickly (Rashbatz).

PERSONALITIES

Rabbi Tarfon – רַבִּי טַרְפוֹן: Rabbi Tarfon was a priest and even participated in the Temple service before the destruction of the Second Temple (*Kiddushin* 71a). He was close to the circle of Rabban Yoḥanan ben Zakkai, even though he was not one of his prominent disciples. Rabbi Tarfon was extremely wealthy (*Nedarim* 62a), but despite his greatness and wealth, he was known to be extremely humble, hesitant to receive honor or benefit due to his status. Rabbi Tarfon was very close with Rabbi Akiva. Rabbi Akiva was initially his disciple–colleague, but ultimately Rabbi Tarfon became Rabbi Akiva's admirer and said in his regard: "Anyone who separates from you, it is as though he has separated from life" (*Kiddushin* 66b).

Beyond his halakhic and aggadic statements, Rabbi Tarfon was known as one who employed pithy and even humorous statements. When he was under the impression that he was liable due to his responsibility for an error in issuing a ruling, he said: "Your donkey is gone, Tarfon" (*Bekhorot* 4:4). When he wanted to express himself exaggeratedly, he would say: "I will bury my sons if I did not…" (*Oholot* 16:1). Rabbi Tarfon lived in the city of Lod and was active during the period of the academy in Yavne, where he deliberated with the leaders of the Sages. He apparently lived a long life. The *tanna* Rabbi Yehuda met him when he was a child (*Tosefta*, *Megilla* 2:8). In *Avot deRabbi Natan* 18, it is related in his regard: "When a Torah scholar came to him and said: 'Teach me,' he would bring him Bible, Mishna, Midrash, halakhot, and *aggadot*. When he would depart from before him, he would depart filled with blessing and good."

Mishna 16

This mishna continues citing statements of Rabbi Tarfon, regarding the considerable labor of Torah study and fulfillment of mitzvot that is incumbent on people in this world.

הוּא הָיָה אוֹמֵר:

He, Rabbi Tarfon, **would say:**

לֹא עָלֶיךָ הַמְּלָאכָה לִגְמֹר, וְלֹא אַתָּה בֶן חוֹרִין לִבָּטֵל מִמֶּנָּה.

It **is not incumbent upon you to complete the** considerable **labor,**[N] **but you are not free to be idle from it;** you are obligated to engage in that labor.

אִם לָמַדְתָּ תּוֹרָה הַרְבֵּה - נוֹתְנִים לְךָ שָׂכָר הַרְבֵּה. וְנֶאֱמָן הוּא בַּעַל מְלַאכְתְּךָ שֶׁיְּשַׁלֶּם לְךָ שְׂכַר פְּעֻלָּתֶךָ.

Although you are not free in this regard, but you are obligated to engage in Torah study, **if you studied much Torah, you are given a great reward, and the employer,** the Holy One blessed be He, **is reliable to pay the reward for your actions.**

וְדַע, מַתַּן שְׂכָרָן שֶׁל צַדִּיקִים לֶעָתִיד לָבֹא.

But know that although it is certain that you will receive your reward, **the granting of the reward of the righteous is in the future.**[N] It is primarily in the World to Come, not in this world.

NOTES

It is not incumbent upon you to complete the labor – לֹא עָלֶיךָ הַמְּלָאכָה לִגְמֹר: This saying is an independent statement, but it is also a continuation and completion of the previous statement. Although the day is short and the task is substantial, it must, nevertheless, be undertaken (Rashbatz). There is much divine work to accomplish, and a person can become discouraged when considering the enormity of the tasks confronting him. That is why Rabbi Tarfon says that a person's obligation is to engage in these matters with full commitment, but not to feel responsibility to complete them or to assess their value based on the outcome.

But know that the granting of the reward of the righteous is in the future – וְדַע, מַתַּן שְׂכָרָן שֶׁל צַדִּיקִים לֶעָתִיד לָבֹא: In other words, do not despair from worshipping God, even if in this world you are not rewarded for it. The reason is that typically an employer pays after a task is completed, and a person's task continues as long as he is alive (Rashbatz). The Sages said something similar in tractate *Pe'a* (1:1), that regarding these matters, the "principal" is kept for the World to Come. Even if one benefits from it in this world, that is only benefit from the "profits" accrued from that principal.

Chapter 3

In contrast to the first two chapters, this chapter contains statements of Sages who do not chronologically follow the Sages cited before them. Rather, it includes a selection of statements of Sages who apparently lived during the Second Temple period and thereafter. That said, these Sages are largely associated with one era, the Yavne era, whether they were elderly or young during that era. The subject matter of this chapter is not uniform, as three primary topics are discussed: engaging in Torah study communally and individually; the relationship between wisdom, on the one hand, and action and fear of God, on the other; and appropriate social conduct.

Mishna 1

עֲקַבְיָא בֶּן מַהֲלַלְאֵל אוֹמֵר: הִסְתַּכֵּל בִּשְׁלֹשָׁה דְבָרִים, וְאִי אַתָּה בָא לִידֵי עֲבֵרָה:

Akavya ben Mahalalel[P] **says:**[N] **Look at,** consider and profoundly analyze,

NOTES

Akavya ben Mahalalel says – עֲקַבְיָא בֶּן מַהֲלַלְאֵל אוֹמֵר: Akavya's saying is one of the best-known sayings of the Sages, due to the widespread custom to begin funeral services with it.

PERSONALITIES

Akavya ben Mahalalel – עֲקַבְיָא בֶּן מַהֲלַלְאֵל: Akavya ben Mahalalel was among the Sages who functioned mainly in Jerusalem at the end of the Second Temple era. Most of what is known about him is related in tractate *Eduyyot* (5:6–7). He was a prominent leader of his generation, and it is said in his regard that there was no one as great as he in wisdom and fear of sin. However, he entered into a dispute with the majority of the Sages regarding several halakhic matters, and he was unwilling to retract his position. When the Sages said to him that if he would recant they would appoint him the president of the court, he refused, saying: I prefer to be characterized as a fool all my life and not to become wicked in the eyes of God for even one moment." Just before his death, he instructed his son to repudiate those matters and to heed the words of the Sages. He explained that he, himself, did not recant, because for him this was a dispute of the many against the many, as he received these matters from his teachers.

three matters,[N] **and you will not encounter transgression:**

דַּע מֵאַיִן בָּאתָ, וּלְאָן אַתָּה הוֹלֵךְ, וְלִפְנֵי מִי אַתָּה עָתִיד לִתֵּן דִּין וְחֶשְׁבּוֹן.

Know, from where you came, to where you are going,[N] **and before whom you are destined to give an accounting.**

מֵאַיִן בָּאתָ - מִטִּפָּה סְרוּחָה.

The mishna elaborates: **From where did you come;** where did your life begin? It was **from a putrid drop**[N] of semen, and there is no basis for taking pride in your origins.

וּלְאָן אַתָּה הוֹלֵךְ - לִמְקוֹם עָפָר רִמָּה וְתוֹלֵעָה.

To where are you going at the end of your days? It is **to a place of dust, maggots,**[N] **and worms,** i.e., to the grave, in which nothing remains of a person's flesh or material possessions.

NOTES

Look at three matters – הִסְתַּכֵּל בִּשְׁלֹשָׁה דְּבָרִים: Some say that these three items engender, respectively, humility, disdain for the pleasures of this world, and vigilance in performance of mitzvot (Rambam, Rabbeinu Yona). Others say that the point is that one should look at the three of them together. If one were to consider only some of them, it would be liable to lead to negative results, e.g., he might say that since he is so lacking in value, there would be no problem with his sinning (*Midrash Shmuel*).

Know, from where you came [*me'ayin bata*], to where you are going – דַּע מֵאַיִן בָּאתָ וּלְאָן אַתָּה הוֹלֵךְ: Some write that this also entails a positive aspect, that a person's soul originated from *ayin*, an extremely exalted level, and it is destined to return to that place. On the other hand, the mishna speaks of the "putrid drop." The manner in which the person is formed, as well as what is ultimately done with him, are not at all exalted (*Pirkei Moshe* and others). Others write that the first clause is directed to people of virtue, who, in order to avoid sin, look to the exalted nature of the soul. The second and third clauses are directed to lesser people, who are directed to look at the origins of their body and its ultimate destiny (*Midrash Shmuel* and others).

From where did you come, from a putrid drop – מֵאַיִן בָּאתָ מִטִּפָּה סְרוּחָה: The straightforward understanding is to indicate the lowliness of man, in order to prevent arrogance. Yaavetz writes that considering the manner in which the person is formed reminds one of the sensitivity of the body's systems and its susceptibility to illness and injury. Alternatively, when considering the formation of an entire person from a putrid drop, one understands that this miracle is inconceivable without God's providence.

To where are you going, to a place of dust, maggots – וּלְאָן אַתָּה הוֹלֵךְ לִמְקוֹם עָפָר רִמָּה: This statement is based on the verses: "For you are dust, and to dust you shall return" (Genesis 3:19) and "how much less so man, a maggot; the son of man, a worm" (Job 25:6). This means that there is consequently no point in amassing property, as it does not descend with the person to his grave, nor flesh or material comforts, which will ultimately become maggots and worms

וְלִפְנֵי מִי אַתָּה עָתִיד לִתֵּן דִּין וְחֶשְׁבּוֹן – לִפְנֵי מֶלֶךְ מַלְכֵי הַמְּלָכִים הַקָּדוֹשׁ בָּרוּךְ הוּא.

And before whom are you destined to give an accounting for your actions? It is **before the King of kings, the Holy One blessed be He.**[N] Considering these matters will promote a sense of both lowliness and reverence, and it will prevent you from transgressing.

Mishna 2

Following the previous mishna, which addressed one's personal contemplations, this mishna presents statements relating to world peace and social order.

רַבִּי חֲנִינָא סְגַן הַכֹּהֲנִים אוֹמֵר:

Rabbi Ḥanina, the deputy High Priest,[P] who was in charge of the Temple service of the priests, **says:**

NOTES

(Rashbatz; see mishna 2:7). Some infer from the use of the present tense [*holekh*] in this mishna that the person gradually nears his death, and in fact he dies a bit each day (Yaavetz). According to this understanding, it is possible to look at the three matters in the mishna as referring to the past, the present, and the future (see Rabbi Matitya HaYitzhari).

Before the King of kings, the Holy One blessed be He – לִפְנֵי מֶלֶךְ מַלְכֵי הַמְּלָכִים הַקָּדוֹשׁ בָּרוּךְ הוּא: This phrase emphasizes two aspects: "King of kings" underscores the aspect of greatness, and "the Holy One blessed be He" underscores the aspect of sanctity. These underscore the enormity of the awe in standing before God (see *Berakhot* 28b), or the greatness of God's kindness. Despite His greatness and sanctity, He judges man Himself (*Pirkei Moshe*).

PERSONALITIES

Rabbi Ḥanina, the deputy High Priest [*segan hakohanim*] – רַבִּי חֲנִינָא סְגַן הַכֹּהֲנִים: The primary meaning of the word "*segan*" is ruler or appointee. The "*segan hakohanim*" was the one appointed to be in charge of the priests [*hakohanim*], and he was given specific areas of authority in the administration of the Temple. He served as the deputy High Priest (see Jeremiah 52:24) and substituted for the High Priest when the latter was unable to perform the service due to impurity, illness, or temporary disqualification (see *Yoma* 1:1, 3:9).

Rabbi Ḥanina (or Ḥananya) served as *segan* in the years just before the destruction of the Temple. After the destruction, he was one of the Sages in Yavne, part of the first generation of *tanna'im*. He gave testimony before the Sages about the details of the Temple service (*Eduyyot* 2:1–3 and elsewhere). Among other things, he related incidents that occurred during the sacred service to him or to his father, who was also a senior figure in the Temple. Besides the halakhot cited in his name, many of his statements are found in the aggadic midrash, especially midrashim that emphasize the value of peace, like his statement cited in this mishna, as well as: "Great is peace as it is the equivalent of the entire act of Creation" (*Sifrei*, *Bemidbar* 42).

הֱוֵי מִתְפַּלֵּל בִּשְׁלוֹמָהּ שֶׁל מַלְכוּת, שֶׁאִלְמָלֵא מוֹרָאָהּ – אִישׁ אֶת רֵעֵהוּ חַיִּים בְּלָעוֹ.

You should pray for the well-being of the monarchy,[N] any monarchy, even a gentile monarchy, and even if it has negative qualities. **As, were it not for fear of it,** the fear that it imposes on people, there would be total anarchy, in which **one person would swallow another alive.**[N] People would dominate others, murder them, and confiscate their property.

From the importance of social order, the mishna pivots to an additional stratum, Torah study as the basis for the resting of the Divine Presence in the midst of Jewish society.

רַבִּי חֲנִינָא בֶּן תְּרַדְיוֹן אוֹמֵר:

Rabbi Ḥananya ben Teradyon[P] **says:**

שְׁנַיִם שֶׁיּוֹשְׁבִין וְאֵין בֵּינֵיהֶן דִּבְרֵי תוֹרָה – הֲרֵי זֶה מוֹשַׁב לֵצִים, שֶׁנֶּאֱמַר: "וּבְמוֹשַׁב לֵצִים לֹא יָשָׁב".

Two who were sitting together, and there is no Torah discourse between them, then even if they are not performing anything evil, **it is** considered **a company of scoffers,**[N] **as it is stated: "And he has not sat in the company of scoffers,** but his desire is the Torah of the Lord" (Psalms 1:1–2).

NOTES

You should pray for the well-being of the monarchy – הֱוֵי מִתְפַּלֵּל בִּשְׁלוֹמָהּ שֶׁל מַלְכוּת: While the mishna refers to any monarchy, in the specific historical context of the time, the monarchy was that of the Roman Empire, which greatly tormented the Jews. This ultimately led to severe clashes with them and uprisings against them. Nevertheless, Rabbi Ḥanina underscores that one must consider the positive aspect of the empire. The source of this is in the verse: "Seek the peace of the city to which I exiled you, and pray to the Lord on its behalf, as in its peace there will be peace for you" (Jeremiah 29:7). When the state ceases to exist, everything ceases to exist, because then every person engages only in the struggle to survive and is unable to devote himself to anything else (Meiri).

Were it not for fear of it, one person would swallow another [*re'ehu*] alive – שֶׁאִלְמָלֵא מוֹרָאָהּ אִישׁ אֶת רֵעֵהוּ חַיִּים בְּלָעוֹ: In tractate *Avoda Zara* (3b–4a) this is derived from the verse: "You made man like the fish of the sea, like crawling creatures with no ruler over him" (Habakkuk 1:14). "Just as the fish of the sea, each one that is larger than another swallows it, so it is with people; were it not for the fear of the monarchy, each one that is greater than another would swallow the other." Some infer that since one would swallow even his friend [*re'ehu*], all the more so would he swallow others (*Midrash Shmuel*).

Two who were sitting…it is a company of scoffers – שְׁנַיִם שֶׁיּוֹשְׁבִין...הֲרֵי זֶה מוֹשַׁב לֵצִים: This is not merely refraining from good, but it is considered a company of scoffers. In other words, it is a gathering in which there is cynicism, mockery, contempt, and lack of seriousness, as indicated by the parallelism in the verse: "And he has not sat in the company of scoffers, but his desire is the Torah of the Lord" (Psalms 1:1–2). Some write that since engaging in Torah study is of prime importance, then even if one does not actually mock Torah study but treats it neglectfully, it is as though he is scoffing at its significance.

אֲבָל שְׁנַיִם שֶׁיּוֹשְׁבִין וְיֵשׁ בֵּינֵיהֶם דִּבְרֵי תוֹרָה – שְׁכִינָה שְׁרוּיָה בֵּינֵיהֶם, שֶׁנֶּאֱמַר: "אָז נִדְבְּרוּ יִרְאֵי ה׳ אִישׁ אֶל רֵעֵהוּ, וַיַּקְשֵׁב ה׳ וַיִּשְׁמָע וַיִּכָּתֵב סֵפֶר זִכָּרוֹן לְפָנָיו לְיִרְאֵי ה׳ וּלְחֹשְׁבֵי שְׁמוֹ".

However, two who were sitting together and there is Torah discourse between them, the Divine Presence rests in their midst, as it is stated: "Then those who fear the Lord spoke one to another, and the Lord listened and heeded; a book of remembrance was written before Him for those who fear the Lord and those who think of His name" (Malachi 3:16). They spoke matters of Torah with each other, and God listened and rested His Divine Presence in their midst.

אֵין לִי אֶלָּא שְׁנַיִם, מִנַּיִן שֶׁאֲפִלּוּ אֶחָד שֶׁיּוֹשֵׁב וְעוֹסֵק בַּתּוֹרָה שֶׁהַקָּדוֹשׁ בָּרוּךְ הוּא קוֹבֵעַ לוֹ שָׂכָר? שֶׁנֶּאֱמַר: "יֵשֵׁב בָּדָד וְיִדֹּם כִּי נָטַל עָלָיו".

The mishna adds: **I have** derived **only** regarding **two** who are engaging in Torah study; **from where** do I derive **that God sets a reward for even one who sits and engages in Torah** study? It is **as it is stated: "Let him sit alone and be silent,**[N] **because he took it upon himself"** (Lamentations 3:22).[N] Even if he studies in silence or a hushed voice, he takes, receives, a reward for himself.

NOTES

And be silent [*veyiddom*] – **וְיִדֹּם**: The commentary understands *yiddom* to mean that one studies silently, as in the phrase: "a faint sound of silence [*demama*]" (I Kings 19:12), because there is no one else with him (Rambam; see Rashbatz). Some explain that this phrase refers to one who studies only in thought, from the word *dimyon*, meaning imagination (Rashi and others).

Sets a reward for him…because he took it [*natal*] upon himself – **קוֹבֵעַ לוֹ שָׂכָר...כִּי נָטַל עָלָיו**: The commentary follows the straightforward understanding, that he receives a reward for doing so. Others explain that this means that he has taken [*natal*] the entire Torah in the sense that it is as though the entire giving of the Torah was for this person (Rambam, Bartenura). Likewise, some cite a variant reading: "The Torah ascribes to him as though he fulfilled the entire Torah" (see Rabbeinu Yona). Others explain that "*natal*" means cover or shade [*tula* in Aramaic], indicating that the Divine Presence rests upon him and protects him (Rashi and others; see mishna 6).

PERSONALITIES

Rabbi Ḥananya ben Teradyon – **רַבִּי חֲנִינָא בֶּן תְּרַדְיוֹן**: Rabbi Ḥanina (or Ḥananya) ben Teradyon was one of the Sages of the Galilee at the end of the Yavne generation, during the bar Kokheva revolt and thereafter. He resided in Sikhni (Sakhnin) and stood there at the head of a great yeshiva. He was a charity collector and is mentioned as the paradigm of a trustworthy collector and distributor of charity. During the edicts of persecution following the bar Kokheva revolt, Rabbi Ḥanina would teach Torah in public despite the prohibition imposed by the authorities. He was ultimately apprehended and sentenced to death, and it is related that they wrapped him in a Torah scroll and burned him along with it. Besides his execution, the Roman Empire decreed harsh punishments on the rest of his family as well (*Avoda Zara* 18a). One of his daughters, Berurya, was the wife of the *tanna* Rabbi Meir and was renowned for her wisdom and her prominence in Torah, which equaled those of the *tanna'im*.

Mishna 3

Incidental to the previous mishna, which addressed the importance of engaging in Torah study when people meet together, as a basis for the resting of the Divine Presence, this mishna cites similar matters regarding a shared meal.

רַבִּי שִׁמְעוֹן אוֹמֵר:

שְׁלֹשָׁה שֶׁאָכְלוּ עַל שֻׁלְחָן אֶחָד, וְלֹא אָמְרוּ עָלָיו דִּבְרֵי תוֹרָה – כְּאִלּוּ אָכְלוּ מִזִּבְחֵי מֵתִים, שֶׁנֶּאֱמַר: "כִּי כָּל שֻׁלְחָנוֹת מָלְאוּ קִיא צֹאָה בְּלִי מָקוֹם".

Rabbi Shimon[P] **says:**

Three who dined[N] **at one table and did not state upon it matters of Torah, it is as though they partook of offerings of the dead,**[N] referring to offerings to idols. A meal of that kind is tantamount to a person sacrificing an offering to his appetites, **as it is stated: "For all tables are full of vomit, excrement, with no room [*makom*]"** (Isaiah 28:8).[N] The word *makom* is expounded as an appellation for the Omnipresent. A meal that does not contain words of God's Torah is morally and religiously revolting.

NOTES

Three who dined – **שְׁלֹשָׁה שֶׁאָכְלוּ**: The previous mishna stated that when two people sit together without Torah discourse between them, it is considered a company of scoffers. This mishna speaks of three because it is a significant number in terms of establishing a formal meal and incurring an obligation to recite the *zimmun* (*Berakhot* 7:1). The Sages dispute the status of Grace after Meals in this regard, as some write that with the joint recital of Grace after Meals by means of the *zimmun*, one satisfies the obligation of Torah discourse during a meal (Bartenura). Others write that the reason that the mishna spoke specifically of three is to emphasize that even though the participants recite the *zimmun* and the Grace after Meals, they are obligated to engage in Torah discourse, and all the more so, if they are two (*Hon Ashir*, *Tosefot Yom Tov*).

Offerings of the dead – **זִבְחֵי מֵתִים**: Most commentaries explain this as offerings to idol worship, as it is written: "They clung to Baal Peor and ate offerings of the dead" (Psalms 106:28). Others write that this refers to the meal of mourners; during their mourning period it is prohibited for them to engage in Torah discourse (Rabbeinu Yosef Ḥayyim). Still others write that those who dine in this manner are like the dead, as it only seems to them that they are alive in this world (Yaavetz). Similarly, some write that since they are eating for the sake of their bodies, and the body will eventually decompose, it is as though they are eating for the dead (*Lev Avot*).

Vomit, excrement, with no room [*makom*] – **קִיא צֹאָה בְּלִי מָקוֹם**: This verse, in which very harsh words are stated, comes to emphasize that even a

אֲבָל שְׁלֹשָׁה שֶׁאָכְלוּ עַל שֻׁלְחָן אֶחָד וְאָמְרוּ עָלָיו דִּבְרֵי תוֹרָה – כְּאִלּוּ אָכְלוּ מִשֻּׁלְחָנוֹ שֶׁל מָקוֹם בָּרוּךְ הוּא, שֶׁנֶּאֱמַר: ״וַיְדַבֵּר אֵלַי זֶה הַשֻּׁלְחָן אֲשֶׁר לִפְנֵי ה׳״.

However, three who dined at one table and stated matters of Torah, it is as though they partook from the table of the Omnipresent, blessed be He. This refers to the altar, which is called the "table," **as it is stated:** "The altar was of wood, three cubits high… **He said to me: This is the table**[N] **that is before the Lord"** (Ezekiel 41:22).

NOTES

table of princes, where they eat all kinds of sumptuous foods, is detestable when there is no Torah discourse at the meal (Yaavetz). The plain understanding of the verse in its original context is that they would eat excessively and get drunk without heeding the word of God. This eating was extremely disgusting, as is typical of the drunk, to the point that the tables would become filled with vomit and excrement, which is unbearable. Here, however, the verse is cited homiletically, with "*beli makom*" meaning that the name of the Holy One blessed be He, who is called "the Omnipresent [*HaMakom*]," was not mentioned (Rashi).

He said to me [*vaydabber elai*], this is the table – וַיְדַבֵּר אֵלַי זֶה הַשֻּׁלְחָן: This is referring to the altar, as proof is cited from the verse in which it is called the table of the Holy One blessed be He. Some write that this is derived from the words "*vaydabber elai*." The man who spoke to Ezekiel in his prophetic vision spoke words of Torah to him and then said: "This is the table that is before the Lord." Likewise, the beginning of the verse, "three cubits [*ammot*]" is expounded to mean "three mothers [*immot*]," which are either Torah, Prophets, and Writings, or Bible, Mishna, and Gemara. If one speaks of all three at his table, it is considered as though he partook from the table of the Omnipresent (Rashi).

PERSONALITIES

Rabbi Shimon – רַבִּי שִׁמְעוֹן: Rabbi Shimon bar Yoḥai, typically cited in the Mishna as Rabbi Shimon without a patronym, was the preeminent disciple of Rabbi Akiva and considered himself his successor. He was great in halakha and *aggada*, and his many statements of Torah are cited frequently in rabbinic literature in a variety of areas. While the halakha is not always ruled in accordance with his opinion, especially in disputes with Rabbi Yosei and Rabbi Yehuda, in many instances it is ruled in accordance with his opinion. Rabbi Shimon has a unique approach, in that he "expounds the rationale of the verse," drawing halakhic conclusions from a verse based on the spirit of the verse. *Sifrei*, the halakhic midrash on Numbers and Deuteronomy, was produced in his study hall. The *Zohar* is also attributed to him.

Rabbi Shimon is renowned as one of the most outstanding righteous men and as a miracle worker, and many incidents are related about wondrous acts that he performed. His most prominent disciples were his son Rabbi Elazar, Rabbi Yehuda HaNasi, and Rabbi Shimon bar Yehuda.

Crypt of Rabbi Shimon bar Yoḥai in Meron.

Mishna 4

As a continuation of the previous *mishnayot*, which addressed disparagement of idleness and the significance of Torah discourse between people, this mishna addresses these matters as they relate to the individual.

רַבִּי חֲנִינָא בֶּן חֲכִינַאי אוֹמֵר: הַנֵּעוֹר בַּלַּיְלָה, וְהַמְהַלֵּךְ בַּדֶּרֶךְ יְחִידִי, וְהַמְפַנֶּה לִבּוֹ לְבַטָּלָה –

Rabbi Ḥanina ben Ḥakhinai[P] **says:** With regard to **one who is awake at night**[N] and does nothing during that time, **one who walks along the way alone,**[N] which is dangerous, **and one who directs his heart to idleness**[N] and engages in insignificant matters,

NOTES

One who is awake at night – הַנֵּעוֹר בַּלַּיְלָה: Some explain that this entire mishna is a single continuing series. One who is awake at night and walks along the way alone, and thereby directs his heart to idleness, incurs liability to be put to death, as he could have been studying Torah during that time (Rashi, Rabbeinu Yona, and others). Alternatively, it is a time when demons have dominion, and if he is not studying Torah, he has no protection from them (Bartenura). Some write that staying awake at night is a shortcoming in and of itself, as one who does not get enough sleep causes himself harm (Meiri).

One who walks along the way alone – הַמְהַלֵּךְ בַּדֶּרֶךְ יְחִידִי: One who sets out on a long trip unaccompanied may encounter danger from robbers and the like, and therefore "incurs liability to be put to death" (Meiri), especially when he is not engaging in Torah study, which could protect him (Bartenura). This is as the Sages expounded in tractate *Eiruvin* (54a): One who is walking along the way without a companion should engage in Torah study, as it is stated about words of Torah: "For they shall be a graceful wreath" (Proverbs 1:9; Rashbatz).

And one who directs his heart to idleness – וְהַמְפַנֶּה לִבּוֹ לְבַטָּלָה: Some explain that this is one who is idle from matters of Torah (Rashi). Others explain that he does not engage in study of matters of wisdom or worldly matters, but is completely idle. Thereby, he could arrive at a condition of oblivion of the heart and astonishment of thought, i.e., insanity (Meiri). In a different formulation, one who is awake at night or walks along the way alone lacks a supportive group of friends to direct him and guide him. As a result, he may sometimes make a conscious decision to engage in matters of no serious or positive value.

PERSONALITIES

Rabbi Ḥanina ben Ḥakhinai – רַבִּי חֲנִינָא בֶּן חֲכִינַאי: Rabbi Ḥanina (or Ḥananya) ben Ḥakhinai was one of the prominent (and apparently oldest) disciples of Rabbi Akiva, not only in matters of halakha, but also in matters of the Design of the Divine Chariot. It is related that he sat and studied for thirteen consecutive years with Rabbi Shimon bar Yoḥai before Rabbi Akiva in Bnei Brak. His wife is mentioned as the paradigm of a woman who accepted upon herself a life of loneliness and enabled her husband to spend years away from home studying Torah. Like Shimon ben Zoma, he is enumerated among those who "deliberate before the Sages" in Yavne. The difference is that the deliberators did not receive rabbinic ordination, while he is called Rabbi. Rabbi Ḥanina ben Ḥakhinai lived a long life, until age ninety-five. In the liturgy, he is mentioned among the Ten Martyrs executed by the Romans.

הֲרֵי זֶה מִתְחַיֵּב בְּנַפְשׁוֹ.

he incurs liability to be put to death in both a physical sense, as he endangers himself, and in the spiritual sense, due to the idleness that grips him.

Mishna 5

רַבִּי נְחוּנְיָא בֶּן הַקָּנָה אוֹמֵר: כָּל הַמְקַבֵּל עָלָיו עוֹל תּוֹרָה – מַעֲבִירִין מִמֶּנּוּ עֹל מַלְכוּת וְעֹל דֶּרֶךְ אֶרֶץ.

Rabbi Neḥunya ben HaKana[P] **says: Anyone who accepts upon himself the yoke of Torah**[N] as a framework for life that determines his practical and internal worlds, **the yoke of the monarchy,** the obligations to and entanglements with the authorities, **and the yoke of livelihood,** needing to work hard to earn a livelihood, and the business and social aspects of this world, **are removed from him.**[N]

NOTES

Anyone who accepts upon himself the yoke of Torah – כָּל הַמְקַבֵּל עָלָיו עֹל תּוֹרָה: Rabbi Neḥunya ben HaKana is referring to one who decides to be totally immersed in the matters of wisdom in the Torah, in the manner of acceptance of a yoke. In other words, he not only engages in Torah study, but accepts it upon himself as a framework for life, with total commitment (Rambam). It is true that in practice one is unable to totally avoid worldly commitments or the laws and statutes of the monarchy; but since he does not identify with those systems in his heart, he is not subjugated to them, and they do not determine the course of his life (see 6:2).

The yoke of the monarchy and the yoke of livelihood are removed from him – מַעֲבִירִין מִמֶּנּוּ עֹל מַלְכוּת וְעֹל דֶּרֶךְ אֶרֶץ: The Meiri writes that this could occur naturally. Since this person engages in Torah study all his life, the monarchy does not monitor him to impose a yoke upon him, as it is under the impression that he has nothing. The same is true of the yoke of livelihood; the labor of the righteous is blessed, and in addition, he is content with little money, so matters of livelihood are not upon him as a cumbersome yoke (Rabbeinu Yona and others). Some write that "the yoke of monarchy is removed from him" refers even to that of the kingship of Heaven, as it is stated regarding the righteous (*Ketubot* 103b) that the Holy One blessed be He fulfills their decrees (*Midrash Shmuel*).

PERSONALITIES

Rabbi Neḥunya ben HaKana – רַבִּי נְחוּנְיָא בֶּן הַקָּנָה: It appears that the beginning of the activity of Rabbi Neḥunya, who was also known as "Rabbi Neḥunya the great," was during the Second Temple era. According to tradition, he was a disciple of Rabban Yoḥanan ben Zakkai, but some say he was his colleague. In tractate *Berakhot* (4:2), it is stated that he would recite a prayer upon his entry into the study hall and upon his exit, and recital of this prayer was instituted as halakha. Rabbi Neḥunya apparently founded a distinctive approach to halakhic midrash, and his foremost disciple, Rabbi Yishmael, developed it after him. There are several fundamental differences between his approach and the approach of Rabbi Akiva (*Shevuot* 26a).

When Rabbi Neḥunya's students asked him what he did to merit living a long life, he answered: "In all my days, I did not attain veneration at the expense of another's degradation; another's curse did not go up with me upon my bed, and I was always generous with my money" (*Megilla* 28a). According to a later tradition, Rabbi Neḥunya engaged in Torah mysticism. Some attribute to him authorship of *Sefer HaBahir* and additional books of *kabbala*, as well as the liturgical poem "*Ana bekho'aḥ*."

וְכָל הַפּוֹרֵק מִמֶּנּוּ עֹל תּוֹרָה – נוֹתְנִין עָלָיו עֹל מַלְכוּת וְעֹל דֶּרֶךְ אֶרֶץ.

Conversely, **anyone who removes the yoke of Torah from upon himself,**[N] **they place upon him the yoke of the monarchy and the yoke of livelihood.**

Mishna 6

In continuation of the previous *mishnayot,* this mishna, too, addresses the importance of engaging in Torah study communally and individually.

רַבִּי חֲלַפְתָּא אִישׁ כְּפַר חֲנַנְיָה אוֹמֵר:

Rabbi Ḥalafta of Kefar Ḥananya[BP] **says:**

עֲשָׂרָה שֶׁיּוֹשְׁבִין וְעוֹסְקִין בַּתּוֹרָה – שְׁכִינָה שְׁרוּיָה בֵינֵיהֶם, שֶׁנֶּאֱמַר: "אֱלֹהִים נִצָּב בַּעֲדַת אֵל".

When there are **ten** men **who are sitting and engaging in Torah** study, **the Divine Presence rests in their midst,** as the Holy One blessed be He gives to them from His wisdom and His strength, both covertly and openly. This is **as it is stated: "God stands in the assembly** [*baadat*] **of the Almighty"** (Psalms 82:1);[N] *eda* is ten people, and if it is the "*eda* of the Almighty," meaning that its members accept upon themselves the yoke of Heaven and the yoke of Torah, the Holy One blessed be He stands in its midst.

NOTES

Anyone who removes the yoke of Torah from upon himself – וְכָל הַפּוֹרֵק מִמֶּנּוּ עֹל תּוֹרָה: Some write that one "who accepts upon himself" refers to one who has the yoke of monarchy and the yoke of livelihood upon him and, nevertheless, makes the effort to accept the yoke of Torah upon himself. As a result, a miracle is performed on his behalf, and the yoke of earthly constraints that had been upon him is removed. Conversely, one who had no yoke upon him at all but nevertheless was indolent in the study of Torah is subject to natural forces, and the yoke of the monarchy and the yoke of livelihood are imposed upon him.

As it is stated: God stands in the assembly [*baadat*] of the Almighty – שֶׁנֶּאֱמַר אֱלֹהִים נִצָּב בַּעֲדַת אֵל: "*Eda*" is ten men, as the Sages derived from the verses; it is stated regarding the spies that Moses sent to scout the Land: "How long will it be with this evil assembly [*haeda*]" (Numbers 14:27). Since Joshua son of Nun and Caleb son of Yefuneh did not sin with the rest of the scouts, the reference was to only ten (*Sanhedrin* 1:6). Ten is the minimal number of a congregation of Jews in which the name of the Holy One blessed be He is sanctified, and every communal occasion of sanctity, e.g., communal prayer or public Torah reading (see *Megilla* 4:3), cannot be performed with fewer than ten Jewish men.

However, the Holy One blessed be He rests His Divine Presence even on fewer than ten, as the *tanna* proceeds to detail:

וּמִנַּיִן אֲפִילּוּ חֲמִשָּׁה? שֶׁנֶּאֱמַר: "וַאֲגֻדָּתוֹ עַל אֶרֶץ יְסָדָהּ".

From where is it derived with regard to **even five** who engage in Torah study, that the Divine Presence is in their midst? It is **as it is stated: "And has established His coterie [*vaagudato*] upon the earth"** (Amos 9:6).[N] Even an *aguda*, formed by the five fingers of the hand, is called by the name of the Holy One blessed be He.

NOTES

Although, as stated previously, the Divine Presence rests upon every individual who engages in Torah study, it was necessary to mention that it rests upon ten and five, etc., because each of these numbers has greater value, and enjoys a special form of resting of the Divine Presence (see *Berakhot* 6a; see Maharal of Prague and Rabbeinu Yona).

Even five as it is stated, "And has established His coterie [*vaagudato*] upon the earth" – אֲפִילּוּ חֲמִשָּׁה שֶׁנֶּאֱמַר וַאֲגֻדָּתוֹ עַל אֶרֶץ יְסָדָהּ: The understanding of most commentaries is the one that appears in the commentary, that the simplest *aguda* is the *aguda* of fingers in a hand. Likewise, when a person seeks to gather [*le'egod*] something in his hand, he does so by grasping it in his fingers (Rashi, Rambam, and others). Some write that this is expounded from the end of the verse: "Upon the earth." Actions performed on earth, in this world, are tied to the number five, as the Sages said that this world was created with the letter *heh*, which has the numerical value five (see *Tiferet Yisrael*).

PERSONALITIES

Rabbi Ḥalafta of Kefar Ḥananya – רַבִּי חֲלַפְתָּא אִישׁ כְּפַר חֲנַנְיָה: This Sage, also called Rabbi Ḥalafta ben Dosa of Kefar Ḥananya in some variant readings, is mentioned few times. It appears that he was a member of the final generation of *tanna'im*, as in several places he cites statements of the *tanna* Rabbi Meir, who was a member of the penultimate generation of *tanna'im*. His place of residence is mentioned to distinguish him from another *tanna* of the same name, who lived in the previous generation and was the father of the *tanna* Rabbi Yosei.

BACKGROUND

B1Kefar Ḥananya – כְּפַר חֲנַנְיָה: Kefar Ḥananya is located in the Beit HaKerem valley, approximately 1 km north of the modern-day Kefar Ḥananya cooperative settlement on the boundary between the Upper Galilee and the Lower Galilee (*Shevi'it* 9:2). The Jewish settlement there existed from the First Temple period until the sixteenth century CE. In the days of the Sages, it was quite a large central village, in which Sages resided. There was a well-developed ceramic industry in the village, and the vessels crafted there were especially durable (*Shabbat* 120b). In archaeological digs in the area, remnants of the kilns utilized in that industry were unearthed.

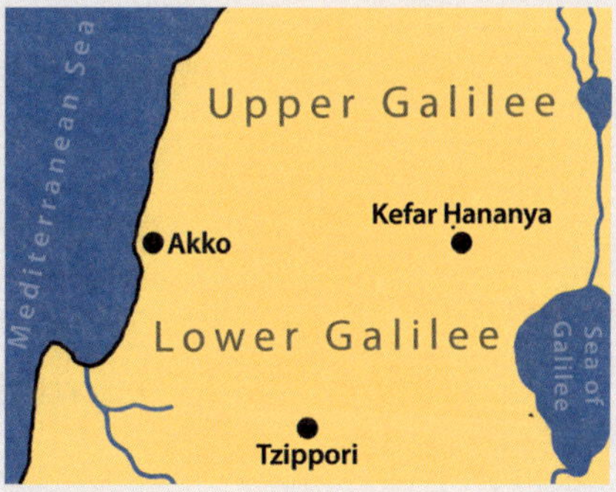

Kefar Ḥananya

וּמִנַּיִן אֲפִילּוּ שְׁלֹשָׁה? שֶׁנֶּאֱמַר: "בְּקֶרֶב אֱלֹהִים יִשְׁפֹּט".

From where is it derived **even** with regard to **three?** It is **as it is stated** in the verse: "God stands in the assembly of the Almighty, **in the midst of the judges** [*elohim*] **He renders judgment**" (Psalms 82:1); a standard court has three judges, and the Holy One blessed be He is found in their midst.

וּמִנַּיִן אֲפִילּוּ שְׁנַיִם? שֶׁנֶּאֱמַר: "אָז נִדְבְּרוּ יִרְאֵי ה׳ אִישׁ אֶל רֵעֵהוּ וַיַּקְשֵׁב ה׳ וַיִּשְׁמָע וְגוֹ׳".

From where is it derived **even** with regard to **two?** It is as it is stated: **"Then those who fear the Lord spoke one to another, and the Lord listened and heeded;** and a book of remembrance was written before Him for those who fear the Lord and those who think of His name" (Malachi 3:16). The phrase "one to another" indicates two.

וּמִנַּיִן אֲפִילּוּ אֶחָד? שֶׁנֶּאֱמַר: "בְּכָל הַמָּקוֹם אֲשֶׁר אַזְכִּיר אֶת שְׁמִי אָבוֹא אֵלֶיךָ וּבֵרַכְתִּיךָ".

From where is it derived with regard to **even one** who engages in Torah study, that the Divine Presence is with him? It is **as it is stated: "In every place**[N] **where I mention My name, I will come to you and I will bless you"** (Exodus 20:21).

NOTES

Even one, as it is stated, "In every place" – אֲפִילּוּ אֶחָד שֶׁנֶּאֱמַר בְּכָל הַמָּקוֹם: Since "I will come to you [*elekha*]" is in the singular, the mishna interprets the verse to mean that everywhere that the name of the Holy One blessed be He is mentioned, He comes even to a single individual and rests His Divine Presence upon him. Torah study and God's wisdom are tantamount to invoking God's name, as the entire Torah is composed of the names of the Holy One blessed be He (*Pirkei Moshe*). Although the verb in the verse is "I mention," Rashi explains that God is essentially saying: I will place the thought in your heart to invoke My name. Some write that "the place where I mention My name" alludes to Torah mysticism dealing with the ineffable name of the Holy One blessed be He, in which only an individual may engage (Rabbi Matitya HaYitzhari and others; see *Ḥagiga* 2:1). Some cite here, too, as in mishna 2, the verse: "Let him sit alone and be silent, because he took it [*natal*] upon himself" (Lamentations 3:28). They explain that "*natal*" is an expression of cover or shade (*tula* in Aramaic), meaning that the Divine Presence rests upon him and protects him (Bartenura).

Mishna 7

רַבִּי אֶלְעָזָר אִישׁ בַּרְתּוֹתָא אוֹמֵר:	**Rabbi Elazar of Bartota**[P] **says:**
תֶּן לוֹ מִשֶּׁלּוֹ, שֶׁאַתָּה וְשֶׁלְּךָ שֶׁלּוֹ.	**Give to Him,** the Holy One blessed be He, through performance of mitzvot with your body and your possessions, with a sense that you are giving Him **of what is His, as** both **you and** all that is **yours are** completely **His.**
וְכֵן בְּדָוִד הוּא אוֹמֵר: "כִּי מִמְּךָ הַכֹּל וּמִיָּדְךָ נָתַנּוּ לָךְ".	**Likewise, regarding David, it says,** when he summarizes everything that he collected and consecrated for the purpose of the Temple: **"For everything comes from You, and from Your hand we have given to You"** (I Chronicles 29:14).

The mishna returns to address the significance of engaging in Torah study communally and individually.

רַבִּי שִׁמְעוֹן אוֹמֵר: הַמְהַלֵּךְ בַּדֶּרֶךְ וְשׁוֹנֶה, וּמַפְסִיק מִמִּשְׁנָתוֹ, וְאוֹמֵר: "מַה נָּאֶה אִילָן זֶה" וּ"מַה נָּאֶה נִיר זֶה" – מַעֲלֶה עָלָיו הַכָּתוּב כְּאִלּוּ מִתְחַיֵּב בְּנַפְשׁוֹ.	**Rabbi Shimon**[P] **says:**[N] With regard to **one who walks along the way and is reviewing** Torah that he studied, **and he interrupts his**

NOTES

Rabbi Shimon says – רַבִּי שִׁמְעוֹן אוֹמֵר: This is the version in some editions. However, in many manuscripts this statement is cited in the name of a *tanna* named Rabbi Yaakov, and that is the version that appears in most commentaries.

PERSONALITIES

Rabbi Elazar of Bartota – רַבִּי אֶלְעָזָר אִישׁ בַּרְתּוֹתָא: Rabbi Elazar ben Yehuda, from the village of Bartota, was one of the disciples of Rabbi Yehoshua ben Ḥananya and transmitted halakhot in his name (*Tevul Yom* 3:4–5 and elsewhere). Likewise, Sages of the next generation transmitted halakhot in the name of Rabbi Elazar (*Orla* 1:4; *Tosefta*, *Zavim* 1:5). Some say that he is Elazar of Bireta, of whom it is related (*Taanit* 24a) that he would give everything that he had to charity, leaving nothing in his possession, to the extent that the charity collectors sought to avoid him so he would not exhaust his funds.

Rabbi Elazar's place, Bartota, is not familiar from other sources. Some explain that the meaning of the name is "the spring [*be'er*] alongside the berry [*tut*] tree." It is presumably in the Judean lowlands (B. Z. Segal). Others identify it with the settlement Migdal Tuta, whose ruins are located near Gaza (Z. Safrai).

Rabbi Shimon, Rabbi Yaakov – רַבִּי שִׁמְעוֹן, רַבִּי יַעֲקֹב: As noted, most versions cite the second statement in the name of Rabbi Yaakov, and the identity of this

study[N] **and says: How beautiful this tree** that he encountered on the way **is, or how beautiful this plowed field**[B] **is, the verse ascribes to him as though he incurs liability to be put to death.**[N] He endangers his life by interrupting his Torah study for that purpose.

PERSONALITIES

tanna is unclear. Some write that he is the father of Rabbi Eliezer ben Yaakov, who lived at the end of the Second Temple era (*Midrash Shmuel*). Others say that this is Rabbi Yaakov ben Korshai, who was a contemporary of the second Rabban Shimon ben Gamliel (*Horayot* 13b), from whom Rabbi Yehuda HaNasi learned the fundamentals of his Torah.

NOTES

One who walks along the way and is reviewing Torah, and he interrupts his study – הַמְהַלֵּךְ בַּדֶּרֶךְ וְשׁוֹנֶה וּמַפְסִיק מִמִּשְׁנָתוֹ: Some write that this is stated regarding all instances of Torah study, but that this scenario is more common when walking along the way (*Maḥzor Vitri*). Alternatively, it could underscore that although he is not interrupting a regular study session but merely walking along the way, nevertheless, one must be strict regarding this matter (Meiri). When one is engaging in Torah study, he must do so with great awe and refrain from engaging in any other matter (Rabbeinu Yona). Others write that this comes to emphasize that although he says: "How beautiful this tree is" in order to praise God, he nevertheless incurs liability to be put to death, because he interrupted his Torah study (Bartenura, Yaavetz; see *Tiferet Yisrael*). A Hasidic interpretation states homiletically that the fact that one incurs liability to be put to death is because he considers it an interruption of his study and not a direct continuation of it. In other words, he does not consider his appreciation for the beauty of Creation to be part of his cleaving to God (*Meor Einayim*; see *Keter Shem Tov* 235).

The verse ascribes to him as though he incurs liability to be put to death – מַעֲלֶה עָלָיו הַכָּתוּב כְּאִלּוּ מִתְחַיֵּב בְּנַפְשׁוֹ: The mishna mentions a verse but does not cite one as a source for this. Indeed, there are some whose version eliminates the words "the verse ascribes to him"; they explain that he incurs liability to be put to death and endangers himself, as one who sets out on the way is in danger, and the Torah alone protects him (Rashi). Some explain that this is derived from the verse: "Who pick saltwort [*malluaḥ*] from bushes [*alei siaḥ*]" (Job 30:4), as the Sages expounded the verse (*Ḥagiga* 12b): "Anyone who pauses from matters of Torah," which was given on tablets [*luḥot*], "to occupy himself with mundane conversation [*siḥa*]" is punished for doing so (*Maḥzor Vitri*). Others explain that this relies on the verse cited in the following mishna, that one who forgets one matter of his Torah studies incurs liability to be put to death, as it is stated: "Only beware, and protect yourself greatly, lest you forget the matters that your eyes saw, and lest they move from your heart all the days of your life" (Deuteronomy 4:9), cautioning against forgetting any matter of his studies (Maharal of Prague).

Plowed field

BACKGROUND

B1Plowed field – נִיר:

Mishna 8

This mishna continues to address the importance of continuity in Torah study and of avoiding distraction from it.

רַבִּי דּוֹסְתַּאי בְּרַבִּי יַנַּאי מִשּׁוּם רַבִּי מֵאִיר אוֹמֵר:

Rabbi Dostai son of Rabbi Yannai[P] **says in the name of Rabbi Meir:**

כָּל הַשּׁוֹכֵחַ דָּבָר אֶחָד מִמִּשְׁנָתוֹ – מַעֲלֶה עָלָיו הַכָּתוּב כְּאִלּוּ מִתְחַיֵּב בְּנַפְשׁוֹ, שֶׁנֶּאֱמַר: ״רַק הִשָּׁמֶר לְךָ וּשְׁמֹר נַפְשְׁךָ מְאֹד פֶּן תִּשְׁכַּח אֶת הַדְּבָרִים אֲשֶׁר רָאוּ עֵינֶיךָ״.

Anyone who forgets one matter of his Torah study, because he does not review it and is not studying Torah, **the verse ascribes to him as though he incurs liability to be put to death.**[N] He endangers his life, as this conduct is an indication that the Torah is not important to him. This is **as it is stated: "Only beware, and protect yourself greatly, lest you forget the matters that your eyes saw"** (Deuteronomy 4:9). Remembering these matters is crucial to protecting one's life.

NOTES

As though he incurs liability to be put to death – כְּאִלּוּ מִתְחַיֵּב בְּנַפְשׁוֹ: Some write that it is his forgetting itself that is the reason it is "as though he incurs liability to be put to death," as he is liable to stumble and violate those matters that he forgot. This is in accordance with the mishna that states (4:13): "An unwitting error in study is considered intentional" (Rabbeinu Yona, Bartenura, and others). So it seems in the version cited in tractate *Semaḥot* (*of Rabbi Ḥiyya* 4:4) and in *Avot deRabbi Natan*, version B, chap. 35. In tractate *Menaḥot* (99b) it is explained that he incurs liability because in forgetting he lost something valuable upon which his life depends, as it is said: "It is comparable to a person who gave a sparrow to his slave. He said to him: Are you under the impression that if you lose it I will take an *issar* from you in payment? I will take your soul from you" (Rashbatz; see *Tiferet Yisrael*). Others write in addition that this is because the Torah protects a person; if he loses it, then it no longer protects him (Bartenura).

PERSONALITIES

Rabbi Dostai son of Rabbi Yannai – רַבִּי דּוֹסְתַּאי בְּרַבִּי יַנַּאי: Rabbi Dostai was a member of the last generation of *tanna'im*, during the period of Rabbi Yehuda HaNasi, and it is possible that he was older than Rabbi. However, it appears that he was a preeminent student of Rabbi Meir, in whose name he stated most of his statements, as he does here. Several aggadic statements are cited in his name (see *Pesaḥim* 8b, *Bava Batra* 10a, *Nidda* 31b, and elsewhere).

Rabbi Dostai adds a caveat:

יָכוֹל אֲפִילּוּ תָּקְפָה עָלָיו מִשְׁנָתוֹ? תַּלְמוּד לוֹמַר: "וּפֶן יָסוּרוּ מִלְּבָבְךָ כֹּל יְמֵי חַיֶּיךָ", הָא אֵינוֹ מִתְחַיֵּיב בְּנַפְשׁוֹ עַד שֶׁיֵּשֵׁב וִיסִירֵם מִלִּבּוֹ.

Could it be so **even if his studies overwhelmed him,**[N] that he studied much material and forgot some of it, which is a natural occurrence in the course of study? Is it possible that even then he would incur liability for forgetting? No, as **the verse states: "And lest they move from your heart all the days of your life" (Deuteronomy 4:9); he is liable to receive the death penalty only if he sits and removes them from his heart**[N] in an intentional and conscious manner.

Mishna 9

After the previous mishna addressed the importance of reviewing one's studies and not forgetting the Torah learned, this mishna addresses the manner in which the Torah will be present and enduring over time in a person's life.

רַבִּי חֲנִינָא בֶּן דּוֹסָא אוֹמֵר: כֹּל שֶׁיִּרְאַת חֶטְאוֹ קוֹדֶמֶת לְחָכְמָתוֹ – חָכְמָתוֹ מִתְקַיֶּימֶת. וְכֹל שֶׁחָכְמָתוֹ קוֹדֶמֶת לְיִרְאַת חֶטְאוֹ – אֵין חָכְמָתוֹ מִתְקַיֶּימֶת.

Rabbi Ḥanina ben Dosa[P] **says: Anyone whose fear of sin precedes,** in its significance for him, **his wisdom,**[N] the wisdom of the Torah, and he works first and foremost on perfecting his character traits and only then turns to acquiring wisdom and knowl-

NOTES

His studies overwhelmed him – תָּקְפָה עָלָיו מִשְׁנָתוֹ: The commentary explains that he forgot details of his studies, which is common after one learns a great deal. This is similar to what the commentaries state, that he forgot due to circumstances beyond his control, because the subject matter was difficult for him (Rashi), or he was old or ill (Rabbeinu Yona and others; see *Nedarim* 41a). The *Notzer Ḥesed* states that he forgot because he was overcome with the desire to study more Torah and consequently did not review his studies properly.

Only if he sits and removes them from his heart – עַד שֶׁיֵּשֵׁב וִיסִירֵם מִלִּבּוֹ: The Rashbatz cites a variant reading: "Only if he understands and removes them from his heart." This is a person who consciously and purposely takes action so that he will no longer remember his Torah, or he refrains from reviewing it.

Anyone whose fear of sin precedes his wisdom – כֹּל שֶׁיִּרְאַת חֶטְאוֹ קוֹדֶמֶת לְחָכְמָתוֹ: This means that in everything that one does, fear of sin is the first matter that he considers. In that way, he will not fail

edge, **his wisdom endures,**[N] because it is not merely an intellectual, abstract matter, unconnected to his life, but an indivisible part of his life. Conversely, with regard to **anyone whose wisdom precedes his fear of sin,**[N] **his wisdom does not endure** over time.

הוּא הָיָה אוֹמֵר: כָּל שֶׁמַּעֲשָׂיו מְרוּבִּין מֵחָכְמָתוֹ – חָכְמָתוֹ מִתְקַיֶּימֶת. וְכָל שֶׁחָכְמָתוֹ מְרוּבָּה מִמַּעֲשָׂיו – אֵין חָכְמָתוֹ מִתְקַיֶּימֶת.

In addition, **he,** Rabbi Ḥanina, **would** similarly **say:** With regard to **anyone whose** good **deeds exceed his wisdom,**[N] **his wisdom endures,** because it is not merely a theoretical matter, but a means of improving

NOTES

in his actions or his concerns ("his wisdom") and will succeed in all his endeavors. But if fear of sin is not first, his wisdom will not endure (Rashi). In *Avot deRabbi Natan* 22, this verse is added as a source: "Wisdom begins with fear of the Lord" (Psalms 111:10). Perfecting one's character traits is included in this caution, as one who perfects his character appreciates wisdom and is diligent in its regard. But one whose character is flawed will be unable to withstand the moral challenges posed by wisdom, and he will reject it.

His wisdom endures – חָכְמָתוֹ מִתְקַיֶּימֶת: The plain understanding is that the wisdom endures and is preserved because it is a practical matter tied to life. Rashi states that this means that all of this person's actions endure; because fear of sin stands at the foundation of his deeds, he does not fail, but rather succeeds in all his endeavors.

Anyone whose wisdom precedes his fear of sin – וְכָל שֶׁחָכְמָתוֹ קוֹדֶמֶת לְיִרְאַת חֶטְאוֹ: Some write that not only does his wisdom not endure, but it itself causes him to fail. This is because in anyone who is greater than another, his evil inclination is also greater than his. That is why fear of sin must precede wisdom (*Ḥafetz Ḥayyim*).

Anyone whose deeds exceed his wisdom – כָּל שֶׁמַּעֲשָׂיו מְרוּבִּין מֵחָכְמָתוֹ: Some write that this cannot be understood plainly, as how can a person perform a deed about which he has learned nothing at all? Rather, the reference is to one who accepts upon himself the matters that he learns (Rashbatz). *Avot deRabbi Natan* 22 states that this is derived from what the children of Israel declared when they received the Torah: "We will perform and we will heed" (Exodus 24:7).

PERSONALITIES

Rabbi Ḥanina ben Dosa – רַבִּי חֲנִינָא בֶּן דּוֹסָא: Rabbi Ḥanina ben Dosa, a disciple of Rabban Yoḥanan ben Zakkai, was a *tanna* who lived at the end of the Second Temple era. Little is known of the events of his life other than the fact that he was a simple laborer and lived all his life in abject poverty. No halakhic statements of his remain, but several aggadic statements remain. Already during his lifetime, he was known as a person whose prayers generate miracles, to the extent that his teacher, Rabban Yoḥanan ben Zakkai, said about him that in that regard Rabbi Ḥanina was greater than he (see *Berakhot* 5:5, 34b). The many stories related about him reflect his humble personality, his numerous distinguished character traits, and the fact that he commonly performed wondrous acts that altered the natural order. It is said in his regard: "The entire world is sustained by My son Ḥanina, and yet, for Ḥanina, My son, a *kav* of carobs is sufficient from Shabbat eve to Shabbat eve" (see *Taanit* 24b–25a).

his behavior and perfecting it. Conversely, with regard to **anyone whose wisdom exceeds his deeds,** meaning that he does not implement his extensive knowledge in practice, **his wisdom does not endure,**[N] because it is detached from practical reality.

Mishna 10

This mishna begins by citing another statement of Rabbi Ḥanina ben Dosa, which continues the basic train of thought that the Torah's essence and significance are realized only when it is implemented in practice, in this case, in one's attitude toward others.

הוּא הָיָה אוֹמֵר: כָּל שֶׁרוּחַ הַבְּרִיּוֹת נוֹחָה הֵימֶנּוּ – רוּחַ הַמָּקוֹם נוֹחָה הֵימֶנּוּ. וְכָל שֶׁאֵין רוּחַ הַבְּרִיּוֹת נוֹחָה הֵימֶנּוּ – אֵין רוּחַ הַמָּקוֹם נוֹחָה הֵימֶנּוּ.

He, Rabbi Ḥanina ben Dosa, **would say:** With regard to **anyone with whom people are pleased,**[N] i.e., people relate to him with appreciation or love, **the Omnipresent,** too, **is pleased with him; and** conversely, with regard to **anyone with whom people are displeased,** it indicates that **the Omnipresent is displeased with him.**

NOTES

Anyone whose wisdom exceeds his deeds, his wisdom does not endure – וְכָל שֶׁחָכְמָתוֹ מְרוּבָּה מִמַּעֲשָׂיו אֵין חָכְמָתוֹ מִתְקַיֶּימֶת: Rashi explains that this person does not fulfill what he learns, and "his wisdom does not endure" means that it would be preferable had he not learned Torah at all. He says that one who studies but does not fulfill what he learns may be likened to a woman who bears a child and buries him, or to a man who sows but does not reap. He provides an alternative explanation, that this person studies Torah more than he performs mitzvot and gives charity. In that case, even his Torah does not endure. However, if one performs more acts of charity and mitzvot than he studies Torah, he merits that his Torah will also endure (Rashi).

Anyone with whom people are pleased – כָּל שֶׁרוּחַ הַבְּרִיּוֹת נוֹחָה הֵימֶנּוּ: Rabbi Ḥanina ben Dosa emphasizes that when a person is good to others, and people relate to him with appreciation and love, it has significance that goes beyond his social standing. It extends to his standing vis-à-vis the Holy One blessed be He. By contrast, one might have no shortcomings, and even be righteous in certain areas and perform good deeds; nevertheless, if people are not pleased with him, then the Holy One blessed be He is not satisfied with him. This is because a person's ability to build positive social connections with others is, itself, a barometer of his internal personality. Some write that the less-common word for people, *beriyyot*, underscores that people were created [*nivre'u*] by the Holy One blessed be He, in His image, so their opinion reflects His opinion (Yaavetz). Moreover, this expression alludes even to simple people, who are not particularly wise (*Notzer Ḥesed*).

The mishna proceeds to cite a statement of another Sage that completes the statement of Rabbi Ḥanina ben Dosa regarding the nature of good relations with people.

רַבִּי דּוֹסָא בֶּן הַרְכִּינַס אוֹמֵר:

Rabbi Dosa ben Harkinas[P] **says:**

שֵׁינָה שֶׁל שַׁחֲרִית, וְיַיִן שֶׁל צָהֳרַיִם, וְשִׂיחַת הַיְלָדִים, וִישִׁיבַת בָּתֵּי כְנֵסִיּוֹת שֶׁל עַמֵּי הָאָרֶץ – מוֹצִיאִין אֶת הָאָדָם מִן הָעוֹלָם.

Extended **sleep in the morning,** as one thereby wastes the hours of the day; **wine at noon,** a long midday break that includes drinking wine or participating in a meal where people become inebriated; engaging in idle **conversation** with **children**[N] to pass the time; **sitting in gathering places of** ***amei***

NOTES

Conversation [*siḥa*] with children – וְשִׂיחַת הַיְלָדִים: This is referring to spending time in conversation and games with children and youth (see Rashi), as one does not learn from them and it is merely to pass the time. The word *siḥa*, when it appears in the Mishna and the Talmud, has a very clear meaning: insubstantial, insignificant conversation, e.g., social prattle (see 1:5). At times, an adjective is added, like "insubstantial conversation [*siḥa kalla*]" or "idle conversation [*siḥa betela*]." This term is different from the term *dibbur*, which refers to transmission of content. The *Notzer Ḥesed* adds that the mishna mentions conversation specifically with children because conversation with elders and wise men is of value and requires study, as expounded (*Avoda Zara* 19b) from the verse: "Whose leaf does not wither" (Psalms 1:3).

PERSONALITIES

Rabbi Dosa ben Harkinas – רַבִּי דּוֹסָא בֶּן הַרְכִּינַס: Rabbi Dosa ben Harkinas was a younger contemporary of Rabban Yoḥanan ben Zakkai; however, it appears that he was an independent Sage, not subordinate to Rabban Yoḥanan (see *Ketubot* 13:1–2). He was among the elder Sages in the generation of the disciples of Rabban Yoḥanan during the Yavne era. He was one of the prominent members of Beit Hillel, and Rabbi Yehoshua was very close to him. It is related (*Yevamot* 16a) that his younger brother, Yonatan, was one of the sharpest and most prominent members of Beit Shammai.

While little is known about his place of residence or the course of his life, it is known that he was very wealthy, lived a very long life, and that Sages would come and visit him at his home seeking his counsel or his knowledge of ancient traditions. Although he did not participate in the deliberations in the Yavne study hall, he was aware of everything that transpired in the Torah world (*Yevamot* 16a; Jerusalem Talmud, *Yevamot* 1:6). He emphasized the importance of accepting the rulings of Rabban Gamliel's court as part of the chain of transmission of the Torah (see *Rosh HaShana* 2:8–9).

Burial site of Rabbi Dosa ben Harkinas, Safed

haaretz,[N] unrefined people, lacking in knowledge and manners; all these, although they are not prohibited per se, **expel a person from the world,**[N] because they are appealing and lead people to waste time on frivolous matters.

Mishna 11

רַבִּי אֶלְעָזָר הַמּוֹדָעִי אוֹמֵר:

Rabbi Elazar HaModa'i[P] **says:**

הַמְחַלֵּל אֶת הַקֳּדָשִׁים,

With regard to **one who profanes the** Temple **consecrations,**[N] rendering them non-sacred and treating them with contempt;

וְהַמְבַזֶּה אֶת הַמּוֹעֲדוֹת,

and likewise, **one who scorns the appointed times,**[N] the intermediate days of a festival, performing unnecessary labor on those days;

NOTES

Sitting in gathering places of *amei haaretz* – וְיִשִׁי־בַת בָּתֵּי כְּנֵסִיּוֹת שֶׁל עַמֵּי הָאָרֶץ: The mishna may be referring to people who gather and prattle in synagogues [*batei keneset*], as that is a place where people tend to gather (see *Shabbat* 32a). Some variant readings have "sitting in *kenesiyyot*" without the word *batei*, thereby referring to gathering places in general. The explanation in the commentary is along these lines, that the mishna is referring to places where uneducated people [*amei haaretz*] gather (see *Avot deRabbi Natan* 21).

Expel a person from the world – מוֹצִיאִין אֶת הָאָדָם מִן הָעוֹלָם: One is very easily drawn into all these activities, and, since their duration is not defined and limited, to spend extended time on them. These activities lead to a waste of one's life on worthless matters, and cause him to be idle from Torah study and fulfillment of mitzvot during those times (see *Avot deRabbi Natan* 21). Ultimately, they cause the person to deviate from the good path. In this way, they are different from other, necessary, matters, which have a set and limited time frame, like sleeping at night or eating appropriately and as necessary at the proper time. Moreover, when a person spends his days on frivolous matters, beyond the fact that he loses his share in the World to Come, he truncates his life in this world, both in terms of health and in terms of morality (see Rabbeinu Yona, Yaavetz).

One who profanes the consecrations – הַמְחַלֵּל אֶת הַקֳּדָשִׁים: Some explain that this person does not properly protect his consecrations from ritual impurity and the like (Rashi; see Yaavetz), or that he benefits from them illegally and misappropriates them (Rashbatz). Others explain that he does not treat offerings with the proper regard and acts as though their sacrifice is contemptuous in his eyes, as is related regarding the High Priest Yissakhar of Kefar Barkai, who would cover his hands when sacrificing offerings because he found it repulsive. It is stated that he honored himself and profaned the consecrations of Heaven (*Pesaḥim* 57a).

One who scorns the appointed times – הַמְבַזֶּה אֶת הַמּוֹעֲדוֹת: Almost everyone explains that this refers to one who scorns the intermediate days of a festival by performing all kinds of labor and by failing to have special meals in keeping with the significance of the days. Nevertheless, it says "scorn," not "profane," because in terms of the halakha, these days are like weekdays, with a few defined limitations, as

וְהַמַּלְבִּין פְּנֵי חֲבֵרוֹ בָּרַבִּים,

and, likewise, **one who humiliates another in public;**[N]

וְהַמֵּפֵר בְּרִיתוֹ שֶׁל אַבְרָהָם אָבִינוּ עָלָיו הַשָּׁלוֹם,

and one who violates the covenant of Abraham our forefather,[N] **of blessed memory,**[B]

NOTES

articulated in tractate *Moed Katan*. Still, they are characterized as "holy" and one must respect them and minimize labor performed on these days as much as possible (see *Ḥagiga* 18a). The Rashbatz adds that because these days are holy, one who scorns them is tantamount to one who profanes the consecrations.

One who humiliates [*malbin penei*] another in public – הַמַּלְבִּין פְּנֵי חֲבֵרוֹ בָּרַבִּים: This matter is extremely severe, as he not only humiliates him, but he does so in public, which magnifies and exacerbates the shame. The early Sages discussed why one who humiliates another is called literally, "one who whitens his face [*malbin panav*]," when, typically, people's faces redden when they are embarrassed. Indeed, there is a variant reading, which says literally: "One who reddens the face of another." In *Bava Metzia* (58b), it is stated that after the face turns red due to shame, it whitens again. Causing the blood to flow from his face is likened to a murderous act.

One who violates the covenant of Abraham our forefather – הַמֵּפֵר בְּרִיתוֹ שֶׁל אַבְרָהָם אָבִינוּ: Some explain that this is one who does not wish to be circumcised (Rashi, Rambam). Others say that this is referring to one who performs certain procedures on his body so he will appear uncircumcised. Such people would pull their foreskin in order to extend it, and thereby violate the physical manifestation of the covenant of Abraham. In other words, it is referring to violation not of the very essence of the covenant with Abraham, but of the sign of the covenant.

PERSONALITIES

Rabbi Elazar HaModa'i – רַבִּי אֶלְעָזָר הַמּוֹדָעִי: Rabbi Elazar (or Eliezer) HaModa'i was one of the Sages of the academy at Yavne in the generation after the destruction of the Temple. He was apparently close to the circle of disciples of Rabban Yoḥanan ben Zakkai. Based on his name, and as it is stated in several places, he was from the city of Modi'in. It is possible that he was a member of one of the families of priests that were located there, where, generations earlier, the Hasmoneans had been members of those families. Almost all his statements address aggadic matters, and they are found primarily in the *Mekhilta*, the Talmud, and aggadic midrash. He was renowned for his homiletical interpretations, and Rabban Gamliel would sometimes say: "We still need Moda'i" (*Shabbat* 55b), i.e., the Sages must hear his statements and innovations regarding this matter. It is related that he was bar Kokheva's uncle, and he prayed each day for his success. However, a false accusation led bar Kokheva to cause his death, and due to that sin, the city of Beitar was destroyed (Jerusalem Talmud, *Taanit* 4:5).

BACKGROUND

B1One who violates the covenant of Abraham our forefather, of blessed memory – הַמֵּפֵר בְּרִיתוֹ שֶׁל אַבְרָהָם אָבִינוּ עָלָיו הַשָּׁלוֹם: Throughout the Second Temple era and thereafter, circumcision was the identification mark of the Jews and a conspicuous expression of Torah observance. This was in contrast to Hellenistic culture, which viewed the body as something perfect that must not be marred. As a result, decrees against circumcision date back to the days of the Greek king Antiochus, although they also existed in later periods, especially during Hadrian's reign. It is described that Hellenized Jews would "pull their foreskin" to appear uncircumcised and to not be identified as Jews, and this occurred in the Roman era as well, for both ideological and utilitarian reasons, e.g., to seek entry into Roman institutions. There are descriptions of surgeries of that kind in the first century BCE by a renowned Alexandrian physician, Aulus Cornelius Celsus. This phenomenon, which Rabbi Elazar HaModa'i was addressing, was also manifest among the early Christians, disciples of Jesus of Nazareth. Some suggest instead that Rabbi Elazar HaModa'i was referring to the time of Hadrian's decrees.

i.e., one who does not wish to be circumcised or conceals the fact that he is circumcised;

וְהַמְגַלֶּה פָּנִים בַּתּוֹרָה שֶׁלֹּא כַּהֲלָכָה –

and one who interprets the Torah inappropriately,[N] in a manner that runs counter to accepted halakha;

אַף עַל פִּי שֶׁיֵּשׁ בְּיָדוֹ תּוֹרָה וּמַעֲשִׂים טוֹבִים, אֵין לוֹ חֵלֶק לָעוֹלָם הַבָּא.

even though he has Torah and good deeds in other areas to his credit, **he has no share in the World to Come,**[N] because by performing these actions, he compromises fundamental matters.

Mishna 12

This mishna continues to address the matters addressed in mishna 10 regarding the proper attitude toward various people.

רַבִּי יִשְׁמָעֵאל אוֹמֵר:

Rabbi Yishmael[P] **says:**

הֱוֵי קַל לְרֹאשׁ,

Be vigilant for a leader,[N] be vigilant in fulfilling the will of a person greater than you,

NOTES

One who interprets the Torah inappropriately – הַמְגַלֶּה פָּנִים בַּתּוֹרָה שֶׁלֹּא כַּהֲלָכָה: This means that one discusses matters of Torah but interprets them in a manner that runs counter to halakha (see Meiri; *Megilla* 4:9), mocks them, or makes inappropriate comments (see Rashi). Some explain (*Sanhedrin* 99a; Jerusalem Talmud, *Pe'a* 1:1) that this is one who states that Torah is not from Heaven, who transgresses Torah matters in public, or who is impudent toward Torah scholars (Rambam, Rabbeinu Yona, and others).

He has no share in the World to Come – אֵין לוֹ חֵלֶק לָעוֹלָם הַבָּא: Formally, none of these matters is as severe as the transgressions for which one incurs liability for excision [*karet*] (see *Karetot* 1:1). One component of *karet* is loss of a share in the World to Come. However, each undermines a primary, fundamental matter, and that is why the punishment is so severe. This was expounded in tractate *Sanhedrin* (99a) from the verse: "Because he scorned the word of the Lord, and he violated His commandment; that person shall be excised [*hikkaret tikkaret*]; his iniquity is upon him" (Numbers 15:31). Moreover, it was derived from the doubled expression *hikkaret tikkaret* that beyond the fact that he has no share in the World to Come, he also loses his life in this world. Another reason for the severity of these matters is that they are not performed due to weakness or appetites, but with heretical intent (Meiri).

Be vigilant [*kal*] for a leader [*lerosh*] – הֱוֵי קַל לְרֹאשׁ: Some explain that one should humble [*kal*] himself before people of exalted standing, so it will not be onerous for him to serve them (Rambam, Rabbeinu Yona). Others explain that a person should

וְנוֹחַ לְתִשְׁחוֹרֶת,

and, on the other hand, **solicitous** and easygoing **to dark-haired** youth,[N]

וֶהֱוֵי מְקַבֵּל אֶת כָּל הָאָדָם בְּשִׂמְחָה.

and, in general, **receive every person,** regardless of their status, **joyfully.**[N]

NOTES

be humble [*kal*] and gentle in his early [*reshit*] days to perform the will of the Creator (Rashi), or that one should be vigilant to be first [*rishon*] in fulfillment of mitzvot (Rav Natan *Av HaYeshiva*). Some explain homiletically that the word *lerosh* [spelled *lamed*, *reish*, *alef*, *shin*] is an acronym for *laasot retzon avikha shebashamayim*, meaning "to perform the will of your Father in Heaven" (Yaavetz).

Solicitous to dark-haired youth [*letishhoret*] – נוֹחַ לְתִשְׁחוֹרֶת: The explanation of *tishhoret* in the commentary is youth. Similarly, the Rambam explains that one should treat them patiently and seriously and should not be dismissive of them. However, many explain that *tishhoret* is from the Aramaic term *shahvar*, meaning appointee, or treasurer, and that *rosh* refers to a mayor [*rosh ir*]; it would thus mean that one should serve prominent people vigilantly and loyally, so they will not harm him (Rashi and others). Likewise, it says in tractate *Kalla Rabbati* (4:8): "Be vigilant *lerosh* – this is the monarchy; and solicitous to *tishhoret* – the tax collectors."

Receive every person [*kol haadam*] joyfully – וֶהֱוֵי מְקַבֵּל אֶת כָּל הָאָדָם בְּשִׂמְחָה: One must speak pleasantly to every person (Rashi). The Rambam writes in continuation of the previous statement that one should treat those younger than he respectfully and patiently. Rather than receiving them with an angry look, he should receive them joyfully and good-heartedly. The *Tiferet Yisrael* notes that Rabbi Yishmael includes in his statements the proper way that a person should relate to those greater than he (*lerosh*), to those lesser than he (*letishhoret*), and with those who are his equal (*kol haadam*).

PERSONALITIES

Rabbi Yishmael – רַבִּי יִשְׁמָעֵאל: Rabbi Yishmael ben Elisha was one of the Sages during the Yavne era. Although he was apparently younger than the others, he was so accomplished in Torah that the great Sages of that generation treated him as a colleague, not as a student. He was a priest, and it is related that when he was a young child, he was taken captive from Jerusalem to Rome, where he later encountered Rabbi Yehoshua, who had traveled there to engage in communal matters. Rabbi Yehoshua redeemed him for a large ransom after becoming aware of his wisdom (*Gittin* 58a).

Rabbi Yishmael resided in Kefar Aziz, in the southern Hebron hills (see *Kilayim* 6:4).Rabbi Yishmael was a colleague and disputant of Rabbi Akiva, although he was younger than Rabbi Akiva. Following the approach of his teacher, Rabbi Nehunya ben HaKana, he developed an independent methodology of halakhic midrash, which seeks to approximate the plain understanding of the verses and their standard syntax. In that framework, he formulated the thirteen hermeneutical principles of halakhic midrash. Regarding his concern for Jewish women and their honor, see *Nedarim* 9:10.

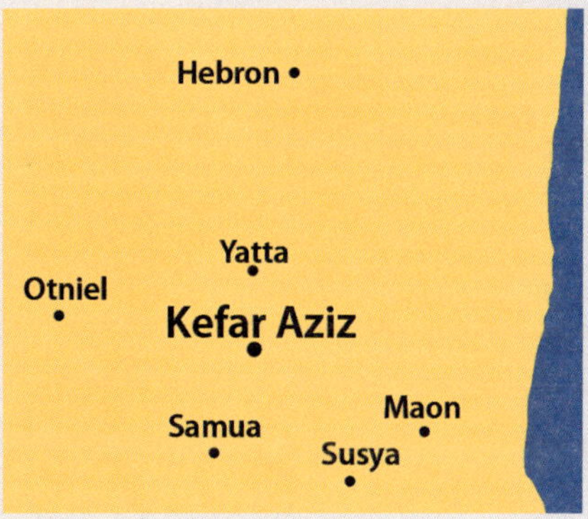

Kefar Aziz, location of Rabbi Yishmael's residence

Mishna 13

Following the statement of Rabbi Yishmael in the previous mishna regarding friendly conduct with various people, the mishna cites the statement of his colleague, Rabbi Akiva, who completes his statement.

רַבִּי עֲקִיבָא אוֹמֵר:	**Rabbi Akiva**[P] **says:**
שְׂחוֹק וְקַלּוּת רֹאשׁ – מַרְגִּילִין לְעֶרְוָה.	**Flippancy and frivolity**[N] **accustom** and lead **a person to** matters of **lewdness.**

Conversely, there are positive matters that serve as a barricade safeguarding aspects of the positive and the good.

מָסוֹרֶת – סְיָיג לַתּוֹרָה.	**Tradition,**[N] precisely counting the verses, words, and letters of the Torah, is **a safeguard for the Torah,** so that it will not be lost due to errors in its transmission from generation to generation.
מַעַשְׂרוֹת – סְיָיג לָעֹשֶׁר.	Meticulousness in giving **tithes** from one's property to Levites and to the poor is **a safeguard** and protection **for** maintaining **wealth.**[N] One who handles his property as the Torah commands is worthy of retaining his wealth.

NOTES

Flippancy and frivolity – שְׂחוֹק וְקַלּוּת רֹאשׁ: Typically, a certain atmosphere or certain conditions are required for a person to commit a sin involving forbidden sexual relations. The standard formula that facilitates this atmosphere is flippancy and frivolity, when people laugh with one another and conduct themselves with one another as though they are playing games and lacking seriousness. Consequently, when one minimizes flippancy and frivolity, he distances himself from transgression and fences himself off from it.

Tradition – מָסוֹרֶת: This can be understood in two ways. One explanation relates to the tradition of the Sages in general, that one accepts their interpretation of the Torah based on the tradition that they received from earlier Sages (Meiri, *Mirkevet HaMishne*, and others). However, most commentaries state that Rabbi Akiva is referring here to what is called *mesora*, which is a precise tally of the number of letters in the Torah, ensuring that the text of the Torah remains intact throughout the generations, so it will not be corrupted or lost. Moreover, many halakhot can be inferred based on the spelling of the words (Rashbatz, Bartenura, and more), as it is stated especially regarding Rabbi Akiva himself that he would expound numerous halakhot from each and every letter (*Menaḥot* 29b).

Tithes are a safeguard for wealth – מַעַשְׂרוֹת סְיָיג

נְדָרִים – סְיָג לַפְּרִישׁוּת.

Vows that a person accepts upon himself to undertake positive matters or refrain from negative matters are **a safeguard for abstinence.**[N] They help a person be abstinent and detached from subservience to worldly matters, because they reinforce his good decisions and compel him to implement them.

סְיָג לַחָכְמָה – שְׁתִיקָה.

Likewise, **a safeguard for wisdom,** a fence against nonsense and foolishness, is **silence**[N]

NOTES

לְעוֹשֶׁר: The commentaries explain that this is like the matter that the Sages expounded from the verse: "*aser te'aser*" (Deuteronomy 14:22): "Tithe [*aser*] so you will become wealthy [*shetitasher*]; one who is scrupulous in tithing will thereby merit wealth (Rashi and others; see *Taanit* 9a). Some state that it says here, "a safeguard for wealth," and not "a safeguard for property," in order to underscore that if one tithes, he merits not only to maintain his belongings, but also thereby to become wealthy (Rashbatz).

Vows are a safeguard for abstinence – **נְדָרִים סְיָג לַפְּרִישׁוּת**: This refers to abstaining from material matters, being content with only what is needed, and shunning luxury (Rabbeinu Yona). At times, a person is unsuccessful in abstaining from prohibited matters or from matters with which he would prefer to be extremely cautious, because his habits cause him to stagnate spiritually. But when that person vows to perform a certain action or to refrain from an action, the vow guards him against breaching his boundary of abstinence; the reason is that after he vows, it is not merely a good decision, but it is a matter proscribed by an actual, substantive prohibition.

A safeguard for wisdom is silence – **סְיָג לַחָכְמָה שְׁתִיקָה**: In other words, in order to safeguard wisdom, a person should remain silent as much as possible, as prattle inevitably leads to speaking nonsense (see 1:17). Moreover, silence itself reflects the wise man's good character.

PERSONALITIES

Rabbi Akiva – **רַבִּי עֲקִיבָא**: Rabbi Akiva, from the third generation of *tanna'im*, was one of the Sages of the Yavne generation, and is considered the greatest of them. In his youth, the Temple was destroyed, and toward the end of his life, the bar Kokheva revolt took place. Little is known of Rabbi Akiva's origins, other than the fact that his father's name was Yosef. He began studying Torah at a relatively advanced age, and his primary teachers were Rabbi Eliezer ben Hyrcanus and Rabbi Yehoshua ben Ḥananya. He also studied many years with Naḥum of Gimzo, and was influenced by his approach to expounding the Torah, using the method of amplification and restriction [*ribbui umiut*]. Rabbi Akiva developed this approach further, expounding each word and each letter in the Torah in the belief that nothing in the Torah could possibly be extraneous.

Rabbi Akiva studied and produced works in all areas of Torah: midrash, halakha, *aggada*, and mysticism. According to tradition, he had twenty-four thousand students who perished in a plague. Some suggest that they died in the bar Kokheva revolt, which he *supported*. Five who remained his students after the plague, Rabbi Meir, Rabbi Yehuda bar Ilai, Rabbi Yosei bar Ḥalafta, Rabbi Shimon bar Yoḥai, and Rabbi Elazar ben Shamoa, were the pillars who formed the foundation for the Oral Torah in the generation that followed him (see *Sanhedrin* 86a). Toward the end of his life, the Roman Empire prohibited Torah study, but Rabbi Akiva continued to study and teach. He was subsequently apprehended, incarcerated, and cruelly executed. An *aggada* counts him among the prominent leaders of the nation who lived 120 years.

Mishna 14

This mishna continues to cite statements of Rabbi Akiva. He speaks about the special virtue of the human race in general and of the Jewish people in particular.

הוּא הָיָה אוֹמֵר: חָבִיב אָדָם שֶׁנִּבְרָא בְּצֶלֶם.

He, Rabbi Akiva, **would say: Beloved** and special **is the human** race beyond all other creations, in **that it was created in** God's **image.**[N]

חִבָּה יְתֵירָה נוֹדַעַת לוֹ שֶׁנִּבְרָא בְּצֶלֶם, שֶׁנֶּאֱמַר: ״כִּי בְּצֶלֶם אֱלֹהִים עָשָׂה אֶת הָאָדָם״.

Moreover, there is **added love** in **that he was informed**[N] by God **that he was created in** His **image, as it is stated: "As He made man in the image of God"** (Genesis 9:6).

חֲבִיבִין יִשְׂרָאֵל שֶׁנִּקְרְאוּ בָנִים לַמָּקוֹם.

Beloved are Israel beyond all other people, in **that,** not only were they created in His image, but **they were also called children of the Omnipresent.**

חִבָּה יְתֵירָה נוֹדַעַת לָהֶם שֶׁנִּקְרְאוּ בָנִים לַמָּקוֹם, שֶׁנֶּאֱמַר: ״בָּנִים אַתֶּם לַה׳ אֱלֹהֵיכֶם״.

Moreover, there is **added love** in **that they were informed that they were called children of the Omnipresent, as it is stated: "You are children to the Lord your God"** (Deuteronomy 14:1).

NOTES

Beloved is the human race, that it was created in God's image [*betzelem*] – חָבִיב אָדָם שֶׁנִּבְרָא בְּצֶלֶם: Being created in God's image means that the person has the intelligence to acknowledge his Creator (Rashbatz; see *Guide of the Perplexed* 1:1). The Meiri writes that it means that humans have a spiritual image, which is the source of their strength and might.

Added love in that he was informed – חִבָּה יְתֵירָה נוֹדַעַת לוֹ: This means that these are not virtues that were granted due to pity, which entails a certain contempt for the recipient, who is not told what good was performed on his behalf. Rather, these are matters of which he is informed; they are bestowed in a loving and respectful manner (Rambam, Rabbeinu Yona). Rashi writes that the added love is that He created him in His image.

חֲבִיבִין יִשְׂרָאֵל שֶׁנִּתַּן לָהֶם כְּלִי חֶמְדָּה.

Moreover, **beloved are Israel,** beyond the fact that they were called children of the Omnipresent, **that a precious vessel,** the Torah, which is the most magnificent and pleasant vessel, **was given to them.**[N]

חִבָּה יְתֵירָה נוֹדַעַת לָהֶם שֶׁנִּתַּן לָהֶם כְּלִי חֶמְדָּה, שֶׁבּוֹ נִבְרָא הָעוֹלָם, שֶׁנֶּאֱמַר: "כִּי לֶקַח טוֹב נָתַתִּי לָכֶם, תּוֹרָתִי אַל תַּעֲזֹבוּ".

It is a great gesture of love that they were informed that a precious vessel, with which the world was created,[N] **was given to them, as it is stated: "For a good lesson I have given you: My Torah; do not forsake it"** (Proverbs 4:2). Not only did the Holy One blessed be He give them the Torah, but He described its virtue to them, that it is a uniquely "good lesson."

NOTES

Beloved are Israel that a precious [*hemda*] vessel was given to them – חֲבִיבִין יִשְׂרָאֵל שֶׁנִּתַּן לָהֶם כְּלִי חֶמְדָּה: Some write that this refers not only to the elevated status of Israel, who received the Torah, but to an additional virtue possessed by Torah scholars, who engage in Torah study in practice. This is why they are informed of additional love beyond that of all of Israel, as their virtue is "that they were called children of the Omnipresent" (*Tiferet Yisrael*). *Tosefot Yom Tov* comments that the adjective *hemda* is especially tied to wisdom and education, as it appears in the verse: "And the tree was desirable [*venehmad*] for wisdom" (Genesis 3:6).

A precious vessel [*keli hemda*] with which the world was created – כְּלִי חֶמְדָּה שֶׁבּוֹ נִבְרָא הָעוֹלָם: The fact that the Holy One blessed be He created the world with the Torah is derived from the verse where the Torah is the subject, saying: "I was with Him, as a protégé [*amon*]" (Proverbs 8:30). The Sages expounded that verse (*Bereshit Rabba* 1:1): "I was the tool [*keli*] of the trade [*omanut*] for the Holy One blessed be He...the Holy One blessed be He would look in the Torah and create the world" (Rashi). It is also explicit in the Bible that matters of Torah are "more desirable [*nehmadim*] than gold, than quantities of fine gold" (Psalms 19:11). The Meiri writes that *keli hemda* also comes to indicate the heights that human comprehension can reach, as through grasping this vessel, through studying Torah, one is capable of understanding divine knowledge.

Mishna 15

This mishna continues citing statements of Rabbi Akiva. He speaks regarding free choice and reward and punishment.

הַכֹּל צָפוּי, וְהָרְשׁוּת נְתוּנָה,

Everything is foreseen;[N] the Holy One blessed be He foresees everything that is destined to transpire. **But,** at the same time, **license is given** to a person to choose how he will behave, and he is judged on the basis of his actions, for better or for worse.

וּבְטוּב הָעוֹלָם נִדּוֹן.

And in general, although when a person chooses evil he is punished for it, ultimately, **the world is judged favorably.**[N]

וְהַכֹּל לְפִי רוֹב הַמַּעֲשֶׂה.

And everything, a person's entire sentence, **is according to the majority of the actions,**[N] whether most of his actions are good, or are not good.

NOTES

Everything is foreseen [*tzafui*] – הַכֹּל צָפוּי: The Holy One blessed be He sees everything, and He knows what transpires even in secret; however, God does not compel a person and does not rob him of his freedom to choose between good and evil (Rashi and others; see Rambam, *Hilkhot Teshuva* 5). Some cite a variant reading, "everything is hidden [*tzafun*]," meaning that every person's deeds are secured and preserved in the hand of the Holy One blessed be He (*Maḥzor Vitri*).

And the world is judged favorably – וּבְטוּב הָעוֹלָם נִדּוֹן: In other words, ultimately, although a person has the choice between various paths and actions, and there is punishment for the wicked; nevertheless, God's attribute of good is greater than that of evil. God, in His stewardship of the world, employs the path of kindness. Only on the Day of Judgment is He exacting regarding one's various deeds (Rashi), and even then, He tilts the scale in favor of kindness (Rambam; see Rashbatz and Yaavetz). Moreover, a person has the possibility of repenting from his sins (Meiri). Some say that even judgment of the wicked is undertaken not as revenge, but rather in order to benefit their soul and prepare it for life in the World to Come (*Tiferet Yisrael*).

And everything is according to the majority of the actions – וְהַכֹּל לְפִי רוֹב הַמַּעֲשֶׂה: Some explain that one is judged according to the majority of his actions. His good deeds constitute his merits, and the opposite is also true. That is why a person must increase the number of his good deeds and do anything that is right to do (Rashi and others). Another possibility is that a person is judged on the basis of most of his actions, not on the basis of the exceptions (see *Maḥzor Vitri*). The Rambam explains differently, that Rabbi Akiva is referring to how a person acquires good character traits. It is dependent not upon the scope of the deed, but rather on the number of deeds. The more a person repeats a good deed, the more he reinforces good traits and incorporates goodness into his soul, as opposed to performing one great, illustrious deed. An example would be one who gives a small amount of charity many times, as opposed to one who gives a large amount all at once.

Mishna 16

This mishna continues citing statements of Rabbi Akiva regarding free choice, reward, and punishment.

הוּא הָיָה אוֹמֵר:

He, Rabbi Akiva, **would say:**

הַכֹּל נָתוּן בְּעֵרָבוֹן, וּמְצוּדָה פְּרוּסָה עַל כָּל הַחַיִּים.

Everything that a person possesses in this world **is given as collateral,**[N] from which the Holy One blessed be He can exact repayment; **and a** trapper's **net is spread**[B] **over all the living,** and no one can escape from it.

הַחֲנוּת פְּתוּחָה, וְהַחֶנְוָנִי מַקִּיף, וְהַפִּנְקָס פָּתוּחַ, וְהַיָּד כּוֹתֶבֶת,

The store, the whole world, **is open,**[N] and it is possible to take anything that one wants from it. **The storekeeper,** the Holy One blessed be

NOTES

Everything is given as collateral – הַכֹּל נָתוּן בְּעֵרָבוֹן: In other words, everything that exists in the world, and anything that belongs to a person and is in his control, all of it is collateral against a person's actions, as the Holy One blessed be He can exact payment from him for everything that he does. Others explain differently, that the world in its entirety is given to people merely as collateral, and in practice it remains under the ownership of the Holy One blessed be He (see Rabbeinu Yona). Rashi explains that all people are guarantors for one another, or that the body and the soul are guarantors for one another, in terms of receiving recompense.

The store is open – הַחֲנוּת פְּתוּחָה: This is a metaphor for a person's freedom of choice in this world. As a "buyer," he may acquire anything that his heart desires, and the Holy One blessed be He allows it. There is no immediate payment or punishment for the deeds he performs. However, all these things are not given as an unconditional gift, but on credit. Ultimately, it will be incumbent upon him to pay for everything, with no possibility of evading settlement.

BACKGROUND

A net [*metzuda*] is spread – מְצוּדָה פְּרוּסָה: A *metzuda*, from the word for hunting or trapping [*tzayid*], is a trapper's net that is spread on a path taken by a beast or bird, into which the creature becomes entangled. Occasionally *metzuda* is used to refer to a basket lowered into the water to catch fish (see *Shabbat* 1:6, *Kelim* 23:5, and elsewhere). The metaphor of the net as an expression of the transitory nature of the life of man who is trapped in it appears in the book of Ecclesiastes (9:12): "For man also does not know his time, like the fish that are trapped in an evil net [*bimtzoda*]."

Apparatus for catching fish. Similar tools are described in records from ancient Egypt

He, does not demand immediate payment, whether it is punishment or reward, but instead, he **extends credit. And the** storekeeper's writing **tablet** [*pinkas*][B] **is open, and the hand is writing** the person's actions, so they are not forgotten.

וְכָל הָרוֹצֶה לִלְווֹת יָבֹא וְיִלְוֶה. וְהַגַּבָּאִים מַחֲזִירִים תָּדִיר בְּכָל יוֹם, וְנִפְרָעִין מִן הָאָדָם מִדַּעְתּוֹ וְשֶׁלֹּא מִדַּעְתּוֹ, וְיֵשׁ לָהֶם עַל מַה שֶּׁיִּסְמוֹכוּ.

Anyone who wishes to borrow may come and borrow from what is in the "store"; however, he must remember that everything he uses has a price. **The** debt **collectors,** emissaries of the Holy One blessed be He in this world, **regularly circulate** in the world, **each** and every **day. And they collect** the debt **from a person with or without his awareness. But they have** a basis **upon which they can rely,** as everything is done with uprightness and justice.

וְהַדִּין דִּין אֱמֶת, וְהַכֹּל מְתוּקָּן לַסְּעוּדָה.

And one must know that **the judgment is a just judgment,** even though we do not know how it is made, and even if it appears to us to be too lenient or too severe; **and everything is prepared for the banquet,**[N] for the granting of the great reward in the future, in the World to Come.

NOTES

Everything is prepared for the banquet – וְהַכֹּל מְתוּקָּן לַסְּעוּדָה: This means that despite any suffering imposed by the "collectors," and, in general, the entire process of "the store is open and the storekeeper extends credit," the essence is that "everything is prepared for the banquet," in other words, for life in the World to Come. Even the worldly punishments are designed only so that everyone will be worthy of getting there, as, after all, "all of the Jewish people have a share in the World to Come" (*Sanhedrin* 10:1). However, for that purpose, preparation is required, as well as cleansing from unworthy actions. Another commentary explains "prepared for the banquet" in a totally different manner, that it is a reference to the meal eaten by mourners, as, ultimately, everyone is destined to die (Rabbi Natan *Av HaYeshiva*).

BACKGROUND

Pinkas – פִּנְקָס: From the Greek *pinaks*, meaning writing tablet. In the time of the Sages, a *pinkas* was a binder of wooden tablets that were coated with wax. People would write upon the wax with a stylus.

Illustration of wax tablet [*pinkas*] in wall fresco, Pompeii, first century CE

Mishna 17

This mishna cites statements of Rabbi Elazar ben Azarya. It begins with a series of statements that appear paradoxical regarding matters that are mutually dependent, meaning that the existence of one requires the existence of the other.

רַבִּי אֶלְעָזָר בֶּן עֲזַרְיָה אוֹמֵר:

Rabbi Elazar ben Azarya[P] **says:**

אִם אֵין תּוֹרָה – אֵין דֶּרֶךְ אֶרֶץ, אִם אֵין דֶּרֶךְ אֶרֶץ – אֵין תּוֹרָה.

If there is no Torah, there is no[N] **civility;** it is not sustainable over time without Torah. **If there is no civility, there is no Torah.** Civility is considered a preface, foundation, and framework for Torah. Torah that is not accompanied by civility is deficient.

NOTES

If there is no...there is no – אִם אֵין...אֵין: The essence of the paradoxical statements cited here has been explained in two ways. Some say that the meaning is that one needs both parts of each pair to occur simultaneously, because the absence of one does not allow the other to exist. That is why one must embrace both of them together in order to proceed. Others explain that each pair addresses two separate stages that are performed one upon the other iteratively, as different levels of the same matter. For example, the statement "If there is no wisdom there is no fear" refers to a basic level of wisdom that engenders fear and facilitates it. However, after the profound analysis of fear and the consequent spiritual elevation, one arrives at a higher level of wisdom. The same is true regarding the other pairs.

PERSONALITIES

Rabbi Elazar ben Azarya – רַבִּי אֶלְעָזָר בֶּן עֲזַרְיָה: Rabbi Elazar ben Azarya, one of the most prominent Sages in Yavne, was a priest of distinguished lineage, tenth generation from Ezra the scribe, and was also exceedingly wealthy. When he was very young, the Sages ousted Rabban Gamliel from his position of *Nasi* of the Sanhedrin, and they selected Rabbi Elazar ben Azarya in his stead. Rabbi Elazar knew that his appointment might be only temporary, until the Sages reconciled with Rabban Gamliel. Indeed, that is what happened. However, even after Rabban Gamliel was restored to his position, Rabbi Elazar ben Azarya remained *Nasi* of the Sanhedrin for one of every four weeks, with Rabban Gamliel serving during the other three. On the day he was appointed *Nasi*, he opened the study hall to anyone who sought to attend, and clarified many halakhot. These were later collected in tractate *Eduyyot* and in additional places (*Berakhot* 27b; Jerusalem Talmud, *Berakhot* 4:1). While several halakhic statements are cited in his name, his homilies were especially exemplary, and even Sages older than he would listen attentively, to the extent that Rabbi Yehoshua, who was many years older than he, said in his regard: No generation is considered orphaned when Rabbi Elazar ben Azarya dwells in its midst (*Tosefta, Sota* 7:9–12). His children and grandchildren followed his path, and the Gemara mentions Sages who descended from him many generations later (see *Menaḥot* 53a).

אִם אֵין חָכְמָה – אֵין יִרְאָה, אִם אֵין יִרְאָה – אֵין חָכְמָה.

If there is no wisdom, there is no fear[N] of God, because fear of God is an outgrowth of understanding His greatness. On the other hand, **if there is no fear** of God, **there is no wisdom.** If fear of God does not precede wisdom, wisdom by itself can lead a person to haughtiness, which will blind him from a true perception of reality, and all the more so from understanding of the Torah.

אִם אֵין בִּינָה – אֵין דַּעַת, אִם אֵין דַּעַת – אֵין בִּינָה.

If there is no understanding, i.e., intellectual ability to analyze and synthesize concepts, **there is no knowledge;**[N] it is impossible to grasp matters properly, to assess their value, and to arrive at a determination in one direction or another. On the other hand, **if there is no knowledge,** if there is no basic grasp of the matters, **there is no understanding,** as without basic knowledge of what anything is, a person has just an accumulation of items that he sensed or intuited that cannot amount to an ordered system of analysis and synthesis.

NOTES

If there is no wisdom, there is no fear – אִם אֵין חָכְמָה אֵין יִרְאָה: Some write that fear must take precedence over wisdom chronologically, and wisdom must take precedence in terms of its elevated standing. However, fear without wisdom indicates a flaw in the fear. Likewise, wisdom without fear of Heaven indicates a flaw in the wisdom (Meiri, Rabbeinu Yona). Moreover, without wisdom, the person is incapable of examining and searching for what is true fear of Heaven (*Maḥzor Vitri*). See mishna 9.

If there is no understanding [*bina*], there is no knowledge [*daat*] – אִם אֵין בִּינָה אֵין דַּעַת: The Mishna commentaries discussed extensively the precise definition of these terms, which are related and very similar. The explanation in the commentary here is that *bina* is the intellectual ability to analyze and synthesize, while *daat* is the ability to consider matters and determine points for evaluating which of them are desirable and necessary and which are not. Others say that *daat* is the intellect introduced into the person from birth, and *bina* is the effort and exertion expended in developing that ability (Meiri). Alternatively, *daat* represents the matters that one learns from his teacher, and *bina* is what he understands on his own (*Maḥzor Vitri*; see Rashi on Exodus 31:3). A different type of explanation is that *daat* is recognizing God and cleaving to Him, while *bina* is practical knowledge of mitzvot (Yaavetz).

אִם אֵין קֶמַח – אֵין תּוֹרָה, אִם אֵין תּוֹרָה – אֵין קֶמַח.

If there is no flour, sustenance, **there is no Torah,** as a person is not free to engage in it. On the other hand, **if there is no Torah, there is no flour,**[N] as the person does not merit it.

הוּא הָיָה אוֹמֵר: כָּל שֶׁחָכְמָתוֹ מְרוּבָּה מִמַּעֲשָׂיו, לְמָה הוּא דוֹמֶה? לְאִילָן שֶׁעֲנָפָיו מְרוּבִּין וְשָׁרָשָׁיו מוּעָטִין, וְהָרוּחַ בָּאָה וְעוֹקַרְתּוֹ וְהוֹפַכְתּוֹ עַל פָּנָיו, שֶׁנֶּאֱמַר: "וְהָיָה כְּעַרְעָר בָּעֲרָבָה וְלֹא יִרְאֶה כִּי יָבוֹא טוֹב וְשָׁכַן חֲרֵרִים בַּמִּדְבָּר אֶרֶץ מְלֵחָה וְלֹא תֵשֵׁב".

He, Rabbi Elazar ben Azarya, **would say: Any** person **whose wisdom exceeds his** good **deeds,** as he does not implement wisdom and ethics in his life, **to what is he comparable?** It is **to a tree whose branches are many and its roots are few, and** despite its beauty and splendor, it will not endure long; because it is not sturdy, **a wind comes and uproots it**[N] from its place **and overturns it.** It is **as it is stated: "He will be like a solitary tree in the desert and will not see when good comes; he will inhabit the parched places in the wilderness, a salty land and uninhabited"** (Jeremiah 17:6). So, the lack of solid roots in the world of good deeds creates a personality lacking in endurance, and in a time of crisis, intellectual ability alone is unable to save the person from collapse of his world and his personality.

NOTES

If there is no Torah, there is no flour – אִם אֵין תּוֹרָה אֵין קֶמַח: Some explain that if one does not study Torah, he is not truly worthy of a livelihood, as the objective of a Jewish person's existence in the world is only to study Torah (Rabbeinu Yona). Others explain that this is like what is stated (4:9): "Anyone who is idle from the Torah in wealth, he will ultimately be idle from it in poverty" (*Tiferet Yisrael*). Some cite a variant reading: "If there is Torah, there is flour," meaning that a person who engages in Torah study will succeed in his business. This reading omits "if there is no Torah, there is no flour," as most of the world earns a livelihood even though they do not engage in Torah study (Rashbatz).

To a tree whose branches are many…and a wind comes and uproots it – לְאִילָן שֶׁעֲנָפָיו מְרוּבִּין...וְהָרוּחַ בָּאָה וְעוֹקַרְתּוֹ: This is also true regarding the appropriate ratio within wisdom itself between intellectual, abstract development, on the one hand, and grasp of actual reality through experience and facts, on the other hand. When the factual roots are few, even if one is capable of producing a multifaceted theory, it does not have lasting existence, as at any point a factor could be introduced that would turn the entire work on its head.

אֲבָל כָּל שֶׁמַּעֲשָׂיו מְרֻבִּין מֵחָכְמָתוֹ, לְמַה הוּא דוֹמֶה? לְאִילָן שֶׁעֲנָפָיו מוּעָטִין וְשָׁרָשָׁיו מְרֻבִּין, שֶׁאֲפִלּוּ כָּל הָרוּחוֹת שֶׁבָּעוֹלָם בָּאוֹת וְנוֹשְׁבוֹת בּוֹ – אֵין מְזִיזִין אוֹתוֹ מִמְּקוֹמוֹ, שֶׁנֶּאֱמַר: "וְהָיָה כְּעֵץ שָׁתוּל עַל מַיִם וְעַל יוּבַל יְשַׁלַּח שָׁרָשָׁיו, וְלֹא יִרְאֶה כִּי יָבֹא חֹם, וְהָיָה עָלֵהוּ רַעֲנָן, וּבִשְׁנַת בַּצֹּרֶת לֹא יִדְאָג, וְלֹא יָמִישׁ מֵעֲשׂוֹת פֶּרִי".

But by contrast, **anyone whose deeds exceed his wisdom, to what is he comparable? To a tree whose branches are few** relative to **its roots,** which **are many.** The existence of this proper ratio leads to the fact **that even if all the winds in the world were to come and blow at it, they would not move it from its place.** Distress and crises of all kinds do not shake him, as the stability of his roots, i.e., his deeds, his steadfastness, and his constancy, enable him to avoid collapse even at the most difficult times. He is able to continue to be productive and creative, **as it is stated: "He will be like a tree planted by water, that spreads its roots near a stream;**[B] **it does not see when heat comes, and its leaves flourish. During a year of drought it is not concerned, and it does not cease from producing fruit"** (Jeremiah 17:8).

BACKGROUND

That spreads its roots near a stream – וְעַל יוּבַל יְשַׁלַּח שָׁרָשָׁיו:

"That spreads its roots near a stream"

Mishna 18

In continuation of the previous mishna, which distinguished between matters that are basic and what is built upon them, this mishna cites matters in which there is a distinction between primary and ancillary, in the area of Torah and wisdom.

רַבִּי אֱלִיעֶזֶר בֶּן חִסְמָא אוֹמֵר:

Rabbi Elazar ben Ḥisma[P] **says:**

קִנִּין וּפִתְחֵי נִדָּה, הֵן הֵן גּוּפֵי הֲלָכוֹת.

With regard to the halakhot of bird **nests,**[N] which deal with cases when pairs of birds that would be brought as an offering in the Temple intermingled with other birds; **and the beginnings of menstruation,**[N] the hal-

NOTES

Nests [*kinnin*] – קִנִּין: A *ken* is a pair of turtledoves or young pigeons that were brought as offerings. When the *ken* was brought as an obligatory offering, one of the birds was a sin offering and the other a burnt offering. When it was brought as a gift offering, the two birds were sacrificed as burnt offerings. If the priest erred and exchanged the birds, or if one of the birds flew away and was lost or intermingled with another pair, it was necessary to enter into many logical and mathematical calculations in order to determine the halakha and resolve the situation. An entire tractate in the order of *Kodashim* was devoted to this matter, tractate *Kinnim*.

The beginnings of menstruation – פִּתְחֵי נִדָּה: These are halakhot that apply to women whose monthly cycle is not fixed (see *Arakhin* 2:1), and, likewise, to women who forgot or became confused in counting the days. Regarding these matters too, there is a need for complicated calculations to determine the woman's halakhic status (Rashi and others). Some explain that this is referring to knowledge regarding identifying the appearance of the woman's blood or spotting with the source in her body where it originated, in order to determine whether she is ritually pure or impure (Rabbeinu Yona).

PERSONALITIES

Rabbi Elazar ben Ḥisma – רַבִּי אֱלִיעֶזֶר בֶּן חִסְמָא: Rabbi Elazar Ḥisma is called Rabbi Elazar ben Ḥisma in some versions; however, it appears that that is a mistaken version. He was one of the Sages who lived in the generation after the destruction of the Temple and were active in the academy in Yavne. It is possible that the name Ḥisma, which means strengthened, is an appellation that was attached to his name because he became stronger in areas of study in which he was not expert at the outset (*Vayikra Rabba* 23:4).

Very little is known about his life or his family. Apparently, he was primarily a disciple of Rabbi Yehoshua (see *Tosefta*, *Sota* 7:9 and *Zavim* 4:4). Rabbi Elazar Ḥisma was a friend of Rabbi Yoḥanan ben Gudgeda, and both of them were extremely poor until Rabbi Yehoshua advocated on their behalf before Rabban Gamliel to appoint them to positions that would provide them with a livelihood. Due to their humility, they refused to accept the appointment. Rabban Gamliel persuaded them to accept by saying: "Are you under the impression that I am granting you authority? I am imposing servitude upon you" (*Horayot* 10a–b).

It is also stated about Rabbi Elazar that he was accomplished in general knowledge as well, especially in mathematics. This quality is closely tied to his statements in the mishna (see *Tosefot Yom Tov*).

akhot associated with a woman's menstrual period; these two areas are notable in that they require logical and mathematical calculations in order to resolve them. Although they are, ostensibly, technical matters, nevertheless, **these are the fundamentals of halakhot,**[N] part of the essence of the Torah, and one should relate to them in this way; it is appropriate to engage in them and clarify them.

תְּקוּפוֹת וְגִימַטְרִיאוֹת, פַּרְפְּרָאוֹת לַחָכְמָה.

By contrast, **seasons,**[N] referring to calculations of the precise time of solstices and equinoxes, which integrate astronomy and

NOTES

These are the fundamentals of halakhot – **הֵן הֵן גּוּפֵי הֲלָכוֹת**: Several explanations have been advanced as to the reason it is specifically regarding these matters that it was emphasized that they are "the fundamentals of halakhot." Rashi says that this is stated because they require analysis and great effort in studying them. Others write that this emphasis is necessary because they appear like matters that are not worthy of analysis, either because, in the case of the birds, their cost is negligible, or, in the case of menstruation, because addressing them seems repugnant. Moreover, all the cases to be studied regard uncertainties that developed and not the primary, *ab initio*, halakha (*Tosefot Yom Tov*).

The Meiri points out that *kinnim* are the halakhot at the end of the order of *Kodashim*, and the beginnings of menstruation are halakhot at the end of the order of *Teharot*. This comes to emphasize that a person should not engage in other pursuits that are not the crux of the Torah, until he knows his Talmud, even these matters.

Seasons – **תְּקוּפוֹת**: Many explain that this is referring to the study of astronomy (Rashi). Others say that astronomy is one of the fundamentals of Torah, because it is necessary for calculating intercalation of the year and determination of the months. That is why these commentaries explain that this is referring

Rabban Gamliel using illustrations of the appearance of the moon when accepting testimony used for determining the new month

Mosaic of the signs of the zodiac in ancient synagogue from Roman era, Tzippori

mathematics, **and** calculations based on **the numerical value of letters**[N] and the various combinations that can be calculated on their basis, are **appetizers to wisdom.**[N]

NOTES

to matters bordering on astrology (Rashbatz) or to matters of astronomy that have no halakhic relevance (*Tosefot Yom Tov*). These matters are not fundamentals of Torah. Nevertheless, there is virtue in engaging in their study, as the verse was expounded in this regard (see *Shabbat* 75a): "You shall observe and you shall perform, as this is your wisdom and your understanding in the eyes of the peoples" (Deuteronomy 4:6). The following verse was expounded regarding anyone who does not engage in their study: "But they will not regard the work of the Lord, and they did not see His handiwork" (Isaiah 5:12).

The numerical value of letters [*gimatriot*] – **גִּימַטְרִיאוֹת**: Some explain this as the Greek term *geometria*, which refers to all aspects of mathematics, particularly the areas of measurement and geometry (Meiri, *Tosefot Yom Tov*). However, most commentaries say that this is referring to the numerical value of letters and the various acronyms (Rashi). These are also used in the homiletic interpretations of the Sages, at least as an allusion to reinforce existing traditions among the Sages.

Appetizers to wisdom – **פַּרְפְּרָאוֹת לַחָכְמָה**: This means that even though the matters enumerated here involve calculations and mathematics, their value is determined by their place in the world of Torah. Matters that are part of the Torah itself are significant, even if they are not central in it. By contrast, other matters, which are not part of the essential Torah, are considered only as "appetizers" that are ancillary to the main course of the meal, even if their use is more extensive (see *Berakhot* 6:5). By contrast, a different explanation speaks in praise of these appetizers. They whet the appetite of the diner and add taste to the main course of the meal. In other words, by means of these matters, one is drawn to study the wisdom of the Torah (Rashi, Rabbeinu Yona, and others).

Chapter 4

In the previous chapter, the statements cited were primarily those of the Sages of Yavne. This chapter begins with statements by Sages who were present in Yavne but were not members of the court. Next it presents statements from the generation after the generation of Yavne, which was the generation of Rabbi Akiva's disciples after the bar Kokheva revolt, and then statements of later Sages. The chapter concludes with words of reproof from Rabbi Elazar HaKappar, who was from the generation that bridged the tannaitic and amoraic periods.

Mishna 1

In this mishna, the Sage Shimon ben Zoma, one of the Sages of the academy in Yavne who were not formally ordained as Sages and did not receive the title "Rabbi," details original perspectives on valued human qualities.

בֶּן זוֹמָא אוֹמֵר: אֵיזֶהוּ חָכָם? הַלּוֹמֵד מִכָּל אָדָם, שֶׁנֶּאֱמַר: "מִכָּל מְלַמְּדַי הִשְׂכַּלְתִּי כִּי עֵדְוֺתֶיךָ שִׂיחָה לִּי".

Ben Zoma[P] **says: Who is wise?**[N] **One who** is capable of **learning from any person,**[N] **as it is stated: "I have gained enlightenment from all my teachers [*mikol melamdai hiskalti*], for Your precepts are my conversation"** (Psalms 119:99).

NOTES

Ben Zoma says: Who is wise – בֶּן זוֹמָא אוֹמֵר אֵיזֶהוּ חָכָם: The commentaries note that the gist of the matters enumerated in the mishna appear in the verse: "So said the Lord: Let the wise not glory in his

אֵיזֶהוּ גִּבּוֹר? הַכּוֹבֵשׁ אֶת יִצְרוֹ, שֶׁנֶּאֱמַר: "טוֹב אֶרֶךְ אַפַּיִם מִגִּבּוֹר וּמֹשֵׁל בְּרוּחוֹ מִלֹּכֵד עִיר".

Who is mighty? One who subdues his inclination,[N] **as it is stated** regarding controlling one's temper: **"One who controls his spirit is better than the mighty; and the ruler of his spirit, than the conqueror of a city"** (Proverbs 16:32)

אֵיזֶהוּ עָשִׁיר? הַשָּׂמֵחַ בְּחֶלְקוֹ, שֶׁנֶּאֱמַר: "יְגִיעַ כַּפֶּיךָ כִּי תֹאכֵל אַשְׁרֶיךָ וְטוֹב לָךְ"; 'אַשְׁרֶיךָ' – בָּעוֹלָם הַזֶּה, 'וְטוֹב לָךְ' – לָעוֹלָם הַבָּא.

Who is wealthy? One who is happy with his lot,[N] with the portion that came into his possession through his toil, and it is sufficient for him, **as it is stated: "When you eat of the labor of your hands, you are happy, and it is good for you"** (Psalms 128:2). It can be inferred from the verse that this person benefits twice: **"You are happy" in this world,** as he lacks nothing; **"and it is good for you," in the World to Come,** because he does not perform monetary transgressions, and is also free to engage in serving God.

NOTES

wisdom, and let the valiant not glory in his valor; let the rich not glory in his riches. Rather, let the one who glories glory in this: perceiving and knowing Me" (Jeremiah 9:22–23). Although these matters are fundamentally straightforward, ben Zoma interprets them by expounding verses in a manner that ostensibly deviates from their plain understanding. For example, the clause from the verse: "*mikol melamdai hiskalti*," whose straightforward understanding is: "I have become more enlightened than all my teachers," he interprets to mean: "Thanks to the ability and the merit of all my teachers, I have become enlightened." He did the same regarding the other qualities.

Who is wise? One who is capable of learning from any person – **אֵיזֶהוּ חָכָם הַלּוֹמֵד מִכָּל אָדָם**: This definition relates to the fundamental conception of the essence of wisdom, which is, first and foremost, the ability to grasp the truth of matters in a direct manner. In that sense, the ability of the wise man to learn from all people is the ability to discern the content of what another says, and accept it, even if that person is ignorant or a child, without prejudice. An additional explanation is that one who learns from any person indicates thereby that he seeks wisdom, even a small bit of wisdom, and he is willing to demean himself in order to grasp it (Rabbeinu Yona, Rashbatz). Some explain that he is called wise because he ultimately becomes wise, by learning from all people (Meiri).

Who is mighty? One who subdues his inclination – **אֵיזֶהוּ גִּבּוֹר הַכּוֹבֵשׁ אֶת יִצְרוֹ**: The essence of might, both in its general sense and its spiritual sense, is the ability to fight and emerge victorious, whether referring to might in physical strength or in military leadership. However, the most difficult battle is one's battle with his evil inclination, because it is an internal battle, where he occupies both sides. That is why this battle and victory in it manifest the essence of might.

Who is wealthy? One who is happy with his lot – **אֵיזֶהוּ עָשִׁיר הַשָּׂמֵחַ בְּחֶלְקוֹ**: The standard definition of "wealthy" is a function of one's financial situation as well as a person's wealth relative to the society in which he lives. In that sense, it is impossible to give

אֵיזֶהוּ מְכֻבָּד? הַמְכַבֵּד אֶת הַבְּרִיּוֹת, שֶׁנֶּאֱמַר: "כִּי מְכַבְּדַי אֲכַבֵּד וּבֹזַי יֵקָלּוּ".

Who is honored? One who honors people,[N] because an attitude of that kind leads other people to honor him, **as it is stated: "For those who honor Me, I will honor,**[N] **but those who scorn Me will be lowly"** (I Samuel 2:30).

NOTES

wealth an absolute definition, as the criteria for these matters varies greatly in different places and at different times. However, here there is another aspect of the definition of wealth; when does a person himself know and decide that he is wealthy? It is when he feels that he lacks nothing, and he does not long for anything that he does not have. That is why a person who is happy with his lot, who is satisfied with what he has, whether it be substantial or meager, and experiences no sense of lack, has thereby achieved the pinnacle of wealth (see Rashbatz).

Who is honored? One who honors people – אֵיזֶהוּ מְכֻבָּד הַמְכַבֵּד אֶת הַבְּרִיּוֹת: One who is honored is typically defined as one honored by others; however, such honor often gets expressed externally, because of social conventions, and does not reflect people's true, internal feelings about him. That is why ben Zoma says that the honored one is one who has true regard for people as well as the ability to express it. As a result, other people will truly honor him, both as a natural emotional reaction, and in recognition of the fact that a person like that recognizes how important it is to honor people (see Meiri and Rashbatz).

For those who honor Me, I will honor – כִּי מְכַבְּדַי אֲכַבֵּד: Although this verse speaks of those who honor God and not of honor among people, ben Zoma expounds it as a kind of *a fortiori* inference. If God repays those who honor Him by honoring them, certainly a person who is accorded honor will honor his counterpart in return (Rabbeinu Yona). Some explain that the intent of the verse is that one who honors God and follows His path acts in a way that is honored by other people (Rashi).

PERSONALITIES

Ben Zoma – בֶּן זוֹמָא: Ben Zoma is a shortened version of the name Shimon ben Zoma. He was one of the Sages active in the academy at Yavne, where he was enumerated among the five students who would deliberate before the Sages, meaning that they would raise halakhic questions and deliberate regarding problems that came before the court; however, for external reasons, they did not receive official rabbinic ordination and therefore they are not addressed with the title "Rabbi" (*Sanhedrin* 17b). Nevertheless, his statements are cited in various places in the Talmud with appreciation for his wisdom.

Ben Zoma is enumerated among the four who entered the "orchard," the world of Torah mysticism, but he did not emerge intact, as he suffered psychological damage (*Tosefta*, *Ḥagiga* 2:3). He is considered one of the great exegetists in his generation and in the generations that followed, which is reflected clearly in his interpretations of the verses here; it was later said: "When ben Zoma died, the exegetists ceased" (*Sota* 9:15).

Mishna 2

Following ben Zoma's statement in the previous mishna, this mishna cites a statement of ben Azzai, who was also one of the Sages of Yavne not formally ordained as Sages.

בֶּן עַזַּאי אוֹמֵר: הֱוֵי רָץ לְמִצְוָה קַלָּה כְּבַחֲמוּרָה, וּבוֹרֵחַ מִן הָעֲבֵירָה.

Ben Azzai[P] **says: One should pursue** with desire and enthusiasm fulfillment of **a mitzva** considered **minor,**[N] **just** as one pursues a mitzva considered **major. And,** on the other hand, **flee from transgression,** even a minor transgression, as one must distance himself from anything liable to lead to sin.

שֶׁמִּצְוָה גּוֹרֶרֶת מִצְוָה, וַעֲבֵירָה גּוֹרֶרֶת עֲבֵירָה. שֶׁשְּׂכַר מִצְוָה – מִצְוָה, וּשְׂכַר עֲבֵירָה – עֲבֵירָה.

As, the reason is, **a mitzva generates a mitzva**[N] in its wake, **and transgression generates transgression** in its wake. Therefore, the importance of the act is not only regarding the solitary mitzva or transgression that a person performs, but in the fact that he thereby creates a causative chain reaction. Ben Azzai adds that this system is due to the fact **that the recompense for a mitzva is** another **mitzva**[N] that the person will have the opportunity to perform, **and** conversely, **the recompense for transgression is transgression.**

NOTES

A mitzva considered minor – מִצְוָה קַלָּה: Some explain that a minor mitzva is one that seems easy (Rashi). Others say that a minor mitzva is one that involves little exertion (Rabbeinu Yona), or does not cause monetary loss (*Notzer Ḥesed*). Another interpretation is that it is specifically a minor mitzva that one should pursue, as perhaps another person will hurry and grab it. But if there is a major mitzva, which is perceived to be difficult, he need not be concerned that others will precede him and fulfill it (Rabbi Yosef Ḥayyim).

The Rambam cites the example of Moses performing a minor mitzva. Moses designated the three cities of refuge on the east bank of the Jordan, despite the fact that they would not attain the status of being actual cities of refuge until the three cities on the west bank of the Jordan were designated.

As a mitzva generates a mitzva – שֶׁמִּצְוָה גּוֹרֶרֶת מִצְוָה: This is true both in terms of man's nature and in terms of the essential nature of this matter (Meiri, Rabbeinu Yona). A good or bad choice is not limited to that specific act, but it affects the future as well and creates a reality, a constellation of good or evil. Therefore, even a minor mitzva ultimately generates an entire reality of good, and even a minor transgression ultimately generates an entire system of evil.

The recompense for a mitzva is a mitzva – שֶׁשְּׂכַר מִצְוָה מִצְוָה: On a basic level, this statement is an

Mishna 3

In the previous mishna, ben Azzai indicated that a person is unable to properly value mitzvot that seem minor. Similarly, here he addresses the significance of people and items in the world that appear to have little value.

הוּא הָיָה אוֹמֵר: אַל תְּהִי בָז לְכָל אָדָם, וְאַל תְּהִי מַפְלִיג לְכָל דָּבָר, שֶׁאֵין לְךָ אָדָם שֶׁאֵין לוֹ שָׁעָה, וְאֵין לְךָ דָבָר שֶׁאֵין לוֹ מָקוֹם.

He, ben Azzai, **would say: Do not scorn any person,** whoever he may be, even if he appears contemptible or insignificant, **and do not dismiss,**[N] distance

NOTES

explanation for how "a mitzva generates a mitzva." When one performs a mitzva, at least some of the reward that he receives comes in the form of an opportunity to perform another mitzva. But the statement also has a more comprehensive meaning. A mitzva itself or a transgression itself has great positive or negative value, respectively. As a result, the reward for a mitzva is not a good life in this world or even recompense in the World to Come. It is, rather, in the essence of the mitzva itself, as the value of the mitzva is incomparable.

Some explain that "a mitzva generates a mitzva" is what happens naturally, while "the recompense for a mitzva is a mitzva" is what is performed from Heaven (Rashbatz and others). Others add that the recompense for a mitzva is also a mitzva; in other words, one who rejoices in performance of a mitzva and feels that the mitzva itself is its own reward, receives an additional reward for that joy (Bartenura).

Do not scorn any person and do not dismiss – אַל תְּהִי בָז לְכָל אָדָם וְאַל תְּהִי מַפְלִיג: The commentary follows Abravanel's interpretation, that this is a continuation of the previous mishna. It impossible to assess not only the value of mitzvot and transgressions, but also the value of people and items in this world, even if they appear to be of little value. Some write that by treating even the lowly with respect, one demonstrates an element of deference to Heaven; as, if he treats them with contempt and distances them, it is as though he is saying that God created something that is inappropriate or that is unnecessary for the world (Yaavetz).

PERSONALITIES

Ben Azzai – בֶּן עַזַּאי: Ben Azzai is the appellation for the Sage Shimon ben Azzai, who was also among the five who deliberated before the Sages. In his youth he was not a Torah scholar, and he went to study Torah due to a promise made to him by Rabbi Akiva's daughter that she would marry him if he did so (*Ketubot* 63b). However, despite the fact that he spoke vehemently against one who does not take a wife, he never married, because his soul yearned for Torah to the extent that he was not free to enter into and commit to a marriage relationship (*Yevamot* 63b).

Ben Azzai was one of the most prominent Sages, famous for his diligence and keen intellect. He resided in Tiberias, and was renowned as one who could answer any question posed to him, to the extent that generations later coined the colloquial expression: "I am like ben Azzai in the marketplaces of Tiberias" (*Eiruvin* 29a and elsewhere). He had great admiration for Rabbi Akiva, and stated in his regard: "All the Sages of Israel seem to me like a garlic peel, except for this bald one" (*Bekhorot* 58a). He too was one of the four who entered the "orchard"; but it is stated in his regard that he "glimpsed [it] and died" (*Tosefta, Ḥagiga* 2:4). That is why he did not live a long life.

and denigrate, **any item.**[N] This is because it turns out **that** ultimately **you have no person**[N] **who does not have his moment** of success or significance. One who treats another with disdain will not be able to receive his help in a time of need, and is even liable to be harmed by him. **And** likewise, **there is no item that does not have its place** in which it will prove to be necessary and in which its absence could cause significant damage.

Mishna 4

This mishna begins with the statement of one of the Sages of Yavne regarding humility.

רַבִּי לְוִיטָס אִישׁ יַבְנֶה אוֹמֵר:

Rabbi Levitas of Yavne[P] **says:**

מְאֹד מְאֹד הֱוֵי שְׁפַל רוּחַ, שֶׁתִּקְוַת אֱנוֹשׁ רִמָּה.

Be extremely, extremely humble,[N] as regarding this quality one must go to the extreme, as there is no room

NOTES

And do not dismiss [*maflig*] any item – וְאַל תְּהִי מַפְלִיג לְכָל דָּבָר: Here *maflig* is explained in the sense of distancing or minimizing the value of something. Some explain *maflig* as procrastination; do not delay hearing words of wisdom, even if the matter is extremely small, as perhaps you will be unable to hear it later and one day you will need it (Rashi; see 2:4).

That you have no person – שֶׁאֵין לְךָ אָדָם: Some point out that regarding a person the mishna says that he has "a moment," and regarding an item it says that it has "a place." This is because people, who have freedom of choice, undergo constant change and are different from moment to moment. However, regarding items, which do not change, the matter is dependent upon the place that they are situated, as that accords them their significance and their value (*Tiferet Yisrael*).

Be extremely, extremely humble [*shefal ruaḥ*] – מְאֹד מְאֹד הֱוֵי שְׁפַל רוּחַ: This means not only that one should not be arrogant and superior vis-à-vis others, but also that in terms of his own self-assessment he should consider himself inferior and lowly. Although, in general, a person should choose for himself the middle path, and in any character trait not to go to either extreme, for example, one should be neither profligate nor miserly; in terms of distancing oneself from arrogance, one should be as extreme as possible for pride. The reason for this is **that the expectancy of humanity,** the ultimate end of each person, **is maggots;**[N] he becomes food for maggots in the grave, regardless of his standing and circumstances while alive. Through introspection on this matter a person can refrain from taking pride in his virtues, and will instead consider himself like dust and ashes.

The mishna proceeds to the statement of another Sage, which addresses the matter of profaning the name of God.

רַבִּי יוֹחָנָן בֶּן בְּרוֹקָא אוֹמֵר: **Rabbi Yoḥanan ben Beroka**[P] **says:**

NOTES

(Rambam). The Rashbatz states that the doubling of the word "extremely" suggests that one should be even more humble than Moses, in whose regard it is stated: "The man Moses was extremely humble" (Numbers 12:3).

That the expectancy of [*tikvat*] humanity is maggots – שֶׁתִּקְוַת אֱנוֹשׁ רִמָּה: Many explain *tikvat* here not in its usual sense of hopeful anticipation, but rather in the sense of a person being resigned to his fate, as in the verse: "How much less is man, a maggot; the son of man, a worm." (Job 25:6). Some understand *tikva* in its standard sense of hope, explaining that while typically people hope and aspire for the body's well-being, its ultimate lot is maggots (*Pirkei Moshe*). Others explain that the matters to which a person should aspire and in which he should take pride are spiritual matters, whose main impact is when a person dies and becomes maggots (*Tiferet Yisrael*).

PERSONALITIES

Rabbi Levitas of Yavne – רַבִּי לְוִיטַס אִישׁ יַבְנֶה: We know virtually nothing about this Sage, and he is not mentioned elsewhere in the Talmud or midrash, with the exception of some mentions in *Pirkei deRabbi Eliezer*. In addition, in *Avot deRabbi Natan* (version B, chap. 34) an additional statement of his is cited that also addresses aspects in which a person is more contemptible than even an animal. His appellation suggests that he had been a resident of the city of Yavne even before other Sages came and established the academy there. His name is from Greek, and means Levite.

Rabbi Yoḥanan ben Beroka – רַבִּי יוֹחָנָן בֶּן בְּרוֹקָא: Rabbi Yoḥanan ben Beroka was one of the Sages who was in the academy at Yavne. He considered himself a disciple of Rabbi Yehoshua (*Ḥagiga* 3a), and also had close ties with Rabbi Yoḥanan ben Nuri (*Tosefta*, *Terumot* 7:14), who was older than he was. Some of his statements appear in the Mishna and in halakhic midrash. His son, Rabbi Yishmael, is also mentioned among the Sages, as can be seen in the following mishna.

כָּל הַמְחַלֵּל שֵׁם שָׁמַיִם בַּסֵּתֶר – נִפְרָעִין מִמֶּנּוּ בְּגָלוּי.

With regard to **anyone who desecrates the name of Heaven clandestinely,**[N] meaning that he commits a transgression that involves demeaning the name of God, e.g., idol worship, **payment is exacted from him** from Heaven; God will take vengeance against him and punish him **openly,**[N] in public.

אֶחָד שׁוֹגֵג וְאֶחָד מֵזִיד בְּחִלּוּל הַשֵּׁם.

Furthermore, regarding the severity of profaning the Name, **both** one who sins **unwittingly and** one who sins **intentionally**[N] are equal **regarding** matters **of profaning the Name.** Even when the matter is not performed with premeditation, diminution of the honor of Heaven causes great damage.

NOTES

Anyone who desecrates the name of Heaven clandestinely – **כָּל הַמְחַלֵּל שֵׁם שָׁמַיִם בַּסֵּתֶר**: Many commentaries found these matters difficult, because "desecrating the name of Heaven" is an action typically performed in the presence of others, corresponding to the parallel concept of sanctifying the name of God. As a result, various explanations were provided for this matter. Some say that this is one who clandestinely performs an action that would have constituted a desecration of the Name had he performed it openly (*Maḥzor Vitri*). Others suggest that he performed an act that is a desecration of God in and of itself, e.g., idol worship or a false oath (Rabbeinu Yona). An additional explanation is that he performs an act that is not a desecration of God per se, but he does so in a rebellious, insubordinate manner (Meiri; see *Tiferet Yisrael*). There are also those who explain that performance of a transgression clandestinely itself constitutes desecration of the Name. It is as though the person is saying that God does not see him there, and as though he is saying that there is no room for the Divine Presence in the world (see *Ḥagiga* 16a).

Payment is exacted from him openly – **נִפְרָעִין מִמֶּנּוּ בְּגָלוּי**: Rashi says that Heaven will see to it that people will discover that this person has sinned, so that they will not say that a righteous, transgression-free person was punished. He cited a source for this from what Natan the prophet said to David: "For you acted clandestinely, but I will perform this matter before all Israel, and before the sun" (II Samuel 12:12). The *Maḥzor Vitri* explains simply that the reason that payment is exacted from him openly is so that people will know that this person is a hypocrite and they will not learn from him.

Both unwittingly and intentionally – **אֶחָד שׁוֹגֵג וְאֶחָד מֵזִיד**: This does not mean that the punishment for these two is equal, but that payment is exacted from both of them openly. In terms of the punishment itself there is a difference between an unwitting sin and an intentional transgression (Rambam and others; see Rashi).

Mishna 5

Following the statement of Rabbi Yoḥanan ben Beroka in the previous mishna, the statement of his son is cited in this mishna.

רַבִּי יִשְׁמָעֵאל בְּנוֹ אוֹמֵר:

Rabbi Yishmael his son, the son of Rabbi Yohanan ben Beroka[P] **says** matters relating to the proper motivation for and objective of Torah study

הַלּוֹמֵד עַל מְנָת לְלַמֵּד – מַסְפִּיקִין בְּיָדוֹ לִלְמֹד וּלְלַמֵּד.

One who studies in order to teach,[N] whose primary motivation in his study is not for himself, but to teach, **is given the opportunity** from Heaven **to study** properly **and to teach** as well.

וְהַלּוֹמֵד עַל מְנָת לַעֲשׂוֹת – מַסְפִּיקִין בְּיָדוֹ לִלְמֹד וּלְלַמֵּד, לִשְׁמֹר וְלַעֲשׂוֹת.

However, **one who studies in order to perform** the matters that he has studied **is given the opportunity to study and to teach,** as well as **to observe and to perform** everything that he learned.

NOTES

One who studies in order to teach – הַלּוֹמֵד עַל מְנָת לְלַמֵּד: He is greater than one who studies just in order to learn, because it is action, not study, that is primary (Rashi). The mishna is not referring to one who studies only in order to teach but not in order to perform, but rather to one whose primary passion is to study, not to perform (Rabbeinu Yona, *Tosefot Yom Tov*). Alternatively, the mishna may be referring to study of matters that do not involve action, like mitzvot that are not practical today, or rare, unusual mitzvot (*Tiferet Yisrael*).

Rashi cites a variant reading (that also appears in *Avot deRabbi Natan*, version B, chap. 32): "One who studies in order to teach is not given the opportunity to study and to teach." He explains that this is referring to one who studies so that he will be honored and called "Rabbi." Such a person does not succeed at all. This is similar to Rabbi Tzadok's statement later in the mishna.

PERSONALITIES

Rabbi Yishmael…son of Rabbi Yohanan ben Beroka – רַבִּי יִשְׁמָעֵאל בְּנוֹ: Rabbi Yishmael son of Rabbi Yoḥanan ben Beroka was apparently also his father's student. In his youth, he lived in Yavne (*Yevamot* 42b), but his main activity was in the following generation, when Rabban Shimon ben Gamliel (the second) was the *Nasi* and the seat of the Sanhedrin was in the city of Usha. He lived a long life, and he engaged in discourse with Rabbi Natan, who was younger than he. His statements are cited twice in the Mishna (*Bava Kamma* 10:2, *Sanhedrin* 11:1), as well as in the *Tosefta*, halakhic midrash, the Babylonian Talmud, and the Jerusalem Talmud.

The mishna cites additional statements relating to Torah study that is not primarily for oneself.

רַבִּי צָדוֹק אוֹמֵר:

Rabbi Tzadok[P] **says:**

אַל תַּעֲשֵׂם עֲטָרָה לְהִתְגַּדֵּל בָּהֶם, וְלֹא קַרְדֹּם לַחְפּוֹר בָּהֶם.

Do not render them, your Torah studies, **a crown for self-aggrandizement,** as an instrument to attain honor. **And not as a pickax**[B] **with which to dig,**[N] a tool or means for accruing assets.

וְכָךְ הָיָה הִלֵּל אוֹמֵר: "וּדְיִשְׁתַּמֵּשׁ בְּתָגָא – חֲלָף". הָא לָמַדְתָּ, כָּל הַנֶּהֱנֶה מִדִּבְרֵי תוֹרָה – נוֹטֵל חַיָּיו מִן הָעוֹלָם.

Likewise, Hillel would say (1:13): **One who exploits the crown will pass. You learned** from Hillel's statement: **Anyone who benefits from matters of Torah,** who exploits them to attain property or honor, **removes his life from the world.**

NOTES

A crown for self-aggrandizement…a pickax with which to dig – עֲטָרָה לְהִתְגַּדֵּל בָּה...קַרְדֹּם לַחְפּוֹר בָּהֶם: The Maharal writes that it was necessary to caution people about both matters, because it is possible to think that it is inappropriate to exploit one's Torah studies in order to be honored, but that it is permitted in order to earn a livelihood, as, "if there is no flour there is no Torah" (3:17). That is why it was necessary to caution against using Torah as a pickax with which to dig. But it is also possible to think the converse, that exploiting Torah in order to earn a livelihood is a demeaning use, but that using one's Torah studies in order to be honored is permitted, as that honor is an outgrowth of the importance of the Torah. Therefore, Rabbi Tzadok cautioned that one should not exploit the Torah as a crown for self-aggrandizement either.

PERSONALITIES

Rabbi Tzadok – רַבִּי צָדוֹק: At least two *tanna'im* were named Rabbi Tzadok, and it is unclear which of them is referred to here. That said, because his statement is positioned here adjacent to the statement of Rabbi Yishmael son of Rabbi Yohanan ben Beroka, it is likely that it is referring to the Sage from the generation of the disciples of Rabbi Akiva who is mentioned as having deliberated with the other disciples. Rabbi Elazar ben Rabbi Tzadok, who appears in the following generation, may have been the son of this Rabbi Tzadok. Some believe that the grandfather of this Rabbi Tzadok was the first, more renowned, Rabbi Tzadok, who was one of the prominent Sages at the end of the Second Temple period and at the beginning of the Yavne period.

Pickax

BACKGROUND

Pickax [*kardom*] – קַרְדֹּם: The *kardom* is a tool similar to a pickax. Its head has two sides, one a flat blade, and the other a long, sharp protrusion. The flat side was used for chopping down and splitting trees, and the sharp side was used for digging, hoeing, and weeding.

Mishna 6

This mishna continues to cite statements of the Sages regarding honoring matters of Torah.

רַבִּי יוֹסֵי אוֹמֵר:	**Rabbi Yosei**[P] **says:**
כָּל הַמְכַבֵּד אֶת הַתּוֹרָה – גּוּפוֹ מְכֻבָּד עַל הַבְּרִיּוֹת.	**Anyone who respects the Torah,**[N] **he himself is respected by the people;**[N] the reward of this person is that he too is respected, because he accorded respect to what is worthy of respect.
וְכָל הַמְחַלֵּל אֶת הַתּוֹרָה – גּוּפוֹ מְחֻלָּל עַל הַבְּרִיּוֹת.	**And** conversely, **anyone who disdains the Torah will himself be disdained by the people;**[N] even in this world he will not be respected.

NOTES

Anyone who respects the Torah – כָּל הַמְכַבֵּד אֶת הַתּוֹרָה: This is one who respects it in every sense. He respects the Torah in the simple sense that he treats the Torah scroll with deference, placing it in a place of honor, and not engaging in any other activity during the Torah reading (Rashi). He also honors the Torah in his speech and attitude, and is exacting and industrious in studying it (Bartenura; see *Sota* 9:15 regarding honoring the Torah). An additional manner of honoring the Torah is by according honor to those who engage in it and study it (see Rambam).

He himself is respected by the people – גּוּפוֹ מְכֻבָּד עַל הַבְּרִיּוֹת: The *Tiferet Yisrael* explains that this is a continuation of what is stated in the previous mishna regarding one who uses the Torah as a pickax with which to dig, that it constitutes a desecration of the Torah and ultimately leads to his being disdained by others. By contrast, one who respects the Torah and does not seek to earn a livelihood from it, even if, as a result, he earns his livelihood from the most menial labor, will be respected by others. In certain respects, this mishna is also a continuation and completion of the mishna before the previous one, which addressed profaning the name of Heaven, as the Torah is a revelation of the Glory of God.

Will himself be disdained by the people – גּוּפוֹ מְחֻלָּל עַל הַבְּרִיּוֹת: Not only does he have no portion or honor in the World to Come (see mishna 11), but even in this world he will not be respected.

PERSONALITIES

Rabbi Yosei – רַבִּי יוֹסֵי: The Rabbi Yosei who is mentioned in the Mishna is Rabbi Yosei ben Rabbi Ḥalafta. He and his father were among the prominent Sages of Tzippori in the Lower Galilee. Rabbi Yosei studied under his father, but later received most of his Torah from Rabbi Akiva, and he became one of his preeminent students. Rabbi Yosei ben Rabbi Ḥalafta was quiet by nature (*Shabbat* 33b and elsewhere) and his statements were made after careful consideration, to the extent that they said: "Rabbi Yosei, his reasoning is with him" (*Eiruvin* 46b). For this reason, the halakha is always ruled in accordance with his opinion. Rabbi Yehuda HaNasi, who was his disciple, held him in high esteem and considered him the preeminent leader of the generation in terms of his Torah scholarship and his holiness. He deferred to Rabbi Yosei's opinion, saying: "The Sage has already ruled" (*Shabbat* 51a). Rabbi Yosei had five sons, all of them ordained Sages. He stated in their regard: "I planted five cedars in Israel" (*Shabbat* 118b). The greatest of them was Rabbi Yishmael ben Rabbi Yosei, who is mentioned in the next mishna.

Mishna 7

Following Rabbi Yosei's statement in the previous mishna, this mishna cites the statement of his eldest son, Rabbi Yishmael.

רַבִּי יִשְׁמָעֵאל בְּנוֹ אוֹמֵר: הַחוֹשֵׂךְ עַצְמוֹ מִן הַדִּין – פּוֹרֵק מִמֶּנּוּ אֵיבָה, וְגָזֵל וּשְׁבוּעַת שָׁוְא.

Rabbi Yishmael, his, Rabbi Yosei's, **son,**[P] **says: One who recuses himself from judgment,**[N] from serving as a judge or from suing another in court, **spares himself enmity** with people, **robbery,** resulting from a mistaken ruling, **and an oath** taken in **vain,**[N] which he is liable to cause in the course of the litigation.

וְהַגַּס לִבּוֹ בְּהוֹרָאָה – שׁוֹטֶה, רָשָׁע, וְגַס רוּחַ.

By contrast, **one who is arrogant in issuing rulings,**[N] a person who issues halakhic rulings to the public but does so with haughtiness, **is a fool,** as, ultimately, no person knows everything. He is also **a wicked person,** because he thereby arrives at mistaken rulings, which create stumbling blocks for himself and others, **and a lout,** because he arrogantly engages in delicate and sensitive matters.

NOTES

One who recuses himself from judgment – הַחוֹשֵׂךְ עַצְמוֹ מִן הַדִּין: Some explain that this is referring to a judge not agreeing to sit in judgment if the litigants are unwilling to enter into mediation. Alternatively, this is referring to the litigant himself compromising with the other litigant in order to avoid judgment (Rashi and others). Some say that although there is a mitzva and an obligation to sit and judge the people, that is only when there is no other judge in that location. As long as there is an alternative, and there are others who are capable of judging and greater than he is, it is preferable to recuse himself (Rabbeinu Yona, Bartenura).

An oath taken in vain – שְׁבוּעַת שָׁוְא: The concern is that the judge will err and require one who is not obligated to take an oath to take an oath; this is an oath taken in vain, not a false oath (Rabbeinu Yona, *Tiferet Yisrael*). According to the understanding that the reference here is to a litigant, Rashi explains that conceivably, he mistakenly thinks that the facts are as he claims, and he takes a false oath to that effect, albeit unwittingly. Another writes that this is referring to a gratuitous oath, as in many cases the other litigant knows the truth and could admit it and prevent the oath. The oath was therefore avoidable, but by not admitting the truth, the other litigant made it necessary for the first litigant to take an oath that could have been avoided (*Midrash Shmuel*).

One who is arrogant in issuing rulings – הַגַּס לִבּוֹ בְּהוֹרָאָה: This quality is the opposite of that of "one who recuses himself from judgment," as the arrogant person has no fear of sitting in judgment or issuing rulings. He is confident that he will not err, and is not concerned about any pitfalls liable to ensue from

Mishna 8

This mishna continues citing statements of Rabbi Yishmael ben Rabbi Yosei with warnings to judges.

הוּא הָיָה אוֹמֵר:	**He,** Rabbi Yishmael ben Rabbi Yosei, **would say:**
אַל תְּהִי דָן יְחִידִי, שֶׁאֵין דָּן יְחִידִי אֶלָּא אֶחָד.	**Do not judge alone,**[N] do not sit in judgment alone, even in situations where it is permitted to do so, **as there is only One who judges alone;** only God is worthy of sitting in judgment alone.
וְאַל תֹּאמַר: "קַבְּלוּ דַעְתִּי", שֶׁהֵן רַשָּׁאִין וְלֹא אַתָּה.	On a similar note, when there are two other judges with you, and they disagree with you, **do not say** to them: **Accept my opinion,**[N] even if

NOTES

his rulings, whether in this world or in the World to Come. The commentaries write that regarding a person like this it is stated: "There is more hope for a fool than for him" (Proverbs 29:20), as this is one who is "wise in his own eyes" (Proverbs 26:12) and "hasty in his affairs" (Proverbs 29:20). Conceivably, a fool could repent and begin studying, but one who is "wise in his own eyes" and thinks that he knows everything will not reform his ways (Rabbeinu Yona and others).

Do not judge alone – אַל תְּהִי דָן יְחִידִי: In this mishna Rabbi Yishmael ben Rabbi Yosei continues speaking about the caution required when sitting in judgment. He says that even in cases where it is fundamentally permitted to sit in judgment alone, e.g., in cases of monetary law, when the judge is considered a recognized expert or when the litigants accepted him as a judge (see *Sanhedrin* 5:1), it is inappropriate to judge in that manner. One should include additional judges, because empaneling numerous judges helps avoid errors. Moreover, if they do err, responsibility will be distributed among them all (Rabbeinu Yona and others).

Do not say, accept my opinion – וְאַל תֹּאמַר קַבְּלוּ דַעְתִּי: This is true regarding every court case with several judges together; the senior judge among them should not impose upon the others to accept his opinion, but rather each of the judges must state his own opinion (see *Sanhedrin* 4:2). However, the mishna is emphasizing that in cases where, fundamentally, the judge is fit to judge alone, he should not say that because he added his colleagues beyond the letter of the law, it is he who should ultimately determine the ruling (Rabbeinu Yona, Bartenura, and others).

PERSONALITIES

Rabbi Yishmael…Rabbi Yosei's son – רַבִּי יִשְׁמָעֵאל בְּנוֹ: Of the *tanna* Rabbi Yosei's five sons, who were ordained to issue halakhic rulings, Rabbi Yishmael was the eldest. He lived during the last generation of *tanna'im*, during the era of Rabbi Yehuda HaNasi. It was said that he was "a surrogate for his fathers," meaning that he was their equivalent (*Shabbat* 51a and elsewhere). Rabbi Yishmael had a close scholarly and personal relationship with Rabbi Yehuda HaNasi, and the two of them treated one another with deference. His Torah statements as well as stories of incidents demonstrating his righteousness appear in many places in the Talmud.

you are the most highly regarded and prominent among them. **As, they are permitted** to accept or reject, **and you are not** permitted to impose your opinion upon them; they are the majority, and according to the Torah one follows the majority.

Mishna 9

רַבִּי יוֹנָתָן אוֹמֵר: כָּל הַמְקַיֵּם אֶת הַתּוֹרָה מֵעֹנִי – סוֹפוֹ לְקַיְּמָהּ מֵעֹשֶׁר.

Rabbi Yonatan[P] **says: Anyone who fulfills the Torah in poverty,**[N] even though he is impoverished and it is difficult for him to fulfill it, **will ultimately** be blessed and be able to **fulfill it in wealth.**

וְכָל הַמְבַטֵּל אֶת הַתּוֹרָה מֵעֹשֶׁר – סוֹפוֹ לְבַטְּלָהּ מֵעֹנִי.

And the converse is true. **Anyone who is idle from the Torah in wealth,** when he is wealthy and has the ability to study Torah, **will ultimately** become poor and continue **to be idle from it in poverty.**

NOTES

Anyone who fulfills the Torah in poverty – **כָּל הַמְקַיֵּם אֶת הַתּוֹרָה מֵעֹנִי**: The simple understanding of the mishna is that it is referring to one who engages in Torah study and practice while impoverished (Rashi, Rambam, and others). However, some explain that the reference is to one who is impoverished intellectually. Although he does not know much, he tries to fulfill what he has heard. Ultimately, God will provide for him in that area, and he will become much wiser. Conversely, one who is idle regarding the Torah but is wealthy in terms of his wisdom and his knowledge will ultimately forget his studies (*Midrash Shmuel*). Some explain that "fulfills" and "is idle" in the mishna, beyond addressing Torah study and fulfillment of mitzvot, also address support of those who study Torah (*Tiferet Yisrael*).

PERSONALITIES

Rabbi Yonatan – **רַבִּי יוֹנָתָן**: Rabbi Yonatan, whose father's name was Rabbi Yosef, or Yosei, was a disciple of the *tanna* Rabbi Yishmael. He also learned Torah from Rabbi Akiva, and he lived in the generation of the latter's disciples. Little is known about Rabbi Yonatan's history and the events of his life. There are many disputes between him and his colleague, Rabbi Yoshiya, but their statements rarely appear in the Mishna, because the Mishna is primarily in accordance with the opinion of Rabbi Akiva, and they were disciples of Rabbi Yishmael. However, in halakhic midrash and in citations in the Talmud that are taught in accordance with the opinion of Rabbi Yishmael, they are among the primary speakers.

Mishna 10

Following the previous mishna, which spoke of one who fulfills the Torah when impoverished, this mishna cites the related statement of Rabbi Meir.

רַבִּי מֵאִיר אוֹמֵר:

Rabbi Meir[P] **says:**

הֱוֵי מְמַעֵט בְּעֵסֶק, וַעֲסוֹק בַּתּוֹרָה.

Minimize business activities as much as possible, **and engage in Torah** during every free moment.

PERSONALITIES

Rabbi Meir – רַבִּי מֵאִיר: Rabbi Meir was a prominent Sage of the Galilee, in the fourth generation of *tanna'im*, in the period between the bar Kokheva revolt and the redaction of the Mishna. His origins were from a family of proselytes, and he was a scribe by profession. While he was a preeminent student of Rabbi Akiva, he also studied with Rabbi Yishmael and apparently served on occasion as an emissary between the study halls of those two Sages (*Eiruvin* 13a). He also learned from Elisha ben Avuya, known as Aḥer, meaning "other." Even after the latter strayed from the path of Torah (see mishna 20), Rabbi Meir continued to learn from him critically and selectively, as they would say: "Rabbi Meir found a pomegranate, and he ate its inside and cast away its peel" (*Ḥagiga* 15b).

It is said regarding Rabbi Meir that he was so great that the other Sages were unable to fully comprehend his opinions in all their profundity. Similarly, there was no one in his generation who was his equal. In the Sanhedrin in Usha, where Rabban Shimon ben Gamliel was *Nasi*, he was appointed to the position of "Sage," the third in the hierarchy after the *Nasi* and the deputy *Nasi*. His great project was redaction of the first version of the Mishna, upon which Rabbi Yehuda HaNasi, who was his disciple, relied when redacting the Mishna. This is the reason for the principle that "an unattributed mishna is in accordance with the opinion of Rabbi Meir" (*Sanhedrin* 86a); i.e., unattributed statements in the Mishna are, in most cases, those of Rabbi Meir.

Rabbi Meir was married to Berurya, daughter of Rabbi Ḥananya ben Teradyon. She would deliberate with the Sages in matters of halakha, and is known as one of the outstanding, scholarly women in Jewish history (see 3:2).

Tomb of Rabbi Meir Baal HaNes, Tiberias

וֶהֱוֵי שְׁפַל רוּחַ בִּפְנֵי כָל אָדָם.

Be humble before every person.[N] One must not lord himself over others, but rather be cognizant of his own insignificance and aware of his shortcomings relative to others.

וְאִם בָּטַלְתָּ מִן הַתּוֹרָה – יֵשׁ לְךָ בְּטֵלִים הַרְבֵּה כְּנֶגְדְּךָ, וְאִם עָמַלְתָּ בַּתּוֹרָה – יֵשׁ לוֹ שָׂכָר הַרְבֵּה לִתֶּן לָךְ.

Moreover, in terms of minimizing the time devoted to earning a livelihood in order to engage in Torah study, you must remember: **If you were idle from Torah** for any reason, e.g., to enable you to devote more time to earning a livelihood, know that **there are many factors causing idleness,** lined up **against you;**[N] various life events will cause you to be idle from what you planned to perform. Ultimately, you will gain nothing from having been idle from engaging in Torah study. **And,** conversely, **if you toil extensively in Torah, there is much reward to be given to you.**[N] Even though he earns little livelihood, he will receive more than he would have received had he been idle from Torah study.

NOTES

Be humble before every person – וֶהֱוֵי שְׁפַל רוּחַ בִּפְנֵי כָל אָדָם: Ostensibly, this statement interrupts the Mishna's statements about Torah study. Some explain that these matters are stated specifically regarding the study of Torah; one must be willing to receive Torah even from one who is inferior to him in wisdom (Bartenura). Another explains that one who is not humble is not willing to live frugally, and will devote extensive time to his business dealings. Therefore, in order to minimize one's business dealings and engage in Torah study, he must be humble before every person (Abravanel). On the other hand, some commentaries explain that this statement comes to underscore the significance of humbleness before every person. Even one who abandons his business dealings and engages in Torah study must cultivate a sense of humbleness before every person, even lowly people who are not worthy of it (Meiri, Yaavetz).

There are many factors causing idleness [*betelim*] against you – יֵשׁ לְךָ בְּטֵלִים הַרְבֵּה כְּנֶגְדְּךָ: The commentary here follows the explanation of most commentaries, that this is referring to matters that impede a person and cause him to be idle from his labor (Rashi, Rambam, and others). This is similar to what Rabbi Neḥunya ben HaKana said (3:5), that if anyone removes the yoke of Torah from upon himself, the yoke of the monarchy and the yoke of livelihood are placed upon him. Others explain that "factors causing idleness against you" are various types of suffering sent by God that befall a person as a punishment for dereliction in the study of Torah (Rabbeinu Yona, Bartenura).

Another explanation is that "*betelim*" are most of the people of the world, who engage in their business extensively. If you seek to be like them, you will not have any special virtue, but will merely be one of many. By contrast, with regard to engaging in Torah study, beyond the fact that its individual virtue is great, there are very few people who adopt this path. If you engage in it, you will be extremely special, greater than the rest of the people (Meiri).

There is much reward to be given to you – יֵשׁ לוֹ שָׂכָר הַרְבֵּה לִתֶּן לָךְ: This means that if you engage in Torah study and are not derelict in its regard in order

Mishna 11

This mishna cites additional statements of Rabbi Akiva's disciples.

רַבִּי אֱלִיעֶזֶר בֶּן יַעֲקֹב אוֹמֵר: הָעוֹשֶׂה מִצְוָה אַחַת – קוֹנֶה לוֹ פְּרַקְלִיט אֶחָד. וְהָעוֹבֵר עֲבֵירָה אַחַת – קוֹנֶה לוֹ קַטֵּיגוֹר אֶחָד.

Rabbi Eliezer ben Yaakov[P] **says: One who performs one mitzva**[N] **acquires one advocate for himself,** who will advocate on his behalf on the Day of Judgment, as the merit of the mitzva functions like a defense attorney does in court. Each and every mitzva serves as an advocate of that kind. **And,** conversely, **one who performs one transgression** thereby **acquires one accuser for himself.**

NOTES

to engage in other pursuits, God will give you a great reward, and provide you with all your needs and everything that you lack (Meiri). Some explain that *betelim harbe*, translated here as "many factors causing idleness," is referring to the fact that in contrast to the attribute of punishment, which God administers by means of intermediaries [*betelim harbe*], He Himself gives reward, and thereby gives it generously (Rabbeinu Yona, Bartenura).

One who performs one mitzva – הָעוֹשֶׂה מִצְוָה אַחַת: Some say this means that a person should not think that if he performed one mitzva and one transgression, they balance each other in the general accounting, so he will neither receive a reward nor be punished. In fact, the mitzva is like an advocate and the transgression is like an accuser, and the person receives reward for the mitzva and punishment for the transgression (Meiri).

PERSONALITIES

Rabbi Eliezer ben Yaakov – רַבִּי אֱלִיעֶזֶר בֶּן יַעֲקֹב: A Sage named Rabbi Eliezer ben Yaakov was from the second generation of *tanna'im* and lived at the end of the Second Temple era. After the destruction of the Temple, he transmitted many testimonies regarding the structure of the Temple and related halakhot. According to rabbinic tradition, he was the author of tractate *Middot*, which describes the structure of the Temple (*Yoma* 16a and elsewhere). He is considered very precise in his statements, and it is stated in his regard: "The mishna of Rabbi Eliezer ben Yaakov is measured and immaculate" (*Yevamot* 49b), meaning that his statements were few, but precise. For this reason, the halakha is almost always ruled in accordance with his opinion, although there are exceptions (see the Talmudic Encyclopedia, entry Halakha, paragraph 15).

A Sage named Rabbi Eliezer ben Yaakov is also mentioned as a disciple of Rabbi Akiva (see *Bereshit Rabba* 61:3; Jerusalem Talmud, *Ḥagiga* 3:1). That is why the prevalent theory is that there was an additional *tanna* by that name, who was a member of the fourth generation of *tanna'im*.

תְּשׁוּבָה וּמַעֲשִׂים טוֹבִים, כִּתְרִיס בִּפְנֵי הַפֻּרְעָנוּת.

But one must remember that **repentance and good deeds** become for a person **a shield** [*teris*][B] **against punishment,**[N] so that he will not be harmed.

רַבִּי יוֹחָנָן הַסַּנְדְּלָר אוֹמֵר: כָּל כְּנֵסִיָּה שֶׁהִיא לְשֵׁם שָׁמַיִם – סוֹפָהּ לְהִתְקַיֵּם. וְשֶׁאֵינָהּ לְשֵׁם שָׁמַיִם – אֵין סוֹפָהּ לְהִתְקַיֵּם.

Rabbi Yohanan HaSandlar[P] **says: Any assembly that is for the sake of Heaven,**[N] whose objective is one of sanctity, **will ultimately endure;** the gathering and the connection will endure. **And,** conversely, any assembly **that is not for the sake of Heaven will not ultimately endure.** Even if the people ostensibly have good reasons to gather and be together, reasons will arise to disperse that assembly.

NOTES

Repentance and good deeds become a shield against punishment [*hapuranut*] – תְּשׁוּבָה וּמַעֲשִׂים טוֹבִים כִּתְרִיס בִּפְנֵי הַפֻּרְעָנוּת: Not only is every mitzva an advocate, but even if a person sinned extensively, repentance and good deeds protect him at the moment of punishment (Meiri). Some say that *hapuranut* is referring to natural disasters that befall the world, and not to disasters that come as punishment for sin (*Tosefot Yom Tov*). There is a variant reading: "Torah and good deeds" (Rashbam, *Tosefot Yom Tov*).

Any assembly that is for the sake of Heaven – כָּל כְּנֵסִיָּה שֶׁהִיא לְשֵׁם שָׁמַיִם: Some say that "for the sake of Heaven" means for the sake of Torah and good deeds (Rabbeinu Yona). Others say that it is for the sake of discovering the truth, even regarding profane matters (Meiri; see *Tiferet Yisrael*). There are also those who derive meaning from the fact that the mishna does not say, "for the sake of a mitzva," but, "for the sake of Heaven." It is possible that people will assemble for the sake of performing a mitzva, but if their primary motive is to attain honor or authority, then ultimately this assembly will not endure (*Midrash Shmuel*).

BACKGROUND

Reproduction of a scutum, a Roman shield

Shield [*teris*] – תְּרִיס: From the Greek *tireos*, meaning a large shield. Such a shield was used by the Roman army, and was called a scutum in Latin. A curved rectangular shield, 1 m high and weighing approximately 10 kg, it was crafted from several thin layers of wood, covered in leather, and had a metal protrusion at its center. Its size enabled groups of soldiers to form a protective wall that reached over their heads and enabled them to maneuver while defending themselves.

Mishna 12

This mishna continues citing statements of Rabbi Akiva's disciples.

רַבִּי אֶלְעָזָר בֶּן שַׁמּוּעַ אוֹמֵר: יְהִי כְבוֹד תַּלְמִידְךָ חָבִיב עָלֶיךָ כְּשֶׁלְּךָ,

Rabbi Elazar ben Shammua[P] **says:**[N] **The honor of your student should be as precious to you as your own**[N] honor. Although he is obligated to honor you, treat him with respect, as though he is your equal.

NOTES

Rabbi Elazar ben Shammua says – רַבִּי אֶלְעָזָר בֶּן שַׁמּוּעַ אוֹמֵר: The commentary here is in accordance with most commentaries and with *Avot deRabbi Natan*, that one should honor all others more than they deserve by right. Others explain that it does not mean to honor others beyond what they deserve, but that one should make certain to accord the appropriate honor to each person, just as he is meticulous in according honor to those who are more important than he is. One must be careful to accord his student the honor due him, just as he is careful not to diminish the honor that he accords himself, or his peer, and so on (Rabbeinu Yona, *Pirkei Moshe*).

The honor of your student should be as precious to you as your own – יְהִי כְבוֹד תַּלְמִידְךָ חָבִיב עָלֶיךָ כְּשֶׁלְּךָ: Rashi writes that this is borne out by the fact that the true honor of a teacher is derived from the honor accorded his students. In *Avot deRabbi Natan* (27), this is derived from what Moses said to his disciple Joshua: "Select people for us" (Exodus 17:9). He considered Joshua as his equal.

A variant text reads: "The honor of your student should be as precious to you as that of your peer." According to this, the mishna is explained as an ascending hierarchy of honor. He should honor his student like his peer, his peer like his teacher, and his teacher like the honor of Heaven.

PERSONALITIES

Rabbi Yoḥanan HaSandlar – רַבִּי יוֹחָנָן הַסַּנְדְּלָר: Rabbi Yoḥanan HaSandlar was a disciple of Rabbi Akiva, in the fourth generation of *tanna'im*. It is related that he would learn halakhot from Rabbi Akiva when the latter was in prison (see Jerusalem Talmud, *Yevamot* 12:5). Rabbi Yoḥanan was probably called HaSandlar because he was a cobbler, who crafted sandals. Some suggest that he was a diamond cutter (*Sefer Yuḥasin*). Others suggest that the name of his birthplace, Alexandria, in Egypt (Jerusalem Talmud, *Ḥagiga* 3:1) was the source of his name (*Maharatz Ḥayyut*).

After the bar Kokheva revolt, Rabbi Yoḥanan HaSandlar moved along with the Torah center to the Galilee. Once he sought to go with Rabbi Elazar ben Shammua to study Torah with Rabbi Yehuda ben Beteira in Netzivin in Babylonia, but when they reached the border of the Land of Israel, their anguish over leaving the Land overcame them. They then declared: "Residence in the Land of Israel is equivalent to all the mitzvot in the Torah" (*Sifrei*, *Devarim* 80), and turned around and returned.

Rabbi Elazar ben Shammua – רַבִּי אֶלְעָזָר בֶּן שַׁמּוּעַ: Rabbi Elazar ben Shammua was one of the preeminent students of Rabbi Akiva, and he is the Rabbi Elazar typically cited in the Mishna. He was a priest, and it is stated that he lived an especially long life (*Megilla* 27b). According to tradition, he was one of the ten martyrs who were executed at the end of the period of edicts issued against the Jews in the wake of the bar Kokheva revolt (*Midrash Eleh Ezkera*). He was one of the teachers of Rabbi Yehuda HaNasi, who reported that when people came to learn from him, it was very crowded. Likewise, when they sought to draw a comparison between Rabbi Akiva's generation and the generation of his students, Rabbi Elazar was chosen as the representative of that generation (*Eiruvin* 53a and elsewhere).

וּכְבוֹד חֲבֵרְךָ – כְּמוֹרָא רַבְּךָ,

And the honor of your peer, who is your equal, should be more important to you than your own honor. Treat him **as** you are commanded to do regarding **the awe of your teacher,**[N] being very careful not to demean him or upset him.

וּמוֹרָא רַבְּךָ – כְּמוֹרָא שָׁמַיִם.

And be very exacting regarding **the awe of your teacher,** and relate to him **as** with **the awe of Heaven.**[N]

Mishna 13

This mishna continues citing statements of Rabbi Akiva's disciples.

רַבִּי יְהוּדָה אוֹמֵר: הֱוֵי זָהִיר בַּתַּלְמוּד, שֶׁשִּׁגְגַת תַּלְמוּד עוֹלָה זָדוֹן.

Rabbi Yehuda[P] **says: Be vigilant with study**[N] regarding matters that you learn, in terms of both remembering them and understanding them. **As, an unwitting error** that stems from a misunderstanding **in study is considered intentional.** One who engages in Torah study must be very exacting and avoid errors, both in his own studies and when teaching others.

NOTES

And the honor of your peer as the awe of your teacher – **וּכְבוֹד חֲבֵרְךָ כְּמוֹרָא רַבְּךָ**: Some ask: How is it possible to present honor and awe as comparable? They explain that the similarity is regarding the commitment to each matter. He must consider himself as committed to the honor of his peer as he is committed to the awe of his teacher.

And the awe of your teacher as the awe of Heaven – **וּמוֹרָא רַבְּךָ כְּמוֹרָא שָׁמַיִם**: Since he is the teacher from whom you receive the Torah, he is for you the source of the Torah and continues the chain of tradition from Heaven. That is why you must relate to him with profound honor, just as we are obligated to relate to God with awe. Rashi and others say that the source of this matter is what the Sages expounded from the verse: "You shall fear *et* the Lord your God" (Deuteronomy 6:13). The word *et* is expounded to include the awe of Torah scholars like the awe of Heaven, and all the more so one who is a person's preeminent teacher (*Pesaḥim* 22b).

Be vigilant with study [*batalmud*] – **הֱוֵי זָהִיר בַּתַּלְמוּד**: The term *talmud* here is explained as referring to careful analysis of the rationales of the laws (Rashi), as well as to achieving expertise in them (see Meiri). Regarding this matter, in the Talmud Rabbi Yehuda expounded from biblical verses that for Torah scholars, their "unwitting sins are transformed for them into intentional transgressions." That is why they must expend great effort in engaging in Talmud study (see *Bava Metzia* 33a–b). Although every person must be vigilant regarding this matter when studying, this statement is directed primarily to Sages and teachers, who must be very careful in this regard. In other words, a teacher must be very careful to ensure that his student will not err in his studies, because a student's unwitting error is considered an intentional transgression for the teacher. Some have a variant reading: "Regarding the unwitting error of the student, it is considered intentional" (*Midrash Shmuel*, citing Ritva).

רַבִּי שִׁמְעוֹן אוֹמֵר: שְׁלֹשָׁה כְּתָרִים הֵם: כֶּתֶר תּוֹרָה, וְכֶתֶר כְּהֻנָּה, וְכֶתֶר מַלְכוּת. וְכֶתֶר שֵׁם טוֹב עוֹלֶה עַל גַּבֵּיהֶן.

Rabbi Shimon says: There are three crowns,[N] three virtues in Israel: **The crown of Torah,** the greatness accorded to a person as a result of his studying Torah; **the crown of priesthood,** the greatness of the priests, belonging to the tribe with distinguished lineage, who were privileged to serve

NOTES

There are three crowns – שְׁלֹשָׁה כְּתָרִים הֵן: It is said based on the Talmud (*Yoma* 72b, and see Rabbeinu Yona) that there is an allusion to these crowns in the three crowns [*zerim*] of three of the Temple vessels: the incense altar, corresponding to the priesthood; the shewbread Table in the Sanctuary, corresponding to the kingship; and the Ark of the Testimony in the Holy of Holies, which is the most esteemed and sacred of them all and corresponds to the Torah (see Rambam).

Golden crown that adorns the incense altar

Golden crown that adorns the Ark of the Testimony

PERSONALITIES

Rabbi Yehuda – רַבִּי יְהוּדָה: Rabbi Yehuda, when mentioned in the Mishna, is Rabbi Yehuda ben Rabbi Ilai. His father, Rabbi Ilai, was one of the students of Rabbi Eliezer ben Hyrcanus, and Rabbi Yehuda was one of the students of Rabbi Akiva. He received Torah from other Sages as well, among them, Rabbi Tarfon, Rabbi Yishmael, and Rabbi Elazar ben Azarya. During most of his life he was very poor, but nevertheless, his face was beaming and joyful, as though he were wealthy (*Nedarim* 49b).

Rabbi Yehuda tended to see the positive elements of Roman rule in the Land, which was why the Romans proclaimed that he would be "first among the speakers in every place" (*Shabbat* 33b), meaning that his status was more respected than that of the other Sages. He lived a long life and would issue halakhic rulings in the house of the *Nasi* (*Menaḥot* 104a). This meant that in practice, the house of Rabbi Yehuda HaNasi acted in accordance with his rulings. It is stated that the *Sifra*, also called *Torat Kohanim*, the halakhic midrash on the book of Leviticus, is based primarily on the opinion of Rabbi Yehuda. His son, Rabbi Yosei ben Rabbi Yehuda, was also a significant Torah scholar.

Gravesite of Rabbi Yehuda bar Ilai on the road to Safed

God in the Temple; **and the crown of monarchy,** the greatness of kingship. **But,** although these three are greatly significant crowns, one must remember that **the crown of** a person's **good name,** which he earned through his actions as expressions of his character, **surpasses them.**[N] This is the most significant crown, because it is independent of any external factor.

Mishna 14

This mishna continues citing statements of Rabbi Akiva's disciples regarding Torah study.

רַבִּי נְהוֹרַאי אוֹמֵר:

Rabbi Nehorai[P] **says** statements regarding the importance of Torah study in a place that is a center of Torah and its Sages:

הֱוֵי גוֹלֶה לִמְקוֹם תּוֹרָה. וְאַל תֹּאמַר שֶׁהִיא תָּבוֹא אַחֲרֶיךָ,

Exile yourself from your place **to a place of Torah,**[N] a center of Torah study, even if you are considered wise. **And do not say that it will come after you** to your place because you are a great, important person. As a rule, that does not happen, and even a great man can find himself isolated in his place.

NOTES

The crown of good name surpasses them [*oleh al gabeihen*] – **וְכֶתֶר שֵׁם טוֹב עוֹלֶה עַל גַּבֵּיהֶן**: This crown stems from a person's actions being deemed proper by people, who are impressed by his acts of kindness, his uprightness, and his sanctification of God and His Torah (Meiri; see *Yoma* 86a). Nevertheless, this is not a fourth crown, as the possessor of a good name has no standing that obligates others to honor him, unlike the mitzva to honor the sage, the priest, and the king. But in practice, all of the crowns are measured according to this one. When the bearer of a crown has a good name, his honor is exalted, but if he does not have a good name, he is not worthy of honor (Bartenura). Rashi says likewise that "*oleh al gabeihen*" means that the crown of a good name comes by means of the three crowns. When one engages in Torah, priesthood, and monarchy properly, he acquires a good name for himself.

Exile yourself to a place of Torah – **הֱוֵי גוֹלֶה לִמְקוֹם תּוֹרָה**: When a person seeks to study Torah, and especially to become accomplished in Torah, he must go to a place that is a center of Torah study. This is true not only regarding one who is a student, but also regarding those with wisdom and knowledge (Meiri, Bartenura). Some say that the entire mishna

שֶׁחֲבֵרֶיךָ יְקַיְּמוּהָ בְּיָדֶךָ,

Likewise, do not say when you have a limited group of colleagues **that your colleagues will sustain it for you,**[N] as a small, insular community does not advance its members, especially when these colleagues are not really Torah scholars.

"וְאֶל בִּינָתְךָ אַל תִּשָּׁעֵן".

And in general one should abide by the principle: **"Do not lean on your understanding"** (Proverbs 3:5),[N] as every person requires both teachers and the company of other Sages. In this way he will be confronted with the facts of reality and the opinions of other Sages.

NOTES

is directed toward young students, and is saying that even if they live in a place of Torah, they should exile themselves to another place of Torah. Uprooting oneself from his natural surroundings is advantageous for acquiring the Torah.

That your colleagues will sustain it for you – שֶׁחֲבֵרֶיךָ יְקַיְּמוּהָ בְּיָדֶךָ: The explanation in the commentary follows the simple understanding that this too is one of those matters that "one should not say." He should not say that if he stays in his place, his colleagues will sustain Torah for him; or that it is sufficient for his colleagues to exile themselves to a place of Torah, and when they return, they will transmit to him the lessons that were stated in the study hall (Rashi, Rabbeinu Yona, and others). Others explain that this statement is an explanation of the advantage of a place of Torah. Joint study with one's colleagues is what sustains the Torah for him (Rashi, Rambam, and others).

And do not lean on your understanding – וְאֶל בִּינָתְךָ אַל תִּשָּׁעֵן: This phrase can be understood as a continuation and explanation of what preceded it. A person cannot rely solely on his knowledge and understanding and leave the Torah center. But this also contains a more general statement, which relates to the essential necessity to study together with others. Because a person's thoughts are a self-contained body of knowledge, one who studies by himself in the absence of supervision or criticism is liable to arrive at mistaken conclusions or to engage in insignificant matters. Therefore, only an encounter with the world outside him, with the facts of reality, with life, and with Sages, can create a flow of true knowledge. This does not exist in a person who is by himself.

PERSONALITIES

Rabbi Nehorai – רַבִּי נְהוֹרַאי: There are many opinions regarding the identity of this *tanna*, because in different places in the Talmud various Sages were called by this name, among them Rabbi Elazar ben Arakh, Rabbi Meir, and others (see *Shabbat* 147b and *Eiruvin* 13b). Many explain that the mishna is referring to one of those *tanna'im*. However, it appears simply that this Sage was a *tanna* whose real name was Rabbi Nehorai, and he was a contemporary of the disciples of Rabbi Akiva. He is mentioned in the Mishna, the *Tosefta*, and both the Jerusalem and the Babylonian Talmuds. It also appears that he studied with Rabbi Tarfon.

Among his other statements, Rabbi Nehorai transmitted statements in the name of Rabbi Yehoshua. It is likewise related that he lived when the seat of the Sanhedrin was in Usha, meaning, when Rabban Shimon ben Gamliel was *Nasi* (*Tosefta*, *Rosh HaShana* 1:16). Elsewhere, it is cited in his name: "I set aside all the trades in the world, and I teach my son only Torah, as a person partakes of its reward in this world, and the principal remains for him in the World to Come" (*Kiddushin* 4:4).

Mishna 15

In contrast to the previous mishnayot, which addressed Torah study, this mishna cites statements of Sages that relate to a person's affairs in this world.

רַבִּי יַנַּאי אוֹמֵר:

Rabbi Yannai[P] **says,** describing a person's life in this world:

אֵין בְּיָדֵינוּ לֹא מִשַּׁלְוַת הָרְשָׁעִים, וְאַף לֹא מִיִּסּוּרֵי הַצַּדִּיקִים.

We have in our purview neither the tranquility of the wicked, as they have no pangs of conscience, and at times achieve success in this world, **nor the suffering of the righteous,**[N] who constantly engage in self-assessment and find flaws in themselves, and whose lives in this world are filled with hardship because they seek to follow the straight and narrow path.

רַבִּי מַתְיָא בֶּן חָרָשׁ אוֹמֵר:

Rabbi Matya ben Ḥarash[P] **says,** regarding the appropriate social conduct that a person should follow:

הֱוֵי מַקְדִּים בִּשְׁלוֹם כָּל אָדָם.

Be first in extending **a greeting** to **every person,** even to the simplest people, who, in terms of social hierarchy, are not worthy to be greeted first.

NOTES

We have in our purview neither...nor – אֵין בְּיָדֵינוּ לֹא...וְאַף לֹא: In contrast to the statements of most of the Sages in this tractate, Rabbi Yannai's statement does not contain any specific guidance or direction, but rather a sober description of reality, according to which, peoples' lives cannot be described as extremely good or extremely evil. They are found somewhere between those two poles.

Most commentaries understand this to be addressing the question of the suffering of the righteous and the tranquility of the wicked, an extremely ancient question that appears several times in the Bible (see, e.g., Jeremiah 12:1). Some explain that the meaning of Rabbi Yannai's statement is that it is not in our purview why the world is conducted in this manner. Rashi explains additionally that although from the perspective of simple justice it is not fitting that the righteous suffer while the wicked sin in tranquility, in practice, the world order is not in our hands but in the hands of God, whose thoughts and considerations are far more profound and comprehensive.

וֶהֱוֵי זָנָב לָאֲרָיוֹת, וְאַל תְּהִי רֹאשׁ לַשּׁוּעָלִים.

Be a tail to lions and not a head to foxes.[N] In other words, it is preferable for a person to cleave to great people who perform great deeds, even if he, himself, fills a less valuable role, rather than assuming a leadership position in an inferior, insignificant place.

NOTES

Be a tail to lions and not a head to foxes [*shualim*] – וֶהֱוֵי זָנָב לָאֲרָיוֹת וְאַל תְּהִי רֹאשׁ לַשּׁוּעָלִים: Some say that this is stated not only in terms of joining great people, but with regard to actions as well. Peripheral elements of a weighty matter are more significant than central elements of matters of less value (Yaavetz). In addition, it is always appropriate for a person to bring himself close to those greater than he, as in that way he can learn from their actions (Meiri and others), as it is written: "One who walks with the wise will become wise, and one who shepherds fools will be broken" (Proverbs 13:20).

The term *shual* can be used for both a fox and a jackal. *Tosefot Yom Tov* suggests that it is referring to a fox, due to its reputation for slyness and trickery. This alludes to inferior Torah scholars, who seek to prevail over their colleagues with ploys such as sarcasm and rhetoric.

However, the mishna may be referring to jackals rather than foxes. Foxes are solitary animals, whereas jackals roam in packs. Since the mishna refers to the head of a group of *shualim*, a jackal would seem to be a better identification for this animal. In addition, jackals often follow lions, to scavenge the remains of their prey. Accordingly, the contrast in the mishna between *shualim* and lions may indicate that it is referring to jackals (R. Natan Slifkin).

PERSONALITIES

Rabbi Yannai – רַבִּי יַנַּאי: Rabbi Yannai in this mishna is apparently the Sage who appears throughout the Talmud. He was a disciple of Rabbi Yehuda HaNasi, and lived in the generation that bridged the tannaitic and amoraic periods. Rabbi Yannai played a significant role in the generation of the disciples of Rabbi Yehuda HaNasi. In the Talmud, he is called "Rabbi Yannai Rabba," meaning "the great," and he apparently had a large contingent of disciples, perhaps in the yeshiva that he headed. His Torah statements were transmitted directly and indirectly in various places in the Babylonian and Jerusalem Talmuds. His daughter married Yehuda ben Rabbi Ḥiyya, whom Rabbi Yannai greatly admired and who died at a young age (see *Ketubot* 62b). The most prominent and renowned among his disciples was the *amora* Rabbi Yoḥanan, who eventually became a prominent leader of his generation and a leader of Israel. It is also stated that Rabbi Yehuda Nesia, grandson of Rabbi Yehuda HaNasi, received Torah from Rabbi Yannai.

Rabbi Matya ben Ḥarash – רַבִּי מַתְיָא בֶּן חָרָשׁ: It appears that Rabbi Matya ben Ḥarash was one of the Sages of the Land of Israel, and he was tied to the Sages in Yavne, especially Rabbi Yehoshua and Rabbi Eliezer, to whom he posed a variety of halakhic questions. Sometime later, he established residence in Rome. It was said in his regard that it is worthwhile to go that far in order to receive Torah from him (*Sanhedrin* 32b). Several places in the Talmud describe his meetings with the Sages of Israel, who came to visit the city of Rome in order to make efforts on behalf of the Jewish people. It is conceivable that he served as both their host and their translator.

From his statements, it appears that he was involved in the life of the Roman city and was well versed in the popular local sayings. Presumably, this statement of Rabbi Matya ben Ḥarash is the converse of what Julius Caesar is said to have stated when he was in a small village in Gaul, that he prefers to be the most important person in that village than the second-most important in Rome. Other than in this mishna, Rabbi Matya ben Ḥarash is mentioned in a mishna in tractate *Yoma* (8:6), and other statements in his name are cited in both Talmuds and in midrash.

Mishna 16

In continuation of the previous mishna, this mishna cites matters connected to a person's situation in this world.

רַבִּי יַעֲקֹב אוֹמֵר: הָעוֹלָם הַזֶּה דּוֹמֶה לִפְרוֹזְדוֹר בִּפְנֵי הָעוֹלָם הַבָּא; הַתְקֵן עַצְמְךָ בִּפְרוֹזְדוֹר, כְּדֵי שֶׁתִּכָּנֵס לַטְּרַקְלִין.

Rabbi Yaakov[P] **says:** This is the way a person should view this world and the events that transpire in it. **This world is similar to a vestibule** [*perozedor*][B] **before the World to Come.**[N] In other words, it is not a place of permanence and not the center of human aspirations. It is merely a place of preparation, the only entrance into the World to Come. As a result, **prepare yourself in the vestibule,**[N] as people typically adjust their garments and appearance there, **so that you may enter the great hall** [*teraklin*][N] in the most honorable and appropriate manner.

NOTES

This world is similar…before the World to Come – הָעוֹלָם הַזֶּה דּוֹמֶה...בִּפְנֵי הָעוֹלָם הַבָּא: Rabbi Yaakov's statements address the relationship between this world and the World to Come. In rabbinic literature, these concepts are interpreted in two different ways. In one usage, this world is the corporeal world in which we live, and the World to Come is the world to which the soul goes after a person dies. In the other usage, this world is the entire world known to us from the history of man until now, and the World to Come is the time that will be in the future, after the revival of the dead. Thus, the commentaries explained these *mishnayot* according to these two meanings.

Prepare yourself in the vestibule – הַתְקֵן עַצְמְךָ בִּפְרוֹזְדוֹר: Some say this means not merely that this world serves as a precursor to the World to Come, but that it is possible to transform it into a microcosm of the World to Come. When a person engages in this world in the spiritual matters that prepare him for the World to Come, he transforms this world into a great hall (Yaavetz).

So that you may enter the great hall – כְּדֵי שֶׁתִּכָּנֵס לַטְּרַקְלִין: Some explain that the point is to underscore that all the toil in this world is only to merit entry into the great hall. However, after one enters, remaining there is a gift of kindness, as it is explained in the following mishna that one hour of the World to Come is better than an entire lifetime in this world, even if it was filled with repentance and good deeds (*Midrash Shmuel*).

PERSONALITIES

Rabbi Yaakov – רַבִּי יַעֲקֹב: There were several *tanna'im* with this name, and they were roughly contemporaries, so it is difficult to identify which of them made the statement cited in the mishna. However, it appears that he was the son of the daughter of Elisha ben Avuya, also known as Aḥer (see mishna 20), as Sages commented that his statement, relating to the relationship between this world and the World to Come, blatantly counters a statement by Elisha ben Avuya (*Kiddushin* 39b). They added that if only Elisha had understood the matters that his grandson had stated, he would not have gone astray. It is also conceivable that this Rabbi Yaakov is Rabbi Yaakov ben Kurshai, who was Rabbi Yehuda HaNasi's teacher for a time.

Mishna 17

This mishna cites an additional statement of Rabbi Yaakov regarding the relationship between this world and the World to Come.

הוּא הָיָה אוֹמֵר: יָפָה שָׁעָה אַחַת בִּתְשׁוּבָה וּמַעֲשִׂים טוֹבִים בָּעוֹלָם הַזֶּה, מִכָּל חַיֵּי הָעוֹלָם הַבָּא.

He, Rabbi Yaakov, **would say:** Although this world is transitory, and one remains in it for only a brief time, nevertheless, it has great significance. As, **better is one hour of repentance**[N] **and good deeds**[N] **in this world,** where the possibility exists to grow genuinely close to God by means of internal, practical changes, **than the entire lifetime in the World to Come.** In the World to Come, a person leads a primarily passive existence, and it is merely a consequence and reward for life in this world. That is why the possibility that exists to achieve a substantive ascent in this world is of much greater value than the entire life in the World to Come.

NOTES

Repentance [*teshuva*] – תְּשׁוּבָה: Some say that this is referring not only to repentance for sins, but also to refraining from transgression. That too is called *teshuva*, because the person recoils [*shav*] and withdraws from his natural attraction to the transgression (Ri ibn Shoshan in *Midrash Shmuel*).

Better is one hour of repentance and good deeds – יָפָה שָׁעָה אַחַת בִּתְשׁוּבָה וּמַעֲשִׂים טוֹבִים: Many explain that this is referring to the very performance of mitzvot in this world, as it is impossible to perform them in the World to Come. It is written in the *Tanya* that the reason that one hour in this world is greater is that the spiritual virtue of the performance of a mitzva is incalculably greater than the spiritual virtue of satisfaction that one experiences in the World to Come. However, in the World to Come the soul is able to enjoy that satisfaction, while in this world, the pleasure of the virtue of performing the mitzva is not sensed. Others write that not every moment of good deeds in this world is greater than the entire lifetime in the World to Come. However, there are decisive moments during which a person can gain extremely great benefit, as the Sages said: "There is one who acquires his world in one moment" (Meiri and others).

BACKGROUND

Perozedor and teraklin – פְּרוֹזְדוֹר וּטְרַקְלִין: The word *perozedor* apparently derives from the Greek *prostada*, meaning before the entry, in other words, the vestibule leading to the great hall, where one entertains guests. The word *teraklin* is from the Greek *teraklinion*, meaning "a dining room with three divans," but its meaning expanded to "a great hall for entertaining guests."

וְיָפָה שָׁעָה אַחַת שֶׁל קוֹרַת רוּחַ בָּעוֹלָם הַבָּא, מִכָּל חַיֵּי הָעוֹלָם הַזֶּה.

On the other hand, one must remember that in terms of delight and happiness, **better is one hour of satisfaction [*korat ruaḥ*]**[N] **in the World to Come than the entire lifetime in this world.** Life in this world, with all the sources of delight that it can provide, is ultimately limited, in terms of the physical receptors of feeling and sensation, which are unable to bear more than a certain level of stimulation. This is true even from a spiritual perspective; since the person's soul is connected to the body, it too is greatly limited. That is why life in the World to Come, where these limitations no longer exist, contains exponentially greater delight than the entire life in this world.

Mishna 18

This mishna cites guidance by Rabbi Shimon ben Elazar regarding considerate, intelligent interpersonal conduct.

רַבִּי שִׁמְעוֹן בֶּן אֶלְעָזָר אוֹמֵר:

Rabbi Shimon ben Elazar[P] **says:**[N]

אַל תְּרַצֶּה אֶת חֲבֵרְךָ בִּשְׁעַת כַּעֲסוֹ,

Do not attempt to **conciliate your counterpart when he is angry,** as at that moment it is ineffective and unwise to seek to pacify him. Due to his enflamed anger, he will ignore the words of conciliation, and might react even more angrily.

וְאַל תְּנַחֲמֶנּוּ בְּשָׁעָה שֶׁמֵּתוֹ מֻטָּל לְפָנָיו,

On a similar note, **do not** attempt to **console him when his dead relative is laid out before him**

NOTES

Satisfaction [*korat ruaḥ*] – קוֹרַת רוּחַ: Rashi explains that this is from the expression "he was placated [*nitkarera daato*], meaning that his spirit achieved calm and tranquility because it achieved its desire (see *Tiferet Yisrael*).

Rabbi Shimon ben Elazar says – רַבִּי שִׁמְעוֹן בֶּן אֶלְעָזָר אוֹמֵר: There is one fundamental principle behind the various sayings of Rabbi Shimon ben Elazar: Be considerate of someone when he is in a tense situation. Attempting to intervene, even with the best of intentions, is generally not effective, and sometimes just exacerbates the problem.

before burial, as at that time his pain is extremely acute. Words of consolation at a time like that are ineffective, and sometimes only exacerbate the grief.

וְאַל תִּשְׁאַל לוֹ בִּשְׁעַת נִדְרוֹ,

Do not ask him questions whose objective is to find an extenuation to dissolve the vow, **at the** very **moment of his vow,**[N] as then, he is still influenced by the experience and the emotion that caused him to vow. Discussing those matters at that moment is ineffective, and could even cause the one who took the vow to reinforce his vow and add to it.

וְאַל תִּשְׁתַּדֵּל לִרְאוֹתוֹ בִּשְׁעַת קַלְקָלָתוֹ.

Do not seek to see him at the moment of his failure,[N] as the awkwardness and embarrassment involved in having been seen can continue much longer than the failure itself.

NOTES

Do not ask him questions at the moment of his vow – וְאַל תִּשְׁאַל לוֹ בִּשְׁעַת נִדְרוֹ: In general, when a person takes a vow and commits to perform a certain action, refrain from actions or certain pleasures, or prohibits himself from maintaining ties with another person, he usually does so at a moment of great emotion, due to anger or to extricate himself from a difficult situation. Therefore, even though from a halakhic standpoint it is possible to bring about dissolution of a vow, by indicating to the one who vowed that he did not take into account all the potential problems that could arise from this vow, and thereby enable dissolution of the vow (see *Nedarim* chapter 9), one should not suggest these possibilities at the moment of the vow, while he is still in the midst of the experience that led him to take the vow. Some offer an additional explanation: When one takes a vow to perform an action, do not ask him to fulfill the vow immediately after he takes it. It is possible that if you wait, he might later regret the vow and seek to dissolve it, and then he would not need to pay the price (Rashi).

Do not seek to see him at the moment of his failure – וְאַל תִּשְׁתַּדֵּל לִרְאוֹתוֹ בִּשְׁעַת קַלְקָלָתוֹ: This refers both to a moment when the other sinned, and to a moment when he was injured (Rabbeinu Yona). Some explain that typically a person goes to a friend to visit him and support him in his time of trouble. For this reason, a special warning is necessary to caution against going to another in his moment of failure. Doing so could be misinterpreted as rejoicing at his downfall, which would have the opposite of the intended effect of increasing connection between them. Therefore, one must wait a bit and approach the friend only after the moment of failure has passed (*Pirkei Moshe*).

PERSONALITIES

Rabbi Shimon ben Elazar – רַבִּי שִׁמְעוֹן בֶּן אֶלְעָזָר: Rabbi Shimon ben Elazar, the preeminent student of Rabbi Meir, lived in the final generation of the *tanna'im*. He was a contemporary and a colleague of Rabbi Yehuda HaNasi, and there are several places where they disagreed. Likewise, because he was a member of the final generation, few statements are cited in the Mishna in his name, and most of his statements appear in the *Tosefta*, other *baraitot*, and the two Talmuds. Among the little that is known about him is the fact that he lived most of his life in the city of Tiberias. Furthermore, he lived a very long time, so that various Sages from the early generations of the *amora'im* received Torah from him directly and indirectly.

Mishna 19

In the previous mishna Rabbi Shimon ben Elazar cautioned against seeing one's counterpart at the moment of his failure. This mishna continues that topic with the statement of an earlier Sage.

שְׁמוּאֵל הַקָּטָן אוֹמֵר:

Shmuel HaKatan[P] **says;** he cites a verse from the book of Proverbs:

"בִּנְפֹל אוֹיִבְךָ אַל תִּשְׂמָח וּבִכָּשְׁלוֹ אַל יָגֵל לִבֶּךָ, פֶּן יִרְאֶה ה' וְרַע בְּעֵינָיו וְהֵשִׁיב מֵעָלָיו אַפּוֹ".

"With the fall of your enemy[N] **rejoice not,**[N] **and in his stumbling let your heart not be glad, lest the Lord see it, and it is evil in His eyes, and He turn away His wrath from him"** (Proverbs 24:17–18);[N] He will remove His wrath from him.

NOTES

With the fall of your enemy – בִּנְפֹל אוֹיִבְךָ: Some understand that because Shmuel HaKatan would cite this verse regularly, it became a saying identified with him, as the choice of a certain verse can constitute a personal statement.

With the fall of your enemy rejoice not – בִּנְפֹל אֹיִבְךָ אַל תִּשְׂמָח: Many commentaries note that this is referring to hatred that exists between two people for personal reasons, but not to the downfall of the wicked or of enemies of Israel, regarding which it is appropriate to rejoice (Rashbatz; see Maharal of Prague and *Megilla* 16a). However, others note that it is permitted for the righteous to rejoice over the downfall of the wicked only if he is not his enemy; as if he is his enemy, there is room for concern that his joy is tainted by personal feelings. It is also conceivable that this enemy is not, in fact, deserving of punishment, but that hatred is skewing the judgment of the person rejoicing, who is certain that his counterpart is deserving of punishment for his wickedness (*Tiferet Yisrael*).

PERSONALITIES

Shmuel HaKatan – שְׁמוּאֵל הַקָּטָן: Shmuel HaKatan was a Sage who lived during the end of the Second Temple period and in the Yavne period. Later generations venerated him greatly, and it was stated that he was called by that name because his stature was only slightly lower than that of Samuel [Shmuel] the prophet (Jerusalem Talmud, *Sota* 9:13). It is also possible that he was the first one named Shmuel after many generations, and he was called that in order to distinguish between him and Samuel the prophet. It was said in his praise that had the generation been worthy, he would have merited being a prophet of Israel. Likewise, it is related that as he was dying he said several matters of prophecy about the prominent leaders of Israel, all of which came to pass (*Sota* 48b).

While few of his Torah statements remain, it is known that he was extremely humble, and he would accept the guilt of others upon himself (*Sanhedrin* 11a). It was specifically for that reason that he was selected during the Yavne period to compose the blessing of the heretics. This is the additional blessing added to the original eighteen blessings of the *Amida* prayer, and it includes a curse on heretics and informants (*Berakhot* 28b). He was chosen because it was known that he bore no personal grudge against anyone, and this ensured that no hatred or personal revenge was intermingled into the formula of the blessing.

Mishna 20

In this mishna, the focus returns to Torah study, with various distinctions drawn between young and old.

אֱלִישָׁע בֶּן אֲבוּיָה אוֹמֵר:

Elisha ben Avuya[P] **says:**

הַלּוֹמֵד יֶלֶד לְמַה הוּא דוֹמֶה? לִדְיוֹ כְּתוּבָה עַל נְיָר חָדָשׁ. וְהַלּוֹמֵד זָקֵן לְמַה הוּא דוֹמֶה? לִדְיוֹ כְּתוּבָה עַל נְיָר מָחוּק.

With regard to **one who studies when** he is **a child,** a young man, **to what is** what **he** learned **comparable?**[N] **To ink**

NOTES

And He turn away [*veheshiv*] His wrath from him – וְהֵשִׁיב מֵעָלָיו אַפּוֹ: Some explain that when one's enemy rejoices at his downfall, the result is that his punishment becomes greater than what he deserves; therefore, the wrath of God is removed from him. Moreover, God agonizes, as it were, when He exacts punishment against someone, and when one who hates that person rejoices, rather than grieving along with God, he is destined to be judged for it (Yaavetz, *Tiferet Yisrael*; see Bartenura, and see Malbim on the verse in Proverbs). Likewise, some infer from the use of the transitive verb *veheshiv* rather than the intransitive verb *veshav*, that not only will the punishment cease from the enemy, but it will afflict the person who rejoiced (Rashi and others).

One who studies when a child, to what is he comparable – הַלּוֹמֵד יֶלֶד לְמַה הוּא דוֹמֶה: Many commentaries say that this is stated regarding memory. What one learns at a young age is etched in his memory, and what is learned at an advanced age is quickly forgotten (Rashi, Rambam, and others). Some say that it is stated regarding the acuity of study and the clarity stemming from concentration (*Tiferet Yisrael*). Another says that it is referring to one who began studying when he was a child and continued studying until he was elderly. In that case, his Torah is clear and lucid, like writing on new paper, because he had an extended period to order and delve into it (*Midrash Shmuel*).

PERSONALITIES

Elisha ben Avuya – אֱלִישָׁע בֶּן אֲבוּיָה: Elisha ben Avuya is one of the tragic figures among the *tanna'im*. He was born in Jerusalem to a wealthy family that was apparently not very involved with Torah; however, he engaged in Torah study and became one of the most significant Sages. He is enumerated among the four who "entered the orchard," i.e., engaged in Torah mysticism, and was apparently a disciple-colleague of Rabbi Akiva. Eventually, he underwent a severe spiritual crisis that was apparently caused by a combination of failure to comprehend certain matters of Torah mysticism and national tragedies that transpired after the suppression of the bar Kokheva revolt. As a result, he completely abandoned the world of Judaism, and even collaborated with the Romans, who persecuted those who engaged in Torah study. The Sages of Israel shunned him and called him by the appellation *Aḥer*, meaning the other.

It seems that in his later years he returned and engaged in Torah study, at least as an intellectual pursuit, and the *tanna* Rabbi Meir, learned Torah from him, despite the complexity involved in learning Torah from such a figure. Rabbi Meir even sought to encourage Elisha to repent (see *Ḥagiga* 15a–b).

The mention of his statements in tractate *Avot*, as well as in other sources, constitutes, to a certain extent, a distinction between his tragic life and character, and his Torah in and of itself (see Rashbatz). In *Avot deRabbi Natan* (24) an entire chapter is devoted to his sayings, many of which relate to the contents of his statement cited in this mishna.

[*deyo*][B] **written on new paper [*neyar*],**[B] as everything that is written on the paper emerges bright and clear, and never becomes completely erased even after time has passed. But, by contrast, **one who studies when elderly, to what is he comparable? To ink written on erased paper,** as the paper was written upon, then erased, and then written upon again; the writing is not clear, and is easily erased.

The mishna cites a different aspect of this distinction.

רַבִּי יוֹסֵי בַּר יְהוּדָה אִישׁ כְּפַר הַבַּבְלִי אוֹמֵר:

Rabbi Yosei bar Yehuda of Kefar HaBavli[P] **says:**

הַלּוֹמֵד מִן הַקְּטַנִּים לְמַה הוּא דוֹמֶה? לְאוֹכֵל עֲנָבִים קֵהוֹת וְשׁוֹתֶה יַיִן מִגִּתּוֹ. וְהַלּוֹמֵד מִן הַזְּקֵנִים לְמַה הוּא דוֹמֶה? לְאוֹכֵל עֲנָבִים בְּשׁוּלוֹת וְשׁוֹתֶה יַיִן יָשָׁן.

One who learns from the young, from young people, **to what is it comparable? To one eating grapes** that are **not** sufficiently **ripe, and** likewise, to one **drinking wine directly from the winepress,**[N] grape juice fresh from the winepress, with none of the characteristics of wine. Similarly, the

NOTES

To one eating grapes that are not ripe [*kehot*], and drinking wine directly from the winepress – לְאוֹכֵל עֲנָבִים קֵהוֹת וְשׁוֹתֶה יַיִן מִגִּתּוֹ: Grapes that are *kehot* are unripe grapes that set one's teeth on edge, as the verse states: "Each man who eats unripe grapes, his teeth will be set on edge [*tik'hena*]" (Jeremiah 31:29). The premise is that when young people have something to say or teach, their thoughts are not fully

Unripe grapes

Wine from the winepress

Torah of young people lacks maturity and completeness. By contrast, **one who learns from the elderly, to what is it comparable? To one eating ripe grapes and drinking old wine,** as their words are based on extensive knowledge, judgment, and experience, and they are profound and established.

NOTES

developed, and they lack the broad, profound ability to reason that comes with experience. The commentaries write that the two allegories, unripe fruit and wine from the winepress, constitute an allusion to two different aspects of Torah study: the preparations necessary for study and the conclusions that emerge from it (Yaavetz), or the revealed plain understanding and the concealed mysticism (*Midrash Shmuel*).

PERSONALITIES

Rabbi Yosei bar Yehuda of Kefar HaBavli – רַבִּי יוֹסֵי בַּר יְהוּדָה אִישׁ כְּפַר הַבַּבְלִי: This Sage had this appellation to distinguish him from Rabbi Yosei ben Rabbi Yehuda bar Ilai. Virtually nothing is known about him other than his having lived in Kefar HaBavli, which could be one of the villages of the Babylonian Jews who arrived in the Land of Israel during Herod's reign. Some suggest identifying it, based on similarity between the names, with Ḥirbat al Babliya, in the western Negev, adjacent to the Gevaram ridge, near Beror Ḥayil (Y. Peres). An additional Sage who resided in that village was Rabbi Neḥunya ben Elinatan; he is mentioned in tractate *Eduyyot* (6:2), and was a member of the generation of Rabbi Yehoshua and Rabbi Eliezer.

Kefar HaBavli

BACKGROUND

Deyo – דְּיוֹ: *Deyo* is a general term for substances used for writing, as far back as the biblical era. *Deyo* in the time of the mishna was made of soot or coal dust mixed with tree sap or with glue to make the pigment adhere to the writing surface, i.e., parchment or paper. It would be preserved as a solid block of pigment that would be ground and then dissolved in water before use.

Neyar – נְיָר: *Neyar* was the primary writing surface in ancient times. Its primary origins were in Egypt, where it was prepared from papyrus stalk (*Cyperus papyrus*), and it may have been produced in the Land of Israel as well. The papyrus stalk reaches a thickness of 5 cm and a height of 4 m, and it is white and spongy inside. They would spread out long, thin strips of it, which they would then stretch and attach to one another with the liquid of the plant and with glue. After it dried they would attach an additional layer, creating a thin surface for writing. They would finish preparing it by smoothing it with a round stone. This paper-like material was also utilized in wrapping food, and in preparation of utensils and even garments (*Kelim* 2:2, 5:2).

Blank papyrus

The mishna cites a response to the statement of Rabbi Yosei bar Yehuda, which utilizes the same imagery that he utilized himself.

רַבִּי אוֹמֵר: אַל תִּסְתַּכֵּל בַּקַּנְקַן, אֶלָּא בְּמַה שֶּׁיֵּשׁ בּוֹ; יֵשׁ קַנְקַן חָדָשׁ מָלֵא יָשָׁן, וְיָשָׁן שֶׁאֲפִילּוּ חָדָשׁ אֵין בּוֹ.

Rabbi Yehuda HaNasi **says: Do not look at the jug**[N] of wine, the age of the person speaking, **but rather at its contents,** the contents of his statement, as there is not always a direct correlation between a person's age and his knowledge. At times, **there is a new jug that contains old** wine, a young person who is wise, with all the virtues of the words of the elders. **And,** on the other hand, there could be **an old** jug **that does not contain even new** wine, an elderly person who is completely lacking in knowledge.

NOTES

Rabbi Yehuda HaNasi says, do not look at the jug – רַבִּי אוֹמֵר אַל תִּסְתַּכֵּל בַּקַּנְקַן: Rabbi does not actually dispute the statement of Rabbi Yosei bar Yehuda. Rather, he says that one should not draw conclusions from the principle, as there are specific instances where the contents of the jug could be different from its appearance (*Tiferet Yisrael*). There is an additional explanation that this was not stated specifically about Torah study, but rather about respect. One should not respect a person based on his appearance, but rather one should examine his character to determine what "wine" he contains (Rashi).

Jugs from the Cave of Letters, bar Kokheva era

Mishna 21

רַבִּי אֶלְעָזָר הַקַּפָּר אוֹמֵר:

Rabbi Elazar HaKappar[P] **says:**

הַקִּנְאָה, וְהַתַּאֲוָה, וְהַכָּבוֹד – מוֹצִיאִין אֶת הָאָדָם מִן הָעוֹלָם.

Envy of others, **lust** for matters like physical pleasure or wealth, **and** pursuit of **honor**[N] **banish a person from the world.** Each of these is liable to constitute a stumbling block, lead him to perform prohibited acts, and dominate his conduct. Consequently, he will ultimately lose his life, both in this world and in the World to Come.

NOTES

Envy, lust, and honor – הַקִּנְאָה וְהַתַּאֲוָה וְהַכָּבוֹד: There is an element of irrationality in each of these matters. When a person becomes entangled in one of them, he is unable to limit it or compartmentalize it, but rather, he is drawn after it to the point of self-destruction and the ruin of others. That is "banishment from the world."

Some explain that these three matters are stages in a person's development. At a young age, envy is one of the central, conspicuous motives in a person's emotional life. Years then follow in which appetites of all kinds become a central motive. Later, when a person physically and spiritually transcends this motive, he reaches the stage of pursuit of honor, which does not leave him until his final day.

PERSONALITIES

Rabbi Elazar HaKappar – רַבִּי אֶלְעָזָר הַקַּפָּר: Rabbi Elazar HaKappar lived in the generation that bridged the tannaitic and amoraic periods. That is why his statements can be found in the *Tosefta*, the Talmud, and midrash. His statements are primarily aggadic; however, some halakhic matters are cited in his name, as well as traditions from previous generations. It appears that his initial place of residence was the city of Lod; later he resided in the Golan, where remnants of his study hall were discovered. The prominent *amora* Rabbi Yehoshua ben Levi was his disciple.

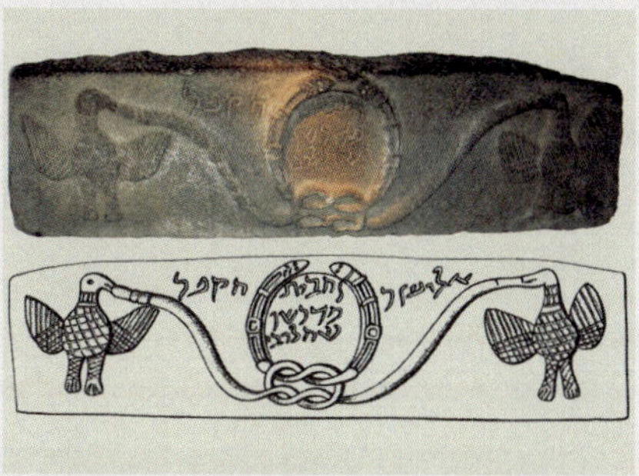

Inscription: "This is the study hall of Rabbi Elazar HaKappar," Golan Heights

Mishna 22

This mishna continues citing statements of Rabbi Elazar HaKappar.

הוּא הָיָה אוֹמֵר:

He, Rabbi Elazar HaKappar, **would say:**

הַיִּלּוֹדִים – לָמוּת, וְהַמֵּתִים – לְהֵחָיוֹת, וְהַחַיִּים – לִידּוֹן.

The born will ultimately **die, and the dead will** ultimately **be revived** in the End of Days. **The** people **living** in this world, as well as those who will be resurrected in the revival of the dead, **will be judged**[N] and sentenced on the basis of their actions.

לֵידַע לְהוֹדִיעַ וּלְהִוָּדַע שֶׁהוּא אֵל, הוּא הַיּוֹצֵר, הוּא הַבּוֹרֵא, הוּא הַמֵּבִין,

These matters a person must himself **know, inform** others, **and be informed**[N] with absolute certainty: **that** the Holy One blessed be **He is** the only **God, He is the Maker, He is the Creator**[N] of the world and of humanity, **and He is the One who understands** everything in the world.

NOTES

The born will die and the dead will be revived. The living will be judged – הַיִּלּוֹדִים לָמוּת וְהַמֵּתִים לְהֵחָיוֹת וְהַחַיִּים לִידּוֹן: This underscores that there is a circle of life and death, and all its aspects are fixed. One must take into account that this is the way of the world, and there is no alternative to accepting it. Everyone born will ultimately die, and they must remember this during their lifetime. The dead will ultimately be resurrected and stand trial, as it is written: "Many of those sleeping in the dust of the earth will awaken; these to eternal life, and those to reviling and eternal disgrace" (Daniel 12:2). This has significance for people, as stated explicitly later in the mishna, as death is not the end of reality. It means that ultimately people have tasks and responsibilities which they can never disregard.

Know, inform, and be informed – לֵידַע לְהוֹדִיעַ וּלְהִוָּדַע: There are certain matters that a person simply knows, sometimes based on faith or on a clear perspective. But other matters can be learned only in a more complicated manner, and a person becomes aware of these matters only after the passage of time. This is the explanation here: Of the matters here, some are known now, and some will be known in the future, when God will be revealed before all His creations, who will know the truth with certainty and clarity (see Rabbeinu Yona). The Rambam says that "know" is referring to the living, "inform" is referring to the dead, and those resurrected are to "be informed," "that He is God, He is the Maker…."

He is God, He is the Maker, He is the Creator – שֶׁהוּא אֵל הוּא הַיּוֹצֵר הוּא הַבּוֹרֵא: Some say that "He is God" relates to human mortality, as that is a clear indication that the Holy One blessed be He alone is God. "He is the Maker" relates to when a person is born, and the fact that "He is the Creator" will become clear in the future, with the revival of the dead, which is an act of *ex nihilo* creation (Yaavetz). Meiri explains that

הוּא הַדַּיָּן, הוּא עֵד, הוּא בַּעַל דִּין, וְהוּא עָתִיד לָדוּן.

Likewise, He knows all the actions that were performed and all the thoughts that were contemplated; **He is the Judge,** and **He is** the **Witness** in the trial and sentence. **He is** also the **Plaintiff,**[N] as He has demands from and claims against those standing trial, **and He is destined to judge** in the ultimate, final trial after the revival of the dead.

בָּרוּךְ הוּא, שֶׁאֵין לְפָנָיו לֹא עַוְלָה, וְלֹא שִׁכְחָה, וְלֹא מַשּׂוֹא פָנִים, וְלֹא מִקַּח שֹׁחַד, שֶׁהַכֹּל שֶׁלּוֹ.

Blessed is He, the Judge of the world, **before whom,** as opposed to a judge of flesh and blood, **there is** during trial **no injustice, no forgetfulness, no favoritism, and no taking of bribes,**[N] not even bribes of good deeds, **as everything is His,** and His judgment cannot be swayed.

NOTES

"He is God" in the sense that He is mighty, zealous, and vengeful; "Maker" in the sense that He renews Creation each and every day; and "Creator" in the sense that He created the world in the beginning.

He is the Plaintiff – הוּא בַּעַל דִּין: In other words, all people are obligated to worship God, and when they conduct themselves improperly, He is the plaintiff against them. This comes to underscore that this is not a standard trial between two litigants in which God is a neutral judge. Rather, He Himself has demands and claims from the world that is standing trial before Him.

No favoritism and no taking of bribes – וְלֹא מַשּׂוֹא פָנִים וְלֹא מִקַּח שֹׁחַד: The source of this phrase is in the verse: "Now let the fear of the Lord be upon you; observe and perform, for there is no injustice, favoritism, and taking bribes with the Lord our God" (II Chronicles 19:7). The commentaries explain that this means that God is not "bribed" by performance of mitzvot and good deeds, and those positive actions do not expunge the transgressions. Rather, He punishes for transgressions separately, and recompenses for mitzvot separately, each according to its value and its reckoning (Rambam and others, based on *Sifrei*, *Devarim* 33:6).

וְדַע, שֶׁהַכֹּל לְפִי הַחֶשְׁבּוֹן. וְאַל יַבְטִיחֲךָ יִצְרְךָ שֶׁהַשְּׁאוֹל בֵּית מָנוֹס לָךְ, שֶׁעַל כָּרְחֲךָ אַתָּה נוֹצָר, וְעַל כָּרְחֲךָ אַתָּה נוֹלָד, וְעַל כָּרְחֲךָ אַתָּה חַי, וְעַל כָּרְחֲךָ אַתָּה מֵת, וְעַל כָּרְחֲךָ אַתָּה עָתִיד לִתֵּן דִּין וְחֶשְׁבּוֹן לִפְנֵי מֶלֶךְ מַלְכֵי הַמְּלָכִים הַקָּדוֹשׁ בָּרוּךְ הוּא.

Know that everything that is performed in this trial **is according to** a precise **reckoning**[N] of matters. **Do not allow your** evil **inclination to assure you that the grave is a refuge for you.** Death is not a place where a person can flee the troubles of this world and the responsibility that he bears. The great course of a person's life is not a matter of choice, but a matter of compulsion, **as perforce you are formed** in your mother's womb, which requires neither your will nor your consent, **and perforce you are born** and emerge into the world, **and perforce you live** thereafter, **and perforce you die, and perforce you are destined to give an accounting before the King of kings, the Holy One blessed be He.**

NOTES

That everything is according to a reckoning – שֶׁהַכֹּל לְפִי הַחֶשְׁבּוֹן: Yaavetz explains that when judging, God takes into consideration that people were created different from one another regarding their life circumstances and their abilities, to the extent that at times an act that appears to be a transgression is primarily an act of the wicked person overcoming his inclination, which sought to entice him to commit a much greater transgression. Likewise, an act that appears to be a mitzva could be in actuality an act of indolence and wickedness, because the one who performed it could have accomplished much more. Only God truly understands these matters, and He considers them when sitting in judgment.

Chapter 5

The fifth chapter of tractate *Avot* is its final chapter. Chapter 6 is a later addition. This chapter is based primarily on unattributed statements, and is structured as a series of numbers, a format that also appears in the Bible (see Proverbs, chap. 30); the statements in this chapter are arranged in descending order, from ten down. The beginning of the chapter is devoted to matters of Creation and of providence over Israel. Later, the Mishna focuses on the conduct of groups of people, on both the group level and on the level of the individuals who are components of the group. At the end of the chapter, the Mishna returns to address the special matters relating to studying Torah and adhering to it.

Mishna 1

The first *mishnayot* of the chapter detail, in chronological order, matters with ten components, beginning with the creation of the world.

בַּעֲשָׂרָה מַאֲמָרוֹת נִבְרָא הָעוֹלָם.

With ten statements of the Holy One blessed be He, **the world was created,**[N] as described at the beginning of the book of Genesis, e.g., "God said: Let there be light" (Genesis 1:3); "God said: Let there be a firmament" (Genesis 1:6).

NOTES

With ten statements the world was created – בַּעֲשָׂרָה מַאֲמָרוֹת נִבְרָא הָעוֹלָם: This is referring to the number of times that "God said" is stated in the course of an act of Creation: "let there be light" (Genesis 1:3); "let there be a firmament" (Genesis 1:6); "let the water be gathered" (Genesis 1:9); "let the earth sprout grass" (Genesis 1:11); "let there be lights" (Genesis 1:14); "let the water swarm" (Genesis 1:20);

וּמַה תַּלְמוּד לוֹמַר? וַהֲלֹא בְּמַאֲמָר אֶחָד יָכוֹל לְהִבָּרְאוֹת!

The question arises: **What does** all **this** detail **teach,** since, after all, **couldn't** the world **have been created with one statement,**[N] such as, "Let there be a world"?

אֶלָּא לְהִפָּרַע מִן הָרְשָׁעִים, שֶׁמְּאַבְּדִין אֶת הָעוֹלָם שֶׁנִּבְרָא בַּעֲשָׂרָה מַאֲמָרוֹת, וְלִיתֵּן שָׂכָר טוֹב לַצַּדִּיקִים, שֶׁמְּקַיְּימִין אֶת הָעוֹלָם שֶׁנִּבְרָא בַּעֲשָׂרָה מַאֲמָרוֹת.

Rather, the detail of the statements **is** intended to underscore the utmost significance of each component of Creation, and, as a result, **to exact punishment** with greater vigor **from the wicked,**[N] **who,** with their evil deeds, **destroy** and ruin **the world,**[N] **which was created with ten statements; and to give fine reward,** with greater vigor, **to the righteous, who sustain the world, which was created with ten statements.**

NOTES

"let the earth produce living creatures" (Genesis 1:24); "let us make man in our image" (Genesis 1:27). Several opinions have been offered as to the identity of the remaining statements, from among the verses: "God said: Behold, I have given you all vegetation yielding seed" (Genesis 1:29); "The Lord God said…I will make for him a helper alongside him" (Genesis 2:18), among others (see *Avot deRabbi Natan*, version B, chap. 36; *Bereshit Rabba* 17:1; *Pirkei deRabbi Eliezer* 3; *Tikkunei Zohar* 47). According to the Talmud, the tenth statement is the verse: "In the beginning, God created the heavens and the earth" (Genesis 1:1), in which the world in its entirety was created, before its completed form was crafted (see *Rosh Hashana* 32a).

Couldn't it have been created with one statement – וַהֲלֹא בְּמַאֲמָר אֶחָד יָכוֹל לְהִבָּרְאוֹת: This question related to the need to detail the acts of Creation, as, if the statement itself is the creative power, then each statement must include an infinite number of statements. For example, the statement that refers to creation of plants includes within it a detailed statement for each and every plant, as each plant is a creation in and of itself. Therefore, since the statements are in any case extremely general, there is room to ask, why were they mentioned and specified at all? Why was it not stated in general that God commanded the creation of the world, as it is stated in the verse: "By the word of the Lord were the heavens made; by the breath of His mouth, all their hosts…For He spoke and it was done; He commanded, and it took form" (Psalms 33:6–9).

To exact punishment from the wicked – לְהִפָּרַע מִן הָרְשָׁעִים: The fact that these statements are detailed in Creation underscores that each one of them is significant in and of itself, and there is a reason for it to be mentioned separately. The conclusion is that the entire world is of great significance. Therefore, the upshot for people is that an extremely great punishment is imposed upon the wicked, who destroy this world with their actions, and that by contrast, the righteous, who sustain this world with their actions, merit an extremely great reward (see Meiri, Rabbeinu Yona). Some say that each statement refers to a new, discrete level of Creation, until the pinnacle, the creation of man, as humanity is the most important creation and constitutes the purpose of the entire Creation. The wicked corrupt the purpose of Creation, and the righteous repair it; and as a result, they corrupt or repair all of Creation (see Rambam).

Who destroy the world – שֶׁמְּאַבְּדִין אֶת הָעוֹלָם: The commentary follows the straightforward meaning, that the wicked person ruins and corrupts the world with his actions, while the righteous person preserves

Mishna 2

The previous mishna dealt with the ten statements with which the world was created and their repercussions for humanity, in whose hands the fate of the world was entrusted; God exacts punishment from the wicked, who destroy the world, and rewards the righteous who sustain it. This mishna continues with a list of ten items that relate to the matter of reward and punishment itself.

עֲשָׂרָה דוֹרוֹת מֵאָדָם עַד נֹחַ, לְהוֹדִיעַ כַּמָּה אֶרֶךְ אַפַּיִם לְפָנָיו, שֶׁכָּל הַדּוֹרוֹת הָיוּ מַכְעִיסִין וּבָאִין עַד שֶׁהֵבִיא עֲלֵיהֶם אֶת מֵי הַמַּבּוּל.

There were ten generations[N] listed in the Torah **from Adam until Noah** (Genesis, chap. 5). The reason that all these generations were listed is **to inform, how much forbearance there is before Him,** in God, **as all** these **generations were increasingly infuriating;**[N] they descended lower and lower and corrupted their actions further from generation to generation. God did not immediately exact retribution against them for their sins, but rather allowed them to exist in that manner for ten generations, in the hope that they would mend their ways and repent, **until He** ultimately **brought the flood waters upon them.**

NOTES

and sustains it. Some explain that "who destroy the world" means that they destroy their souls with their sins, and it is as though they destroyed an entire world. Another explanation is that with their actions they tilt the balance of the entire world to the side of liability. The result is that they destroy the entire world (Bartenura).

There were ten generations – **עֲשָׂרָה דוֹרוֹת**: Ostensibly, the two parts of this mishna are essentially identical, as detailing the ancient generations is designed to inform us of God's forbearance, that He is not quick to exact retribution against the wicked. On the other hand, there is a contrast between the two parts, as the attribute of forbearance does not necessarily lead to an identical result. Noah's righteousness was sufficient only to rescue him and the members of his family from annihilation and to enable a new beginning, after which the succeeding generations continued to be "increasingly infuriating." But the new path that Abraham's righteousness encompassed required only the repair of the corrupt world, not its destruction. As a result, he received the reward for all the accrued merit of the generations since Noah (see *Pirkei Moshe*).

As all these generations were increasingly infuriating – **שֶׁכָּל הַדּוֹרוֹת הָיוּ מַכְעִיסִין וּבָאִין**: Very little is known about the generations from Adam to Noah, but the Torah relates that there was already bloodshed (Genesis, chap. 4), idol worship (Genesis 4:26), and licentiousness (Genesis 6:1–4). Ultimately, "The

עֲשָׂרָה דוֹרוֹת מִנֹּחַ עַד אַבְרָהָם. לְהוֹדִיעַ כַּמָּה אֶרֶךְ אַפַּיִם לְפָנָיו, שֶׁכָּל הַדּוֹרוֹת הָיוּ מַכְעִיסִין וּבָאִין עַד שֶׁבָּא אַבְרָהָם וְקִבֵּל עָלָיו שְׂכַר כֻּלָּם.

Likewise, **there were ten generations** detailed in the Torah **from** after the generation of **Noah until Abraham** (see Genesis 11:10–26),[N] **to inform how much forbearance there is before Him, as all the generations were increasingly infuriating until Abraham.** In contrast to Noah, Abraham **came** and turned to the true faith, **and** therefore **received for himself the reward of all of them.**[N] It is as though he remedied the wickedness of all the generations that preceded him.

NOTES

Lord saw that the wickedness of man was great on the earth, and that every inclination of the thoughts of his heart was only evil all the time. The Lord regretted that He had made man on the earth, and He was saddened in His heart…The earth was corrupted before God, and the earth was filled with villainy" (Genesis 6:5–6, 11).

The flood waters, Phillip Medhurst Collection, England

Ten generations from Noah until Abraham – עֲשָׂרָה דוֹרוֹת מִנֹּחַ עַד אַבְרָהָם: Noah himself is not part of the ten generations "from Noah until Abraham," and their tally begins with his son Shem. This is simply the Mishna's style; since it states, "from Adam until Noah," it then states, "from Noah until Abraham" (*Tosefot Yom Tov*). However, the Maharal of Prague notes that the mishna can be interpreted otherwise, in a mystical manner, according to which Noah's generation was counted twice, first in the ten generations from Adam until Noah, and second in the ten generations from Noah until Terah, Abraham's father. According to this interpretation, Abraham is not included in the second unit of ten generations, because he was considered to have a special, separate status.

And received for himself the reward of all of them – וְקִבֵּל עָלָיו שְׂכַר כֻּלָּם: Some explain that Abraham performed as many good deeds as should have been performed during all those generations. That is why he merited all the goodness that was initially designated for them (Rabbeinu Yona, Bartenura). Likewise, it says in the Talmud: "Each and every person has two portions, one in the Garden of Eden and one in Gehenna. If the righteous one is deemed worthy, he takes his portion and the portion of his counterpart in the Garden of Eden; if the wicked one incurs liability, he takes his portion and the portion of his counterpart in Gehenna (*Ḥagiga* 15a). Some explain that the reward mentioned here is the fact that God appeared to him and chose him and his descendants for special treatment: that the Torah would be given to them, that miracles would be performed on their behalf, and that they would merit prophecy. Had the previous generations conducted themselves properly, they would have merited all of this. Because they did not do so, they were excluded from that reward, which was given to Abraham alone (*Tiferet Yisrael*).

Mishna 3

Following the previous mishna, which dealt with the count of ten generations, starting from Noah and culminating with Abraham, who received the reward of all of them, this mishna cites a facet of Abraham's exalted status related to the number ten.

עֲשָׂרָה נִסְיוֹנוֹת נִתְנַסָּה אַבְרָהָם אָבִינוּ עָלָיו הַשָּׁלוֹם וְעָמַד בְּכֻלָּם, לְהוֹדִיעַ כַּמָּה חִבָּתוֹ שֶׁל אַבְרָהָם אָבִינוּ עָלָיו הַשָּׁלוֹם.

With ten ordeals, challenges that he needed to overcome, **Abraham our forefather**[N] **of blessed memory was tested,**[N] **and he withstood them all,**[N] without voicing any resentment against God. All this was done **to inform** and reveal, **how** great **the love of Abraham**[N] **our forefather of blessed memory was for God.**

NOTES

Abraham our forefather – אַבְרָהָם אָבִינוּ: Some point out that whereas the previous mishna says, "Abraham," this mishna says, "Abraham our forefather," to emphasize that we are his descendants. As such, we must adopt his attribute, that he withstood the ordeals with which God tested him, and by virtue of this, we too will be credited with his merit.

With ten ordeals Abraham our forefather…was tested – עֲשָׂרָה נִסְיוֹנוֹת נִתְנַסָּה אַבְרָהָם אָבִינוּ: Abraham's ten ordeals are mentioned primarily in chapters 12–24 in the book of Genesis. Among them are the requirement to uproot himself from his homeland to another land (Genesis 12:1); the abduction of his wife by two different kings (Genesis 12:15, 20:2); the famine in the Land (Genesis 12:10); and the most difficult ordeal, the binding of Isaac (Genesis, chap. 22). While the number of ordeals in the mishna is a rabbinic tradition, ultimately, since the identity of the ordeals is not stated explicitly, the commentaries cite several different lists that include various incidents stated in the Torah or in the oral tradition (see *Avot deRabbi Natan* 33; *Pirkei deRabbi Eliezer* 26; Rambam, and others).

And he withstood them all – וְעָמַד בְּכֻלָּם: This means that he fulfilled everything that he was commanded, e.g., that he leave his land, circumcise himself, and bind his son. Moreover, he had no second

The binding of Isaac, wall fresco, Dura-Europos synagogue, third century CE

thoughts about God and did not become angry at Him at all, even though he was in dire straits (see Rambam, Meiri, and others). The Sages contrasted Abraham and Job in this regard, as, although both were righteous, Job was filled with grievances against God, whereas Abraham had no misgivings about God's attributes even in his most arduous ordeals (*Midrash Tanḥuma*, *Vayishlaḥ* 8).

To inform how great the love of Abraham…was – לְהוֹדִיעַ כַּמָּה חִבָּתוֹ שֶׁל אַבְרָהָם: The explanation in the commentary is that this refers to how much Abraham loved God, as that is the reason that He

Mishna 4

Following the previous mishna, which addressed Abraham, this mishna continues with a list of ten matters that are tied to his descendants; their enslavement in Egypt, culminating in ten miracles that were performed as part of their redemption from Egypt, was stated to Abraham in the Covenant between the Pieces.

עֲשָׂרָה נִסִּים נַעֲשׂוּ לַאֲבוֹתֵינוּ בְּמִצְרַיִם, וַעֲשָׂרָה עַל הַיָּם.

Ten miracles were performed on behalf of our ancestors in Egypt,[N] as they were spared from the plagues that were visited upon Egypt, **and ten** miracles were performed on their behalf **at the sea,**[N] according to a tradition of the Sages. The miracles at the sea included the pillar of fire that protected them, their crossing through the midst of the sea, and more.

NOTES

chose him (see *Maḥzor Vitri*). However, some explain that it refers to how much Abraham was beloved before God, as these ordeals were designed to inform everyone just how complete was Abraham's faith in God and fear of Him. This was the reason that God was so fond of him and that Abraham was worthy of sustaining a world that was created with ten statements (see *Maḥzor Vitri*). Some say that this phrase is referring to informing Abraham of his own virtue. When the one being tested withstands the ordeal, he knows that he is wholeheartedly devoted to God (*Midrash Shmuel*).

Ten miracles were performed on behalf of our ancestors in Egypt – עֲשָׂרָה נִסִּים נַעֲשׂוּ לַאֲבוֹתֵינוּ בְּמִצְרַיִם: The commentaries explain that these miracles were the fact that Israel was spared from the plagues that afflicted Egypt, as is written in the verses regarding all the plagues, with the exception of the plague of lice, for which there is a tradition to that effect. Some say that the mishna is emphasizing that they were spared from the plagues in Egypt and at the sea, even though, in truth, they were not worthy of it. The merit of their forefathers protected them, as it is stated in *Avot deRabbi Natan* (33), that they experienced these ten miracles due to the merit of the ten ordeals with which Abraham was tested (*Tiferet Yisrael*).

The Plague of Hail, Phillip Medhurst Collection, England

And ten at the sea – וַעֲשָׂרָה עַל הַיָּם: The number of miracles that were performed on Israel's behalf at the sea was transmitted by rabbinic tradition. Some of these miracles are written explicitly in the Bible, and the Sages derived the rest by expounding verses. These miracles include the basic fact of the splitting of the sea, that it was split into many paths, that it

The mishna cites the additional, parallel element of the ten miracles performed on behalf of the children of Israel.

עֶשֶׂר מַכּוֹת הֵבִיא הַקָּדוֹשׁ בָּרוּךְ הוּא עַל הַמִּצְרִיִּים בְּמִצְרַיִם, וַעֲשָׂרָה עַל הַיָּם.

God brought ten plagues upon the Egyptians in Egypt, as recorded explicitly in the Bible, **and** he afflicted them with **ten** corresponding plagues **at the sea,**[N] as the Sages explained based on inferences from the verses.

עֶשֶׂר נִסְיוֹנוֹת נִסּוּ אֲבוֹתֵינוּ אֶת הַמָּקוֹם בָּרוּךְ הוּא בַּמִּדְבָּר, שֶׁנֶּאֱמַר: "וַיְנַסּוּ אֹתִי זֶה עֶשֶׂר פְּעָמִים וְלֹא שָׁמְעוּ בְּקוֹלִי".

With ten trials our ancestors tested[N] **the Omnipresent, blessed be He, in the wilderness:** They complained that He took them out of Egypt, did not believe that He is capable of performing a miracle when they needed one, and violated His commands,

NOTES

was like a tent of sorts, that the seabed was dry, that the pillar of fire illuminated for them, that they could drink potable water from the sea when they passed through it, and more (see *Avot deRabbi Natan* 33, and commentaries on the mishna).

Splitting of the Red Sea; wall fresco; Dura-Europos synagogue; third century CE

Ten plagues…at the sea – עֶשֶׂר מַכּוֹת...עַל הַיָּם: The plagues with which the Egyptians were afflicted on that occasion are derived from what is explicated in the Song at the Sea: "He cast into the sea" (Exodus 15:1); "he cast into the sea" (Exodus 15:4); "were drowned in the Red Sea" (Exodus 15:4); "the deep covered them" (Exodus 15:5); "they descended into the depths" (Exodus 15:5); "shatters an enemy" (Exodus 15:6); "You overthrow those who rise against You" (Exodus 15:7); "it consumes them like straw" (Exodus 15:7); "the sea covered them" (Exodus 15:10); "they sank like lead" (Exodus 15:10). Some commentaries detailed what each of these plagues was (see Rabbeinu Yona). Regarding the matter itself, that the Egyptians were afflicted with numerous plagues at the sea, it is said that there is an allusion in the verse: "This is the God who smote the Egyptians with every plague in the wilderness" (I Samuel 4:8). Although there are Sages who expounded that at the sea the Egyptians were afflicted with even more plagues, as stated explicitly in the Haggadah, ultimately, all the plagues are divided into ten primary categories (Rambam).

With ten trials our ancestors tested – עֶשֶׂר נִסְיוֹנוֹת נִסּוּ אֲבוֹתֵינוּ: These trials include instances when they tested God and instances when they angered Him. These trials, explicated in tractate *Arakhin* (15a), were: they did not believe that God would rescue them from the Egyptians, before the splitting of the Red

thereby testing Him, to see whether or not He would rescue them from their travails, **as it is stated** after the sin of the spies: **"And have tested Me these ten times, and have not heeded My voice" (Numbers 14:22).**

Mishna 5

Following the list of ten miracles that were performed on behalf of Israel when they left Egypt, this mishna continues with the miracles that were performed on Israel's behalf as a continuation of the redemption, after they entered the Land of Israel and constructed the Temple.

עֲשָׂרָה נִסִּים נַעֲשׂוּ לַאֲבוֹתֵינוּ בְּבֵית הַמִּקְדָּשׁ:

Ten miracles were performed on behalf of our ancestors in the Temple[N] on a regular basis.

לֹא הִפִּילָה אִשָּׁה מֵרֵיחַ בְּשַׂר הַקֹּדֶשׁ,

No woman miscarried due to the odor of the consecrated meat[N] sacrificed on the

NOTES

Sea (Exodus 14:11); even afterward, they did not believe that God had saved them until they saw the Egyptians dead (as expounded from Psalms 106:7); they complained about the water at Mara (Exodus 15:24) and the lack of water at Refidim (Exodus 17:2); they defied God twice regarding the proper conduct vis-à-vis the manna (Exodus 16:26–27); they complained twice regarding food, until God sent them quail for their food (Exodus 16:2; Numbers 11:1); they crafted the Golden Calf (Exodus, chap. 32); they promulgated a slanderous report on the Land in the sin of the spies (Numbers 13:32). Some reckon the number of trials differently (see *Avot deRabbi Natan* 34).

Ten miracles were performed on behalf of our ancestors in the Temple – עֲשָׂרָה נִסִּים נַעֲשׂוּ לַאֲבוֹתֵינוּ בְּבֵית הַמִּקְדָּשׁ: Some explain that specifically ten miracles were performed on their behalf because the various mishaps in this world were caused by the sin of Adam the first man. However, in the Temple, where the Divine Presence rests, the situation is as it was prior to the sin (Yaavetz). According to one of the answers in the Jerusalem Talmud (*Yoma* 1:4), this mishna is referring to the situation in the First Temple, not the Second Temple. Some infer from the expression "on behalf of our ancestors" that this is referring specifically to the miracles performed on behalf of our ancestors. That is why the mishna did not enumerate additional miracles described in rabbinic literature that attest to the Divine Presence resting in Israel (*Tiferet Yisrael*). In *Avot deRabbi Natan* (35, and differently in version B, chap. 39), there is a variant reading of ten miracles that were unique to the Temple and ten additional miracles that were unique to Jerusalem.

No woman miscarried due to the odor of the

altar, although, typically, the pungent odor from burning multiple offerings is liable to cause miscarriage.

וְלֹא הִסְרִיחַ בְּשַׂר הַקֹּדֶשׁ מֵעוֹלָם,

The consecrated meat never spoiled,[N] even meat that remained until the following day or beyond.

וְלֹא נִרְאָה זְבוּב בְּבֵית הַמִּטְבָּחַיִם,

No fly was seen in the slaughterhouse, where the offerings were slaughtered and the meat prepared, although flies are typically attracted to a place like that.

וְלֹא אֵרַע קֶרִי לְכֹהֵן גָּדוֹל בְּיוֹם הַכִּפּוּרִים,

No impure **seminal emission befell**[N] **the High Priest on Yom Kippur,** which would have disqualified him from performing the service and necessitated replacing him.

NOTES

consecrated meat – לֹא הִפִּילָה אִשָּׁה מֵרֵיחַ בְּשַׂר הַקֹּדֶשׁ: The explanation in the commentary is that the odor of offerings was typically very powerful, but it nevertheless did not cause a woman to miscarry. Most commentaries, however, explained otherwise, that the aroma of the offerings was like the aroma of roast meat, which could have aroused her desire to partake of it. If that desire were not satisfied, she would be liable to endanger herself and the fetus (see *Yoma* 8:5). On the other hand, it is prohibited to partake of burnt sacrificial meat. That is why it was miraculous that no woman ever needed to do so, and, nevertheless, did not miscarry due to the aroma of the meat.

The consecrated meat never spoiled – וְלֹא הִסְרִיחַ בְּשַׂר הַקֹּדֶשׁ מֵעוֹלָם: Some explain that it never spoiled and the meat never became infested with worms (see *Avot deRabbi Natan*, version B, chap. 39), even though, at times, two or more days passed, e.g., if it was a peace offering, which is eaten for two days, or if it was meat placed atop the altar for an extended period until the opportunity to burn it there presented itself (see Rashi). Some explain that the hands of the priests who tended to the meat never reeked like the hands of butchers typically do (Meiri).

No seminal emission befell – וְלֹא אֵרַע קֶרִי: Some say, based on an incident cited in tractate *Yoma* (12b), that while there were occasions when a High Priest was disqualified on Yom Kippur, the disqualification was not due to a seminal emission. Impurity due to a seminal emission is a demeaning type of impurity, as opposed to impurity caused by a swarming animal and the like (Meiri, Rashbatz, and others; see *Yoma* 88a). On Yom Kippur, when the entire Temple service was performed by the High Priest, it would destabilize the entire system if he were disqualified. Indeed, they would expend extraordinary effort to ensure that no stumbling block of that kind would befall the High Priest (see *Yoma* 1:4–7), because it is prohibited to rely on a miracle (see Jerusalem Talmud, *Yoma* 1:4). They considered it a miracle that no seminal emission took place, even though it was ostensibly due to their own efforts, because "if the Lord does not guard a city, in vain does the watchman keep vigil" (Psalms 127:1; see Yaavetz).

וְלֹא כִבּוּ גְשָׁמִים אֵשׁ שֶׁל עֲצֵי הַמַּעֲרָכָה, וְלֹא נִצְּחָה הָרוּחַ אֶת עַמּוּד הֶעָשָׁן,

Rain did not extinguish the fire of the wood of the arrangement, the wood that was arranged on the altar. **And wind did not divert**[N] **the column of smoke** that would ascend from the altar, to any side.

וְלֹא נִמְצָא פְּסוּל בָּעֹמֶר וּבִשְׁתֵּי הַלֶּחֶם וּבְלֶחֶם הַפָּנִים,

No disqualification was found in the *omer* meal offering that is sacrificed on the sixteenth of Nisan in order to render the new grain permitted, **or in the two loaves,**[N] the public meal offering brought on Shavuot from the new wheat, **or in the shewbread,** which would be placed every Shabbat on the shewbread Table in the Sanctuary and remain there for an entire week.

NOTES

Rain did not extinguish the fire…And wind did not divert – **וְלֹא כִבּוּ גְשָׁמִים אֵשׁ...וְלֹא נִצְּחָה הָרוּחַ**: Since the arrangement of wood on the altar was outside, in the middle of the courtyard, rain naturally fell on it. However, the rain never extinguished the fire. A similar miracle was performed with the smoke of the arrangement; it would ascend like a column, and the wind would not divert it. In *Yoma* 21b it is stated that the smoke would incline somewhat in the direction of the wind, but it would not dissipate. They likened it to a palm tree, which always stands straight and tall, even if the wind causes it to slightly sway.

Fire of the wood of the arrangement

The pillar of smoke

No disqualification was found in the *omer* or in the two loaves – **וְלֹא נִמְצָא פְּסוּל בָּעֹמֶר וּבִשְׁתֵּי הַלֶּחֶם**: The *omer* meal offering, a communal meal offering brought from barley on the sixteenth of Nisan, renders the new grain permitted for consumption (Leviticus 23:10–14). The "two loaves" offering, a communal meal offering brought from wheat on the festival of *Shavuot*, renders the new grain permitted for use in the Temple service (Leviticus 23:15–20). The shewbread was a set of twelve loaves that were placed each Shabbat on the Table in the Sanctuary,

עוֹמְדִים צְפוּפִים וּמִשְׁתַּחֲוִים רְוָוחִים,

When people were in the Temple courtyard, **they would stand crowded, and** yet they could **prostrate themselves** on the ground, extending their hands and their feet, **with ample space.**[N]

וְלֹא הִזִּיק נָחָשׁ וְעַקְרָב בִּירוּשָׁלַיִם מֵעוֹלָם,

No snake or scorpion ever caused harm to the people **in Jerusalem.**

NOTES

and were removed a week later (Leviticus 24:5–9). Although preparation of these meal offerings was very complicated, and many mishaps were liable to occur, these offerings were never disqualified, which was considered a miracle. This was a significant miracle because these were symbolic, central offerings of the Jewish collective. Moreover, if these were disqualified, there was no possibility to bring others in their stead (see Rashi and others).

They would stand crowded [*tzefufim*] and prostrate themselves with ample space – עוֹמְדִים צְפוּפִים וּמִשְׁתַּחֲוִים רְוָוחִים: On occasion, the congregation that entered the Temple was extremely large, and the crowding was so great that "no creature could extend his finger between them" (*Avot deRabbi Natan* 35). Similarly, some (Meiri, Bartenura, and others) say that *tzefufim* means that they would float [*tzafim*] in the air due to the extreme crowding. *Avot deRabbi Natan* says that this was the greatest of the miracles, as prostrating in the Temple was not merely bending at the waist, but was performed with the person lying flat on the floor and extending his arms and his legs.

The shewbread

וְלֹא אָמַר אָדָם לַחֲבֵרוֹ צַר לִי הַמָּקוֹם שֶׁאָלִין בִּירוּשָׁלַיִם.

No person ever said to his counterpart: There is not sufficient space for me to lodge[N] **in Jerusalem**[B] There was always room for lodging, even during the pilgrimage festivals, when multitudes would come to the city.

NOTES

No person ever said to his counterpart, there is not sufficient space for me to lodge – וְלֹא אָמַר אָדָם לַחֲבֵרוֹ צַר לִי הַמָּקוֹם שֶׁאָלִין: The mishna is referring to the many pilgrims who were hosted in the city during the three pilgrimage festivals, particularly on Passover, when the crowding was greatest. This is in accordance with the language of the verse: "The children of your bereavement will yet say in your ears: The place is crowded for me, make way for me and I will sit" (Isaiah 49:20). Some infer from the language of the mishna that not only was there room for everyone to lodge in the city, but no one even complained about his lodging conditions, even though typically people complain about it (*Pirkei Moshe*).

BACKGROUND

No person ever said to his counterpart, there is not sufficient space for me – וְלֹא אָמַר אָדָם לַחֲבֵרוֹ צַר לִי הַמָּקוֹם: The pilgrimage to the Temple included people who had been exiled throughout the Hellenistic and Roman worlds, and many sources from that period attest to the tremendous impression created by the mass pilgrimages to Jerusalem. The pilgrims would assemble in groups and ascend to the city in caravans, adorned with garlands of olive branches and accompanied by music and song. They would also bring the half-shekel payments to Jerusalem in these caravans. Although it is known that there were great numbers of pilgrims during each festival, it is difficult to accurately assess the precise number. The pilgrims would remain within the city limits throughout the days of the festival and the intermediate days, and they would lodge in the city's residences without payment. This was based on the belief that the city of Jerusalem belongs to the entire people, and that the city residences were not considered to be the exclusive property of their owners. In the City of David excavations, a Greek inscription from a synagogue, the "Theodotus inscription," documents the construction of an inn for the benefit of the pilgrims: "He built the inn, the rooms, and the water apparatuses for the purpose of hosting the needy from foreign lands."

Theodotos inscription

Mishna 6

In continuation of the list of ten miracles cited in the previous mishna, this mishna cites a list of ten phenomena that are not part of the natural order.

עֲשָׂרָה דְבָרִים נִבְרְאוּ בְּעֶרֶב שַׁבָּת בֵּין הַשְּׁמָשׁוֹת, וְאֵלּוּ הֵן:

Ten phenomena[N] that incorporate deviation from the natural order **were created** at the concluding moments of the six days of Creation **on the eve of Shabbat during twilight,**[N] **and they are:**

פִּי הָאָרֶץ,

first, **the mouth of the earth,** that the ground opened its mouth and swallowed the assembly of Korah (Numbers 16:30–33).

וּפִי הַבְּאֵר,

Second was **the mouth of the well,** which was the stone that would produce water for Israel for all their needs in the wilderness, and it would accompany Israel in all their travels (Numbers 21:16–20).

NOTES

Ten phenomena – עֲשָׂרָה דְבָרִים: This mishna is cited, with certain changes, in the Talmud (*Pesaḥim* 54a), where it is referred to as a *baraita*. For example, instead of the staff, it lists the cave in which Moses and Elijah stood. And there is an opinion that states: "Fire and the mule as well." An additional variant reading was cited at the end: "Some say the staff of Aaron, its almonds and its flowers, as well. Some say even the demons, and some say the garment of Adam the first man."

Were created on the eve of Shabbat during twilight – נִבְרְאוּ בְּעֶרֶב שַׁבָּת בֵּין הַשְּׁמָשׁוֹת: The items enumerated in the mishna constitute a certain deviation from the fixed order of Creation. That is why it is stated that they were not created during the six days of Creation proper, but rather separately at the conclusion of the labor, just as Shabbat was beginning. The Meiri explains that all these items allude to matters fundamental to the existence of the world and the Jewish people. They were created during twilight to indicate that Creation is incomplete without them. This does not mean that they were actually created then; what was created was the ability of these items to be realized when the time would come (*Tiferet Yisrael*). This underscores that after Creation ended, God did not introduce anything new in the world, as it is written: "There is nothing new under the sun" (Ecclesiastes 1:9). Even matters that appear to be miraculous and totally novel were already established during the six days of Creation (see chapter eight of Rambam's introduction to this tractate, *Shemone Perakim*).

וּפִי הָאָתוֹן,

Third was **the mouth of** Bilam's **female donkey,** as the donkey was given the ability to speak on a special, provisional basis (Numbers 22:28).

וְהַקֶּשֶׁת,

Fourth was **the rainbow,** a sign of God's covenant that there will never be another flood in the world (Genesis 9:16).

וְהַמָּן,

Fifth was **the manna,** the miraculous food that descended to Israel from the heavens when they were in the wilderness (Exodus, chap. 16).

וְהַמַּטֶּה,

Sixth was **the staff**[N] of Moses, with which he performed the signs and wonders in Egypt and in the wilderness (see Exodus 4:17, and elsewhere).

וְהַשָּׁמִיר,

Seventh was **the *shamir*,**[N] a stone or creature capable of splitting even the hardest stones.

וְהַכְּתָב,

Eighth was **the script** that was on the Tablets of the Covenant and written with the finger of God.

וְהַמִּכְתָּב,

Ninth was **the letter** that Elijah the prophet dispatched to the king of Judah after he had already ascended heavenward (II Chronicles 21:12), and which was not written through natural circumstances.

וְהַלּוּחוֹת.

Tenth were **the** first **tablets**[N] upon which the

NOTES

The staff – וְהַמַּטֶּה: The commentary here follows most of the commentaries, that this is referring to the staff of Moses. However, some say, based on a variant reading in *Pesaḥim* 54a, that this is referring to the staff of Aaron the priest, as a miracle was performed, causing his staff to blossom when it was placed in the Tent of Meeting (Numbers 17:23).

The *shamir* – וְהַשָּׁמִיר: The *shamir* is mentioned in tractate *Sota*, where it is stated that it became null and disappeared after the Temple was destroyed. It is stated in the *Tosefta* (*Sota* 15:1) that it was a special creation that "when one places it on stones or on beams, they open before it like the pages of a pamphlet. Moreover, when one places it on iron, the iron splits and descends before the *shamir*, and nothing can withstand it." It is said that Solomon utilized this creature to hew the stones of the Temple, or at least to inscribe the writing on the stones of the breastplate (see *Sota* 48b).

Ten Commandments were inscribed, in whose regard it is written that they are "the work of God" (Exodus 32:16).

וְיֵשׁ אוֹמְרִים: אַף הַמַּזִּיקִין, וּקְבוּרָתוֹ שֶׁל מֹשֶׁה, וְאֵילוֹ שֶׁל אַבְרָהָם אָבִינוּ.

Some say: Also the demons,[N] evil spirits, intelligent, incorporeal beings whose purpose is to cause damage; **Moses's grave,** as God buried him in a wondrous manner (Deuteronomy 34:6); **and the ram of Abraham our forefather;** it appeared suddenly at the site of the binding, and was slaughtered instead of Isaac (Genesis 22:13).

וְיֵשׁ אוֹמְרִים: אַף צְבָת בִּצְבָת עֲשׂוּיָה.

And some say: Also tongs made with tongs, in other words, the first tongs, whose existence enabled the crafting of all the other utensils in the world, as every utensil requires another utensil with which to craft it.

NOTES

The script [*haketav*], the letter [*hamikhtav*], the tablets – וְהַכְּתָב וְהַמִּכְתָּב וְהַלּוּחוֹת: The explanation in the commentary is that the "letter" is an independent matter, unrelated to the Tablets of the Covenant. However, most commentaries maintain that all three are related to the Tablets of the Covenant, and especially to the first tablets, which were "written [*ketuvim*] with the finger of God" (Exodus 31:18), and likewise, "inscribed on both their sides; from this side and from that side they were inscribed. The tablets were the work of God, and the writing was the writing of God [*vehamikhtav mikhtav elohim*], engraved on the tablets" (Exodus 32:15–16). The difference between *ketav* and *mikhtav* was explained in several manners, among them that *ketav* refers to the shape of the letters, and *mikhtav* refers to the utensil with which the letters were inscribed on the tablets (Rashi). Alternatively, *ketav* is the Torah as Moses wrote it in front of God, and *mikhtav* is the inscription of the letters on the tablets that He gave to Moses (Rambam, Rabbeinu Yona); or perhaps *mikhtav* is the special miracle that was in the Tablets, that it could be read from both sides. Likewise, the inner portion of the letters *samekh* and *mem sofit* remained in place miraculously even though they were not attached to the tablets (Bartenura, *Tiferet Yisrael*). Another possibility is that *ketav* is the language and *mikhtav* is the shape of the letters (Meiri).

The demons [*hamazikin*] – הַמַּזִּיקִין: These *mazikin* are known as *shedim* in the Bible (Deuteronomy 32:17, Psalms 106:37; see Ramban on Leviticus 17:7). Although they were not created as part of the natural world during the six days of Creation, they were added to the world at the end of Creation. More detailed descriptions of these beings appear in the Talmud. They are described as intelligent beings that do not have a corporeal body, although they do have a certain form. At times they are emissaries for the performance of evil in the world (see *Tiferet Yisrael*). In *Avot deRabbi Natan* (37) several of their characteristics are enumerated; in some they are like people and in others they are like angels.

Mishna 7

Following the lists of items that number ten, the mishna begins enumerating items that number seven.

שִׁבְעָה דְבָרִים בְּגֹלֶם, וְשִׁבְעָה בְּחָכָם:

There are **seven qualities in an unaccomplished person,**[N] one whose education and training were incomplete, **and** a corresponding **seven** qualities **in a wise person.**

חָכָם אֵינוֹ מְדַבֵּר בִּפְנֵי מִי שֶׁהוּא גָּדוֹל מִמֶּנּוּ בְּחָכְמָה,

A wise person does not speak in the presence of[N] **one who is greater than he in wisdom.**

וְאֵינוֹ נִכְנָס לְתוֹךְ דִּבְרֵי חֲבֵרוֹ,

He does not interrupt the words of another, but he allows him to complete his statement, and only then does he comment, ask a question, or challenge the other's statement.

וְאֵינוֹ נִבְהָל לְהָשִׁיב,

He does not respond rashly, whether in answering a question that is posed to him or in rejecting statements made by others, but rather he waits and considers whether and how to respond.

NOTES

Seven qualities in an unaccomplished person [*golem*] – **שִׁבְעָה דְבָרִים בְּגֹלֶם**: A *golem* is an item whose form is not complete, and it is considered to be still in its undeveloped state (see *Eduyyot* 3:9). Here too, the *golem* is a person who studied but never completely achieved the "form" of a Sage, either because he lacks understanding and is incapable of independent logical reasoning (Rashi, Rabbeinu Yona), or because he is less than accomplished in his character traits (Meiri, *Tiferet Yisrael*), or because he is less than accomplished in both areas (Rambam, Bartenura).

Does not speak in the presence of – **אֵינוֹ מְדַבֵּר בִּפְנֵי**: Some cite a variant reading: "He does not speak before one who is greater than he in wisdom." The difference between the two readings is that according to the reading "in the presence of," he does not speak at all, while according to the reading "before," he does not speak before one who is greater than he has completed his statement; but after he finishes his statement, he too expresses his opinion. That is why it says: "does not speak" and it does not say: "he is silent."

Some say that the fact that he does not speak in the presence of one who is greater is not only in deference to the greater person, but because he seeks to learn wisdom from him (Rabbeinu Yona). According to many readings, the wise man does not speak in the presence of one who is greater than he "in wisdom and in number" (see *Eduyyot* 1:5). "In number" refers to greatness in Torah wisdom and in the number of proper students, or possibly to greatness in the number of years of life (Rashi, Meiri).

שׁוֹאֵל כָּעִנְיָן וּמֵשִׁיב כַּהֲלָכָה,

He asks questions that are **relevant** to the matter discussed and not from another realm. **And he responds appropriately,**[N] and does not say anything without authority or without a basis.

וְאוֹמֵר עַל רִאשׁוֹן רִאשׁוֹן וְעַל אַחֲרוֹן אַחֲרוֹן,

When he responds or speaks, he does so in an orderly fashion, as **he states first things first and last things last.**[N]

וְעַל מַה שֶּׁלֹּא שָׁמַע אוֹמֵר "לֹא שָׁמַעְתִּי",

Regarding matters that he has not heard, he says: I have not heard; both when he is asked about those matters and when he introduces novel ideas on his own, he makes certain that the listener knows that he did not receive this matter from someone else.

וּמוֹדֶה עַל הָאֱמֶת.

He acknowledges the truth. If others challenge his statement or disprove it, he is not insistent on maintaining his position, but can recognize that it is not true.

NOTES

He asks questions that are relevant, and he responds appropriately – שׁוֹאֵל כָּעִנְיָן וּמֵשִׁיב כַּהֲלָכָה: The explanation in the simple sense is that he asks regarding the subject matter that is being studied at that time (see *Tosefta*, *Sanhedrin* 7:7–10). On a similar note, some explain that as a result of the student asking his teacher about the matter that is being studied at that time, he ensures that the teacher's answer will be accurate (Bartenura; see *Shabbat* 3b). From what is written in *Avot deRabbi Natan* (37), where biblical examples are cited for all the characteristics mentioned in the mishna, it appears that it means that he asks in a logical and considered manner.

Some explain that this means that he does not confuse the different methods of study appropriate to each area. Each discipline has its own unique approaches of study and methods of thought and proof with which to deliberate. He is meticulous in that regard, both when he is the one posing the question and when he is responding to questioners (Rambam).

He states first things first and last things last – וְאוֹמֵר עַל רִאשׁוֹן רִאשׁוֹן וְעַל אַחֲרוֹן אַחֲרוֹן: The simple understanding of the matters is that when a wise man presents his statements or responds to questioners, he does so in an orderly fashion. The *Midrash Shmuel* explains that this is stated in a more general sense, as the wise man organizes his thoughts himself and plans the curriculum of his study appropriately. Alternatively, he knows how to distinguish between the status of the different generations and to appreciate the special value of the Sages from the early generations as opposed to the sages of the later generations. That is why he greatly appreciates the traditions that pass from generation to generation, and, as a result, he is careful to say about what he did not hear, "I did not hear this."

וְחִלּוּפֵיהֶן בְּגֹלֶם.

All of these are the virtues of the wise person, one who speaks with civility and consideration. **The opposite** of these virtuous qualities are the seven matters that are in **an unaccomplished person.**

Mishna 8

This mishna and the one that follows continue with a list of seven matters. Here the mishna addresses the meaning of calamities that befall the world, meaning the community, as a result of communal transgressions. The first part of the mishna addresses trouble that results from failure to give *teruma* and tithes, and then the mishna proceeds to other calamities.

שִׁבְעָה מִינֵי פֻרְעָנִיּוֹת בָּאִין לָעוֹלָם, עַל שִׁבְעָה גּוּפֵי עֲבֵרָה:

Seven types of calamities come to the world as punishment **for seven types of transgression.**[N] How so?

מִקְצָתָן מְעַשְּׂרִין וּמִקְצָתָן אֵינָן מְעַשְּׂרִין – רָעָב שֶׁל בַּצּוֹרֶת בָּאָה, מִקְצָתָן רְעֵבִים וּמִקְצָתָן שְׂבֵעִים.

When **some** of the people **tithe** their produce **and some do not tithe,**[N] **famine of drought comes.** Since rain does not fall, there is very minimal produce, and only in certain places. Therefore, **some of them are hungry and some of them are satiated,** and the punishment fits the crime.

NOTES

Seven types of calamities [*puranuyot*]...seven types of transgression – שִׁבְעָה מִינֵי פֻרְעָנִיּוֹת...שִׁבְעָה גּוּפֵי עֲבֵרָה: According to the Meiri, the mishna comes to teach that every calamity that befalls the world is retribution for a specific transgression, with the punishment fitting the crime. That is why a person who experiences trouble must repent. The *Midrash Shmuel* adds that this is the reason calamities are called *puranut*; they are like paying off [*periat*] a debt (see 3:16).

Some tithe and some do not tithe – מִקְצָתָן מְעַשְּׂרִין וּמִקְצָתָן אֵינָן מְעַשְּׂרִין: Tithe is a general name for that part of the produce that is given to priests and Levites, and in some years also to poor people (see mishna 9), in accordance with the interpretation of this mitzva, which is written in several places in the Torah (see, e.g., Numbers, chap. 18). The Sages derive from the verses that a person's receiving blessing and abundance is contingent on meticulous fulfillment of these mitzvot, as the Sages expounded: "'Tithe [*aser te'aser*]' (Deuteronomy 14:22) – so you will become wealthy [*titasher*]" (*Taanit* 9a and elsewhere). This idea is also explicit in the verse: "Bring all the tithes to

גָּמְרוּ שֶׁלֹּא לְעַשֵּׂר – רָעָב שֶׁל מְהוּמָה וְשֶׁל בַּצּוֹרֶת בָּאָה.

If they all **resolved not to tithe, famine of chaos,** wars, **and drought comes.** The chaos makes it impossible to procure the little food that is available, and everyone suffers.

וְשֶׁלֹּא לִיטּוֹל אֶת הַחַלָּה – רָעָב שֶׁל כְּלָיָה בָּאָה.

If they decided **not to take ḥalla**[N] from the dough, **famine of annihilation comes.** The famine not only causes suffering, but it also eradicates the people.

דֶּבֶר בָּא לָעוֹלָם – עַל מִיתוֹת הָאֲמוּרוֹת בַּתּוֹרָה שֶׁלֹּא נִמְסְרוּ לְבֵית דִּין, וְעַל פֵּרוֹת שְׁבִיעִית.

The plague of **pestilence comes to the world** as punishment **for death penalties mentioned in the Torah**[N] **that were not given to** the jurisdiction of **the court** to administer them. Therefore, the punishment is administered by Heaven. **And** it also comes as punishment **for** not declaring **Sabbatical** Year **produce**[N] ownerless and for utilizing it inappropriately.

NOTES

the storehouse…I will pour out an endless blessing for you" (Malachi 3:10). The opposite is true when one is not meticulous regarding separation of tithes.

Not to take *ḥalla* – וְשֶׁלֹּא לִיטּוֹל אֶת הַחַלָּה: In contrast to tithes that are separated from produce, *ḥalla* is separated from dough. It is given to the priests, and its status is like that of *teruma*, as stated explicitly in the Torah (Numbers 15:20–21) and in tractate *Ḥalla*. As long as the people are meticulous regarding this mitzva, its merit will stand on their behalf to protect them from punishment that comes due to failure to tithe, so there will not be total eradication. However, if they fail to fulfill this as well, meaning that no gifts are separated, neither from the grain pile nor from dough, utter famine befalls the world, leading to eradication and death.

Pestilence comes to the world for death penalties mentioned in the Torah – דֶּבֶר בָּא לָעוֹלָם עַל מִיתוֹת הָאֲמוּרוֹת בַּתּוֹרָה: Pestilence is plague (see *Taanit* 3:4). The explanation in the commentary, that these death penalties mentioned in the Torah "were not given to the jurisdiction of the court," follows certain commentaries. Others maintain that this is not referring to plague, but to transgressions punishable by *karet*, or by death at the hand of Heaven; these by definition are not given to the jurisdiction of the court (Rabbeinu Yona). Some understand this as referring to transgressions for which the punishment is one of the four court-administered death penalties, as in practice the courts cannot adjudicate these since they stopped judging capital cases (Rashi).

For Sabbatical Year produce – וְעַל פֵּרוֹת שְׁבִיעִית: The commentaries explain that the reason the punishment for sins regarding Sabbatical Year produce is so severe is that they thereby prevent the poor from gathering produce and cause their death. During the Sabbatical Year, when it is prohibited to till the land, the poor receive no "gifts of the poor" from the field; therefore, their lack is extremely great (Meiri). Some explain that because this person was supposed to declare his produce ownerless and abandoned,

חֶרֶב בָּאָה לָעוֹלָם - עַל עִנּוּי הַדִּין, וְעַל עִוּוּת הַדִּין, וְעַל הַמּוֹרִים בַּתּוֹרָה שֶׁלֹּא כַּהֲלָכָה.

The **sword** of war **comes to the world** as punishment for matters relating to judgments and issuing rulings: **for delay of justice,**[N] when judges delay issuing their sentence, thereby causing the litigants to suffer; **for perversion of justice,** issuing mistaken judgments; **and for those who issue Torah rulings not** in keeping with the correct **halakha,**[N] as they permit the prohibited or prohibit the permitted.

Mishna 9

The beginning of the mishna is a continuation of the previous mishna and enumerates two more calamities that come as punishment for major transgressions.

חַיָּה רָעָה בָּאָה לָעוֹלָם - עַל שְׁבוּעַת שָׁוְא, וְעַל חִלּוּל הַשֵּׁם.

Wild beasts that enter into settled areas and cause damage or death **come to the world for oaths taken in vain,**[N] i.e., false or unnecessary oaths, **and for profaning the name of God.**

NOTES

but he did not do so, his soul is abandoned to the hands of the angel of death (*Tiferet Yisrael*). In *Avot deRabbi Natan* (38) it is said: "Pestilence comes to the world due to iniquity regarding gleanings, forgotten sheaves, produce in the corner of the field, and poor man's tithe," as explained in the following mishna.

Sword comes to the world for delay of justice – חֶרֶב בָּאָה לָעוֹלָם עַל עִנּוּי הַדִּין: The Meiri explains that the punishment fits the crime. When justice is not performed in the world in a fair and just manner, it causes strife between people. Therefore, they are punished with the calamity of the sword (Meiri). Others understand this as meaning that in matters of law and justice, punishment is exacted by sword, as the sword represents the attribute of justice (*Mirkevet HaMishne*).

And for those who issue Torah rulings not in keeping with halakha – וְעַל הַמּוֹרִים בַּתּוֹרָה שֶׁלֹּא כַּהֲלָכָה: The reason is that a ruling not in keeping with halakha is like a miscarriage of justice (Meiri), or because this is the punishment for distortion of the Torah and its abrogation, as the Sages expounded in various places (see *Shabbat* 33a, *Vayikra Rabba* 35:6). Some explain in another manner that "those who issue Torah rulings not in keeping with halakha" are students who were not ordained to issue rulings, but issue rulings nonetheless (Rashbatz and others; see *Sota* 22a).

Wild beasts come to the world for oaths taken in vain – חַיָּה רָעָה בָּאָה לָעוֹלָם עַל שְׁבוּעַת שָׁוְא: The Meiri explains that this is due to the fact that the oath is in the name of God. If a person compromises the

גָּלוּת בָּאָה לָעוֹלָם – עַל עוֹבְדֵי עֲבוֹדָה זָרָה, וְעַל גִּלּוּי עֲרָיוֹת, וְעַל שְׁפִיכוּת דָּמִים, וְעַל הַשְׁמָטַת הָאָרֶץ.

Exile comes to the world for idol worship, for forbidden sexual relations, for bloodshed,[N] **and for** failure to **leave the land fallow** during the Sabbatical Year.

לאחר רשימות של שבעה דברים, עוברת המשנה לרשימות של ארבעה דברים, שהראשון בהם ממשיך את העניין שעסקה בו כעת – פורעניות הבאות כתוצאה מעברות מסוימות:

After the lists containing seven items, the mishna moves to lists containing four items. The first such list continues the theme of calamities that come as a consequence of certain transgressions.

בְּאַרְבָּעָה פְּרָקִים הַדֶּבֶר מִתְרַבֶּה: בָּרְבִיעִית, וּבַשְּׁבִיעִית, וּבְמוֹצָאֵי שְׁבִיעִית, וּבְמוֹצָאֵי הֶחָג שֶׁבְּכָל שָׁנָה וְשָׁנָה.

At four junctures during the Sabbatical cycle, **pestilence increases:**[N] **in the fourth** year; **in the seventh** year, the Sabbatical Year; **at the conclusion of the seventh** year; **and at the conclusion of the festival** of Sukkot **of each and every year.**

NOTES

honor of the Name by taking His name falsely and in vain, or by profaning His name, then his honor as a person is also compromised, and permission is given to the beasts, which are lesser than he is, to harm him.

Exile comes to the world for…bloodshed – גָּלוּת בָּאָה לָעוֹלָם...עַל שְׁפִיכוּת דָּמִים: According to the Meiri, the reason for this is that since transgressions cause the Divine Presence to move from its place, which is with Israel, those who commit these transgressions are punished by being forced to move from their place. The punishment of exile for violating the mitzva of leaving the land fallow during the Sabbatical Year is stated explicitly in the Torah: "And you I will scatter among the nations…your land shall be desolate and your cities shall be ruins…Then the land will be repaid for its Sabbaths…All the days of its desolation it shall rest, that which it did not rest during your Sabbaths, when you lived upon it" (Leviticus 26:33–35; see II Chronicles 36:21). This too is a punishment that fits the crime, as Israel did not conduct themselves in their land as they were commanded.

At four junctures pestilence increases – בְּאַרְבָּעָה פְּרָקִים הַדֶּבֶר מִתְרַבֶּה: As explained in the mishna, pestilence increases at these times for sins tied to robbing the poor of what should be given to them: poor man's tithe, seventh-year produce, and gifts to the poor, as explained below. It is explicit in the verses that stealing the portion of the poor is punishable by death, as it is stated: "Do not rob the impoverished…and do not oppress the poor…for the Lord will fight their battle and will deprive of life those who deprive them" (Proverbs 22:22–23; see *Pe'a* 5:6). The Maharal of Prague explains that the mishna serves to underscore that punishment comes immediately after the poor person's portion is robbed from him, because God is nearby and hears the cry of the poor (see Exodus 22:20–26).

בָּרְבִיעִית – מִפְּנֵי מַעְשַׂר עָנִי שֶׁבַּשְּׁלִישִׁית.

The mishna elaborates: **In the fourth year, because** the people did not give **poor man's tithe,**[N] which should have been given **in the third year** of the Sabbatical cycle.

בַּשְּׁבִיעִית – מִפְּנֵי מַעְשַׂר עָנִי שֶׁבַּשִּׁשִּׁית.

Likewise, **in the seventh** year, **because** they did not give **poor man's tithe,** which should have been given **in the sixth year** as well.

וּבְמוֹצָאֵי שְׁבִיעִית – מִפְּנֵי פֵּרוֹת שְׁבִיעִית.

At the conclusion of the seventh year, **due to Sabbatical Year produce**[N] that was not declared ownerless and was not made available to the poor (see previous mishna).

וּבְמוֹצָאֵי הֶחָג שֶׁבְּכָל שָׁנָה וְשָׁנָה – מִפְּנֵי גֶּזֶל מַתְּנוֹת עֲנִיִּים.

And at the conclusion of the festival of Sukkot **of each and every year,** marking the conclusion of the season of reaping and harvesting, **because of robbery of the gifts of the poor.**[N] The gifts of the field given to the poor – gleanings, forgotten sheaves, and produce of the corners – were not given to them, and they were not included in the celebration of the Sukkot festival, as prescribed in the Torah.

NOTES

Poor man's tithe – מַעְשַׂר עָנִי: Poor man's tithe is one-tenth of the produce remaining after *teruma* and first tithe are separated. It is given to the poor in the third and sixth years of the Sabbatical cycle. Because it has no sanctity, and it is not prohibited to partake of the produce when this tithe has not been separated, people tend to take it lightly and neglect giving it.

Due to Sabbatical Year produce – מִפְּנֵי פֵּרוֹת שְׁבִיעִית: As written in the previous mishna, although Sabbatical Year produce is ownerless and available for all, wealthy and poor, it is especially relevant for the poor, who lack the means to purchase food. Moreover, during the Sabbatical Year, the poor also do not receive the gifts of the field that they receive every year. The right of the poor to Sabbatical Year produce is explicit in the language of the verse: "But the seventh year you shall leave it fallow and relinquish it, and the poor of your people will eat" (Exodus 23:11).

Because of robbery of the gifts of the poor – מִפְּנֵי גֶּזֶל מַתְּנוֹת עֲנִיִּים: Gifts of the poor typically include gleanings, forgotten sheaves, and produce in the corner of the field, as well as individual fallen grapes and incompletely formed clusters of grapes. All of these remain in the field and vineyard for distribution to the poor, as written explicitly in the Torah (Leviticus 19:9–10; Deuteronomy 24:19–21) and detailed extensively in the order of *Zera'im*. After the festival of *Sukkot*, at the conclusion of the agricultural year, the harvest of the grain and produce is brought indoors, and people are judged if they had not made these gifts available.

It is also possible to explain that the mishna is also referring to gifts related to the pilgrimage to Jerusalem on the festivals, as on the festival of *Sukkot*

Mishna 10

Continuing with another list containing four items, this mishna details different qualities in people that are tied to their perception of property.

אַרְבַּע מִדּוֹת בָּאָדָם:

There are four archetypical **qualities** [*middot*], approaches or characteristics, relating to property, **in a person:**[B]

הָאוֹמֵר "שֶׁלִּי שֶׁלִּי, וְשֶׁלְּךָ שֶׁלְּךָ" – זוֹ מִדָּה בֵּינוֹנִית.

In the case of **one who says: Mine is mine, and yours is yours,**[N] meaning that I keep and maintain what is mine, and you keep what is yours, and neither of us involves himself with the property of the other, **this**

NOTES

there is a mitzva of great rejoicing, as it is written: "You shall hold the festival of Tabernacles seven days, upon your gathering from your threshing floor and from your winepress. You shall rejoice on your festival, you, and your son, and your daughter, and your slave, and your maidservant, and the Levite, and the stranger, and the orphan, and the widow, who are within your gates" (Deuteronomy 16:13–14). Often, people would greatly augment their personal rejoicing on the festival but refrain from including the poor, and that is considered as though they robbed them (see Rambam, *Hilkhot Yom Tov* 7:18).

Mine is mine and yours is yours – שֶׁלִּי שֶׁלִּי וְשֶׁלְּךָ שֶׁלָּךְ: In the mishna, two opinions are cited regarding this quality. One is that there is nothing wrong with this quality, and the other is that it is characteristic of Sodom. The Meiri says that the opinions are not contradictory, but refer to different situations. When a person does not wish to allow others to use something that might be damaged or diminished by its use, that is an average quality. But when no harm could transpire, i.e., it is a situation where "one benefits and the other does not incur a loss," that is the quality of the people of Sodom.

Another commentator explains that this quality is average because half of it, "mine is mine," is bad, and half of it, "yours is yours," is good. However, the opinion that it is the quality of Sodom is based on the fact that he said that he does not want to benefit from another only so that the other will not seek to benefit from his property in return (*Midrash Shmuel*). See below.

BACKGROUND

Four qualities [*middot*] in a person – אַרְבַּע מִדּוֹת בָּאָדָם: In the Bible, *midda* means a unit of measurement of length, volume, or time. From this initial meaning, it branched out in the language of the Sages to include additional meanings: "A vessel for measuring the amount of food," as well as "fixed principle," "characteristic," and "mode of behavior." This last meaning is the sense of the term in this mishna and in the *mishnayot* that follow. It suggests methods of assessment and classification of personality traits and conduct.

is an average quality. People typically hold on to what is theirs and do not want to receive anything from others or give anything to them. This is neither particularly praiseworthy nor worthy of condemnation.

וְיֵשׁ אוֹמְרִים – זוֹ מִדַּת סְדוֹם.

But some say that **this is the quality of** the people of **Sodom,**[NB] who were "extremely wicked and sinful to the Lord" (Genesis 13:13). This is because at the root of Sodom's wickedness was the absolute, zealous preservation of each person's private property. This was indicative of lack of consideration for others and their needs.

NOTES

But some say this is the quality of Sodom – וְיֵשׁ אוֹמְרִים זוֹ מִדַּת סְדוֹם: In the Torah, the great wickedness of the city of Sodom is detailed, especially regarding the treatment they afforded guests who happened to come there (Genesis 18:20–19:9). In the Prophets, it is stated that the city's primary sin was that it "had pride, surfeit of bread and tranquil calm, but it did not support the hand of the poor and indigent" (Ezekiel 16:49). In other words, despite the fact that it had plenty, it did not want others, who were in need, to benefit from it.

As written above, the Meiri explains that the mishna is referring to one who does not want to share with others even when the matter does not involve loss and damage. Some explain that the mishna is stated in general terms because even when one consistently refrains from enabling others to benefit from matters that do entail a loss, it can lead to antagonism between people and ultimately to conduct like the people of Sodom (Bartenura, *Tiferet Yisrael*). Another explains that the mishna is not speaking of one who does not give at all, as he is wicked. Rather, it is speaking of one who does give charity but believes privately that it is not right. The dispute in the mishna is over whether this quality is considered an average quality or a quality of Sodom (Rabbeinu Yona).

BACKGROUND

The quality of Sodom – מִדַּת סְדוֹם: This phrase in the mishna is the source of the halakhic concept "the quality of Sodom," which is used to describe a situation in which a person insists upon his legal right and prevents another from benefiting from his property, although the first, thereby, loses nothing and is not harmed. Regarding a situation of that kind, the principle "one coerces concerning the quality of Sodom" is said. In other words, in certain circumstances the court will coerce one who acts in this manner and force him to relinquish his property. This principle, together with the fundamental instruction: "You shall perform the upright and the good" (Deuteronomy 6:18; see Proverbs 3:27), serves as the basis for many of the ordinances and the halakhot of neighbors (see *Shulḥan Arukh*, *Oraḥ Ḥayyim* 386:9, *Ḥoshen Mishpat* 153:8 and 153:4, and more).

״שֶׁלִּי שֶׁלְּךָ, וְשֶׁלְּךָ שֶׁלִּי״ – עַם הָאָרֶץ.

One who says: **Mine is yours, and yours is mine,** wanting to exchange his property for the property of others, is an **am haaretz**[N] in terms of his awareness, as, fundamentally, he supports the existing world order but just wants to change it and divert it for his own benefit. This is nothing other than avarice or envy; it is not a comprehensive philosophy about the world.

״שֶׁלִּי שֶׁלָּךְ, וְשֶׁלְּךָ שֶׁלָּךְ״ – חָסִיד.

One who says: **Mine is yours, and yours is yours,** meaning, I am willing to give my belongings in order to help another, but I do not want to take anything from anyone else, is **pious.** He goes beyond the letter of the law, and relinquishes his property and his rights on behalf of others.

״שֶׁלִּי שֶׁלִּי, וְשֶׁלְּךָ שֶׁלִּי״ – רָשָׁע.

This contrasts to one who says: **Yours is mine, and mine is mine.** He believes that no one has any right to receive anything from him or benefit from him, and he always covets, and sometimes even takes, what belongs to others. This is the quality of a **wicked** person.

NOTES

Mine is yours and yours is mine is an *am haaretz* – שֶׁלִּי שֶׁלָּךְ וְשֶׁלְּךָ שֶׁלִּי עַם הָאָרֶץ: The expression *am haaretz* is used at times as a pejorative term and at other times to mean an ordinary person. According to the explanation in the commentary, *am haaretz* is stated in a negative sense, because it is referring to one who seeks to exchange his portion and his fate with others; his statement reflects simple jealousy and a desire to become wealthy (see Rashi, *Midrash Shmuel*).

Some explain this expression as a neutral, or even positive expression, saying that the mishna is referring to a person willing to allow others to benefit from what is his, and who wishes to benefit from others, as do most people in the world, as this is the way of the world (Rabbeinu Yona, Bartenura, and others). This is what the Meiri maintains, and he notes that there is a variant reading: "This is the quality of every person."

Mishna 11

This mishna continues the theme of dividing character traits and ways of conduct into four categories.

אַרְבַּע מִדּוֹת בַּדֵּעוֹת:

There are four archetypal **qualities in temperament:**

נוֹחַ לִכְעוֹס וְנוֹחַ לִרְצוֹת – יָצָא שְׂכָרוֹ בְּהֶפְסֵדוֹ.

One who is **easy to anger and easy to assuage** is a person with a mercurial temperament, who is not particularly stable. He angers quickly and is quickly mollified. However, **his gain is superseded by his loss,** as, although he is easily appeased, ultimately his life is filled with anger.

קָשֶׁה לִכְעוֹס וְקָשֶׁה לִרְצוֹת – יָצָא הֶפְסֵדוֹ בִּשְׂכָרוֹ.

For one who is **hard to anger,** as he is level-headed and moderate, **and hard to assuage,** as due to that selfsame characteristic he will not change his mind after he is angered, even conciliation is difficult for him. **His loss is superseded by his gain,** as ultimately, he does not get angry often.

קָשֶׁה לִכְעוֹס וְנוֹחַ לִרְצוֹת – חָסִיד.

There is also one who is **hard to anger, but,** if he nevertheless becomes angry, is also **easy to assuage;**[N] in one way he is level-headed and moderate, but in another way he is quick to change his mind. This is not a character trait per se, but rather is the result of his working hard to rectify his personality traits so as never to be in a state of anger. That is why he is characterized as **pious.**

NOTES

Hard to anger, but easy to assuage – קָשֶׁה לִכְעוֹס וְנוֹחַ לִרְצוֹת: Some point out that in the mishna the pious person is not one who never gets angry, but one who seldom gets angry; as, there are situations where anger is necessary and positive (Rashbatz, Yaavetz). Some say simply that it is impossible for a person never to get angry (*Tiferet Yisrael*).

נוֹחַ לִכְעוֹס וְקָשֶׁה לִרְצוֹת – רָשָׁע.

This contrasts with one who is **easy to anger and hard to assuage,** who, similarly, possesses two contradictory qualities. Here too, this is not due to a natural personality trait, but rather due to his philosophy, as he does not consider anger to be a negative quality. That is why he is characterized as **wicked.**[N]

Mishna 12

This mishna continues dividing people's nature into four types. However, this mishna does not address personality traits, but rather the intellectual abilities of students.

אַרְבַּע מִדּוֹת בַּתַּלְמִידִים:

There are four archetypal **qualities in students,** in terms of their scholarly ability:

מַהֵר לִשְׁמֹעַ וּמַהֵר לְאַבֵּד – יָצָא שְׂכָרוֹ בְּהֶפְסֵדוֹ.

In the case of a student who is **quick to absorb and quick to forget, his gain is superseded by his loss.** His advantage stemming from his quick intellect is for naught, due to the speed with which he forgets, as, ultimately, little remains with him.

קָשֶׁה לִשְׁמֹעַ וְקָשֶׁה לְאַבֵּד – יָצָא הֶפְסֵדוֹ בִּשְׂכָרוֹ.

By contrast, with regard to one for whom it is **hard to absorb and hard to forget, his loss is superseded by his gain.** While he absorbs matters only after expending time and effort, he

NOTES

Wicked – רָשָׁע: For both the pious person and the wicked person, the commentary posits that the fact that his conduct is contradictory indicates that his quality is not a natural personality trait but the result of a certain life philosophy that shapes his personality. However, some explain that this conduct is a natural personality trait, but, because anger is an important cause of sin, the result is that one who is almost never angry is extremely close to the level of the pious. By contrast, one who is frequently angry is extremely close to being wicked regarding the rest of his actions. Likewise, they said in the Talmud (*Berakhot* 29a) in the name of Elijah the prophet: "Do not get angry, and you will not sin" (Rashi, Meiri, and others; see *Tiferet Yisrael*).

does not quickly forget them, and they remain with him. Ultimately, his shortcoming stemming from his slow perception is compensated for by his retentive memory, which preserves the matters that he grasped, for a long time.

מַהֵר לִשְׁמֹעַ וְקָשֶׁה לְאַבֵּד – חָכָם.

One who is privileged to be **quick to absorb and hard to forget** will ultimately become **wise;**[N] this is a gift from Heaven.

קָשֶׁה לִשְׁמֹעַ וּמַהֵר לְאַבֵּד – זֶה חֵלֶק רָע.

By contrast, with regard to one for whom it is **hard to absorb and,** on the other hand, he is **quick to forget, this is a bad lot** in life. This is his fate from Heaven that he has two characteristics that render his studies difficult.

Mishna 13

This mishna offers another list of four qualities relating to people's conduct and characteristics.

אַרְבַּע מִדּוֹת בְּנוֹתְנֵי צְדָקָה:

There are four archetypal **qualities among givers of charity,**[N] regarding the manner in which it is given:

NOTES

Quick to absorb and hard to forget will become wise – מַהֵר לִשְׁמוֹעַ וְקָשֶׁה לְאַבֵּד חָכָם: The mishna is not expressing a value judgment, but rather is listing traits that are a gift from Heaven. Ultimately, a person who possesses the combination of understanding and memory can become wise easily. However, there is a variant reading like the end of this mishna, that this quality is "a good lot in life" (Meiri, *Melekhet Shlomo*, and more).

There are four qualities among givers of charity – אַרְבַּע מִדּוֹת בְּנוֹתְנֵי צְדָקָה: Two of those enumerated in the mishna are those who do not want to give of their own; therefore, this statement may be understood as: "There are four qualities among people in their attitude toward givers of charity" (Bartenura). Some say that all the archetypes in the mishna actually give charity, but they differ in their intent, and this influences the nature and amount of the donation (Yaavetz, *Tiferet Yisrael*).

הָרוֹצֶה שֶׁיִּתֵּן וְלֹא יִתְּנוּ אֲחֵרִים – עֵינוֹ רָעָה בְּשֶׁל אֲחֵרִים.

The first type is **one who wants to give** charity himself **but** desires that **others will not give**[N] it, because he wants to do the mitzva all himself. One might say that **he is begrudging regarding what belongs,** pertains, **to others,** as he does not want others to perform good and important actions.

יִתְּנוּ אֲחֵרִים וְהוּא לֹא יִתֵּן – עֵינוֹ רָעָה בְּשֶׁלּוֹ.

With regard to one who wants **others to give but he will not give,**[N] **he is begrudging regarding what belongs to him;** he is a miser and does not want to expend anything of his own.

יִתֵּן וְיִתְּנוּ אֲחֵרִים – חָסִיד.

One who wants to **give and** desires that **others will give** is considered **pious.** His generosity of spirit makes him willing to give of his own and also to share with others in performance of mitzvot and doing good.

לֹא יִתֵּן וְלֹא יִתְּנוּ אֲחֵרִים – רָשָׁע.

By contrast, with regard to one who wants **to not give and** that **others will not give,** he is considered **wicked**, as he does not want charity to be given at all, due to his combination of miserliness and envy.

NOTES

One who wants to give but others will not give – הָרוֹצֶה שֶׁיִּתֵּן וְלֹא יִתְּנוּ אֲחֵרִים: Explaining this matter, some say that this person does not want anyone else to have a good reputation, or he believes that giving charity makes a person wealthy and he does not want others to gain the merit of the mitzva because he wants to be wealthier than they are (Rashi, Meiri). A different explanation is that this is a person who seeks to spare the assets of others, particularly his relatives and friends, more than he seeks to spare his own assets. Although he is willing to give his own money for charity, he does not wish for others to expend their assets for it (Bartenura).

Some explain that the clause "he is begrudging regarding what belongs to others" is referring to the poor; after he provides them with their basic needs, he does not want others to give them more, because he believes they do not deserve more than they already received (Yaavetz, *Tiferet Yisrael*).

Others to give but he will not give – יִתְּנוּ אֲחֵרִים וְהוּא לֹא יִתֵּן: The commentaries note that although this is not a positive attribute, it is less negative than wanting to give but desiring that others not give, because he does not begrudge the poor receiving support; he wants them to receive charity. He also does not begrudge others' merit or good reputation; he is just naturally miserly regarding his own money (Rashi, *Tosefot Yom Tov*, and others).

Mishna 14

This mishna, like the previous one, presents another list of four qualities or modes of people's conduct, returning to the area of Torah study.

אַרְבַּע מִדּוֹת בְּהוֹלְכֵי לְבֵית הַמִּדְרָשׁ:

There are four archetypal **qualities of those who go to the study hall:**

הוֹלֵךְ וְאֵינוֹ עוֹשֶׂה – שְׂכַר הֲלִיכָה בְּיָדוֹ.

One who goes to the study hall and learns material **but does not perform**[N] and fulfill what he learned **has** in any event **received reward for going.** He took the trouble to go and study, although he clearly lacks the practical element.

עוֹשֶׂה וְאֵינוֹ הוֹלֵךְ – שְׂכַר מַעֲשֶׂה בְּיָדוֹ.

If one **performs** the appropriate actions in accordance with what is studied in the study hall, **but** he himself **does not go** to the study hall, **he has received reward for the action,** but not the reward for Torah study.

NOTES

One who goes but does not perform – הוֹלֵךְ וְאֵינוֹ עוֹשֶׂה: The word "perform" in the mishna refers to practical fulfillment of the mitzvot. The mishna is not referring to one who does not fulfill mitzvot at all, as a person of that kind is called wicked; rather, this is one who seeks to concentrate on his studies but not necessarily to fulfill mitzvot, though when the opportunity to perform a mitzva presents itself, he performs it. For example, he fulfills the mitzvot that he is obligated to fulfill, but does not perform acts of kindness and the like (see Rabbeinu Yona, Rashbatz, and others). Some explain that, indeed, he does not fulfill the halakhot that he studied, but this is not out of rebellion but because he is unable to overcome his evil inclination (*Tiferet Yisrael*). There are also those who explain "perform" as relating to Torah study itself, i.e., he goes to the study hall but does not study there, or he is not successful in studying or remembering (Meiri, Bartenura). See below.

הוֹלֵךְ וְעוֹשֶׂה – חָסִיד.

One who goes to the study hall **and performs** what he studied there is **pious,**[N] as he integrates in his character both intellectual drive and adherence to practical halakha.

לֹא הוֹלֵךְ וְלֹא עוֹשֶׂה – רָשָׁע.

One who does not go to the study hall **and does not perform** what is studied there is **wicked.**

Mishna 15

This mishna presents another list of four qualities or modes of conduct that characterize people vis-à-vis Torah study.

אַרְבַּע מִדּוֹת בַּיּוֹשְׁבִים לִפְנֵי חֲכָמִים: סְפוֹג, וּמַשְׁפֵּךְ, מְשַׁמֶּרֶת, וְנָפָה.

There are **four qualities among** students who **sit before the Sages**[N] and absorb their words. They are likened to four household utensils used to absorb and expel: **a sponge, a funnel, a strainer** used for wine, **and a sieve.** The mishna elaborates:

NOTES

One who goes and performs [*oseh*] is pious – הוֹלֵךְ וְעוֹשֶׂה חָסִיד: Some explain "performs" in all these cases to mean that he counsels others and encourages them to go and study, like the Hebrew word *me'aseh*. According to this explanation, "one who goes but does not perform" is one who goes to study alone, who receives reward only for his own Torah study, while "performs but does not go" refers to one who sends others to study but does not himself join them. The latter is nevertheless rewarded, for having counseled others to go and study. One who goes and studies and even encourages others to go with him, is pious.

Another suggested explanation is that the mishna is referring to one who is on his way to the study hall when the opportunity to perform a mitzva presents itself, and he cannot manage to perform it and to study as well. One in this situation is rewarded for what he chooses. But if he expends great effort and manages to perform them both, he is called pious (*Midrash Shmuel*).

Among those who sit before the Sages – בְּיוֹשְׁבִים לִפְנֵי חֲכָמִים: The mishna teaches that those who sit before the Sages absorb their words in different ways. Beyond the differences that exist in each individual's understanding and his ability to draw conclusions on that basis, there are also differences in personality and intellectual disparities. These cause each person to learn and understand all his Torah in a different manner.

סְפוֹג – שֶׁהוּא סוֹפֵג אֶת הַכֹּל.

The first is **a sponge,**[B] **as it absorbs everything.**[N] This is a student who absorbs and understands everything that he hears, both significant and useful matters and insignificant and useless matters, and he does not distinguish between them.

מַשְׁפֵּךְ – שֶׁמַּכְנִיס בְּזוֹ וּמוֹצִיא בְּזוֹ.

A funnel[B] represents the opposite quality, as **it takes in on this** end **and expels on that** end. This is a person who hears everything, and immediately thereafter, he forgets and loses everything that he learned.

NOTES

A sponge, as it absorbs everything – סְפוֹג שֶׁהוּא סוֹפֵג אֶת הַכֹּל: The explanation in the commentary follows the simple understanding, of *Avot deRabbi Natan* (40). A "sponge" remembers everything, primary and secondary. A "funnel" remembers nothing. A "strainer" remembers only the secondary. A "sieve" remembers what is primary and most developed.

Some, however, explain the mishna otherwise. The "sponge" understands nothing on his own. Only if he is asked and prodded – squeezed – will he respond. The "funnel" is one who knows how to study and speak, and immediately when he studies, he articulates his Torah and teaches it to the multitudes. However, he does not have the intelligence to arrive at the deep understanding of the matters and to develop them. Similarly, a "strainer" is a student who knows how to separate the quality "wine," and then he teaches it to others but keeps the secondary matters in his heart and dismisses them. The "sieve" is one who is stingy regarding the honor of the Sages from whom he learns; he keeps their primary teachings to himself, and disseminates only their secondary teachings (see *Midrash Shmuel*, *Tiferet Yisrael*, and *Avot deRabbi Natan* 29).

BACKGROUND

Sponge [*sefog*] – סְפוֹג: From the Greek *sefongos*, this word moved to the Latin spongia, then to other languages, including Hebrew, where the root *samekh*, *peh*, *gimmel* then developed. This root connotes absorption of liquids, and more broadly, absorbing or receiving other matters, like the expression regarding one who incurs liability to be flogged in court: "He incurs [*sofeg*] the forty lashes." The *sefog* mentioned in the mishna is the natural bath sponge, made from the soft, flexible skeleton of *Spongia officinalis*, from the sea bed. After the living tissue of the creature decomposes, it is rinsed, and the skeleton is dried. The *sefog* has a wool-like texture, with many air holes, which is why it absorbs liquids well.

Sponge

Funnel – מַשְׁפֵּךְ:

Roman funnel, first to third centuries CE

מְשַׁמֶּרֶת – שֶׁמּוֹצִיאָה אֶת הַיַּיִן וְקוֹלֶטֶת אֶת הַשְּׁמָרִים.

Third is **a strainer**[B] **that lets out the wine and retains the sediment** that remains in it. Such a student has the ability to absorb, but his ability to discern is lacking, and he fixates specifically on those parts of what he heard that are not significant, even those that are worthy of rejection. It is specifically the important matters, which are analogized to wine, that he forgets and loses.

וְנָפָה – שֶׁמּוֹצִיאָה אֶת הַקֶּמַח וְקוֹלֶטֶת אֶת הַסֹּלֶת.

And by contrast, there is one who is like **a sieve**[B] **that lets out the flour,** the very fine flour considered to be of low quality, **and retains the high-quality flour,**[B] with larger particles, which is the most select portion. This is the student who has both

BACKGROUND

Strainer [*meshameret*] – מְשַׁמֶּרֶת: This refers to a utensil used for filtering wine. Its name apparently derives from the word *shemarim*, meaning dregs (Rashi, Rambam), because it was used primarily to filter the dregs from wine before drinking. The strainer is made from fabric of a garment or from sackcloth, and the wine would be poured through it. The strainer would be stretched onto pegs and suspended over a vessel, or sometimes stretched over the vessel itself.

Strainer

Sieve – נָפָה: The sieve is fine mesh material, crafted from rubber, palm branches, or other materials. It was used for sifting flour and high-quality flour after the grains had been ground.

Sieve

High-quality flour [*solet*] – סֹלֶת: In the language of the Bible, *solet* is high-quality, sifted flour, perhaps "white flour." This was pure flour ground from kernels from which the bran was removed, while regular flour is "whole flour," with the bran mixed in. This understanding of *solet* appears in rabbinic literature in various contexts, e.g., meal offerings (*Menaḥot* 8:2). An additional meaning of *solet* in rabbinic literature and in modern Hebrew, and which is also the basis for the commentary here, is the thicker particles that are formed from the center of the kernel, the endosperm, while grinding wheat kernels. They remain in the sieve during the sifting, as opposed to flour, which falls through the small holes (T. Dickstein).

the ability to grasp material and the ability to appropriately discern what he heard. He remembers and maintains only the essence, the best and most meaningful matters, but not the matters of secondary importance.

Mishna 16

The mishna turns to discuss matters that have two aspects, a positive aspect and a corresponding negative aspect. The first matter discussed is love.

כָּל אַהֲבָה שֶׁהִיא תְלוּיָה בְדָבָר, בָּטֵל דָּבָר – בְּטֵלָה אַהֲבָה.

With regard to **any love that is contingent**[N] **on a circumstance,** that it is not directed toward the loved one himself but toward an objective to acquire something else, i.e., money, influence, or anything else; **when the circumstance,** the motive for the love, **is nullified,**[N] e.g., if the lover does not need him anymore, **the love is nullified** with it.

וְשֶׁאֵינָהּ תְּלוּיָה בְדָבָר – אֵינָהּ בְּטֵלָה לְעוֹלָם.

And, by contrast, love **that is not contingent on a circumstance,** but is love of the beloved himself, **is never nullified,** as no reason can arise to nullify it.

NOTES

Any love that is contingent – כָּל אַהֲבָה שֶׁהִיא תְלוּיָה: Various behaviors look like love but in truth have no inner emotion, because their intent is to acquire something. Showing love in order to acquire money or honor from another person is not love at all; it is merely a pretense. But an emotion could also look like love, and the person himself experiences it as love, even if it is not in fact actual love, as it is contingent upon acquiring something.

Any love that is contingent on a circumstance, when the circumstance is nullified – כָּל אַהֲבָה שֶׁהִיא תְלוּיָה בְדָבָר בָּטֵל דָּבָר: There is a variant reading: "Any love that is contingent on an ephemeral circumstance, when the circumstance is null the love is null. And love that is not contingent on an ephemeral circumstance is never null" (Bartenura). Even according to the version here it can be understood in this manner, that it is referring to something ephemeral, meaning that it is external and temporary; but love that is dependent upon a matter that is not ephemeral, but rather eternal, directed to the ultimate truth and fulfillment of God's will, endures forever (see Rambam and Bartenura). On a similar note, love that is natural, like the love of a person for his family, is not considered null (*Tiferet Yisrael*).

The mishna cites examples of this from the Bible.

אֵיזוֹ הִיא אַהֲבָה הַתְּלוּיָה בְּדָבָר? זוֹ אַהֲבַת אַמְנוֹן וְתָמָר.

Which is love that is contingent on a circumstance? This is the love of Amnon and Tamar.[N] Although it appeared that Amnon exceedingly loved Tamar (II Samuel 13:1), in fact, this love was based on his powerful lust for her body. That is why, once he satisfied his lust, he no longer had any feelings of love toward her (II Samuel 13:15).

וְשֶׁאֵינָהּ תְּלוּיָה בְּדָבָר? זוֹ אַהֲבַת דָּוִד וִיהוֹנָתָן.

And which is love **that is not contingent on a circumstance? This is the love of David and Yehonatan,**[N] which was not meant to attain anything beyond their love for one another. That is why, even with all the peaks and valleys in the external circumstances of their relationship, when David's status was ascendant and when it was descendant, this love remained intact. Even after Yehonatan's death it was not nullified (II Samuel 1:26).

NOTES

This is the love of Amnon and Tamar – זוֹ אַהֲבַת אַמְנוֹן וְתָמָר: The incident of Amnon and Tamar is related in II Samuel (chap. 13). Amnon son of David fell in love with his half sister (whom, from a halakhic perspective, he was permitted to marry), to the extent that he became ill due to his great love for her. He was not satisfied until he brutally raped her. The Bible relates that just after he satisfied his lust, his love was transformed into "exceedingly great hatred, as the hatred that he hated her was greater than the love that he had loved her…and said: Please send this one away from me, and lock the door behind her" (II Samuel 13:15–17). There is a variant reading: "The love of Amnon for Tamar," as Tamar did not love Amnon (*Melekhet Shlomo*).

This is the love of David and Yehonatan – זוֹ אַהֲבַת דָּוִד וִיהוֹנָתָן: The love that existed between David and Yehonatan son of Saul is described in the verse: "The soul of Yehonatan became attached to the soul of David, and Yehonatan loved him as his soul" (I Samuel 18:1–2). It constitutes an expression of love that is not contingent on a circumstance, as it stood contrary to Yehonatan's simple interests. The choice of David and his success constituted, for all intents and purposes, a threat to Yehonatan's future reign as his father Saul's heir, as Saul said to him: "For all the days that the son of Yishai lives upon the earth, you and your kingdom will not be established" (I Samuel 20:31).

Mishna 17

Following the previous mishna, which dealt with two types of love, this mishna deals with two similar types of disputes.

כָּל מַחֲלוֹקֶת שֶׁהִיא לְשֵׁם שָׁמַיִם – סוֹפָהּ לְהִתְקַיֵּים.

In **any dispute that is for the sake of Heaven,** when one group of people disagrees with another in an attempt to seek the truth and not because of any personal agenda based on envy, pride, or hatred, even if that group did not prevail in that dispute, the dispute **will ultimately endure.**[N]

וְשֶׁאֵינָהּ לְשֵׁם שָׁמַיִם – אֵין סוֹפָהּ לְהִתְקַיֵּים.

But a dispute **that is not for the sake of Heaven,** that is not purely to ascertain the truth but is based on other motives, **will ultimately not endure;** it is destined to disappear.

The mishna cites examples of this.

אֵיזוֹ הִיא מַחֲלוֹקֶת שֶׁהִיא לְשֵׁם שָׁמַיִם? זוֹ מַחֲלוֹקֶת הִלֵּל וְשַׁמַּאי.

Which is a dispute that is for the sake of Heaven? This is the dispute of Hillel and Shammai.[N] Hillel and Shammai themselves, and their disciples, Beit Hillel and Beit Shammai after them, all endured, and their

NOTES

Any dispute that is for the sake of Heaven will ultimately endure – כָּל מַחֲלוֹקֶת שֶׁהִיא לְשֵׁם שָׁמַיִם סוֹפָהּ לְהִתְקַיֵּים: The term "dispute" here is interpreted as one faction disagreeing with another faction. If those who disagree with the others do so for the sake of Heaven, their position will endure over time (Meiri). Many explain that this is referring to a gathering where there is a difference of opinion. If the intent of all of them is for the sake of Heaven, they will clarify their opinions with one another and will thereby converge on the truth, and the issue for which they convened will endure. However, if one faction disagrees, not in pursuit of the truth but for the sake of ancillary and personal matters, their opinion will not endure (see Bartenura and *Tiferet Yisrael*). Some explain that this statement means that the dispute itself will endure, that each of the disputants will live a long life adhering consistently to his own approach in a series of disputes, and they will not die or disperse after their initial dispute, unlike the case of Korah (Rabbeinu Yona).

The dispute of Hillel and Shammai – מַחֲלוֹקֶת הִלֵּל וְשַׁמַּאי: The idea that the dispute between

statements endured, even though one of the parties prevailed in the dispute.

וְשֶׁאֵינָהּ לְשֵׁם שָׁמַיִם? זוֹ מַחֲלוֹקֶת קֹרַח וְכָל עֲדָתוֹ.

And which is a dispute that is **not for the sake of Heaven? This is the dispute of Korah and his entire congregation.**[N] Some of them were actually eradicated from the world, when they were swallowed by the earth or consumed by fire, and the rest scattered in all directions.

Mishna 18

This mishna continues with the presentation of two contrary types of conduct and their correspondingly opposite consequences.

כָּל הַמְזַכֶּה אֶת הָרַבִּים – אֵין חֵטְא בָּא עַל יָדוֹ.

Anyone who, through his actions or his words, **confers merit upon the multitudes** receives help from Heaven that unwitting **sin will not come** upon him or upon the multitudes, **by means of him.**[N]

NOTES

Shammai and Hillel was for the sake of Heaven can be derived from the fact that they treated one another with deference and on occasion conceded to the opinion of the other (see *Yevamot* 1:4; *Eduyyot* 1:12–14). Although it might appear that the words of Beit Shammai did not endure, as the halakha was ruled in accordance with the opinion of Beit Hillel, the meaning is that their words were written in the Mishna for the generations, because they have value and significance (*Melekhet Shlomo*; see *Eduyyot* 1:4–6). Their dispute actually continues over time, as the Sages study the reasoning of both of them and deliberate in their regard, despite the fact that the halakha was established in accordance with only one of the parties (*Midrash Shmuel*). Some explain the mishna according to a mystical tradition that in the future, the halakha will be ruled in accordance with the opinion of Beit Shammai (Ḥida in *Petaḥ Einayim*).

The dispute of Korah and his entire congregation – מַחֲלוֹקֶת קֹרַח וְכָל עֲדָתוֹ: Some note that the mishna says: "The dispute of Korah and his entire congregation," and not, "the dispute of Korah and Moses." The reason is that Moses's intent was for the sake of Heaven (*Leḥem Yehuda*). Moreover, there was division and dissent among the congregation of Korah, as each one wanted authority and honor for himself and they were not united (*Melekhet Shlomo*).

Anyone who confers merit upon the multitudes, unwitting sin will not come by means of him – כָּל הַמְזַכֶּה אֶת הָרַבִּים אֵין חֵטְא בָּא עַל יָדוֹ: The fact that sin is not facilitated by one who confers merit upon the multitudes is explicit in *Avot deRabbi Natan* (40): "So there would not be a situation where his disciples inherit the World to Come and he descends to the netherworld." According to that, it appears that the

וְכָל הַמַּחֲטִיא אֶת הָרַבִּים – אֵין מַסְפִּיקִין בְּיָדוֹ לַעֲשׂוֹת תְּשׁוּבָה.

By contrast, with regard to **anyone who causes the multitudes to sin,** not only are their sins assessed against him, but **opportunity,** conditions and circumstances, **to repent is not given him.**[N] He will forever remain in the lowly status that he brought upon himself.

The mishna cites examples of this:

מֹשֶׁה זָכָה וְזִכָּה אֶת הָרַבִּים – זְכוּת הָרַבִּים תָּלוּי בּוֹ, שֶׁנֶּאֱמַר: "צִדְקַת ה' עָשָׂה וּמִשְׁפָּטָיו עִם יִשְׂרָאֵל".

Moses was worthy of merit himself **and conferred merit upon the multitudes.** Therefore, not only are his own actions credited to him, but also, **the merit of the multitudes,** of the mitzvot that all Israel performed, **is attributed to him,** as though he himself performed them, **as it is stated: "He performed the righteousness of the Lord, and His judgments with Israel"** (Deuteronomy 33:21). In other words, although some of the actions that Moses performed with Israel were God's commands and instructions, nevertheless, the righteousness and judgments are attributed to Moses himself.

NOTES

mishna is referring primarily to personal sin that the person will commit. However, some say that it is referring to the fact that he will not err when issuing rulings to the multitudes. Even if he errs, matters will develop such that no stumbling block will result from his error (Yaavetz; see *Avoda Zara* 22a).

Opportunity to repent is not given him – **אֵין מַסְפִּיקִין בְּיָדוֹ לַעֲשׂוֹת תְּשׁוּבָה**: One who causes the multitudes to sin does not receive assistance from Heaven to arrive at a situation where he will be able to repent, "so there would not be a situation where his disciples descend to the netherworld and he inherits the World to Come" (*Avot deRabbi Natan*

Site in Tel Dan that some scholars identify as the site of Yorovam's worship; tenth century BCE

יָרָבְעָם חָטָא וְהֶחֱטִיא אֶת הָרַבִּים – חֵטְא הָרַבִּים תָּלוּי בּוֹ, שֶׁנֶּאֱמַר: ״עַל חַטֹּאות יָרָבְעָם (בן נבט) אֲשֶׁר חָטָא וַאֲשֶׁר הֶחֱטִיא אֶת יִשְׂרָאֵל״.

By contrast, **Yorovam** son of Nevat **sinned and caused the multitudes to sin.** After he revolted against the royal house of David and established the kingdom of Israel, he crafted the golden calves and caused the entire people of Israel to sin (see I Kings, chap. 12). **The sin of the multitudes,** even after his death, **is** therefore **attributed to him, as it is stated: "For the sins of Yorovam that he sinned and that he caused Israel to sin"** (I Kings 15:30).

Mishna 19

The previous *mishnayot* addressed actions that are for the sake of Heaven and those that are not, and one who confers merit upon the multitudes and one who causes them to sin. This mishna continues the theme of two opposite legacies, one positive and one negative.

כָּל מִי שֶׁיֵּשׁ בְּיָדוֹ שְׁלֹשָׁה דְּבָרִים הַלָּלוּ – מִתַּלְמִידָיו שֶׁל אַבְרָהָם אָבִינוּ. וּשְׁלֹשָׁה דְּבָרִים אֲחֵרִים – מִתַּלְמִידָיו שֶׁל בִּלְעָם הָרָשָׁע.

Anyone who possesses these three characteristics that are enumerated below **is among the disciples,** who follow the virtuous path, **of Abraham our forefather,** and is affiliated with his spiritual path. **But** anyone who possesses **three other,** contrary, **characteristics is among the disciples of the wicked Bilam.**[N]

NOTES

40). According to the Rambam this means that he is actually prevented from repenting; but many other commentaries say it means that although the person will not receive assistance from Heaven to repent, if he tries anyway and rouses himself to repent, his repentance is accepted (see *Tosefot Yom Tov*). Another explains that the mishna is also referring to the natural course of things. One who confers merit upon the multitudes is found in good company that protects him so he will not stumble. By contrast, one who causes the multitudes to sin is found in bad company, which prevents him from repenting for his evil deeds (*Midrash Shmuel*).

Among the disciples of Abraham our forefather… of the wicked Bilam – מִתַּלְמִידָיו שֶׁל אַבְרָהָם אָבִינוּ... שֶׁל בִּלְעָם הָרָשָׁע: The contrast between Abraham and Bilam is accentuated because of the similarities in their backgrounds. Externally, both of them originated from Aram and came to the

עַיִן טוֹבָה, וְרוּחַ נְמוּכָה, וְנֶפֶשׁ שְׁפָלָה – מִתַּלְמִידָיו שֶׁל אַבְרָהָם אָבִינוּ.

The mishna elaborates: One who possesses **a generous eye** and looks favorably upon the success and prominence of others without envying them, hating them, or seeking to stymie them; **and** likewise, he possesses **a humble spirit** and does not aspire to prominence or honor for himself; **and** likewise, he possesses **a modest soul,** in that he is satisfied with little as far as matters of this world are concerned, is **among the disciples of Abraham our forefather.**

עַיִן רָעָה, וְרוּחַ גְּבוֹהָה, וְנֶפֶשׁ רְחָבָה – מִתַּלְמִידָיו שֶׁל בִּלְעָם הָרָשָׁע.

By contrast, one who possesses **a miserly eye,**[N] in that he hates people, and the success of others pains him and troubles him; **and** likewise, he possesses **an arrogant spirit,**[N] in the sense of haughtiness and aspiration

NOTES

boundaries of Israel, and internally, they were in essence not leaders of a nation, and not prophets who received a particular, defined mission from God, but rather private individuals with prophetic ability and inspiration, who apparently were leaders or mentors of groups of people. There is also some similarity between the stories related in their regard (see, e.g., Genesis 22:3 and Numbers 22:21). It is specifically that similarity that underscores the polar differences between these two personalities; Abraham represents the epitome of good, while Bilam, despite being a prophet, was a wicked person in terms of his personality traits.

The difference between these two types of people is primarily a difference of approach, philosophy, and perspective. The personality traits mentioned in the mishna are not mentioned explicitly in the Torah, whether regarding Abraham or regarding Bilam, but they emerge from their statements and their conduct. The statement that each of them has "disciples" means, therefore, that there are people who follow their path. They can consequently be called disciples even if they follow that path not in imitation of their "teacher" but on their own initiative (see Meiri).

A miserly eye – **עַיִן רָעָה**: A generous eye is the attribute of a person who is happy with his lot and does not want anything beyond what he has, but, on the other hand, is happy that others have plenty (Meiri, Yaavetz, and others; see 2:9). The fact that Abraham possessed that quality is derived from what is stated: "I will not take so much as a thread or a sandal strap of what is yours" (Genesis 14:23), and, in general, from how he sought to benefit other people.

By contrast, Bilam had a miserly eye. He wanted much money for himself, as he said: "If Balak would give me his house full of silver and gold" (Numbers 22:18, 24:13). He also sought to impose an evil eye upon Israel (see Numbers 24:2 and Rashi there). Moreover, ultimately, when he was unable to curse as he was asked to, he counseled Balak on how he could cause Israel to be debased, because he was unable to bear seeing Israel succeed.

An arrogant spirit – **רוּחַ גְּבוֹהָה**: A humble spirit connotes humility, as Abraham said: "I am dust and ashes" (Genesis 18:27). By contrast, Bilam was arrogant, as he said: "As the Lord refused to allow me to go with you" (Numbers 22:13), implying, "but only with those greater than you." Likewise, he boastfully said about

for great honor and greater accomplishments; **and** likewise, he possesses **an avaricious soul,**[N] in that he is filled with a sense of greatness and desires many things in this world for himself, is **among the disciples of the wicked Bilam.**

מַה בֵּין תַּלְמִידָיו שֶׁל אַבְרָהָם אָבִינוּ לְתַלְמִידָיו שֶׁל בִּלְעָם הָרָשָׁע?

What is the difference **between** the fate of **the disciples of Abraham our forefather and** that of **the disciples of the wicked Bilam?**

תַּלְמִידָיו שֶׁל אַבְרָהָם אָבִינוּ – אוֹכְלִין בָּעוֹלָם הַזֶּה וְנוֹחֲלִין בָּעוֹלָם הַבָּא, שֶׁנֶּאֱמַר: "לְהַנְחִיל אֹהֲבַי יֵשׁ, וְאֹצְרֹתֵיהֶם אֲמַלֵּא".

The disciples of Abraham our forefather live and **benefit in this world,** because the attributes of their nature provide them with a decent way of life with suitable gratification, **and** since they conduct themselves in the proper manner, **they inherit** their share **in the World to Come, as it is stated: "To bequeath substance to those who love me, and I will fill their storehouses"** (Proverbs 8:21);[N] "substance" – in the World to Come; and "fill their storehouses" – in this world.

NOTES

himself: "The utterance of one who hears the sayings of God, and knows the knowledge of the Most High, he shall see the vision of the Almighty" (Numbers 24:16), claiming that he sees and can speak about everything, and that kings must obey him.

An avaricious soul – **נֶפֶשׁ רְחָבָה**: "A modest soul" is the attribute of not seeking prominence and of being content with what one has. Abraham did not seek great things for himself at all, not from others and not from God (see *Maḥzor Vitri*). Some explain that "a modest soul" refers to refraining from lust to the point of extreme caution, as it was inferred from the verses that Abraham did not look at Sarah's beauty (see Genesis 12:11, and see Rambam and others).

By contrast, it is stated that Bilam was steeped in desires, as is clear from the fact that he wanted much silver and gold, as well as from his counsel to Balak to send the daughters of Moav to engage in harlotry with Israel (see Rambam). Rashi explains that "a modest soul" is one who involves himself with people and is not condescending to others. He cites a variant reading: "A curt soul," instead of "an avaricious soul," meaning an impatient person whose interchanges with other people are harsh.

To bequeath substance to those who love me, and I will fill their storehouses – **לְהַנְחִיל אֹהֲבַי יֵשׁ וְאֹצְרֹתֵיהֶם אֲמַלֵּא**: This verse contains two segments. That is why it is expounded as relating to both the share designated for the righteous in the World to Come, which is the true substance – "to bequeath substance to those who love me" – and the share that the righteous receive in this world, in which they have everything that is good – "and I will fill their storehouses." Even if they do not always receive

אֲבָל תַּלְמִידָיו שֶׁל בִּלְעָם הָרָשָׁע – יוֹרְשִׁין גֵּיהִנֹּם וְיוֹרְדִין לִבְאֵר שַׁחַת, שֶׁנֶּאֱמַר: ״וְאַתָּה אֱלֹהִים תּוֹרִידֵם לִבְאֵר שַׁחַת, אַנְשֵׁי דָמִים וּמִרְמָה לֹא יֶחֱצוּ יְמֵיהֶם. וַאֲנִי אֶבְטַח בָּךְ״.

But, by contrast, **the disciples of the wicked Bilam** have no tranquility in this world, due to their covetousness. Their evil deeds lead them to **inherit Gehenna** after their death, **and to descend to the pit of destruction,** as their souls will be excised and will completely disappear, **as it is stated: "You, God, will bring them down to the pit of destruction. Men of bloodshed and deceit will not live out half their days,**[N] **but I will trust in You"** (Psalms 55:24). "Bring them down to the pit of destruction" – after their death; "will not live out half of their days" – they will die or be killed during their best years.

Mishna 20

The mishna begins by enumerating four special traits taken from the animal world, each of which should be adapted for and employed in the appropriate context and at the appropriate time in fulfilling God's will.

יְהוּדָה בֶּן תֵּימָא אוֹמֵר:

Yehuda ben Teima[P] **says:**[N]

NOTES

everything, still, since jealousy, ambition, and arrogance are absent, they have the ability to enjoy the portion that they acquired. Another explains that the phrase, "to bequeath substance to those who love me," which is in present tense, relates to this world, and that "I will fill their storehouses," which is in future tense, relates to the World to Come (*Pirkei Moshe*). The commentaries say that this verse relates particularly to the disciples of Abraham, who is called: "Abraham who loved Me" (Isaiah 41:8).

Men of bloodshed and deceit will not live out half their days – אַנְשֵׁי דָמִים וּמִרְמָה לֹא יֶחֱצוּ יְמֵיהֶם: The commentaries say that this verse is stated regarding the wicked, Bilam among them, who were killed before they lived even half of a typical life expectancy, in other words, before they reach the age of thirty-five (Rashi and others, based on *Sanhedrin* 106b). By contrast, it is described that Abraham toward the end of his life was "old, advanced in years, and the Lord blessed Abraham with everything" (Genesis 24:1), and he "died at a good old age, aged and content" (Genesis 25:8).

Yehuda ben Teima says – יְהוּדָה בֶּן תֵּימָא אוֹמֵר: This mishna contains two statements that were

הֱוֵי עַז כַּנָּמֵר, וְקַל כַּנֶּשֶׁר, וְרָץ כַּצְּבִי, וְגִבּוֹר כָּאֲרִי, לַעֲשׂוֹת רְצוֹן אָבִיךָ שֶׁבַּשָּׁמַיִם.

Be bold like a leopard,[NB] be **light like a**

NOTES

established for the generations as foundation stones of the Jewish world. The initial statement of the mishna was chosen as the beginning of the *Arbaa Turim*, a work that was the first to divide Jewish halakha into the four sections that ultimately served as the basis for the *Shulḥan Arukh*. The *Shulḥan Arukh* also begins with a selection from this mishna. The concluding statement, "May it be Your will….," was established (using a variant reading that includes "that the Temple will be constructed"), as a brief prayer recited immediately after the end of each *Amida* prayer, and is well known as the essence of Israel's hopes and prayers.

Bold [*az*] like a leopard – **עַז כַּנָּמֵר**: *Az* means bold, impudent, and inconsiderate of others. The trait is characteristic of the leopard, as even though it is not the largest predator, it is bolder than other beasts. Its boldness, along with its physical strength, aids it in overcoming its prey or its enemies. In the context of service of God, this trait refers to the ability of a servant of God to be daring and to stay true to his path without fearing criticism from those taunting him, and to stand firm in his convictions even without support.

Light like a vulture – **קַל כַּנֶּשֶׁר**: The vulture reaches great heights and can move from place to place with great speed and little effort. In the context of service of God, the vulture's lightness refers to the ability to sever oneself from a certain place and matter and to move on to another matter that is more significant at that moment. The *Tur* says that this refers to how quickly one closes his eyes when encountering inappropriate matters. Commentaries on the mishna say that it refers to one's general effort in performing mitzvot (Rashi), and especially to the ease with which one reviews his Torah studies, as he will thereby ascend ever higher (Rashbatz, Bartenura).

PERSONALITIES

Yehuda ben Teima – **יְהוּדָה בֶּן תֵּימָא**: Yehuda ben Teima is mentioned once in the Mishna and very few times in the *Tosefta* and *baraitot*. In the Talmud, he and his colleagues were characterized with the title "Masters of the Mishna," and it is stated that in their time, six or seven hundred orders of Mishna were taught (*Ḥagiga* 14a). Some see this depiction as an allusion to the fact that he was from an earlier period and was one of the earliest *tanna'im*.

BACKGROUND

Leopard [*namer*] – **נָמֵר**: The leopard was commonly found in the Land of Israel in ancient times. A few individual leopards can still be found in the country's deserts. Leopards feed off small and medium-sized animals, e.g., birds, hares, gazelles, and ibexes, and those who live near human residential areas attack cattle and sheep as well. The word "*namer*" in the Bible and in rabbinic literature may also include the cheetah, *Acinonyx jubatus*, which resembles the leopard.

Bold like a leopard, Arabian leopard

vulture,[NB] **run** quickly **like a gazelle,**[NB] **and** be **strong** in your confrontations **like a lion,**[NB] all **to perform the will of your Father in Heaven,** even if in other areas it is out of character for you to conduct yourself in that manner.

הוּא הָיָה אוֹמֵר: עַז פָּנִים לְגֵיהִנֹּם, וּבֹשֶׁת פָּנִים לְגַן עֵדֶן.

However, these characteristics per se are not necessarily desirable, especially the first of them, just as **he,** himself, **would say: The bold,** an impertinent person, will ultimately go **to Gehenna,** as he does not accept authority, **but,** by contrast, one who has **shame** over his improper actions and regrets them will ultimately reach **the Garden of Eden.**

The mishna continues with a comment in the form of a prayer, relating to the previous matter.

יְהִי רָצוֹן מִלְּפָנֶיךָ ה׳ אֱלֹהֵינוּ שֶׁתִּבְנֶה עִירְךָ בִּמְהֵרָה בְּיָמֵינוּ, וְתֵן חֶלְקֵנוּ בְּתוֹרָתֶךָ.

May it be Your will,[N] **Lord, our God, that You will build Your city,** Jerusalem, and the Temple will be constructed **speedily in our days,** restoring the way of life that existed in the nation's glorious past. **And** may it

NOTES

Run like a gazelle – רָץ כַּצְּבִי: The gazelle runs quickly and is capable of surmounting various obstacles. In the context of service of God, this refers to the ability to run around and energetically perform every mitzva, and do everything that is necessary and fitting to perform, with alacrity.

Strong like a lion – גִּבּוֹר כָּאֲרִי: To be strong like a lion means to bolster one's strength in order to overcome all enemies, like a lion that fights for what belongs to it and does not withdraw. Commentaries say that this refers primarily to overcoming the evil inclination (Rashbatz, Bartenura; see 3:1) and to fulfilling mitzvot with all one's might (Rabbeinu Yona). Likewise, the *Tur* depicted this trait as relating to the willpower necessary to rise early in the morning.

May it be Your will – יְהִי רָצוֹן מִלְּפָנֶיךָ: The construction of the Temple is a manifestation and symbol of the spiritual renaissance of the Jewish people, and the betterment of the world in general. This request at the end of the mishna explains and clarifies what was stated previously, that the fact that a person must take all sorts of extreme measures in order to perform the will of his Father in Heaven is because the reality of this world is not proper and its ways are not true. The proper situation is to have the Temple rebuilt and the general reality supporting fulfillment of God's will, so there will be no need for extraordinary efforts like these (see *Tosefot Rabbi Akiva Eiger*). In practice, this prayer may serve to teach that one must pray not only for the perfection of various minor details, but for the fundamental, general betterment of everything.

be Your will to **grant us our portion,** the course of our lives, to be connected **with Your Torah.** Then there will be no need for extraordinary efforts in order to perform the will of God, because one's entire way of life will conform and correspond to it.

BACKGROUND

Vulture [*nesher*] – נֶשֶׁר: The griffon vulture, *Gyps fulvus*, is a bird of prey mentioned many times in the Bible. The book of Micah (1:16) mentions the *karaḥat*, a short, white tuft of hair that grows on the vulture's head and neck and is a characteristic sign of this bird. Presumably, the vulture's name derives from the word *neshira*, meaning shedding, due to its bald appearance. The vulture is mentioned in the Mishna only here, a few times in the *Tosefta* and *baraitot*, and many times in the two Talmuds. From the contexts where it appears in rabbinic literature, it may be concluded *that nesher* also relates occasionally to the eagle, which was one of the symbols of the Greek god Zeus, and the eagle appears among the symbols of the Roman army. As a result, *nesher* was also an appellation for the Roman army.

While in modern Hebrew a *nesher* is an eagle, it is clear that the *nesher* here refers to a griffon vulture and not an eagle. The Bible describes the *nesher* as a bird that is bald and feeds on carrion. The eagle, even the bald eagle, is not bald, and it is a bird of prey (R. Natan Slifkin).

Gazelle [*tzevi*] – צְבִי: The gazelle is a wild animal of which several species can be found in the Land of Israel. In the time of the Sages, the gazelle was commonly found near human habitation, and they were typically hunted. The gazelle has advanced running ability, which enables it to quickly flee when it senses danger. The lightness of the legs of the gazelle is mentioned in additional places in the Bible and rabbinic literature, like in the verse: "Asa'el was swift of foot like one of the gazelles in the field" (II Samuel 2:18).

Proof that the *tzevi* is a gazelle and not a deer can be cited from the Talmud where it is described as having horns that are not branched. The deer's antlers are branched.

The *namer*, *nesher*, and *tzevi* are often misidentified as the tiger, eagle, and deer respectively. This is because the leopard, vulture, and gazelle did not exist in Europe and the Jewish communities that lived there identified these animals with those with which they were familiar (R. Natan Slifkin).

Lion – אֲרִי: The lion, *Panthera leo persica*, was the largest, most threatening predator in the ancient Land of Israel. A male lion can reach a weight of 250 kg. Lions attack herds of livestock and flocks in places where their habitats are adjacent to grazing pastures. They do not typically attack people, although there are recorded instances of lions who mauled people during times of famine. Lions disappeared from the Land of Israel and from all of Europe during the Crusades. The tremendous impression created by the lion's size, strength, and roar led to its serving as a symbol in several contexts. It appears in mosaics and wall drawings in synagogues.

Light like a vulture

Run like a gazelle

Strong like a lion

Mishna 21

This mishna continues the numbers-based theme, presenting a complete program for the various levels and stages that a person goes through during the course of his lifetime. This program largely parallels the standard practice in those days, although it has changed somewhat from generation to generation.

הוּא הָיָה אוֹמֵר:

He, Yehuda ben Teima, **would say:**[N]

בֶּן חָמֵשׁ שָׁנִים לַמִּקְרָא,

Five years old for study of the **Bible,**[N] the Written Torah, which includes the Torah, Prophets, and Writings.

בֶּן עֶשֶׂר לַמִּשְׁנָה,

Ten years old for study of **Mishna,**[N] the principles and the laws contained in the Oral Torah, which are studied in an orderly, systematic manner.

NOTES

He would say – הוּא הָיָה אוֹמֵר: According to the version that appears in the mishna, "he" refers to the Sage, Rabbi Yehuda ben Teima. However, there are variant readings that attribute this statement to Shmuel HaKatan. Other variant readings do not include this statement in this tractate. According to those readings, it is an external *baraita* (see Meiri, Rashbatz, and others).

The commentaries expounded several sources from verses as derivations for these times; however, this mishna is primarily a description of the appropriate course a person's life should take, one that accords with the nature of the world.

Five years old for Bible – בֶּן חָמֵשׁ שָׁנִים לַמִּקְרָא: The commentaries say that a father begins to teach his child at age three so that two years later, when the child is strong and mature enough and can read properly, he is enrolled in school where he can begin learning the verses of the Bible (see *Ketubot* 50a). However, there are some who explain that the mishna means that one begins teaching the child to read at age five (Meiri).

Children studying Torah in Tiznit, Morocco, 1935

בֶּן שְׁלֹשׁ עֶשְׂרֵה לְמִצְוֹת,

Thirteen years old for the obligation to fulfill mitzvot, as that is when the body begins physical maturity, which is accompanied by emotional and intellectual maturity. That point was determined as the transitional point, after which the young man is obligated in mitzvot like any other Jewish adult. For a young woman the age is twelve years old.

בֶּן חֲמֵשׁ עֶשְׂרֵה לְתַלְמוּד,

When he is **fifteen years old,** after having properly engaged in acquiring the foundation of Bible and Mishna, he is prepared **for** beginning to study **Talmud** – the analysis and deliberation regarding all those matters he studied previously.

בֶּן שְׁמוֹנֶה עֶשְׂרֵה לְחֻפָּה,

When he is **eighteen years old,** that is the appropriate time **for standing under the wedding canopy,** i.e., marrying a woman, as by then he has attained some emotional and physical maturity.

בֶּן עֶשְׂרִים לִרְדּוֹף,

Typically, during the initial period of marriage, the couple lives without obligations and without an onerous financial burden. However, after two years, when the man is **twenty years old,** the time arrives **for pursuit**[N] of his livelihood and for finding a profession that will enable him to support himself and his family.

NOTES

Ten years old for Mishna – בֶּן עֶשֶׂר לְמִשְׁנָה: The mishna allots a period of five years for each of the disciplines of Bible, Mishna, and Talmud. The commentaries (Rashi and others) say that this is derived from the Levites in the wilderness, who were allotted five years to learn their service (see *Ḥullin* 24a). Similarly, the phrase: "thirty years old for strength" is also derived from the Levites, because in the wilderness, where the Levites engaged in dismantling the Tabernacle, bearing its parts, and reassembling it, they began to serve at the age of thirty.

Twenty years old for pursuit – בֶּן עֶשְׂרִים לִרְדּוֹף: This phrase is difficult to understand, and the commentary explains that it refers to pursuit of a livelihood (Bartenura and others). The commentaries provide additional explanations, among them that if he has not found a wife by that age, he must pursue

בֶּן שְׁלֹשִׁים לְכֹחַ,

When a person is **thirty years old,** he reaches the stage **for strength,** the peak of his physical maturity and strength, and to a large extent, his spiritual maturity as well.

בֶּן אַרְבָּעִים לְבִינָה,

Forty years old is the age **for understanding,** as then a person has a sufficient critical sense and the life experience to discern matters and grasp them from a proper perspective.

בֶּן חֲמִשִּׁים לְעֵצָה,

When a person has engaged in development of his character over the years, then when he is **fifty years old** he reaches the proper age **for counsel;** his understanding is sufficiently developed by that time to enable him to give advice to others.

בֶּן שִׁשִּׁים לְזִקְנָה,

Sixty years old is the time **for aging,**[N] for the wisdom that establishes a person in a position of being one of the leaders of society, e.g., an elder of the congregation, due to the combination of characteristics that he acquired over the course of his many years.

בֶּן שִׁבְעִים לְשֵׂיבָה,

At **seventy years old** a person has reached the stage **for old age,** when a person deserves respect due to his age, for having traversed a

NOTES

a woman and make an effort to marry (Meiri). Some explain that the mishna is referring to the age when one is conscripted into the army and goes to pursue his enemies (*Melekhet Shlomo*; see Numbers, chap. 1). Others say that it is referring to the age when one incurs liability to receive punishment administered by Heaven, when the Heavenly court begins to pursue that sinner (Rashbatz, based on Numbers 32:11; see Rashi). Alternatively, one must pursue Torah study and fulfillment of mitzvot (see Rashbatz), as well as learning a profession with which to earn a livelihood. Another commentary maintains that the mishna is referring to all of these together; they are all interdependent, as fundamentally, at that age, a person becomes completely independent and must make an effort in all these areas (*Mirkevet HaMishne*).

Sixty years old for aging [*lezikna*] – בֶּן שִׁשִּׁים לְזִקְנָה: The commentary explains that this is an expression of honor, as it is stated in *Torat Kohanim* (on Leviticus 19:32) that "*zaken* is nothing other than a wise man," as Rabbi Yosei HaGelili expounded there that the word is an acronym for "one [*zeh*] who acquired [*shekana*] wisdom." Some even cite a variant reading in the mishna: "Sixty years old for wisdom" (see *Tosefot Yom Tov*).

complete course of life. It is appropriate to respect him even if he did not acquire wisdom or accomplish notable achievements.

בֶּן שְׁמוֹנִים לִגְבוּרָה,

Eighty years old for might; people who are still working, functioning, and taking action in the world at this age manifest a degree of personal might that entails both a physical element and an element of character traits, as he is not idle despite his advanced age.

בֶּן תִּשְׁעִים לָשׁוּחַ,

Ninety years old for hunching over,[N] as most people who reach that age are no longer capable of innovating or controlling large enterprises. It may be said that at that age a person is hunched over, whether physically or in other respects, and he gives way to his successors.

בֶּן מֵאָה כְּאִלּוּ מֵת וְעָבַר וּבָטֵל מִן הָעוֹלָם.

At **one hundred years old it is as though he were dead, left, and gone from the world,** both because after so many years a person can no longer be an active participant in life and because when a person reaches that age he must detach himself from the calculations and actions of this world and engage in matters relating to the spiritual realm. Once he becomes like that it is as though he no longer exists, even though he is still alive.

NOTES

Ninety years old for hunching over – בֶּן תִּשְׁעִים לָשׁוּחַ: The simple understanding of this phrase is that a person at this age walks hunched over, bowed in his body and in his spirit. Some explain that it is from the word "ditch [*shuḥa*]," indicating that as a person approaches this age he approaches his grave (Rashi and others). Others cite a variant reading with the letter *sin* instead of *shin*, from the word "conversation [*siḥa*]," connoting that at that age the person lacks the ability to take action, but he merely converses and speaks (*Mirkevet HaMishne*); this is especially so since it is appropriate for him to engage in Torah study and prayer, as the time of his passing from the world is gradually approaching (Rabbeinu Yona, Rashbatz, and others).

Mishna 22

The mishna cites statements in praise of the Torah and of the study of Torah.

בֶּן בַּג בַּג אוֹמֵר: הֲפוֹךְ בָּהּ וַהֲפוֹךְ בָּהּ, דִּכֹלָּא בָּהּ.

Ben Bag Bag says: Search it, Torah and wisdom, **thoroughly, search it thoroughly, as everything is in it,**[N] and it is the key to the questions and answers of life. The more you analyze it, the more you will discover.

וּבָהּ תֶּחֱזֵי, וְסִיב וּבְלֵה בָּהּ, וּמִינַּהּ לָא תָזוּעַ, שֶׁאֵין לְךָ מִדָּה טוֹבָה הֵימֶנָּה.

Consider it[N] always, as in it you will see all the matters worth considering, and the proper ways to consider them. **Grow old and devote yourself to it;** engage in Torah study all your life, and even when you grow old continue to engage in it. **And do not deviate from it** to engage in other disciplines, **as there is no greater portion for you than it.**[N]

NOTES

Search it thoroughly, search it thoroughly, as everything is in it – **הֲפוֹךְ בָּהּ וַהֲפוֹךְ בָּהּ, דִּכֹלָּא בָּהּ**: in other words, it is not enough to know matters of Torah in one simple manner; one must review them again and again, and each time consider them and analyze them from different angles, as it is stated regarding wisdom: "Prize it, and it will elevate you; it will honor you when you embrace it" (Proverbs 4:8). This verse means both that you should venerate it greatly and not forsake it at all, and that you should search it again and again (see *Nazir* 3a). In the Kaufman manuscript there is a variant reading: "Search it thoroughly, search it thoroughly, as all of it is in you and all of you is in it."

Consider it [*uva teḥezei*] – **וּבָהּ תֶּחֱזֵי**: It means both that you should constantly consider and analyze the Torah, similar to the first statement in the mishna, and that you should know and see the truth, because "everything is in it." In some early variant readings, it states: "You should always be in it [*uva tehevei*]" (see Maharal of Prague and *Tosefot Yom Tov*).

The *Tiferet Yisrael* explains that this statement is a continuation of the previous mishna and it means, "search it thoroughly, search it thoroughly" even between the ages of twenty and forty, during which you are engaged in earning your livelihood. "Consider it" between the ages of forty and sixty, during which you reach the level of understanding and counsel, and use that ability to understand the Torah. "Grow old and devote yourself to it" between the ages of sixty and eighty, when a person grows old and weakens. "And do not deviate from it" from age eighty and beyond, as engaging in Torah study continues even at that stage, and even after a person dies, in the World to Come.

As there is no greater portion [*midda*] for you than it – **שֶׁאֵין לְךָ מִדָּה טוֹבָה הֵימֶנָּה**: The simple understanding is that this is the best and most upright

Mishna 23

בֶּן הֵא הֵא אוֹמֵר: לְפוּם צַעֲרָא אַגְרָא.

Ben Heh Heh[P] **says: According to the effort is the reward.**[N] In other words, reward is commensurate with effort, pain, or investment.

NOTES

path to follow, and one may not forsake it in order to engage in foreign wisdom. Some infer from the term "*midda*," which can also mean "standard," that the Torah is the most appropriate standard against which to measure all matters and actions (*Pirkei Moshe*).

According to the effort is the reward [*agra*] – לְפוּם צַעֲרָא אַגְרָא: The simple understanding of the mishna is that it is referring to a person's reward as given to him from Heaven (Rashi and others). In this world, reward is determined primarily on the basis of the value of the product of one's labor, combined with many and varied factors, such as his abilities, life circumstances, and even luck. By contrast, it is primarily one's effort and investment that is taken into consideration for the reward given from Heaven. Others say that for every mitzva there is a double reward, the great reward for the mitzva itself (see 2:1) and the reward for the effort expended in performing it, and that the statement of ben Heh Heh addresses only the reward for the effort (Maharal of Prague).

Some explain that this is stated regarding success and memory in Torah study, as only a matter that is studied with effort, toil, and fear of God is truly preserved and results in blessing (Rambam, *Tiferet Yisrael*). The Meiri writes that according to this explanation, the term *agra* is not interpreted literally, as "reward," but rather, in the sense of "product" or "consequence."

PERSONALITIES

Ben Bag Bag and ben Heh Heh – בֶּן בַּג בַּג בֶּן הֵא הֵא: Ben Bag Bag is mentioned only once in the Mishna and a few times in the *Tosefta* and in *baraitot*. Ben Heh Heh is mentioned only in this mishna. They are presumed to have been from earlier generations. Others believe that they were proselytes, perhaps contemporaries of Hillel the Elder (see Rashi). Elsewhere (*Avot de Rabbi Natan* 12), the statements stated here appear as part of a compendium of statements attributed to Hillel the Elder. Conceivably, ben Bag Bag is the *tanna* Yoḥanan ben Bag Bag, who appears in the midrash *Seder Eliyahu Zuta* (17).

Chapter 6

This chapter addresses one central topic: acquiring the Torah, encompassing both how one does so and the reward that it entails. For this reason, the commentaries call this chapter: "the chapter of acquisition of the Torah." Some *mishnayot* in this chapter are from the last generations of the *tanna'im* and some are from the generation after the redaction of the Mishna. This chapter is not part of the Mishna, but it was added as a sixth chapter to the five chapters of tractate *Avot*, apparently due to the ancient custom to engage in the study of tractate *Avot* during the six *Shabbatot* between the end of the Passover festival and the festival of *Shavuot*, in preparation for the occasion of the giving of the Torah.

The chapter begins with an introduction that explains its essence.

שָׁנוּ חֲכָמִים בִּלְשׁוֹן הַמִּשְׁנָה,

The Sages taught matters relating to the essence of the Torah **in the language** and the style **of the Mishna,** even though they are not part of the Mishna.

בָּרוּךְ שֶׁבָּחַר בָּהֶם וּבְמִשְׁנָתָם.

The mishna adds words of praise for the Sages: **Blessed is** the Holy One blessed be **He, Who chose them and their teaching.**[N]

NOTES

Blessed is He, Who chose them and their teaching – בָּרוּךְ שֶׁבָּחַר בָּהֶם וּבְמִשְׁנָתָם: Some maintain that this is praise for the Sages who taught this chapter, as, even though this chapter is not part of the Mishna as redacted by Rabbi Yehuda HaNasi, blessed are the Sages whose teaching approximates the quality of the *mishnayot*, and who therefore arranged their statements in a style close to the language of the Mishna (*Midrash Shmuel*). Some write that this is praise for the Sages of the Mishna, as the Sages of this chapter taught their statements in the language of the Mishna due to the outstanding quality of the Torah and its students, which this chapter addresses (*Pirkei Moshe*; see *Tiferet Yisrael*).

Mishna 1

The chapter begins by detailing matters that a person who engages in Torah study merits.

רַבִּי מֵאִיר אוֹמֵר: כָּל הָעוֹסֵק בַּתּוֹרָה לִשְׁמָהּ – זוֹכֶה לִדְבָרִים הַרְבֵּה. וְלֹא עוֹד, אֶלָּא שֶׁכָּל הָעוֹלָם כֻּלּוֹ כְּדַי הוּא לוֹ.

Rabbi Meir says: Anyone who engages in Torah study for its own sake, and not for the sake of external motives, **merits many things** that will be detailed below. **Moreover, the entire world is worthwhile for his sake;** a person like this justifies the existence of the entire world.

These are the matters that a person who engages in Torah study for its own sake merits:

נִקְרָא: רֵעַ, אָהוּב, אוֹהֵב אֶת הַמָּקוֹם, אוֹהֵב אֶת הַבְּרִיּוֹת, מְשַׂמֵּחַ אֶת הַמָּקוֹם, מְשַׂמֵּחַ אֶת הַבְּרִיּוֹת. וּמַלְבַּשְׁתּוֹ עֲנָוָה וְיִרְאָה, וּמַכְשַׁרְתּוֹ לִהְיוֹת צַדִּיק וְחָסִיד וְיָשָׁר וְנֶאֱמָן, וּמְרַחַקְתּוֹ מִן הַחֵטְא, וּמְקָרַבְתּוֹ לִידֵי זְכוּת, וְנֶהֱנִין מִמֶּנּוּ עֵצָה וְתוּשִׁיָּה בִּינָה וּגְבוּרָה, שֶׁנֶּאֱמַר "לִי עֵצָה וְתוּשִׁיָּה אֲנִי בִינָה לִי גְבוּרָה".

He is called friend to the Holy One blessed be He, **beloved** to the Holy One blessed be He. His engaging in Torah study brings him to be a **lover of the Omnipresent** and to be a **lover of people,** whoever they may be, as well. Likewise, he **brings joy to the Omnipresent and brings joy to people** with his actions and his wisdom. **And the** Torah **clothes him,** provides him with exalted attributes, e.g., **humility and reverence** in his entire character. **And it primes him,** directs him to his objective and assists him, **to be righteous,** in that he observes the halakha; **pious,** in that he performs good deeds far beyond the obligations incumbent upon him; and **upright**[N] **and**

NOTES

Righteous, pious, and upright – צַדִּיק וְחָסִיד וְיָשָׁר: The commentary follows the standard interpretation of these terms: Righteous [*tzaddik*] refers to one who fulfills all of the halakhot according to their legal requirements, whereas one who is pious [*ḥasid*] goes beyond the letter of the law (Rashi and others; see Ran on *Moed Katan* 18a). Some say, moreover, that it was necessary to write both *tzaddik* and *ḥasid*,

loyal,[N] both in his relations with others and in his perception of wisdom. The Torah **distances him from sin and** also **draws him near to merit. And** on the basis of the gifts that one receives from the Torah, other people **benefit from him** and receive **counsel and resourcefulness** to answer their questions, as well as **understanding and might,**[N] **as it is stated: "Counsel and resourcefulness are mine; I am understanding; might is mine"** (Proverbs 8:14).

וְנוֹתֶנֶת לוֹ מַלְכוּת וּמֶמְשָׁלָה וְחִקּוּר דִּין, וּמְגַלִּין לוֹ רָזֵי תוֹרָה, וְנַעֲשֶׂה כְּמַעְיָן הַמִּתְגַּבֵּר וּכְנָהָר שֶׁאֵינוֹ פּוֹסֵק, וֶהֱוֵי צָנוּעַ וְאֶרֶךְ רוּחַ, וּמוֹחֵל עַל עֶלְבּוֹנוֹ, וּמְגַדַּלְתּוֹ וּמְרוֹמַמְתּוֹ עַל כָּל הַמַּעֲשִׂים.

The Torah **grants him sovereignty and government** over all matters, each person according to his importance and his essence. His stature leads to his being appointed to positions of leadership. **In addition,** it provides him with the ability to conduct **judicial inquiry,** to truly analyze the problems that arise before him and to identify genuine claims. Heaven **reveals to him the**

NOTES

because in our corrupted reality there can be a *ḥasid* who is not righteous, but rather, a foolish *ḥasid* (see *Sota* 3:4). One who engages in Torah study for its own sake is righteous, pious, and upright, as his piety lives up to the standards of law and uprightness (*Midrash Shmuel*). Some explain that *tzaddik* relates to matters between man and Heaven, *ḥasid* relates to matters between man and his counterpart, and upright relates to matters within oneself (*Tiferet Yisrael*).

Loyal – וְנֶאֱמָן: Some explain that this is one whose righteousness and piety is steady and permanent (*Tiferet Yisrael*). Others explain that it is one who is a trusted one in God's house (*Midrash Shmuel*; see Numbers 12:7).

Counsel and resourcefulness, understanding and might – עֵצָה וְתוּשִׁיָּה... בִּינָה וּגְבוּרָה: The *Tiferet Yisrael* explains that "counsel" connotes one who knows how to speak and explain well; therefore, people benefit from seeking and hearing his counsel. "Resourcefulness" connotes one whose advice is correct on a practical level as well, and is beneficial when implemented. "Understanding" connotes one whose intellect benefits others, unrelated to practical guidance. "Might" connotes one with the ability to overcome obstacles that arise in his service of God. The author also suggests an alternative explanation: "Counsel" is regarding matters of this world, "resourcefulness" is regarding the eternal matters of the Torah, "understanding" is regarding knowledge of scientific and general disciplines, and "might" is regarding the practical leadership involved in performing justice, saving the oppressed from their oppressors, and the like.

esoterica of Torah; he receives assistance in understanding the profound secrets concealed in it. **He becomes,** with his latent creative ability, **like an ever-flowing spring,** whose waters are continually renewed, **and like a never-ending river,**[N] as he is granted a continuous ability to create and renew. **He becomes modest and forbearing and one who overlooks affronts to him. And,** all in all, the Torah **makes him great and exalts him above all matters,**[N] all of the world's creations.

NOTES

Like an ever-flowing spring and like a never-ending river – כְּמַעְיָן הַמִּתְגַּבֵּר וּכְנָהָר שֶׁאֵינוֹ פּוֹסֵק: The *Tiferet Yisrael* explains that spring water is potable but limited in amount. River water is plentiful, but generally not potable. That is why the metaphor is doubled: What flows from him will be potable like spring water and plentiful like river water. Some have a variant reading: "like a never-ending spring" (*Midrash Shmuel*). In *Kalla Rabbati* (5:2), there is a variant reading: "Like a never-ending spring and like an ever-flowing river." They explained there that on the one hand, his wisdom is permanent like the flow of a spring, but on the other hand, he is constantly renewing himself like an ever-flowing river.

Like a never-ending river, the Jordan River

And Torah makes him great and exalts him above all matters – וּמְגַדַּלְתּוֹ וּמְרוֹמַמְתּוֹ עַל כָּל הַמַּעֲשִׂים: Ultimately, one who engages in Torah study for its own sake and merits all the positive attributes and virtues enumerated in the mishna does indeed become greater and more important than any other person or matter, as he becomes perfect in every aspect of his character: in his knowledge and understanding, in his actions and attributes, in his ability to provide for others, and in the fact that despite all these attributes he lives and acts with humility and modesty.

Mishna 2

The previous mishna detailed the virtues that one merits if he engages in Torah for its own sake. This mishna addresses the converse, a person who does not engage in Torah study.

אָמַר רַבִּי יְהוֹשֻׁעַ בֶּן לֵוִי: בְּכָל יוֹם וָיוֹם בַּת קוֹל יוֹצֵאת מֵהַר חוֹרֵב, וּמַכְרֶזֶת וְאוֹמֶרֶת: "אוֹי לָהֶם לַבְּרִיּוֹת מֵעֶלְבּוֹנָהּ שֶׁל תּוֹרָה".

Rabbi Yehoshua ben Levi[P] **said: Each and every day a Divine Voice,** a clandestine spiritual voice, **emerges from Mount Horev,**[N] Mount Sinai, where the Torah was given, **and it proclaims and says: "Woe unto the people for the affront to the Torah,"**[N] when one forsakes it and does not engage in its study.

NOTES

Each and every day a Divine Voice [*bat kol*] emerges from Mount Horev – בְּכָל יוֹם וָיוֹם בַּת קוֹל יוֹצֵאת מֵהַר חוֹרֵב: This is a voice of sorts that emerges from Heaven. It is called a *bat kol*, which literally means "daughter of a voice," because it is not the voice itself, but an ancillary voice that emerges from it (*Sanhedrin* 11a, and *Tosafot* there). Although the revelation of the giving of the Torah was a one-time phenomenon, nevertheless, it is stated that the voice that was there did not cease (see Deuteronomy 5:19 and *Sanhedrin* 17a). There are aspects of it that never cease, and from that voice, an ancillary voice emerges each day and speaks about the Torah and related matters (*Tiferet Yisrael*). There is a tradition in the name of the Baal Shem Tov that although typically people do not hear this Divine Voice, it has an effect in the world and inspires thoughts of repentance and other good thoughts in people's hearts (Baal Shem Tov on the Torah, *Behukotai* 7–8).

Woe unto the people for the affront to the Torah – אוֹי לָהֶם לַבְּרִיּוֹת מֵעֶלְבּוֹנָהּ שֶׁל תּוֹרָה: Some explain that this is one who does not engage in Torah study properly, for its own sake, as that is an affront to it (Rashi). Others say that this is referring to the fact that not everyone who engages in Torah study acquires all the virtues enumerated in the previous mishna, because there is an additional element involved: When a person does not engage in Torah study properly, he is censured for doing so and loses much of the goodness he would otherwise have had (*Tiferet Yisrael*; see *Berakhot* 5a). Another explanation is that if a Sage was negligent in his studies and cannot provide an appropriate answer to those who ask, he thereby causes an affront to the Torah, as the Torah is belittled through him (*Pirkei Moshe*).

PERSONALITIES

Rabbi Yehoshua ben Levi – רַבִּי יְהוֹשֻׁעַ בֶּן לֵוִי: Rabbi Yehoshua ben Levi, a first generation *amora* of the Land of Israel, is mentioned many times in midrashim and in the two Talmuds. He was the head of the community in the city of Lod, and served as a representative of the Jews before the Romans. Rabbi Yehoshua ben Levi engaged extensively in the study of aggadic material, and in his study hall there was a Sage whose role it was to arrange the aggadic material before him. Many of his sayings address the virtue of Torah study and praise good character traits. Aggadic statements in his name are also cited at the conclusion of the Mishna, at the end of tractate *Okatzin*.

שֶׁכָּל מִי שֶׁאֵינוֹ עוֹסֵק בַּתּוֹרָה נִקְרָא 'נָזוּף', שֶׁנֶּאֱמַר: "נֶזֶם זָהָב בְּאַף חֲזִיר אִשָּׁה יָפָה וְסָרַת טָעַם".

As, anyone who does not engage in Torah study is called censured [*nazuf*],[N] **as it is stated: "A beautiful woman without sense** is like **a gold ring in the snout [*nezem zahav be'af*] of a pig"** (Proverbs 11:22), and nezem zahav be'af is an allusion to nazuf. It means that when wisdom is not utilized for its fitting purpose, it is analogous to a gold ring in the snout of a pig.

Rabbi Yehoshua ben Levi adds words in praise of the Torah, and how meritorious it is to cleave to it.

וְאוֹמֵר: "וְהַלֻּחֹת מַעֲשֵׂה אֱלֹהִים הֵמָּה וְהַמִּכְתָּב מִכְתַּב אֱלֹהִים הוּא חָרוּת עַל הַלֻּחֹת", אַל תִּקְרָא "חָרוּת" אֶלָּא 'חֵירוּת', שֶׁאֵין לְךָ בֶּן חוֹרִין אֶלָּא מִי שֶׁעוֹסֵק בְּתַלְמוּד תּוֹרָה.

And the verse **says: "The tablets were the work of God, and the writing was the writing of God, engraved [*ĥarut*] on the tablets"** (Exodus 32:16).[N] The verse should be expounded in this manner: **Do not read it as ḥarut, but rather as ḥerut, freedom,** as the writing that was on the tablets, the words of the Torah, grant a person freedom, **as only one who engages in Torah study is** truly **a free man.** A person like that is freed from subservience to the opinions, whims, and desires of other people.

NOTES

As anyone who does not engage in Torah study is called censured – שֶׁכָּל מִי שֶׁאֵינוֹ עוֹסֵק בַּתּוֹרָה נִקְרָא נָזוּף: The simple understanding of this verse is that it is referring to one who receives a worthy gift when he himself is not worthy, e.g., a woman who is beautiful externally but who lacks intelligence and character, like a pig that uses a gold ring in its snout to burrow in rubbish. Similarly, since the Torah is likened to gold, one who forsakes it thereby demeans it, as though it were a gold ring placed in a pig's snout (*Kalla Rabbati* 5:3). This also applies to one who utilizes his intellect, which he received in order to engage in Torah study, to instead engage in nonsense (*Tiferet Yisrael*).

Engraved [*ḥarut*] on the tablets – חָרוּת עַל הַלֻּחֹת: Rashi writes simply that a person like that is a "free man [*ben ḥorin*]" because he is honored by people and they care for him and see to his needs (see 3:5 and *Eiruvin* 54a). Some point out that *ben ḥorin* is not only an expression of freedom, but also an expression of importance, as in the expression: "The nobles [*ḥorei*] of Judah and Jerusalem" (Jeremiah 27:20). According to this interpretation, we can better understand the connection to the derivation that follows it in the mishna: "Anyone who engages in Torah study becomes exalted" (*Yaavetz*). Others explain that a person's intellect is like the tablets. When he studies Torah, he engraves the script onto

וְכָל מִי שֶׁעוֹסֵק בְּתַלְמוּד תּוֹרָה – הֲרֵי זֶה מִתְעַלֶּה, שֶׁנֶּאֱמַר: "וּמִמַּתָּנָה נַחֲלִיאֵל וּמִנַּחֲלִיאֵל בָּמוֹת".

Anyone who engages in Torah study becomes exalted, as it is stated: "And from Matana to Nahaliel and from Nahaliel to Bamot" (Numbers 21:19).[N] The Sages expounded this verse, saying it contains a spiritual depiction: The Torah, which is called a gift [*mattana*], flows like a stream through which the one studying it ascends to "bamot," i.e., to an elevated place that has significance and prominence.

Mishna 3

This mishna is a continuation of what was stated at the end of the previous mishna, that one who engages in Torah study is exalted and merits honor, as the Torah is honor, and through it, a person is worthy of honor.

הַלּוֹמֵד מֵחֲבֵרוֹ פֶּרֶק אֶחָד, אוֹ הֲלָכָה אַחַת, אוֹ פָּסוּק אֶחָד, אוֹ דִּבּוּר אֶחָד, אוֹ אֲפִילּוּ אוֹת אַחַת – צָרִיךְ לִנְהוֹג בּוֹ כָּבוֹד.

One who learns from another one chapter of Mishna, **one halakha, one verse, one word, or even one letter**[N] **must treat him with honor.** This is not only as an expres-

NOTES

it. This action of engraving the "script" onto the "tablets" is what renders him a free man, as it frees him of enslavement to his physical desires and needs (*Tiferet Yisrael*). Alternatively, he is not influenced by the events of this world, because he has acquired a spiritual acquisition that cannot be damaged or taken from him (*Pirkei Moshe*).

And from Matana to Nahaliel and from Nahaliel to Bamot – **וּמִמַּתָּנָה נַחֲלִיאֵל וּמִנַּחֲלִיאֵל בָּמוֹת**: This verse appears in the "Song of the Well," which the children of Israel recited toward the end of their journey in the wilderness. It describes several of the various stations passed through by the miraculous well that accompanied Israel on their journey (see *Tosefta*, *Sukka* 3:11–12). However, the Sages expounded the song as though it had been stated regarding the Torah as well. "Once it was given to him as a gift [*mattana*], God bequeaths it [*nehalo*] to him, as it is stated: "And from Matana to Nahaliel." And once God bequeaths it to him, he rises to greatness, as it is stated: "And from Nahaliel to Bamot," as *bamot* are elevated places (*Eiruvin* 54a). In *Kalla Rabbati* (5:3), it is explained otherwise: The reward [*mattana*] is given only to one whose Torah is uninterrupted, like a never-ending river [*nahaliel*].

One who learns from another…one letter – **הַלּוֹמֵד מֵחֲבֵרוֹ...אוֹת אַחַת**: This means that at times it is necessary to clarify the proper way to write a certain word (see *Kalla Rabbati* 5:4 and *Shabbat* 77b). Sometimes, halakhic significance can be derived from this, as often occurs in rabbinic literature through expounding verses.

sion of gratitude, but because every part of the Torah is a precious gift. That is why one must honor anyone who served as his teacher in transmitting the Torah.

שֶׁכֵּן מָצִינוּ בְּדָוִד מֶלֶךְ יִשְׂרָאֵל, שֶׁלֹּא לָמַד מֵאֲחִיתוֹפֶל אֶלָּא שְׁנֵי דְבָרִים בִּלְבַד, קְרָאוֹ רַבּוֹ אַלּוּפוֹ וּמְיוּדָּעוֹ, שֶׁנֶּאֱמַר: "וְאַתָּה אֱנוֹשׁ כְּעֶרְכִּי אַלּוּפִי וּמְיֻדָּעִי". וַהֲלֹא דְבָרִים קַל וָחוֹמֶר: וּמַה דָּוִד מֶלֶךְ יִשְׂרָאֵל, שֶׁלֹּא לָמַד מֵאֲחִיתוֹפֶל אֶלָּא שְׁנֵי דְבָרִים בִּלְבַד – קְרָאוֹ רַבּוֹ אַלּוּפוֹ וּמְיוּדָּעוֹ; הַלּוֹמֵד מֵחֲבֵירוֹ פֶּרֶק אֶחָד, אוֹ הֲלָכָה אַחַת, אוֹ פָּסוּק אֶחָד, אוֹ דִּבּוּר אֶחָד, אֲפִילוּ אוֹת אַחַת – עַל אַחַת כַּמָּה וְכַמָּה שֶׁצָּרִיךְ לִנְהוֹג בּוֹ כָּבוֹד!

So we find regarding David king of Israel, who learned from Ahitofel, who was his minister and advisor, **only two matters,**[N] but nevertheless, **he called him his teacher, his guide, and his companion,**[N] **as it is stated** in the psalm speaking of people who betrayed David and rebelled against him, among them Ahitofel: **"But rather it is you, a man who was my equal, my guide, and my companion"** (Psalms 55:14). **Can these matters not be inferred *a fortiori*?**[N] **If David king of Israel, learned from Ahitofel only two matters, and** yet **he called him his teacher, his guide, and his companion,** then in the case of **one who learns from another,** who is his equal or his peer, **one chapter, one halakha, one verse, one**

NOTES

Who learned from Ahitofel only two matters – שֶׁלֹּא לָמַד מֵאֲחִיתוֹפֶל אֶלָּא שְׁנֵי דְבָרִים בִּלְבַד: The verse cited in the mishna is stated in Psalm 55, which David composed when he was forced to flee from Jerusalem in the wake of the revolt of his son Avshalom, and heard that Ahitofel joined those rebelling against him (Radak). In this psalm, David describes his close relationship with Ahitofel with the words: "But rather it is you, a man who was my equal, my guide, and my companion. We took sweet counsel together; we went in the House of God with feeling [*beragesh*]" (Psalms 55:14–15). The Sages expounded that the verse beginning: "We took sweet counsel" describes the two halakhot that David learned from Ahitofel: that one should study Torah with another person, and that one should attend the synagogue in a group [*beragesh*] (*Kalla Rabbati* 5:4; see Rashash and *Hon Ashir*).

He called him his teacher, his guide, and his companion – קְרָאוֹ רַבּוֹ אַלּוּפוֹ וּמְיוּדָּעוֹ: The commentaries note that in the verse cited as proof, the term "teacher [*rabbi*]" is not mentioned, but only "my guide and my companion [*alufi umeyuda'i*]." The *Pirkei Moshe* explains that by David's saying to Ahitofel that he was his guide and his companion, it is understood that he was his teacher as well. The Maharal of Prague writes that this is referring to what David said: "But rather, it is you, a man who is my equal," meaning, just as you are obligated to honor me because I am king, so I am obligated to honor you because you are my teacher.

Can these matters not be inferred *a fortiori* – וַהֲלֹא דְבָרִים קַל וָחוֹמֶר: The explanation in the commentary is simply that the *a fortiori* inference is from

word, or even one letter, all the more so must he treat him with honor.

וְאֵין כָּבוֹד אֶלָּא תּוֹרָה, שֶׁנֶּאֱמַר: ״כָּבוֹד חֲכָמִים יִנְחָלוּ״.

The reason is that **"honor" is nothing other than Torah,**[N] **as it is stated: "The wise will inherit honor"** (Proverbs 3:35). That is the reason that masters of Torah are people deserving of honor and that is the appropriate reward deserved by those who teach Torah.

״וּתְמִימִים יִנְחֲלוּ טוֹב״ – וְאֵין טוֹב אֶלָּא תּוֹרָה, שֶׁנֶּאֱמַר: ״כִּי לֶקַח טוֹב נָתַתִּי לָכֶם תּוֹרָתִי אַל תַּעֲזֹבוּ״.

They add that besides the honor that Torah Sages merit, they merit "good" as well, as it is written: **"And the honest will inherit goodness"** (Proverbs 28:10);[N] **and "good" is nothing other than Torah,** which is the source and the origin of good, **as it is stated: "For a good lesson I have given you: My Torah, do not forsake it"** (Proverbs 4:2).

NOTES

the fact that David, who was a Torah luminary, with significant standing, esteemed and honored his advisor Ahitofel. Some explain that the derivation is from the fact that if David king of Israel, who was righteous and holy, characterized Ahitofel in that manner, after the latter had already been exposed as wicked, it is all the more so true that a person must honor a counterpart who is his equal (Rashi, Yaavetz). Moreover, there is a tradition in the name of Baal Shem Tov that the inference is that because Ahitofel was wicked, his words of Torah do not proliferate, but they are "only two matters." By contrast, when someone learns from another who is respectable and worthy, his words of Torah proliferate; therefore, all the more so must one treat him with respect (Baal Shem Tov on the Torah, *Va'ethanan* 61).

Honor is nothing other than Torah – וְאֵין כָּבוֹד אֶלָּא תּוֹרָה: This means that it is only Torah that makes one who engages in its study entitled to true honor (*Tiferet Yisrael*); therefore, all the more so must a person honor one who taught him Torah (*Maḥzor Vitri*). Moreover, it underscores that the mishna is not speaking of one who taught just anything to another, but only one who taught him a Torah matter (Rashi). Some had a variant reading: "There is honor only for Sages." Some explain according to that variant reading that the mishna means that regarding the statement that a person must honor one from whom he learned one matter, it is referring to an ordinary person; but a person must honor Torah Sages even if he learned nothing from them (*Midrash Shmuel*).

And the honest will inherit goodness – וּתְמִימִים יִנְחֲלוּ טוֹב: The explanation in the commentary is that in this statement, the mishna is adding another virtue merited by those who engage in Torah study. The *Tiferet Yisrael* explains that this too is a continuation of what was stated regarding the honor that must be accorded to one from whom he learned Torah. He adds that one must do so because it was through him that the one who learned merited both honor and good.

Mishna 4

Previous *mishnayot* in this chapter spoke of the honor and the good that a person merits through Torah study. In this mishna, the Sage says that Torah study does not afford any reward or comforts to a person in this world, but, nevertheless, engaging in it and connecting to it constitute sufficient reward in and of themselves.

כָּךְ הִיא דַּרְכָּהּ שֶׁל תּוֹרָה: פַּת בְּמֶלַח תֹּאכַל, וּמַיִם בִּמְשׂוּרָה תִּשְׁתֶּה, וְעַל הָאָרֶץ תִּישַׁן, וְחַיֵּי צַעַר תִּחְיֶה, וּבַתּוֹרָה אַתָּה עָמֵל.

This is the path of Torah,[N] the path by which a person merits to study Torah properly and to be exalted through it. Even if **you will eat bread with salt,** as do the poorest of the poor, who have nothing to add to bread other than salt, **"you will drink water by measure"** (Ezekiel 4:11)[N] and nothing beyond that, **you will sleep on the ground,** not on a bed, **you will live a life of suffering,** due to the privation, **but,** nevertheless, **in the Torah you shall toil**[N] and devote most of your time to it.

NOTES

This is the path of Torah – כָּךְ הִיא דַּרְכָּהּ שֶׁל תּוֹרָה: The *Hon Ashir* states that "this is the path of Torah" means that this was also the path of the Torah itself, as its beginning in the world was in the wilderness, which is lacking in both bread and water.

Some explain that the mishna means that even in the most difficult of circumstances one must engage in Torah study, but not that one must live that sort of life (Rashi; see 4:9). Others explain that this is relevant even to the wealthy; although they have the means to live a life of luxury, they should not accustom themselves to do so, but should minimize to whatever degree possible their devotion to a life of luxury so that they will be free to devote themselves to Torah study (*Midrash Shmuel* and others). Likewise, there are those who explain that indeed, this is the path that is required to acquire the Torah, but only when one begins to study it. Later, one who engages in Torah study merits growing wealthy (*Tiferet Yisrael*).

You will drink water by measure [*bimsura*] – וּמַיִם בִּמְשׂוּרָה תִּשְׁתֶּה: The commentaries inferred a double emphasis here, both that one should drink water and not wine or other beverages, and that even drinking water should be by measure. It is stated in the Babylonian Talmud that a *mesura* is one thirty-sixth of a *log*, approximately 10 cc.

In the Torah you shall toil – וּבַתּוֹרָה אַתָּה עָמֵל: Some explain that this serves to underscore that the primary element is not knowledge of Torah, but one's exertion in it, each according to his ability and his effort. On that basis is a person's reward determined (Yaavetz; see 5:23). Others say that this emphasizes that a person should not think that in order to acquire Torah it is sufficient to live a life of privation; rather, one must exert himself and toil in Torah (*Midrash Shmuel*).

אִם אַתָּה עוֹשֶׂה כֵּן – "אַשְׁרֶיךָ וְטוֹב לָךְ", "אַשְׁרֶיךָ" – בָּעוֹלָם הַזֶּה, "וְטוֹב לָךְ" – לָעוֹלָם הַבָּא.

If you do so, "you are happy, and it is good for you" (Psalms 128:2), as the Sages expounded this verse: **"You are happy" in this world,** as when a person can engage in Torah study despite all the suffering, scarcity, and lack of worldly pleasures, it brings happiness, as he lives a life of inherent meaning, without the complications and concerns tied to owning considerable wealth; **"and it is good for you" in the World to Come,** as he will certainly receive a great reward for having engaged in Torah study.

Moreover, they counsel the Torah Sages and those who study Torah:

אַל תְּבַקֵּשׁ גְּדֻלָּה לְעַצְמְךָ, וְאַל תַּחְמוֹד כָּבוֹד.

Do not seek prominence,[N] a position of authority or importance, **for yourself,**[N] **and do not covet honor.**[N] Although it is appropriate to accord honor to the Sages, the Sages themselves should not desire or covet it.

NOTES

Do not seek prominence – אַל תְּבַקֵּשׁ גְּדֻלָּה: Some understand this mishna as a continuation of what was stated in the previous mishna regarding honor and goodness merited by those who engage in Torah study. They explain that even one who has virtually nothing in his material life is happy if he engages in Torah study, and the Torah study is good for him. Therefore, it is not fitting for the Sages to seek material honor and good, because the Torah itself is the quintessence of good and honor (*Pirkei Moshe*).

Do not seek prominence for yourself – אַל תְּבַקֵּשׁ גְּדֻלָּה לְעַצְמְךָ: Some maintain that the term "for yourself" underscores that even when it is necessary for a Sage to seek honor because Torah scholars should be honored, he should not see the honor as his own; it is not he who deserves the honor, but God and the Torah who do (Yaavetz, *Hon Ashir*). Others say that this means that one should not seek his own honor, but must see to and seek the honor of his counterpart (*Midrash Shmuel*).

Do not covet honor – וְאַל תַּחְמוֹד כָּבוֹד: Some cite a variant reading; instead of "Do not covet honor. Let your actions [*aseh*] exceed what you consumed," as written here, that reading drops the word *aseh*, so that it reads: "Do not covet honor beyond your learning." In other words, when a person is honored, he must ensure that he is not accorded honor beyond what is fitting for him based on the degree of his Torah scholarship. The Maharal of Prague used the version that appears here, but parsed it differently, to read: "Do not covet honor beyond your learning. Engage in Torah study [*aseh*], and do not aspire to the table of kings."

יוֹתֵר מִלִּמּוּדְךָ עֲשֵׂה. וְאַל תִּתְאַוֶּה לְשֻׁלְחָנָם שֶׁל מְלָכִים, שֶׁשֻּׁלְחָנְךָ גָּדוֹל מִשֻּׁלְחָנָם, וְכִתְרְךָ גָּדוֹל מִכִּתְרָם, וְנֶאֱמָן הוּא בַּעַל מְלַאכְתְּךָ שֶׁיְּשַׁלֶּם לְךָ שְׂכַר פְּעֻלָּתֶךָ.

Let your actions exceed what you are accustomed to[N] perform; expend great effort. **And do not aspire to the table of kings,** which contains wealth, prominence, and honor, **as your table,** that of one who engages in Torah study, **is greater than their table, and your crown,** the crown of Torah, **is greater than their crown.** Moreover, beyond the present situation, **your employer,** God, for whom you work, **is trusted to pay you the reward for your action** in the World to Come.

Mishna 5

This mishna and the one that follows it constitute the bulk of this chapter, which is named "Acquisition of the Torah." These *mishnayot* address the means of acquiring the Torah, encompassing the preparation, the toil, the action, ways of life, study, and character traits that a person must acquire, as well as the matters from which he must refrain and distance himself, so that he will merit opening his heart and his mind to acquiring the Torah. Furthermore, those matters themselves are the spiritual and psychological virtues that a person gradually acquires as a result of engaging in Torah study.

NOTES

Let your actions exceed what you are accustomed to [*limudekha*] – יוֹתֵר מִלִּמּוּדְךָ עֲשֵׂה: *Limudekha* could mean, "what you are accustomed [*lamud*] to perform" or "what you have learned [*lamadta*]." According to the latter meaning, one should perform more than he has himself learned, and do according to what others, more learned than he, instruct him. Others explain that in matters regarding which one lacks clear knowledge and is uncertain, he should adopt the more stringent ruling (*Midrash Shmuel*; see Maharal of Prague).

As an introduction, the mishna begins with a comparison between "the crown of Torah," its virtue and its importance, to two other "crowns," which were already mentioned in this tractate (4:13) together with it, the crown of priesthood and the crown of monarchy. These two crowns also have special mitzvot and virtues, and special means of acquisition.

גְּדוֹלָה תוֹרָה יוֹתֵר מִן הַכְּהֻנָּה וּמִן הַמַּלְכוּת, שֶׁהַמַּלְכוּת נִקְנֵית בִּשְׁלֹשִׁים מַעֲלוֹת, וְהַכְּהֻנָּה בְּעֶשְׂרִים וְאַרְבַּע, וְהַתּוֹרָה נִקְנֵית בְּאַרְבָּעִים וּשְׁמֹנָה דְבָרִים:

The virtue of **Torah is greater than** that of **priesthood and monarchy.** Proof for this is **that monarchy is acquired with thirty virtues,**[N] as the greatness of monarchy is manifest in thirty types of special rights and mitzvot that the king has thanks to his special status, as detailed in the Bible and the Mishna; **priesthood is acquired** and manifest **with twenty-four** special virtues, mitzvot, sanctity, and "gifts of the priesthood" that the Torah granted the priests; **and Torah is acquired through forty-eight matters:**[N]

בְּתַלְמוּד,

1. **Through study** – the Torah is acquired by means of engaging in study and understanding, and cannot be acquired in any other way.

NOTES

That monarchy is acquired with thirty virtues – שֶׁהַמַּלְכוּת נִקְנֵית בִּשְׁלֹשִׁים מַעֲלוֹת: These thirty virtues are the additional rights of the king. Some say that these are the rights enumerated in I Samuel, chapter 8. And some say that in order to complete the list, one should add the special laws relating to the king enumerated in the second chapter of tractate *Sanhedrin* (Rashi and others; see *Maḥzor Vitri*). In tractate *Kalla Rabbati* (5:7), other rights of the king are detailed. Many of them come from the descriptions of wealth that appear in the book of Ecclesiastes, e.g., "with silver, gold, women, slaves, maidservants...the advantage of kings, countries, male singers, female singers, pleasures...weapons, armies, spices, and more" (Ecclesiastes 2:4–8). Among the virtues of the monarchy enumerated there were also "justice, kindness, and charity."

Regarding the virtues of the priesthood, the commentary follows the opinion of most commentaries, that this is referring to the twenty-four gifts that priests receive from the people. However, some explain that the reference is to the twenty-four mitzvot unique to the priesthood, which are the virtues of the priesthood (*Maḥzor Vitri*).

Through forty-eight matters – אַרְבָּעִים וּשְׁמֹנָה דְּבָרִים: The commentary is according to the version that appears in the mishna. However, there are many versions in which the matters listed include "with ritual purity" and "minimizing commerce," and, likewise, in which some of the virtues were not enumerated, e.g., "loves charity." In some versions one virtue is listed in the mishna as two separate virtues, e.g., "distances himself from honor" and "does not pursue honor," and, likewise, what is listed in the mishna as two virtues was enumerated as one virtue, e.g., "guides him to the truth and to peace," and the like.

בִּשְׁמִיעַת הָאֹזֶן,

2. **Through attentive hearing** – as a person must prepare himself properly in order to hear matters of Torah and to distinguish between matters of significance, which he must remember, and matters that are insignificant.

בַּעֲרִיכַת שְׂפָתַיִם,

3. **Through well-ordered speech**[N] – the ability to express oneself appropriately and properly, both when asking and when answering.

בְּבִינַת הַלֵּב,

4. **Through understanding of the heart** – the ability to understand matters profoundly, beyond their external, superficial level.

בְּשִׂכְלוּת הַלֵּב,

5. **Through intelligence of the heart**[N] – the ability to grasp the distinctions between matters.

בְּאֵימָה,

6. **Through awe** – as Torah study must be undertaken with the intellectual awe of one who is encountering wisdom and perception of infinite depth and magnitude.

בְּיִרְאָה,

7. **Through reverence**[N] – through a sense of fear and honor, as Torah study must be undertaken with an approach of serious consideration,

NOTES

Through well-ordered speech – בַּעֲרִיכַת שְׂפָתַיִם: The commentary explains that he knows how to express himself appropriately and to ask and answer questions in a prepared and orderly fashion. Some explain that when he studies, he articulates aloud what he is learning and does not merely contemplate it (Rashi). Others explain that the meaning is that one should review what he studies several times, and should make certain to arrange and order the material into its different categories (*Midrash Shmuel*), or that he should remain fluent in the matters as he was when he learned them (*Tiferet Yisrael*).

Through understanding of the heart, through intelligence [*besikhlut*] of the heart – בְּבִינַת הַלֵּב בְּשִׂכְלוּת הַלֵּב: "Understanding of the heart" means to fathom matters, and "intelligence of the heart" is the ability to distinguish between them. The *Tiferet Yisrael* says that "intelligence of the heart" refers to getting a sense [*haskala*] of Torah mysticism. Since it is impossible to fully understand and explain it, one can only peruse it and get a sense of it. Some cite a variant reading: "intent of the heart," instead of "understanding of the heart" (see Yaavetz and *Midrash Shmuel*).

Through awe [*be'eima*], through reverence [*be'yira*] – בְּאֵימָה בְּיִרְאָה: The commentary explains

which stems from acknowledging its greatness and significance. The fear and honor must exist both vis-à-vis the Torah itself and vis-à-vis the one teaching it.

בַּעֲנָוָה, 8. **Through modesty** – the psychological posture based on the acknowledgment that a person has nothing of his own, but only gifts from Heaven. In that way, he can become a receptacle to receive matters of Torah with complete openness.

בְּשִׂמְחָה, 9. **Through joy** – a person acquires the Torah and accepts it in his heart when he learns it with joy, and with an open and expansive heart.

Until this point, the mishna enumerated the qualities of the person who studies. From this point, the mishna begins addressing the methods of study and acquisition of the Torah.

בְּשִׁמּוּשׁ חֲכָמִים, 10. **Through serving the Sages** – when a student serves his teacher on a daily basis, he observes his actions and learns how to act in practice.

בְּדִקְדּוּק חֲבֵרִים, 11. **Through camaraderie** – through joint study in a group, which enables them to analyze, discuss, and precisely infer matters of Torah.

וּבְפִלְפּוּל הַתַּלְמִידִים, 12. **Through in-depth study by the students**[N] – engaging in Torah study with one's students, and in-depth study among the students them-

NOTES

that there are two types of fear, intellectual and emotional, and one should cultivate both of them vis-à-vis both the teacher and the Torah itself. Some write that *eima* is awe of the teacher and *yira* is reverence of Heaven (*Midrash Shmuel*, *Tiferet Yisrael*).

Through serving the Sages, through camaraderie [*bedikduk ḥaverim*]…the students – בְּשִׁמּוּשׁ חֲכָמִים בְּדִקְדּוּק חֲבֵרִים...הַתַּלְמִידִים: These three attributes correspond to the material that a person learns from his teachers, his colleagues, and his students (see 4:12). Some cite a variant reading, "*bedibbuk ḥaverim*," meaning to adhere to one's colleagues, to receive Torah from them and to give to them (this is the version in *Tanna deVei Eliyahu Zuta* 17).

selves, by raising and assessing different possibilities and ways of reasoning, and through questions, riddles, acuity, and sharp intellect.

בְּיִשּׁוּב, 13. **Through consideration**[N] – stability, deliberation, and calmness.

From here, the mishna moves to the basis of knowledge, the Torah itself. It is through engaging in and studying Torah that one acquires it.

בְּמִקְרָא, 14. **Through Bible** – intensive and extensive knowledge of the verses, as expertise in the Bible is an instrument for acquiring the other parts of the Torah, as well.

בְּמִשְׁנָה, 15. **Through Mishna** – memorization of the statements of the early generations, the Sages of the Oral law. These statements have an accepted, fixed text.

The mishna proceeds to address the way of life of one who studies Torah and the manner in which he acquires it. First and foremost, it entails minimizing his engagement in matters of this world. His mind and heart are thereby available and focused on receiving and absorbing the Torah.

בְּמִעוּט שֵׁינָה, 16. **Through minimizing sleep** – as he must devote much time to Torah study.

בְּמִעוּט שִׂיחָה, 17. **Through minimizing conversation** – minimizing speech about insignificant matters and

NOTES

Through consideration [*beyishuv*] – בְּיִשּׁוּב: The commentary follows the plain understanding that Torah study should be undertaken with deliberation and consideration. Some explain additionally that one must be expert in settling the world, meaning, he must be familiar with the practicalities of how the world works, and must also possess general knowledge of the various sciences (*Tiferet Yisrael*). Some cite a variant reading, "*bishiva*," meaning that one should not study just anywhere, but in a "yeshiva," where Sages study (*Midrash Shmuel*; see mishna 2:7).

avoiding inconsequential conversation, as these are a waste of time and a distraction from Torah.

בְּמִעוּט תַּעֲנוּג, 18. **Through minimizing pleasure** – one should not seek the pleasures of this world and should not be steeped in them, as they dominate and captivate his heart.

בְּמִעוּט שְׂחוֹק, 19. **Through minimizing laughter** – one should not overly engage in laughter and games.

בְּמִעוּט דֶּרֶךְ אֶרֶץ, 20. **Through minimizing conjugal relations**[N] – he should not engage in them excessively.

The mishna proceeds to address refinement of personality traits, through which the Torah penetrates a person's heart.

בְּאֶרֶךְ אַפַּיִם, 21. **Through consideration** – patience, and the ability to forgive and to refrain from anger.

בְּלֵב טוֹב, 22. **Through a good heart** – the general attitude of a person's heart, which includes searching for the good in everything, as well as the desire to do good.

בֶּאֱמוּנַת חֲכָמִים, 23. **Through faith in the Sages** – to have faith in the Sages and embrace their opinion, as if a person has doubts regarding the status and wisdom of the Sages, he is unable to learn from them properly.

NOTES

Through minimizing conjugal relations [*derekh eretz*] – בְּמִעוּט דֶּרֶךְ אֶרֶץ: The term "*derekh eretz*" has numerous connotations, and the explanation in the commentary is that it is a euphemism for conjugal relations, meaning that one should not engage in relations excessively, as that will cause him to be idle from Torah study (Yaavetz, *Tiferet Yisrael*, and others). Rashi explains that it means that a person should not spend time with people in the marketplace. Some write otherwise, that the term is referring to politeness in interpersonal relationships; when a person is too rigorous in its regard, it leads to idleness from Torah study, and therefore one must not excessively implement rules for manners (see *Midrash Shmuel*). In any event, for all the matters stated in the mishna that one should minimize, it means that one should minimize them, but not totally abstain from them.

וּבְקַבָּלַת הַיִּסּוּרִין.

24. **And through acceptance of suffering** – if suffering of any kind befalls him, he should accept it with submission to Heaven, with love, and without defiance in his heart. Likewise, one must not allow afflictions that befall him to distract him from his studies.

Mishna 6

This mishna continues with a list of matters with which the Torah is acquired, describing here the traits and attributes of one who studies Torah. These qualities enable one to acquire the Torah and, in turn, studying Torah enables one to acquire these qualities.

הַמַּכִּיר אֶת מְקוֹמוֹ,

25. **One who knows his place** – one who properly assesses his scholarly, ethical, and spiritual standing, so he will neither be drawn to matters that are beyond him at that moment, nor degrade himself below his appropriate station.

וְהַשָּׂמֵחַ בְּחֶלְקוֹ,

26. **One who is happy with his lot** – he is happy with what he has, and does not develop desires for what is not his.

וְהָעוֹשֶׂה סְיָג לִדְבָרָיו,

27. **One who restricts his words** – he is careful with his speech and seeks to clearly articulate what he says. However, he does not say everything that he thinks and knows, so that he will not unwittingly utter prohibited or gratuitous matters.

וְאֵינוֹ מַחֲזִיק טוֹבָה לְעַצְמוֹ,

28. **And does not give himself credit** – although he studied much Torah and performed many deeds, he is not arrogant and does not consider himself particularly important or respectable, but rather, as one who performs what is incumbent upon him. Likewise, he does not believe that he has reached a level that allows him to stop studying.

אָהוּב,	29. **One who is beloved** – he seeks to be a person who does not alienate others and is even beloved by them.
אוֹהֵב אֶת הַמָּקוֹם,	30. **Loves the Omnipresent.**
אוֹהֵב אֶת הַבְּרִיּוֹת,	31. **Loves creatures**[N] – he loves all people and all creations.
אוֹהֵב אֶת הַצְּדָקוֹת,	32. **Loves charity** – he loves performing acts of charity and kindness.
אוֹהֵב אֶת הַתּוֹכָחוֹת,	33. **Loves admonishment** – he loves people's criticism and rebuke, as he subdues his heart to accept it and learn from it.
אוֹהֵב אֶת הַמֵּישָׁרִים,	34. **Loves straightforwardness** – he loves following the straight and narrow path, which has no deceit or deviousness, both regarding worldly matters and matters relating to Torah study.
מִתְרַחֵק מִן הַכָּבוֹד,	35. **Distances himself from honor** – one who not only does not pursue honor, but he distances himself from receiving honor from others.
וְלֹא מֵגִיס לִבּוֹ בְּתַלְמוּדוֹ,	36. **Is not arrogant**[N] **in his studies** – he has no arrogance or haughtiness regarding the matters of Torah in which he engages, even if he has learned much and is expert and successful in his study.

NOTES

Loves creatures [*haberiyot*] – אוֹהֵב אֶת הַבְּרִיּוֹת: In the parlance of the Sages, the term "*beriya*" sometimes means "creation," referring to anything created. However, the Sages often use *beriyot* to mean people, as in the phrase: "loves people [*haberiyot*] and draws them near to the Torah" (1:12).

Is not arrogant [*megis libo*] – וְלֹא מֵגִיס לִבּוֹ: The expression *megis libo* has two possible meanings: One is arrogance, and the other is conduct of excessive intimacy and shamelessness, as in the phrase, "familiar with her [*libo gas bah*]" (see *Yevamot* 4:10).

וְאֵינוֹ שָׂמֵחַ בְּהוֹרָאָה,

37. **Does not delight in issuing rulings** – he is not eager to guide others and issue halakhic rulings for them regarding how they should conduct themselves. He does so only due to compulsion and obligation, and even then, he does so with great care. All matters contain uncertainties and complexities. Eagerness to issue rulings is liable to be accompanied by a sense of arrogance and dominance.

נוֹשֵׂא בְּעֹל עִם חֲבֵרוֹ,

38. **Shares in the burden with others** – he is by his counterpart's side when he is in distress, senses his suffering, assists him as though the burden is upon both of them together, and does not seek to escape responsibility.

מַכְרִיעוֹ לְכַף זְכוּת,

39. **Gives another the benefit of the doubt** – when another's action can be interpreted positively or negatively, he gives him the benefit of the doubt.

מַעֲמִידוֹ עַל הָאֱמֶת,

40. **But on the other hand, guides him to the truth** – when he sees that another is mistaken, he points out his errors to him and does not leave him remaining in error.

מַעֲמִידוֹ עַל הַשָּׁלוֹם,

41. **Guides him to peace**[N] – he helps another avoid entering into dispute. If that other person, nevertheless, enters into dispute, he takes action to appease and defuse the quarrel.

NOTES

Guides him to the truth, guides him to peace – מַעֲמִידוֹ עַל הָאֱמֶת מַעֲמִידוֹ עַל הַשָּׁלוֹם: Rashi explains that "guiding to the truth" refers to during one's studies or to matters of halakha. However, when executing justice, one should seek to take the path of compromise to whatever extent possible. That is, "guides him to peace."

The mishna proceeds to address the manner in which one who studies Torah engages in his study.

מִתְיַשֵּׁב לִבּוֹ בְּתַלְמוּדוֹ,	42. **Reconciles his heart with his studies** – he seeks to integrate what he learns in a manner that avoids any internal conflict and is in concert with his heart. Moreover, engaging in the study of wisdom renders him more moderate and considerate in various respects.
שׁוֹאֵל וּמֵשִׁיב, שׁוֹמֵעַ וּמוֹסִיף,	43. **Asks** when necessary, and knows how to ask good questions, through which the truth can be ascertained. **And responds** – when it is necessary for him to do so, and does not refrain. **Listens** – to the words of his teachers or others, **and** on that basis **adds** his own.
הַלּוֹמֵד עַל מְנָת לְלַמֵּד,	44. **One who studies in order to teach** – from the outset, he does not seek to keep the wisdom for himself, but rather, he intends to teach others. This influences the way he studies.
וְהַלּוֹמֵד עַל מְנָת לַעֲשׂוֹת,	45. **One who studies in order to perform** – one who studies with the intent for his studies to not remain as abstract knowledge, but to be acted on and fulfilled.
הַמַּחְכִּים אֶת רַבּוֹ,	46. **One who makes his teacher wiser**[N] – one who asks his teacher questions through which his teacher will be open to absorbing and understanding new insights.

NOTES

One who makes his teacher wiser [*hamaḥkim*] – הַמַּחְכִּים אֶת רַבּוֹ: The *Tiferet Yisrael* had a different understanding of the term *hamaḥkim*. He explains that the mishna is stated regarding the virtues of one who has already become great in Torah and has already become a Sage. That is why he writes that *hamaḥkim* means one who deems his teacher wise. When he finds one of his teacher's statements difficult, he does not say that his teacher forgot or did not know that matter. Instead, he should remind himself that his teacher is a great Sage, whose thoughts are profound. As a result, he will seek to resolve his statement and establish it as his teacher intended. Likewise, when halakhic statements that he heard from his teacher appear contradictory, he must not reject them, but rather must reconcile them.

וְהַמְכַוֵּן אֶת שְׁמוּעָתוֹ,

47. **One who is precise in his studies** – he seeks to combine and channel the matters that he learned and hears, so they will be systematic and harmonious. Likewise, he seeks to reconcile his own statements with tradition and halakha.

וְהָאוֹמֵר דָּבָר בְּשֵׁם אוֹמְרוֹ.

48. **And one who cites matters in the name of the one who said it** – when he cites something that he heard, he makes certain to preserve the name of the one who made the original statement, and does not attribute to himself statements made by others.

הָא לָמַדְתָּ שֶׁכָּל הָאוֹמֵר דָּבָר בְּשֵׁם אוֹמְרוֹ מֵבִיא גְאֻלָּה לָעוֹלָם, שֶׁנֶּאֱמַר: "וַתֹּאמֶר אֶסְתֵּר לַמֶּלֶךְ בְּשֵׁם מָרְדֳּכָי".

Regarding the previous matter, the mishna adds: **You learned** elsewhere **that anyone who cites a statement in the name of the one who said it**, beyond the fact that this entails integrity and fairness, **he brings redemption to the world, as it is stated: "Esther said to the king in the name of Mordekhai"** (Esther 2:22). Ultimately, the redemption of Purim began and developed from this matter, as when the king was reminded of Mordekhai, he accorded him honor and promoted him.

Mishna 7

This mishna concentrates on the goodness involved in Torah study. Most of these words of praise are based on the book of Proverbs.

גְּדוֹלָה תוֹרָה שֶׁהִיא נוֹתֶנֶת חַיִּים לְעוֹשֶׂיהָ, בָּעוֹלָם הַזֶּה וּבָעוֹלָם הַבָּא.

Torah is great, as it provides life for its practitioners[N] **in this world and in the World to Come.**

NOTES

Torah is great as it provides life for its practitioners – גְּדוֹלָה תוֹרָה שֶׁהִיא נוֹתֶנֶת חַיִּים לְעֹשֶׂיהָ: The *Tiferet Yisrael* explains that this mishna serves as an introduction to the mishna that follows, which details

שֶׁנֶּאֱמַר: "כִּי חַיִּים הֵם לְמֹצְאֵיהֶם וּלְכָל בְּשָׂרוֹ מַרְפֵּא". וְאוֹמֵר: "רִפְאוּת תְּהִי לְשָׁרֶּךָ וְשִׁקּוּי לְעַצְמוֹתֶיךָ".

As it is stated: "For they are life for those who find them, and healing for all one's flesh" (Proverbs 4:22). "Life for those who find them" – in the World to Come; "and healing for all one's flesh" – in this world. **And** moreover, the verse **says: "It will be healing for your navel and an elixir for your bones"** (Proverbs 3:8).[N] The Torah heals those who embrace it, and it is an elixir that strengthens one's bones.

וְאוֹמֵר: "עֵץ חַיִּים הִיא לַמַּחֲזִיקִים בָּהּ וְתֹמְכֶיהָ מְאֻשָּׁר".

And it says: "It is a tree of life for those who hold on to it,[N] and its supporters are happy" (Proverbs 3:18), as it provides life and happiness for those who embrace and fulfill it, as well as for those who provide assistance to others who study Torah.

וְאוֹמֵר: "כִּי לִוְיַת חֵן הֵם לְרֹאשֶׁךָ וַעֲנָקִים לְגַרְגְּרֹתֶיךָ".

And it says: "For they will be a graceful adornment for your head, and necklaces for your neck" (Proverbs 1:26), as matters of Torah provide a person with both beauty and glory.

NOTES

the many qualities that are fitting for the righteous, e.g., wealth, might, and honor. These are qualities that can be achieved in other ways as well; however, life in the World to Come can be achieved only by means of the Torah. That is why "Torah is great." Some comment that the language of the mishna, "for its practitioners," and not "for those who study it," serves to emphasize that the Torah gives life specifically to one who fulfills what is stated in it, and not to one who studies it without fulfilling it.

An elixir for your bones – וְשִׁקּוּי לְעַצְמוֹתֶיךָ: Rashi explains that "an elixir for your bones" means that the Torah will protect a person's bones when he is in the grave. The *Tiferet Yisrael* explains that "healing for all one's flesh" is a cure for external wounds, "healing for your navel" is a cure for illnesses affecting a person's internal organs, and "an elixir for your bones" is a cure for general weakness in a person's body.

It is a tree of life for those who hold on to it – עֵץ חַיִּים הִיא לַמַּחֲזִיקִים בָּהּ: The *Tiferet Yisrael* explains that this is referring to eternal life, as the Sages said regarding the righteous that "even in their death they are characterized as living" (Jerusalem Talmud, *Berakhot* 2:3, and elsewhere). The term "tree of life" alludes to the Tree of Life that was in the Garden of Eden, in whose regard it is stated that one who eats from it lives forever (Genesis 3:22).

וְאוֹמֵר: "תִּתֵּן לְרֹאשְׁךָ לִוְיַת חֵן עֲטֶרֶת תִּפְאֶרֶת תְּמַגְּנֶךָּ".

And it says, similarly: **"It will give your head an adornment of grace; it will bestow upon you a crown of glory"** (Proverbs 4:9).

וְאוֹמֵר: "אֹרֶךְ יָמִים בִּימִינָהּ בִּשְׂמֹאולָהּ עֹשֶׁר וְכָבוֹד".

And it says: "Length of days is on its right; on its left is wealth and honor" (Proverbs 3:16). The Torah provides long life on the one hand and wealth and honor on the other.

וְאוֹמֵר: "כִּי אֹרֶךְ יָמִים וּשְׁנוֹת חַיִּים וְשָׁלוֹם יוֹסִיפוּ לָךְ".

And it says: "For they will add length of days, years of life, and peace to you" (Proverbs 3:2).

Mishna 8

The mishna continues to list matters merited by one who engages in Torah study.

רַבִּי שִׁמְעוֹן בֶּן יְהוּדָה מִשּׁוּם רַבִּי שִׁמְעוֹן בֶּן יוֹחַאי אוֹמֵר: הַנּוֹי, וְהַכֹּחַ, וְהָעֹשֶׁר, וְהַכָּבוֹד, וְהַחָכְמָה, וְהַזִּקְנָה, וְהַשֵּׂיבָה, וְהַבָּנִים – נָאֶה לַצַּדִּיקִים וְנָאֶה לָעוֹלָם,

Rabbi Shimon ben Yehuda says in the name of Rabbi Shimon ben Yoḥai: Beauty, strength, wealth, honor, wisdom,[N] **old age,** the **gray hair** that accompanies it, **and children are fitting for the righteous,** as all these qualities can be found in them, **and** the matter is also **fitting for the world.**[N] When these gifts are given to the righteous, they generate blessing for the entire world as well.

NOTES

Beauty, strength…are fitting for the righteous and fitting for the world – הַנּוֹי וְהַכֹּחַ...נָאֶה לַצַּדִּיקִים וְנָאֶה לָעוֹלָם: See the *Tiferet Yisrael*, who explains at length why these matters are fitting for the righteous and how the entire world benefits when the righteous merit these qualities. The *Midrash Shmuel* explains that these are all matters that can also be used for evil. That is why they are fitting specifically when they are in the hands of the righteous. On a similar note, Yaavetz writes that these are, ostensibly, external and transitory items. However, the righteous channel them for use for eternal objectives. That is why there is benefit for the world in the fact that they are blessed with them.

Wisdom – וְהַחָכְמָה: The Yaavetz writes that this is

The mishna cites proof from the verses that all of these matters are fitting and fine for the righteous and the world.

שֶׁנֶּאֱמַר: "עֲטֶרֶת תִּפְאֶרֶת שֵׂיבָה בְּדֶרֶךְ צְדָקָה תִּמָּצֵא".

As it is stated regarding the beauty of old age: **"Gray hair is a crown of glory; it will be found in the way of righteousness"** (Proverbs 16:31).[N] Gray hair is a crown and glory for those who follow the path of righteousness.

וְאוֹמֵר: "תִּפְאֶרֶת בַּחוּרִים כֹּחָם וַהֲדַר זְקֵנִים שֵׂיבָה".

And it says regarding strength: **"The glory of young men is their strength, and the splendor of elders is gray hair"** (Proverbs 20:29). Both strength and gray hair are among the positive qualities that people have, each at its appropriate time, and old age is something that contains splendor.

וְאוֹמֵר: "עֲטֶרֶת חֲכָמִים עָשְׁרָם".

And it says regarding wealth: **"The crown of the wise is their wealth"** (Proverbs 14:24).

NOTES

not referring to the Torah, as Torah is the primary concern of the righteous, and not a matter that is merely fitting for them. He therefore explains that this is wisdom of the heart, i.e., sharp-wittedness, or perhaps general, secular knowledge, "as it is fitting for the righteous, so they will lack nothing."

Gray hair is a crown of glory; it will be found in the way of righteousness – עֲטֶרֶת תִּפְאֶרֶת שֵׂיבָה בְּדֶרֶךְ צְדָקָה תִּמָּצֵא: It appears from Rashi's explanation that this verse is the source of almost all the matters stated in the mishna, and the verses that follow are meant to explain what is stated in it. The crown, the glory, and the gray hair can be found through righteousness, i.e., with the righteous. "Crown" is wealth, as derived from the verse: "The crown of the wise is their wealth" (Proverbs 14:24). While the simple explanation of "glory," is beauty, here it is also children and strength, as derived from the verses: "the crown of elders is grandchildren, and the glory of children is their fathers" (Proverbs 17:6) and "the glory of young men is their strength" (Proverbs 20:29). Honor and old age are derived from "and glory will be before His elders" (Isaiah 24:23).

The *Tiferet Yisrael* explains that no proof at all is needed that beauty, strength, honor, and wisdom are fitting for the righteous. The verses are cited to prove only what requires proof: The verse: "gray hair is a crown of glory" comes to teach that old age and gray hair are a virtue and a good find. "The crown of elders is grandchildren" (Proverbs 17:6) comes to teach that children are a crown for a person. See also Rabbi Matitya HaYitzhari, who addresses this at length.

וְאוֹמֵר: "עֲטֶרֶת זְקֵנִים בְּנֵי בָנִים וְתִפְאֶרֶת בָּנִים אֲבוֹתָם".

And it says regarding children: **"The crown of elders is grandchildren, and the glory of children is their fathers"** (Proverbs 17:6).

וְאוֹמֵר: "וְחָפְרָה הַלְּבָנָה וּבוֹשָׁה הַחַמָּה, כִּי מָלַךְ ה' צְבָאוֹת בְּהַר צִיּוֹן וּבִירוּשָׁלַיִם וְנֶגֶד זְקֵנָיו כָּבוֹד".

And it says regarding honor: **"The moon will be disgraced and the sun will be ashamed, for the Lord of hosts will reign on Mount Zion and in Jerusalem, and glory will be before His elders"** (Isaiah 24:23). Honor is a fine gift for the righteous.

רַבִּי שִׁמְעוֹן בֶּן מְנַסְיָא אוֹמֵר: אֵלּוּ שֶׁבַע מִדּוֹת שֶׁמָּנוּ חֲכָמִים לַצַּדִּיקִים – כּוּלָּם נִתְקַיְּמוּ בְּרַבִּי וּבָנָיו.

Rabbi Shimon ben Menasya[P] **says: These are seven qualities**[N] **that the Sages enumerated regarding the righteous; they were all fulfilled in Rabbi** Yehuda HaNasi **and** in **his sons.**

NOTES

These are seven qualities – אֵלּוּ שֶׁבַע מִדּוֹת: There are eight matters enumerated in the mishna. Some resolve the discrepancy by saying that wisdom and old age [*zikna*] are considered one matter, because *zikna* here is not longevity, but rather, acquisition of wisdom (*Notzer Ḥesed*). Others say that old age and gray hair are considered one matter (Maharal of Prague). In *Maḥzor Vitri*, *zikna* is not taught at all. Likewise, *zikna* is not enumerated in the version in *Tanna deVei Eliyahu*, which includes "glory" instead of "honor."

PERSONALITIES

Rabbi Shimon ben Menasya – רַבִּי שִׁמְעוֹן בֶּן מְנַסְיָא: Rabbi Shimon ben Menasya was a fifth-generation *tanna* and a contemporary of Rabbi Yehuda HaNasi. Rabbi Shimon and his colleague Rabbi Yosei ben Meshulam were called "the holy congregation," because they would divide their day, one-third Torah, one-third prayer, and one-third labor, or they would toil in Torah during the winter and toil in labor in the summer (*Kohelet Rabba* 9:1). He is mentioned once in the mishna (*Ḥagiga* 1:7), and additional times in the *Tosefta* and in the two Talmuds. According to ancient traditions, his tomb is located between Gush Ḥalav and Safed.

Tomb of Rabbi Shimon ben Menasya, located between Gush Ḥalav and Safed

Mishna 9

In this mishna, an incident is recounted that expresses what was already stated in the previous mishna, that the wealth that the Torah provides is greater than any wealth that a person acquires in this world.

אָמַר רַבִּי יוֹסֵי בֶּן קִיסְמָא: פַּעַם אַחַת הָיִיתִי מְהַלֵּךְ בַּדֶּרֶךְ, וּפָגַע בִּי אָדָם אֶחָד, וְנָתַן לִי שָׁלוֹם, וְהֶחֱזַרְתִּי לוֹ שָׁלוֹם.

Rabbi Yosei ben Kisma[P] **says:**[N] **Once I was walking along the way and a certain person encountered me. He greeted me** in the manner that a person greets one who is greater than him, **and I responded and greeted him.**

אָמַר לִי: רַבִּי, מֵאֵיזֶה מָקוֹם אַתָּה? אָמַרְתִּי לוֹ: מֵעִיר גְּדוֹלָה שֶׁל חֲכָמִים וְשֶׁל סוֹפְרִים אֲנִי. אָמַר לִי: רַבִּי, רְצוֹנְךָ שֶׁתָּדוּר עִמָּנוּ בִּמְקוֹמֵנוּ, וַאֲנִי אֶתֵּן לְךָ אֶלֶף אֲלָפִים דִּינְרֵי זָהָב וַאֲבָנִים טוֹבוֹת וּמַרְגָּלִיּוֹת?

He said to me: Rabbi, from what place are you? I said to him: I am from a large city of Sages and scribes, teachers of Torah. **He said to me: Rabbi, would you like to reside with us in our place,** our city, and become our leader, **and I will give you thousands upon thousands of gold dinars, gems, and pearls?**

NOTES

Rabbi Yosei ben Kisma says – אָמַר רַבִּי יוֹסֵי בֶּן קִסְמָא: The *Tiferet Yisrael* explains that the mishna is saying that despite the fact that advantages such as wealth and honor are fitting for the righteous and fitting for the world, as stated in the previous mishna, nevertheless, one should not pursue them, but should reside in a place of Torah.

He expounded the details of the incident, that the person whom Rabbi Yosei ben Kisma encountered wondered why a great man like Rabbi Yosei needed to wander on the roads to earn a livelihood, and did not serve as a rabbi in his own place. When Rabbi Yosei answered him that he lives in a city of Sages and scribes, who are not sufficiently wealthy to support him, he offered to provide Rabbi Yosei with a livelihood as great as he desires if he would move to his city. Rabbi Yosei answered that he had no need for that, only to reside in a place of Torah, as was explained.

PERSONALITIES

Rabbi Yosei ben Kisma – רַבִּי יוֹסֵי בֶּן קִסְמָא: Rabbi Yosei ben Kisma, a third-generation *tanna* and one of the Sages of Yavne, is mentioned in several places in the Talmud, where aggadic material about him is cited. It is related that he had the special ability to foretell the end of days (*Sanhedrin* 98a, and elsewhere). During the bar Kokheva revolt, he was one of the moderates who believed that they should not rebel against the Romans. It appears that he had close relations with the authorities, and many of the elite of Rome attended his funeral (*Avoda Zara* 18a). He had a son named Rabbi Yoḥanan, who was a Sage.

אָמַרְתִּי לוֹ: בְּנִי, אִם אַתָּה נוֹתֵן לִי כָּל כֶּסֶף וְזָהָב וַאֲבָנִים טוֹבוֹת וּמַרְגָּלִיּוֹת שֶׁבָּעוֹלָם, אֵינִי דָּר אֶלָּא בִּמְקוֹם תּוֹרָה. לְפִי שֶׁבִּשְׁעַת פְּטִירָתוֹ שֶׁל אָדָם, אֵין מְלַוִּין לוֹ לָאָדָם לֹא כֶּסֶף וְלֹא זָהָב, וְלֹא אֲבָנִים טוֹבוֹת וּמַרְגָּלִיּוֹת, אֶלָּא תּוֹרָה וּמַעֲשִׂים טוֹבִים בִּלְבַד, שֶׁנֶּאֱמַר: "בְּהִתְהַלֶּכְךָ תַּנְחֶה אֹתָךְ, בְּשָׁכְבְּךָ תִּשְׁמֹר עָלֶיךָ, וַהֲקִיצוֹתָ הִיא תְשִׂיחֶךָ"; "בְּהִתְהַלֶּכְךָ תַּנְחֶה אֹתָךְ" - בָּעוֹלָם הַזֶּה, "בְּשָׁכְבְּךָ תִּשְׁמֹר עָלֶיךָ" - בַּקֶּבֶר, "וַהֲקִיצוֹתָ הִיא תְשִׂיחֶךָ" - לָעוֹלָם הַבָּא.

I said to him: If you were to give me all the silver, gold, gems, and pearls in the world, I would reside only in a place of Torah, in which Sages reside, and your place is not a place of that kind. This is **because, at the moment of a person's death it is not silver, gold, gems, and pearls that accompany a person,** as these are pertinent only in this world. **But rather,** it is **only Torah and good deeds,** which are spiritual acquisitions, that accompany the soul even after death, **as it is stated: "It will guide you when you walk; when you lie down, it will protect you, and when you awaken, it will be your conversation"** (Proverbs 6:22). **"It will guide you when you walk"** – during your lifetime **in this world; "when you lie down, it will protect you"** – when you are **in the grave; "and when you awaken, it will be your conversation" – in the World to Come,** after the revival of the dead.

וְכֵן כָּתוּב בְּסֵפֶר תְּהִלִּים עַל יְדֵי דָוִד מֶלֶךְ יִשְׂרָאֵל: "טוֹב לִי תוֹרַת פִּיךָ מֵאַלְפֵי זָהָב וָכָסֶף".

Likewise, it is written in the book of Psalms by David king of Israel: "The teaching of Your mouth is better for me than thousands of gold and silver pieces" (Psalms 119:72); Torah is more valuable than all the wealth in the world.

וְאוֹמֵר: "לִי הַכֶּסֶף וְלִי הַזָּהָב נְאֻם ה׳ צְבָאוֹת".

Moreover, **it says: "Mine is the silver, and Mine the gold**[N] **– the utterance of the Lord of hosts"** (Haggai 2:8). Ultimately, silver and gold are also gifts from God, and if He

NOTES

It says, Mine is the silver, and Mine the gold – וְאוֹמֵר לִי הַכֶּסֶף וְלִי הַזָּהָב: In other words, the silver and the gold belong to God, and He can give them to him wherever he is (*Tiferet Yisrael*), and also take them from him if they are not for his benefit (*Midrash Shmuel*). Rashi writes that this means that the purpose of silver and gold is only for the praise and glory of God, and they are not an objective in

wishes for a certain person to have great wealth of that kind, He can provide it to him wherever he may be.

Mishna 10

At the conclusion of this chapter, which praises the Torah and addresses its virtues, a list of significant, primary matters is presented, with Torah first among them.

חֲמִשָּׁה קִנְיָנִים קָנָה הַקָּדוֹשׁ בָּרוּךְ הוּא בְּעוֹלָמוֹ, וְאֵלּוּ הֵן: תּוֹרָה קִנְיָן אֶחָד, שָׁמַיִם וָאָרֶץ קִנְיָן אֶחָד, אַבְרָהָם קִנְיָן אֶחָד, יִשְׂרָאֵל קִנְיָן אֶחָד, בֵּית הַמִּקְדָּשׁ קִנְיָן אֶחָד.

God acquired [*kana*] **five possessions in His world;** although the whole world in its entirety is made by God and is His possession, in any case He characterizes five particular matters as His special possession. **And they are: Torah, one possession,**[N] **the heavens and the earth, one possession, Abraham** our forefather, **one possession, Israel, one possession, the Temple, one possession.** The mishna cites proof from verses for each of these matters:

NOTES

and of themselves. In tractate *Kalla Rabbati* (5:9) it is stated that this verse is cited regarding what was said, that when a person dies, his silver and gold do not accompany him. The point is that a person does not retain ownership of his belongings after he dies, and charity is effective for him only when he gives it during his lifetime, but not after his death.

Roman gold dinar, 41 BCE

Five possessions *kinyanim*…one possession [*kinyan*] – **חֲמִשָּׁה קִנְיָנִים...קִנְיָן אֶחָד:** The commentaries write that these are matters that are dear to God and are extremely significant in His eyes. On the one hand, these possessions are dependent upon one another for existence (*Tiferet Yisrael*; see below), but on the other hand, each of them is significant in and of itself. For this reason, the mishna emphasizes that each of them is "one possession" (*Midrash Shmuel*).

The *Maḥzor Vitri* noted that apparently the Sages disagreed in this regard. In the Babylonian Talmud (*Pesaḥim* 87b), four of the possessions [*kinyanim*] in the mishna appear, with Abraham omitted. The verse: "Master [*koneh*] of heavens and earth," cited in the mishna in his regard, is cited there as proof that the heavens and the earth are considered possessions [*kinyanim*] of God. This is also how it

תּוֹרָה מִנַּיִן? דִּכְתִיב: "ה׳ קָנָנִי רֵאשִׁית דַּרְכּוֹ קֶדֶם מִפְעָלָיו מֵאָז".

With regard to **Torah, from where is it derived? As it is written** in the name of the Torah: **"The Lord acquired me [*kanani*] at the beginning of His way, the earliest of His undertakings from then"** (Proverbs 8:22).

שָׁמַיִם וָאָרֶץ קִנְיָן אֶחָד מִנַּיִן? דִּכְתִיב: "כֹּה אָמַר ה׳ הַשָּׁמַיִם כִּסְאִי וְהָאָרֶץ הֲדֹם רַגְלָי, אֵי זֶה בַיִת אֲשֶׁר תִּבְנוּ לִי וְאֵי זֶה מָקוֹם מְנוּחָתִי". וְאוֹמֵר: "מָה רַבּוּ מַעֲשֶׂיךָ ה׳ כֻּלָּם בְּחָכְמָה עָשִׂיתָ מָלְאָה הָאָרֶץ קִנְיָנֶךָ".

The heavens and the earth, one possession, from where is it derived? As it is written: "So said the Lord: The heavens are My throne and the earth is My footstool; what house could you build for Me, and what place could be My resting place?" (Isaiah 66:1). The heavens and the earth are God's seat. **And,** indicating that they were called possession [*kinyan*], **it says: "Lord, how manifold are Your deeds, in wisdom have You made them all. The earth is full of Your possessions [*kinyanekha*]"** (Psalms 104:24).

אַבְרָהָם קִנְיָן אֶחָד מִנַּיִן? דִּכְתִיב: "וַיְבָרְכֵהוּ וַיֹּאמַר בָּרוּךְ אַבְרָם לְאֵל עֶלְיוֹן קֹנֵה שָׁמַיִם וָאָרֶץ".

Abraham, one possession [*kinyan*], from where is it derived? As it is written in the blessing that Malkitzedek king of Shalem blessed Abraham: **"He blessed him, and he said: Blessed is Abram to God, the Most High,**[N] **Master [*koneh*] of heavens and earth"** (Genesis 14:19). Abraham, who is blessed to God, is also considered to be a kinyan of God.

NOTES

appears in the *Mekhilta* (Exodus 15:16). According to Rashi's version, the Talmud there enumerated only three possessions: Torah, the heavens, and the Land of Israel. In *Sifrei* (Deuteronomy 32:6), a different set of three is enumerated: Torah, the Jewish people, and the Temple.

Abraham, one possession [*kinyan*]...Blessed is Abram to God, the Most High – אַבְרָהָם קִנְיָן אֶחָד...בָּרוּךְ אַבְרָם לְאֵל עֶלְיוֹן: The *Tiferet Yisrael* explains that it would have been sufficient to say that the Holy One blessed be He is "God, the Most High." The fact that it added "Master [*koneh*] of heavens and earth" teaches that just as they are called the *kinyan* of God, Abraham too is called that. The *Maḥzor Vitri* says that some derive the parallel between Abraham and the heavens and the earth from the verse: "This is the legacy of the heavens and of the earth when they were created [*behibare'am*]" (Genesis 2:4), which is expounded by transposing the letters, as though *beAvraham* was written (see *Bereshit Rabba* 12:9).

יִשְׂרָאֵל קִנְיָן אֶחָד מִנַּיִן? דִּכְתִיב: "עַד יַעֲבֹר עַמְּךָ ה׳ עַד יַעֲבֹר עַם זוּ קָנִיתָ". וְאוֹמֵר: "לִקְדוֹשִׁים אֲשֶׁר בָּאָרֶץ הֵמָּה וְאַדִּירֵי כָּל חֶפְצִי בָם".

The people of **Israel, one possession [*kinyan*], from where is it derived? As it is written: "Until the passage of Your people, Lord, until the passage of this people whom You have acquired [*kanita*]"** (Exodus 15:16). Moreover, **it says: "With the holy of the earth and the majestic ones, all My desire is with them"** (Psalms 16:3). Not only are they His possession, but He especially desires them.

בֵּית הַמִּקְדָּשׁ קִנְיָן אֶחָד מִנַּיִן? דִּכְתִיב: "מָכוֹן לְשִׁבְתְּךָ פָּעַלְתָּ ה׳ מִקְּדָשׁ ה׳ כּוֹנְנוּ יָדֶיךָ". וְאוֹמֵר: "וַיְבִיאֵם אֶל גְּבוּל קָדְשׁוֹ הַר זֶה קָנְתָה יְמִינוֹ".

The Temple, one possession [*kinyan*],[N] from where is it derived? As it is written: "The place You fashioned for Your dwelling, Lord, the Sanctuary, my Lord, that Your hands established" (Exodus 15:17), as the Temple is the handiwork of God. Moreover, **it says: "He brought them to the boundary of His holiness, to this mountain owned [*kaneta*] by His right hand"** (Psalms 78:54). The mountain of the Lord that the Lord created with His right hand, as it were, is also called the kinyan of God.

NOTES

The Temple, one possession [*kinyan*] – בֵּית הַמִּקְדָּשׁ קִנְיָן אֶחָד: The fact that the Temple is the possession [*kinyan*] of God is simply derived from the verse: "To this mountain owned [*kaneta*] by His right hand." The *Midrash Shmuel* says that it is derived from the fact that it is more significant than the heavens and the earth, which were created with one hand, as it were, or the Temple, which was created with two hands of God, as it were ("Your hands established"; see *Ketubot* 5a and *Tiferet Yisrael*). Therefore, it can be inferred *a fortiori* that it is called a possession [*kinyan*]. He added that the verse: "This mountain owned [*kaneta*] by His right hand," is necessary in order to indicate that even when the Temple is in ruins, and there is nothing there other than a mountain, it is still called a *kinyan*.

In tractate *Kalla Rabbati* (5:10), it is said regarding this mishna: "Rabbi Yosei says: Just as the heavens and the earth are destined to be renewed, Israel, too, is destined to be renewed…By what merit? It is by the merit of Abraham and the merit of the Torah. And where? It is in the Temple." Similarly, it is stated in the *Mekhilta* (on Exodus 15:16); "Let Israel, who were called *kinyan*, come to the Land that was called *kinyan*, build the Temple that is called *kinyan*, by the merit of the Torah that is called *kinyan*."

This mountain owned by His right hand, the Temple Mount today

Mishna 11

Following the previous mishna, which mentioned the special possessions that God acquired in His world, this mishna addresses the entirety of Creation, which was also created completely in His honor.

כָּל מַה שֶּׁבָּרָא הַקָּדוֹשׁ בָּרוּךְ הוּא בְּעוֹלָמוֹ – לֹא בְרָאוֹ אֶלָּא לִכְבוֹדוֹ, שֶׁנֶּאֱמַר: "כֹּל הַנִּקְרָא בִשְׁמִי וְלִכְבוֹדִי בְּרָאתִיו יְצַרְתִּיו אַף עֲשִׂיתִיו". וְאוֹמֵר: "ה׳ יִמְלֹךְ לְעֹלָם וָעֶד".

Everything that God created in His world, he created only for His glory, to exalt the Creator, as the world is the place where His glory is revealed. **As it is stated: "Everything that is called by My name and for My glory,**[N] **I created it, I fashioned it, indeed, I made it"** (Isaiah 43:7). This is not only true regarding what was already created, but it is also the purpose of the world for all generations, as **it says: "The Lord will reign forever and ever"** (Exodus 15:18).

That passage is an apt conclusion for this chapter and to tractate *Avot* in general. The upshot is that we too should direct our thoughts and actions so that all of them will be for the glory of the Creator.

NOTES

Everything that is called by My name and for My glory – כֹּל הַנִּקְרָא בִשְׁמִי וְלִכְבוֹדִי: The *Midrash Shmuel* explains that this verse is an especially apt proof text for this mishna, because it is one of the clearest sources for the standard division in Torah mysticism regarding the existence of four "worlds" located one beneath the other, and includes the complete created reality, both spiritual and physical: The world of Emanations [*atzilut*], called in the verse: "called by My name and for My glory," as it is, as it were, the place of the glory of God. Beneath it are the worlds of Creation [*beria*] and Formation [*yetzira*], and beneath them is the world of Action [*asiya*], which includes the familiar material world. In this regard, the emphasis is on the phrase "indeed, I made it," because ostensibly this world, in contrast to the spiritual worlds, does not always function in a manner that is for the glory of God. The verse comes to say that this is not the case, but rather, ultimately "the Lord will reign forever and ever."

The *Tiferet Yisrael* explains that the phrase "indeed, I made it" teaches that the precise, wondrous form of all God's creations, to the most minute, subtle details, indicates that everything was designed for the extremely significant purpose of God's glory and dominion, and there is nothing in this world that was created in vain.

KOREN